On Mennonite/s Writing

Selected Essays

Hildi Froese Tiessen

Edited and with an Introduction by
Robert Zacharias

Winnipeg, Manitoba
2023

Contents

1   Editor's Preface | *Robert Zacharias*

Introduction | "Into the Land of MennoLit": On Hildi Froese Tiessen's *On Mennonite/s Writing* | *Robert Zacharias*

One | A Mighty Inner River: "Peace" in the Early Fiction of Rudy Wiebe

Two | The Role of Art and Literature in Mennonite Self-Understanding

61   Three | Mother Tongue as Shibboleth in the Literature of Canadian Mennonites

71   Four | Mennonite Writing and the Post-Colonial Condition

81   Five | Beyond the Binary: Re-Inscribing Cultural Identity in the Literature of Mennonites

93   Six | Mennonite Literature and Postmodernism: Writing the "In-Between" Space

109   Seven | Between Memory and Longing: Rudy Wiebe's *Sweeter Than All the World*

127   Eight | Critical Thought and Mennonite Literature: Mennonite Studies Engages the Mennonite Literary Voice

137   Nine | A Mennonite Novelist's Journey (from) Home: Ephraim Weber's Encounters with S.F. Coffman and Lucy Maud Montgomery

159   Ten | Mennonite/s Writing: State of the Art?

169   **Eleven** | An Imagined Coherence: Mennonite Literature and Mennonite Culture

179   **Twelve** | The Case of Dallas Wiebe: Literary Art in Worship

189   **Thirteen** | Homelands, Identity Politics, and the Trace: What Remains for the Mennonite Reader?

201   **Fourteen** | After Identity: Liberating the Mennonite Literary Text

219   **Fifteen** | Beyond "What We by Habit or Custom Already Know," or, What Do We Mean When We Talk About Mennonite/s Writing?

237   **Sixteen** | Thirty Years of Mennonite Literature: How a Modest Course Became Something Else (A Fragment of Literary Memoir)

249   **Seventeen** | "I didn't have words for it": Reflections on Some of the Early Life-Writing of Di Brandt and Julia Kasdorf

267   **Afterword** | "Some Hidden Rhythm": On Being Right There, Right Then

297   *Author's Note*

299   *Acknowledgements*

301   *Index*

309   *About the Author*

Editor's Preface

Robert Zacharias

The first time I suggested a collection such as this to Hildi Froese Tiessen, she literally waved the idea away. It was well over a decade ago, and my research for a dissertation on Mennonite literature kept turning up essays, special issues, interviews, and collections by the same author. My research notes were filled with cited passages and key terms, often underlined and in bold, all accompanied by the same set of initials: "H.F.T." The essays spanned decades and were scattered across a range of venues; some had been tucked away in small, Mennonite-affiliated publications, others were in leading academic journals. How could there be so many essays by the same author, I wondered, and why had they never been gathered together in a single place? This "H.F.T." had edited half a dozen collections of other people's work in the field; where was her own? Yet when I finally had the opportunity to meet her in person and asked if she ever considered undertaking the project of gathering some of her own essays into a volume, Hildi—then very much still "Dr. Froese Tiessen" to me—responded with a shake of her head and a wave of her hand. "And would I ever consider it?" she continued, suddenly serious. "No."

It was with some trepidation, then, that I suggested this project a second time in the fall of 2022. I had begun work on a large critical anthology of Mennonite literary criticism in North America, and had come upon a problem. The premise for the project was to create an authoritative record of the most significant critical commentary on Mennonite literature in Canada and the United States, and I had reached out to experts in the field for suggestions on what to include. "As for all of the Hildi essays," the first responded, "I have no idea how you will choose just one or two." "And of course you'll need to have any number from Hildi," wrote another; "Good luck deciding which ones to leave out." I was working with Canadian Mennonite University Press for the large anthology, and so I decided I would propose a second collection, this one dedicated solely to collecting Hildi's most notable and influential works. After the press responded enthusiastically, I gathered up my courage and pitched the project to Hildi a second time. The press is already on board, I explained in an email, adding that I could serve as editor, and would do much of the legwork myself. "Let me say enough of a 'yes,'" she wrote back cautiously, "to allow you and me to move forward in conversation." Sometimes you have to take what you can get.

What changed in the intervening period? She had retired nearly a decade earlier, it is true, but she had continued to be as prolific as ever. A press was on board this time, yes, and someone was offering to help with the groundwork, but since when did Hildi Froese Tiessen need help with such trifling matters? My guess, rather, is that the retrospective gaze currently at play in the larger field of Mennonite literary studies—as the field collectively undertakes, in the words of a recent Mennonite/s Writing conference subtitle, the work of "Reflecting on the Past [and] Creating the Future"—made the prospect of gathering this work together suddenly more palpable to her, just as it made it more urgent to me. That is the sense, certainly, that one gets from the remarkable afterword she has written for this volume, where, in the process of reviewing her work for consideration for inclusion, she notes her surprise at finding "a rather peculiarly defined beginning and end" in her own work, and perhaps also in the "literary era to which [she] had been responding" (269 in this volume).

Whatever the reason, I am thankful for the change of heart, and I am thrilled to have been able to help bring *On Mennonite/s Writing* into being. All but two of the essays included here were previously published, and I am thankful for the permission to reprint them. The essays are presented here in their original form, with the exception of citation and note styles, which have been standardized for ease of reading, and some minor changes in language or phrasing made for clarity. As we decided to otherwise retain the original form of the essays, readers may notice some minor repetitions as key ideas or events are returned to throughout. I want to express my deep appreciation to the full team at CMU Press, including Dr. Sue Sorensen, Jonathan Dyck, and

Katie Doke Sawatzky. Sue's patience throughout and her enthusiasm for the project—along with her tireless work with the details of editing, fundraising, and chasing after a tardy editor—were instrumental in moving the project through the various stages to completion. My thanks to Katie, too, for her help with putting the manuscript together and chasing down various permissions required to reprint the essays here, and to Jonathan for overseeing the design of the material book so beautifully.

And, of course, my sincere thanks to Hildi Froese Tiessen, for trusting me to work on this project with her. The opportunity to read through nearly everything she has written in this area over the past 50 years was truly humbling, and I have deeply appreciated the chance to work closely with her once again. It is my hope that the collection will come to serve as the kind of touchstone resource for future scholars that I had been looking for when I first became interested in Mennonite literary studies—both as a home for those H.F.T. essays otherwise scattered across their various journals and collections, and as a key document reflecting the trajectory of the broader field in which Hildi's work has played such a crucial role.

Introduction

"Into the Land of MennoLit": On Hildi Froese Tiessen's *On Mennonite/s Writing*[*]

Robert Zacharias, York University

IT WOULD BE too much to suggest, surely, that Hildi Froese Tiessen *invented* Mennonite literary studies in North America. After all, by the time she first turned her attention to the subject in 1973, American Mennonite scholars like Elizabeth Horsch Bender, Elmer Suderman, and Cornelius Krahn had been publishing on the subject for decades, mostly in places like *Mennonite Quarterly Review* and *Mennonite Life*, and a few essays on Mennonite literature could already be found in academic venues like *Midcontinental* and *Canadian Literature*.[1] The beginnings of a creative infrastructure for Mennonite literature were taking shape, as well. An American "Mennonite Writers' Fellowship" had run conferences as early as the 1950s, and in the early 1970s two literary-minded Mennonite magazines, *Festival Quarterly* and the *Mennonite Mirror*, were launched, the latter of which was published by the newly established

---

[*] Parts of this introduction draw on my earlier tribute to Hildi: "Hildi Froese Tiessen: A Tribute." *Journal of Mennonite Writing* vol. 15, no. 1, 2023, online.

[1] See Elmer Suderman, "Fiction and Mennonite Life," *Midcontinent American Studies*, vol. 10, 1969, pp. 16–24; Jack Thiessen, "Canadian Mennonite Literature," *Canadian Literature*, vol. 51, 1972, pp. 65–72; and Elizabeth Peters, "A Glimpse of Mennonite Literature in Canada," *Canadian Modern Language Review*, vol. 29, no. 2, 1973, pp. 15–19.

Mennonite Literary Society in Winnipeg. When Hildi arrived at Conrad Grebel College as an Assistant Professor in 1988, these scattered efforts had already begun to coalesce into a conversation about the suddenly rich world of Mennonite creative writing. John Ruth's influential *Mennonite Identity and Literary Art* (1977) had been published, and Harry Loewen and Al Reimer were editing scholarly collections where scholars debated questions of literary theme and form in Mennonite poetry and fiction. Hildi herself had just published her second essay on Mennonite literature in 1986, and there were a host of other scholars clambering to join the conversation. In other words: by the time Hildi began to work on Mennonite literature in earnest, the study of Mennonite literature in North America was already underway.

And yet.

And yet there is good reason why, when Hildi retired from Conrad Grebel University College in 2012, the College's announcement confidently declared her to be "widely recognized as the founder and most significant sustainer of the study of Mennonite Literature" ("Champion"). Good reason, too, why her contemporaries, such as Ann Hostetler, single her out as "the scholar to whom the field turns to articulate where the conversation is at," and why Daniel Shank Cruz, a leading voice in the next generation of critics, has christened Hildi the "godmother of Mennonite literary criticism" (1). There is good reason why Magdalene Redekop, after acknowledging herself to be deeply "indebted" to Hildi's work, could safely add "like all who write about Mennonites and literature" (330). And yes, there is good reason why the novelist and essayist Rudy Wiebe, perhaps still the best known of all the Mennonite creative writers, described Hildi's contributions to the study of Mennonite literature as "incalculable," and as a "gift she has given to all of us" (qtd. in "Champion").

On Mennonite/s Writing provides ample evidence that shows why Hildi is so widely recognized as a field-defining voice in Mennonite literary studies. For if it is true that the study of Mennonite literature preceded Hildi's arrival in the field, the essays collected here make clear that she was less joining a critical conversation than she was setting out to initiate a new scholarly discourse. The criticism on Mennonite literature to that date, such as it was, had its focus elsewhere: on the representation of Mennonites in European drama; on the theological implications of the scattered works written by Mennonites in North America; or on German-language fiction and poetry among the Canadian Mennonites. The prospect of a Mennonite literature in English as a body of serious creative writing that would be widely read and open to the rigours of academic critique was only just beginning to come into view. Even Ruth's widely read lectures on the transformative potential that literature could hold for the broader Mennonite community made only passing mention of individual writers or specific literary works, insisting instead that there were "story-tellers needed" (13).

It would take the arrival of a breakthrough generation of Mennonite poets and novelists in the latter decades of the twentieth century to make it possible to think of Mennonite literature in collective terms. In part because of Hildi's work in sketching the history of the field, the central elements of the literature's emergence in this period are well known: in the late 1970s and throughout the 1980s, a loose collection of Russian Mennonite writers working in English, including Patrick Friesen, Di Brandt, Sandra Birdsell, and others, coalesced in Manitoba, from where they worked with major publishers and gained national reputations. So surprising was the emergence of this body of writing—coming, as it did, from a community with a deep suspicion of the arts and correspondingly little experience with literary success—that scholars routinely reach for the most dramatic of terms to describe it, such as a "Mennonite renaissance," a "Mennonite *fin de siècle*," or, most commonly, a "Mennonite miracle."[2] Before long, a corresponding burst of creative writing had begun in the United States—primarily, though not exclusively, among authors of Swiss Mennonite descent, including the poets Jeff Gundy and Julia Spicher Kasdorf.

In the expansive afterword she has contributed to this volume, Hildi recalls the sense of rich possibility afforded by the unexpected arrival of all this "new Mennonite writing," and reflects on her good fortune to find herself in the midst of it. "I had simply been, somehow, all those years, 'in the right place at the right time,'" she suggests. "I had been given an astonishing range of opportunities to observe at close hand and to comment upon a singular literary phenomenon" (267–268). She is not wrong, of course. It was, unquestionably, a fortuitous moment for a Mennonite literary critic to come of age—and not simply because there was a sudden embarrassment of Mennonite literary riches for the young critic to engage. Scholars have recognized a range of overlapping social, political, and historical factors that worked to unlock and foster a movement of creative writing among Mennonites in this period, but

---

2 The phrase "Mennonite *fin de siècle*" is used by historian Royden Loewen. The phrase "Mennonite miracle" is from Andris Taskans, editor of *Prairie Fire*, an established literary magazine based in Winnipeg, which published work by and about many of the Mennonite writers in this period. Hildi picks up on Taskans' phrase several times in the essays collected here, as have I in my own scholarship. Scholars using the language of a literary "renaissance" include Ted Regehr (295), Di Brandt (36), Jeff Gundy (217), and Magdalene Redekop (7).

have rarely paused to consider how these same factors were also working to foster a generation of Mennonite literary critics. The critics, like the creative writers, were animated and enabled by the rise of official multiculturalism and its encouragement of "ethnic" literature and minority cultural productions; they, too, were encouraged by the development of a broad and appreciative audience of a budding Mennonite literary culture. Critics, like creative writers, were participants in the wider post-war migration of Mennonites into urban centres and postsecondary institutions, where they found an academic infrastructure primed to recognize literary texts in collective terms as minority literatures. Indeed, a generation of literary critics was richly enabled and encouraged to turn their critical attention toward Mennonite writing in this period—including Hildi and her husband, Paul Tiessen, Magdalene Redekop, Ervin Beck, Ann Hostetler, and others, alongside predominantly creative writers like Di Brandt, Julia Spicher Kasdorf, and Jeff Gundy. Not one of these scholars had focused on Mennonite literature in their own graduate studies, but all responded to the conditions of their shared historical moment to become central figures in a fast-emerging field.

In another sense, however, Hildi's account of "hav[ing] been given an astonishing range of opportunities to observe at close hand and to comment upon a singular literary phenomenon" strikes me as slightly misplaced. It understates, in my view, the crucial role she played in *creating* this "astonishing range of opportunities," and for offering that opportunity to others—this being the central "gift" that Wiebe suggests she had given to the field. At Conrad Grebel College, Hildi's interest in Mennonite writing was met with strong institutional support. Within five years of her arrival, she had organized and hosted (along with *The New Quarterly*) the first major scholarly conference in Mennonite literature, "Mennonite/s Writing in Canada," alongside of which she undertook a truly herculean series of editorial projects, including: the first fully English-language anthology of Mennonite literature, *Liars and Rascals: Mennonite Short Stories* (U Waterloo P, 1989); the first three special issues of non-Mennonite affiliated literary journals dedicated to Mennonite literature, including a double issue of the respected literary magazine *The New Quarterly* ("Mennonite/s Writing in Canada," Spring–Summer, 1990) and two issues of *Prairie Fire* ("New Mennonite Writing," Summer 1990; "Patrick Friesen," Spring 1992); and *Acts of Concealment: Mennonite/s Writing in Canada* (U Waterloo P, 1992), a collection co-edited with Peter Hinchliffe of *The New Quarterly*, which included essays and creative work emerging from the 1990 conference. In this same five-year period, she also convinced the Social Sciences and Humanities Research Council of Canada to fund a series of extended interviews with dozens of Mennonite literary authors, and also contributed an entry on "Mennonite Poetry" for the *Mennonite Encyclopedia*. Shortly thereafter, she began her "Literary Refractions" series for the *Conrad Grebel Review*, which, over the course of some 14 issues through the next decade, she would use to introduce new work by Mennonite writers in Canada and the United States. If it is true that Hildi always seemed to be "in the right place at the right time" in those early years, in other words, it was usually less a matter of simple good fortune than it was because she had organized the event herself, and was hosting it, too.

By the late 1990s, a new conversation about Mennonite literature in North America was underway. A new generation of critics, most of them Mennonites themselves, were undertaking the project of reading the "new Mennonite writing" as a form of "ethnic" or minority literature, a prominent disciplinary framework of the period. In this new scholarly conversation, especially as it was being articulated in Canada, Mennonite literary studies was repositioned as a thoroughly secular affair, with the theological concerns central to the earlier critics being mostly set aside to explore the literature's complex but close relationship to distinct cultural or ethnic Mennonite communities. Accordingly, this new lens focused nearly exclusively on works written *by* Mennonites, rather than those *about* them. In keeping with the disciplinary norms of the period, this critical discourse elevated "serious" literature—mostly the type of fiction and contemporary poetry being published by major or academic presses—over other popular forms and genres of writing like children's literature, life-writing, or religious fiction. With few exceptions, the focus of this new discourse was also relentlessly contemporary: as scholars worked to grapple with the sudden excess of fast-arriving new works in North America, the German-language works of earlier Mennonite authors in Canada disappeared from critical view, along with the critical commentary they had inspired. Gone, too, was the earlier interest in literary efforts of Dutch and Swiss Mennonites of the early Anabaptists of the sixteenth, seventeenth, and eighteenth centuries. Scholars looking to write the history for this new version of the field marked its beginning just decades before, with the 1962 publication of Rudy Wiebe's landmark debut novel, *Peace Shall Destroy Many*.

The ways in which Hildi was working to foster this conversation can be read across her early work. In the introductions to her editorial projects of this period, for example, she frames the field as engaging the creative writing of "'Mennonites'—a designation some of them would define in religious, others in ethnic terms, and many in both" ("Mennonite/s Writing" 9), an "ethno-religious group" ("Introduction," *Prairie Fire* 9) whose work constitutes "one of the most vigorous minority literary cultures enriching the Canadian mainstream" (*Liars and Rascals* xi). This effort to locate Mennonite literary studies as a minority literature within the secular, critical context of Canadian literary studies is also readable in the venues in which these projects were launched (primarily in university presses and non-Mennonite journals), as well as in the critical genealogies on which Hildi drew. In *Acts of Concealment,* for example, she introduces her landmark collection of work from the first Mennonite/s Writing conference by invoking a host of decidedly non-Mennonite critical figures, including Robert Kroetsch, Bill Ashcroft, and Linda Hutcheon, and drawing on those working in Black, Jewish, and South Asian Canadian literary traditions,[3] in order to argue that "Post-colonial literary theory may well prove to be instructive in any future study of the development and place of the literature of the Mennonites in Canada" (12). Even as she began publishing more widely in Mennonite venues, such as *Mennonite Quarterly Review, Conrad Grebel Review,* and the *Journal of Mennonite Studies,* she continued to position her arguments outside of the field's critical genealogy. Direct quotations from earlier Mennonite literary critics, for example, are notably absent across her work: references to figures like Reimer, Ruth, or Suderman are almost always brief, and offered in anecdote or paraphrase. Later efforts to grapple with the emerging field as a whole, such as Margaret Loewen Reimer's *Mennonites and the Artistic Imagination* (CMBC Publications, 1998) and Douglas Reimer's *Surplus at the Border: Mennonite Writing in Canada* (Turnstone, 2002), are engaged even less. Instead, she draws her major references from established figures in cultural and literary theory more generally (such as Stuart Hall, Homi Bhabha, or, more recently, Franco Moretti, and Wai Chee Dimock), or from critics working in adjacent critical fields, including Asian or Jewish literary studies (such as Tina Chen and Benjamin Schreier). If it is true that early on, as Julia Spicher Kasdorf suggests, Hildi was "determined to drag Mennonite writing out of the margins at a time when it might have seemed exotic or parochial," it seems also to be true that she has remained determined to keep the critical conversation from sliding back into the margins from whence it came.

So yes, it would be too much to say Hildi *invented* Mennonite literary studies in North America. There were earlier scholars working on Mennonite creative writing, and a host of critics that joined the new conversation as it was forming in the 1980s and 90s. But we can also say, given her central role as an organizer, editor, teacher, and scholar at that pivotal moment, that it

---

3 Including Dionne Brand, Matt Cohen, and Michael Ondaatje, respectively.

is altogether fitting that it was Hildi who gave a name to the contemporary version of the field. She coined the phrase "Mennonite/s Writing" for the 1990 conference at Conrad Grebel, and it was promptly adopted as the umbrella term for the discussion to follow, regularly invoked—not least by Hildi herself—in the titles of edited collections, special issues, and essays, and as the organizing term for the field's major bibliographic projects. And, crucially, it became the title for the ongoing series of international conferences on Mennonite literature, nine of which have been held to date—all of which Hildi has helped to plan, naturally.

As one would expect, the critical conversation has shifted and expanded over the decades, as has Hildi's own writing. It has returned to (re)consider earlier authors and texts, as well as the theological aspects of literature; to ask questions of ethnocentrism and race; and to grapple with the shape and even possibility of the field's future. Indeed, the critical conversation about Mennonite creative writing, like the literature itself, is multivocal and varied, contested and conflicted. As Hildi herself suggests, there are multiple and distinct "Mennonite literatures," including those explored by scholars focused on the American and Canadian fields, respectively, but also the little-discussed world of Amish romance novels, as well as the fiction published by church-affiliated Mennonite presses—the latter being a form of writing that scholars "all but ignore" ("Beyond" 26). And yet since the 1990 conference, Hildi's name for the field was effectively synonymous with Mennonite literary criticism itself. In the afterword to this collection, Hildi calls it "something of a brand or trademark denoting a field of literary activity centred around texts written by authors who are Mennonites"; she also notes of that "both the assemblage of my own essays and the cluster of texts these essays engage seem now, in retrospect, to have comprised a perceptible (and in many senses, parallel) surge, wave, or phase" (269). In my assessment, the "brand or trademark" Hildi gave to the field is best understood as designating this "surge, wave, or phase." It is just that the name itself, "Mennonite/s Writing," had become so ubiquitous it had been hard to see; it was so widely employed that it seemed to function less as an argument about how to understand and define Mennonite literary studies than as the terrain on which such arguments could be held. For the better part of three decades, in other words, the conversation about Mennonites and creative writing was being held *on Mennonite/s Writing*.

As she recounts over several of the more personal essays in this volume, Hildi's background and education have richly informed her work in Mennonite literary studies—and thus, I would suggest, the shape of the field itself. Hildi was born and raised in Winnipeg, Manitoba, the child of *Russländer* parents (Russian Mennonites who arrived in Canada in the late 1920s after a dramatic escape from the Soviet Union). Like many other children of Russian Mennonite descent in this period, she grew up in a multilingual context in which she was surrounded by High German at church, Low German at home, and English at school, including her high school years at Mennonite Brethren Collegiate Institute. In a 2008 essay, she declares herself to be "Mennonite Mennonite," or Mennonite in both consent and descent. She writes:

> I am—in the language of the diversity of Canada's heritage groups—Mennonite Mennonite: Mennonite (religious denomination) Mennonite (cultural heritage designation). My religion is Mennonite. My heritage designation is not "Russian," even though my ancestors occupied a "Russian" landscape for some two hundred years. Nor is it Dutch or German, even though the languages I learned in my Canadian home originated in the Dutch and German regions of Europe. Culturally and religiously I am Mennonite, but the two identical-sounding terms I invoke when I say this do not mean the same thing. ("Mennonite/s Writing: State of the Art?" 45)

As readers familiar with the ongoing debates about the nature of the term "Mennonite" will recognize—and those coming new to this discussion will discover in these pages—the claims of this passage are only partially about Hildi herself. They also constitute an argument about the doubled nature of Mennonite identity in Canada, and, implicitly, the terms under which its culture and literature is to be engaged and understood. In that same essay, Hildi goes on to insist that Mennonite creative writing is at least as much about Mennonite cultural and ethnic identity as it is about religious and theological concern—even as she recognizes the contested nature of such a claim. "At the risk of evoking a stormy protest from people I know and people I don't," she writes, "who insist that there can be no such thing as a secular Mennonite, that the term is an oxymoron, I might remark that each of David Bergen and Sandra Birdsell and Miriam Toews, all agreeable enough to be spokespeople for the 'Mennonite miracle,' declared themselves on national radio to be reasonably comfortable with that 'secular Mennonite' nomenclature. As am I" (44).

When Hildi completed her undergraduate degree in English literature at the University of Winnipeg in 1968, however, the prospect of a "'secular Mennonite' nomenclature" being discussed on national radio in relation to a Mennonite "literary miracle" was still unthinkable. "The University of Winnipeg English Department taught little Canadian literature then, if at all," she reflected in 2004, adding: "And certainly no literature by Mennonites" ("Critical Thought" 239). From Winnipeg Hildi moved to Edmonton for her graduate studies at the University of Alberta, where she completed a Masters in 1971, and a PhD in 1981 focusing on the work of British modernist Wyndham Lewis. In Edmonton she reconnected with Rudy Wiebe, who was a faculty member in the English department and also a member of the Lendrum Mennonite Brethren Church, where Hildi attended. It was during her PhD studies that she first read a "Mennonite novel" in an academic setting. Her essay on Wiebe's work, written for a graduate class on "Western Canadian Literature," would be her first academic publication.

While a dissertation on the work of the British modernist may seem far removed from Mennonite studies, Hildi has suggested the project was fortuitous in its focus on "the nature and dynamics, and even the politics, of literary community" ("Thirty"). And indeed, the possibility, shape, and nature of a "Mennonite literary community," along with the place of the artist within it, would prove an enduring concern of her writing—both as an object of critical investigation, as in key essays like "The Role of Art and Literature in Mennonite Self-Understanding" (1988) and "Between Memory and Longing" (2003), and as a practical project, or even "institution," as she tentatively described it in a 2023 essay, built through a series of conferences and public readings, in university courses, book reviews, and, of course, in her scholarship.[4] Importantly, Hildi's exploration of the relationship between Mennonite literature and a broader Mennonite community quickly pushed past the type of ethnographic readings that often weighed down the reception of literatures described as "multicultural" in this period. Far from presenting

---

4 "When I invoke the term 'institution,' I am not referring to a community of writers," she writes. "I refer, rather, to a literary community that includes writers and everyone else: readers and mentors, critics, editors, reviewers, agents, publishers, graphic designers, copy editors, bookstore buyers, bloggers, award jury members, patrons and funders, readings hosts, conference organizers—all those figures we assemble in our minds when we speak of this project called 'Mennonite/s Writing'" ("Fourteen," 136).

Mennonite writing as the transparent expression of a stable ethnic community (or communities), Hildi repeatedly called for critics to push "beyond the binary" of such reductive readings, and to recognize Mennonite literature as a site wherein creative writers were "in large measure *shaping* ... the new cultural memory of the Mennonites" ("State" 48, italics mine). This faith in the constitutive force of creative writing within the broader Mennonite community remains a constant in her work, but was given perhaps its strongest articulation in a 2010 public lecture, published here for the first time as "An Imagined Coherence." "[I]t is without a doubt the literature produced by writers nurtured within the diversity of Mennonite communities [...] that is most palpably shaping how many Mennonites are seeing themselves in our day (and, of course, how Mennonites are being perceived by others)," she writes—before pushing further yet. "Perhaps we could also say that the Mennonites' homeland resides between the covers of books: the Bible, the *Martyrs Mirror*—and (is it so outrageous to say this?) the Mennonite literary discourse of the twentieth and twenty-first centuries" (173).

It was during her time at Conrad Grebel University College, however, that Hildi undertook her life work in Mennonite studies. She moved to Ontario in 1974, and, while completing her dissertation, began teaching at Wilfrid Laurier University. In 1987 she was hired as an Assistant Professor at Grebel, where she would remain through her retirement in 2012. Notably, much of her research in Mennonite studies was undertaken while she also shouldered a substantial administrative load. She arrived at Grebel as both the Associate Academic Dean and the Founding Registrar of the Graduate Program; in the coming years she would serve as the Academic Dean, the Vice President Academic and Academic Dean, and, briefly, as the Acting Director of Grebel's Peace and Conflict Studies Program and as the College's Interim President. Already in 1983, then as a part-time lecturer, she had developed one of the first post-secondary courses in Mennonite literary studies for the College. As she describes at some length in her 2016 essay, "Thirty Years of Mennonite Literature," she would go on to teach Mennonite literature courses at both the undergraduate and graduate levels at the College, sometimes incorporating major reading series into the curriculum, as in her 2012 series, "Celebrating Mennonite Literature." And, of course, she also served as a graduate supervisor or external examiner for multiple dissertations on Mennonite writing (including my own).

On Mennonite/s Writing: Selected Essays is thus but a partial record of Hildi Froese Tiessen's many contributions to the field of Mennonite literary studies. Since publishing that first essay on Wiebe's work in 1973, she has amassed a truly remarkable body of Mennonite literary criticism—including the editing of some 14 books or special journal issues on the subject, such as the aforementioned *Liars and Rascals* and *Acts of Concealment*, and special issues of *Prairie Fire* and *The New Quarterly*. She assembled a chapbook of tributes on Rudy Wiebe (2002), edited multiple special issues of *Conrad Grebel Review* (2004, 2008) and *Rhubarb* (2007, 2017), and co-edited volumes on Ephraim Weber (U Toronto P, 2006) and Woldemar Neufeld (Wilfrid Laurier UP, 2010). Including book chapters, essays, public lectures, introductions, interviews, reviews, reflections, and encyclopedia entries, she has published over 80 works on Mennonite literature in Canada and the United States. From this list, and in close consultation with Hildi, I have chosen the 18 essays that are included in this collection—16 previously published across ten different scholarly venues, one a public lecture published here for the first time, and one commissioned as an afterword to this project. And it is to the essays themselves that we now turn.

How does one best engage a volume like this? As useful as I expect it will be for scholars looking to track down Hildi's key works, I would encourage readers to consider working their way through the full collection chronologically, in the order I have presented them here.[5] It is rare to have the opportunity to follow a major critical figure across decades of her thinking in an area, and rarer still for it to be a scholar whose work has been so central to the trajectory of the field in which she works. For those familiar with the broader world of literary criticism, reading through the full collection in order provides an opportunity to track where Hildi's scholarship follows some of the larger critical trends over this period, as in the shift away from a New Critical emphasis on close reading toward a post-colonial emphasis of context and literary communities, through an engagement with identity-based scholarship in adjacent fields of criticism, and toward her late-career reassessment of identarian literary studies. These readers will also note how her work resists following other trends, such as the high poststructuralism of Derrida, or the most sharply politicized edges of literary theory as expressed, say, in the work of Foucault or Butler. Those familiar with Mennonite literary studies will be able to track lines of influence from and to her work,

---

5 Chapter 11, "An Imagined Coherence," is published for the first time, and has been placed in the table of contents by the date of the original lecture, in 2010.

as well, taking note of which avenues of thought she takes up, such as the cross-border analysis of American Swiss Mennonite writers (as practised by Beck, Hostetler, and Gundy) or the exploration of the intersection of religion and gender (alongside the work of Brandt, Redekop, and Kasdorf)—as well as those she rarely explores, such as the earlier field-building efforts or the later shifts toward theopoetics or queer theory.

Reading across the full collection also provides an opportunity to see the range and development of Hildi's key arguments in the field, and the chance to track her shifts in key terms and concerns. Readers of the full collection will be able to follow those arguments that return and build across the trajectory of her work, and also to take note of those frameworks that get tested and left behind. In several ways, for example, the earliest essays included here are atypical of the larger collection. The first, "A Mighty Inner River: 'Peace' in the Early Fiction of Rudy Wiebe" (1973), published while Hildi was still a graduate student, emphasizes the theological implications of Mennonite fiction; the second, "The Role of Art and Literature in Mennonite Self-Understanding," published 15 years later, is an attempt to explain the function of contemporary Mennonite arts in aesthetic terms. And yet while neither theology nor aesthetics would prove a central concern for her larger career, the essays are valuable as an opening pair both in that they reveal an arc to her thinking on Mennonite writing, and because, in their details, they clearly gesture in the direction of her work to come. It is notable, for example, that the *very first line of her very first essay*, published well before a critical mass of writing by and about Russian Mennonites made it possible for scholars to imagine a well-recognized, contemporary discourse of Mennonite literary studies, Hildi confidently presents Rudy Wiebe as reflecting a distinctly Mennonite form of writing, which she defines in both ethnic and religious terms—all while claiming a place for such work within in the secular realm of Canadian literary studies:

> Rudy Wiebe's *Peace Shall Destroy Many* (1962) and *The Blue Mountains of China* (1970) function within the Canadian literary context not only as works of Prairie fiction but also as documents that illuminate Mennonitism, a particular religious and ethnic orientation which has impressed itself upon the Prairie landscape for the past one hundred years. (169)

If this first essay claims a place for Mennonite literary study within the "Canadian literary context," the second essay included here, first published in a 1988 collection of essays entitled *Mennonite Identity: Historical and Contemporary Perspectives*, makes a compelling counter-gesture, looking to claim a place for secular literary criticism within the world of the Mennonites themselves. "The Mennonites won't fully accept art until they acknowledge what it is," she cautions ("Role" 248), using an argument that she rarely takes up in later work—that the literary artist works by "an ongoing, unselfconscious discovery of the possibility of the aesthetic in the commonplace" (246)—in order to settle on a conclusion that will prove central to her larger work: that Mennonite writers "are forcing new perspectives" both *of* and *for* the community (252).

Readers are also welcome, of course, to leap about the collection by making use of the table of contents or the index at the back of the collection. Those new to the field may be interested in starting with one of Hildi's wide-ranging, historicizing arguments about Mennonite literature given as state-of-the-field addresses at Mennonite/s Writing conferences. These essays will be especially valuable for readers looking for insight on the field at a given moment. They include "Mennonite/s Writing: State of the Art?" first given at the fourth conference, at Bluffton University in Ohio (2006), in which she posits that creative writing has become the primary force "shaping [...] the new cultural memory of the Mennonites" (248); "Homelands, Identity Politics, and the Trace: What Remains for the Mennonite Reader?" from the sixth conference, at Eastern Mennonite University in Virginia (2012), in which she attends closely to the active but shifting role of the audience for Mennonite literature; and "Beyond 'What We by Habit or Custom Already Know,' or, What Do We Mean When We Talk About Mennonite/s Writing?," from the seventh conference, held at Fresno Pacific University in California (2016), in which she reflects on the changing nature of the field. Those looking for the most accessible of the essays might consider beginning with one of the two included here first given as invited talks for a general public—one in honour of the Chair in Mennonite Studies program at the University of Winnipeg, and the other to mark the launch of a Mennonite Studies program at the University of the Fraser Valley. Both these pieces—"Critical Thought and Mennonite Literature" (2004) and the previously unpublished "An Imagined Coherence" (2010)—are engaging and enlightening: when speaking to general audiences, Hildi proves more willing to risk definitions of her key terms, lay out her claims boldly, and reflect openly on the field's accomplishments and potential.

I have also done my best to include all of what I take to be Hildi's most influential, or field-defining, works. These works have become classics in the sense that Jonathan Culler has defined the term: they were the first to articulate arguments that are now accepted as all but self-evident in the field. Well *of course* it's true, as she argues in "The Role of Art and Literature in Mennonite Self-Understanding" (1988), that early Mennonite writers were working self-consciously from the margins of their communities, we think. *Isn't it obvious*, as she insists in "Mother Tongue as Shibboleth in the Literature of Canadian Mennonites" (1988), that in deploying their Low German as a "shibboleth" in their works, the Russian Mennonite writers of the 1980s were invoking the very isolation they are ostensibly writing against? Yes, *of course* we need to move past the either/or logic of the author vs. the community as an interpretative model, as she argues in her seminal essay, "Beyond the Binary" (1998). And yes, it is *obviously true*, as she suggests in "After Identity" (2015), that literary texts sometimes need to be liberated from our critical squabbles.

The state-of-the-field essays, along with the key essays noted above, have been indispensable to the Mennonite/s Writing critical conversation, and are thus some of the most widely read of Hildi's scholarship. For that reason, I am especially pleased to be able to present them here alongside a broader array of her work. The collection also includes examples of Hildi's extended close readings of major figures and key texts, such as "Between Memory and Longing" (2003), a close consideration of the use of the photograph in historicizing Rudy Wiebe's novel *Sweeter Than All the World*, in which she leans deeply into the "transcendent" power of fiction; as well as "'I didn't have words for it': Reflections on Some of the Early Life-Writing of Di Brandt and Julia Kasdorf" (2018), in which she revisits her arguments about cultural hybridity to show how early Mennonite poetry stretched toward a complexity that even its authors were unable to articulate in their own criticism. The collection includes "Mennonite Literature and Postmodernism" (2000), perhaps Hildi's most playful and self-conscious essay, in which she both identifies and performs a type of ironic engagement with Mennonite identity; and "The Case of Dallas Wiebe" (2006), a brief, poignant account of the theological resonance of the work of an ostensibly "secular Mennonite" writer. And it also includes the 2006 essay, "A Mennonite Novelist's Journey (from) Home" an archive-rich essay similar to others she published with her husband and fellow academic Paul Tiessen. Here she recounts her efforts to trace the work of the early Swiss Mennonite Canadian writer Ephraim Weber. The highly readable essay showcases Weber's extended correspondence with writers like Lucy Maud Montgomery of *Anne of Green Gables* fame, and recounts a decades-long adventure that concludes with the discovery of a "lost" Mennonite novel.

Finally, I trust even those readers who know Hildi's work well already will find the collection as a whole worth rereading in the light of the retrospective essay that closes it. Readers will likely note an increasingly personal tone and retrospective gaze as she begins to take stock of the history of the field and its changing dynamics, beginning perhaps as early as her 2010 "Imagined Coherence" lecture, and certainly through the overlapping trilogy of essays that follow: "Homelands, Identity Politics, and the Trace" (2013), "After Identity" (2015), and "Beyond 'What We by Habit or Custom Already Know'" (2016). That retrospective gesture reaches its height, however, in two of the collection's final essays. In the first, "Thirty Years of Mennonite Literature" (2016)—aptly subtitled "A Fragment of Literary Memoir"—Hildi reflects on the personal and cultural contexts that served to animate her early work in the field, and offers an intimate literary history of her organizing and teaching in that period, even as it closes on a note that nears lament. This essay pairs well with the wide-ranging afterword, "'Some Hidden Rhythm.'" Here, Hildi offers a full retrospection on her work in the field, and notes with surprise the various trajectories that can be drawn across the decades of her work and the writing it has engaged. Among the most notable of her insights there is the prospect that the "most dominant *object* of literary representation from an earlier era—Mennonites thoughtfully negotiating their existence within Canada and the USA—had given way to its *subject*, which was now, more clearly than ever before, simply writers writing (and readers reading)" (294). The afterword also shows Hildi at her most reflective, as she takes the occasion, as she puts it, as an invitation to "ponder some of the questions that, for lack of time or courage, [she] had not paused to address" before (297).

With 18 chapters that reflect a full 50 years of criticism, *On Mennonite/s Writing* is a record of a truly remarkable scholarly career. Whether readers are coming to this work for the first time, or returning to it once again as a resource to be built upon or wrestled with, they will find Hildi a most thoughtful guide into what she once called "the land of Mennolit" ("Thirty"). Thanks in no small part to the work collected in this volume, there is now an abundance of literary critics considering—arguing, debating, and reconsidering—what it is we are talking about when we are talking about Mennonite literature. Welcome to the conversation.

WORKS CITED

Brandt, Di. *Dancing Naked: Narrative Strategies for Writing Across Centuries*. Mercury, 1996.

"Champion of Mennonite Literature Retires." *Grebel Now*, Spring 2012, www.uwaterloo. ca/grebel/publications/grebel-now.

Cruz, Daniel Shank. *Queering Mennonite Literature: Archives, Activism, and the Search for Community*. Pennsylvania State UP, 2019.

Gundy, Jeff. *Walker in the Fog: On Mennonite Writing*. Cascadia, 2005.

Hostetler, Ann. Email to the author, 3 October 2023.

Kasdorf, Julia Spicher. Email to the author, 1 October 2022.

Loewen, Royden. "A Mennonite *Fin de Siècle:* Exploring Identity at the Turn of the Twenty-First Century." *After Identity: Mennonite Writing in North America*, ed. Robert Zacharias, Pennsylvania UP, 2015, pp. 37–51.

Redekop, Magdalene. *Making Believe: Questions about Mennonites and Art*. U Manitoba P, 2020.

Regehr, T.D. *Mennonites in Canada: 1939–1970, A People Transformed*. U Toronto P, 1996.

Ruth, John L. *Mennonite Identity and Literary Art*. Herald Press, 1977.

Tiessen, Hildi Froese, "A Mighty Inner River: 'Peace' in the early fiction of Rudy Wiebe." *Journal of Canadian Fiction*, vol. 2, no. 4, 1973, pp. 71–76.

———. "An Imagined Coherence: Mennonite Literature and Mennonite Culture." 2010. *On Mennonite/s Writing: Selected Essays*. CMU P, 2023, pp. 169-177.

———. "Beyond 'What We by Habit or Custom Already Know,' or 'What Do We Mean When We Talk About Mennonite/s Writing'?" *Mennonite Quarterly Review*, vol. 90, 2016, pp. 11–28.

———. "Critical Thought and Mennonite Literature: Mennonite Studies Engages the Mennonite Literary Voice." *Journal of Mennonite Studies*, vol. 22, 2004, pp. 237–246.

———. "Fourteen Reflections After 32 Years." *Mennonite Quarterly Review*, vol 97, no 2, 2023, pp. 135–148.

———. Introduction. *Liars and Rascals: Mennonite Short Stories*, ed. Hildi Froese Tiessen, U Waterloo P, 1989, pp. xi–xiii.

———. "Introduction." *New Mennonite Writing*, spec. issue, *Prairie Fire*, vol. 11, no. 2, 1990, 8–11.

———. "Mennonite/s Writing in Canada: An Introduction." *Mennonite/s Writing in Canada*, spec. issue, *The New Quarterly*, vol. 10, no. 1–2, 1990, pp. 9–12.

———. "Mennonite/s Writing: State of the Art?" *Conrad Grebel Review*, vol. 26, no. 1, 2008, pp. 41–49.

———. "The Role of Art and Literature in Mennonite Self-Understanding." *Mennonite Identity: Historical and Contemporary Perspectives*, ed. Calvin Wall Redekop and Samuel J. Steiner, UP America, 1988, pp. 235–252.

———. "'Some Hidden Rhythm': On Being Right There, Right Then." *On Mennonite/s Writing: Selected Essays*. CMU P, 2023, pp. 267–295.

———. "Thirty Years of Mennonite Literature: How a Modest Course Became Something Else." *Journal of Mennonite Writing*, vol. 8, no. 1, 2016.

One

A Mighty Inner River: "Peace" in the Early Fiction of Rudy Wiebe*

R UDY WIEBE'S *PEACE Shall Destroy Many* (1962) and *The Blue Mountains of China* (1970) function within the Canadian literary context not only as works of prairie fiction but also as documents that illuminate Mennonitism, a particular religious and ethnic orientation that has impressed itself upon the prairie landscape for the past one hundred years. In each novel the material used is Mennonite, and the thematic framework in which it is cast is a theological one, tempered primarily by the author's own interpretation of Anabaptist teaching. Wiebe briefly describes the Mennonites in the Foreword to *Peace Shall Destroy Many* as "Anabaptists of the sixteenth century ... the extreme evangelical wing of the Reformation movement":

> The name "Mennonite" was early attached to them, after Menno Simons, their sole early theological leader to survive persecution. Because the group's literal biblicism expressed itself in believers' baptism, a life of discipleship, separation of church and state, non-participation in war or government,

---

* This very early essay was first published as Hildegard E. Tiessen, "A Mighty Inner River: 'Peace' in the early fiction of Rudy Wiebe." *Journal of Canadian Fiction*, vol. 2, no. 4, 1973, pp. 71–76.

> the "'Brethren," as they preferred to call themselves, were savagely martyred by Catholic and Protestant alike. Restrained from open proselytizing, they could do no more than teach their faith to their children; what in 1523 began as a religious movement became in time a swarming of a particular people from various nationalities bound together by a faith. (7)

In this same Foreword, Wiebe anticipates a major motif in *The Blue Mountains of China*: "they were a religious nation without a country. They were driven from Switzerland to America, from Holland and northern Germany to Prussia, then Russia, finally to North and South America" (7).

The characters of both of Wiebe's Mennonite novels are representatives of the group of Mennonites that originated in Holland and northern Germany and began to emigrate to the steppes of Russia in 1789. By 1914, approximately 100,000 had settled in over two hundred villages spread across the south and east of Russia, even though many had already begun to move to Canada from Russia in 1874. The migration to the New World was undertaken when the privileges originally offered to the Mennonites by Catherine II—religious toleration, exemption from military duty, freedom to establish private educational institutions—were jeopardized; it continued as long as a way out of Russia could be found. The experiences of the fugitives in Moscow, as described in Chapter 4 of *The Blue Mountains*, are representative of what these people had to face when, during the 1920s, they fled from the Communist regime which at that time further stifled their religious and social liberties. The story Wiebe tells of the Mennonites in *The Blue Mountains*—although the details make it a mixture of what he would choose to call "layers of fact" and "prisms of fiction" ("Passage" 257)—is a genuine physical and spiritual history of these people. A sense of the authenticity of Wiebe's account is provided in an individualistic "folk-response" to the novel:

> Brother Wiebe has torn us up by the roots with the black earth still clinging, and for all our people, let us pray.
> ...
> The facts of our history we, many of us, know tolerably well. It is the truth of our history that we have never learned.
> ...
> Our history is a history of fragments; God has torn the veil of our people; He hath scattered us in remnants abroad.

> Wiebe has gathered up the fragments: often, he has grappled with us clumsily, or violently, as we ourselves are a clumsy and a violent people ... often, he has taken us gently like children by the hand, as we also may be gentle and like children. One would think that, gathering fragments from so many diverse places—from Winnipeg to Siberia to South America—Wiebe should be left with a patchwork quilt. But truly, we are all of the same cloth. Truly, gathered together in our kulak boots and our blistered feet and our imported alligator shoes, we are all one family. (Toews 4)

In an interview Wiebe once stated that he would like to think of himself as "someone who's trying to live what the original Anabaptists were about" ("Moving" 148). The early Anabaptist fathers had stressed in their teachings a literal application of Jesus' concept of the brotherhood of humanity. In his fiction Wiebe attempts to demonstrate that those who would seriously wish to express that principle, and so live at peace with their neighbours, must first find peace within their own souls—specifically the peace Jesus spoke of so often, "such as the world cannot give."[1] Wiebe's theology as he provides it in *Peace* and *The Blue Mountains* is concerned above all with a definition of this inner peace and with a fictional exploration of some men's discovery of it:

> In a way I see that as the main thing that Jesus is all about, you know, the conscious knowledge of being at peace, in a state of rest in relation to everything around you, because somehow you are in a state of rest in relation to the God that has made it all. You don't have to be perturbed even if you are violently assaulted, because basically you're still at peace. In Jeremiah's images, it's like a moving stream, irresistibly moving on, but, in relation to its environment, perfectly at rest. ("Moving" 156)

Following the publication of *Peace Shall Destroy Many*, most critics expressed an apprehensive, casually dismissive attitude towards Wiebe. The initial reviews, which appeared in newspapers and periodicals that ranged broadly in interest and sophistication, were relatively insensitive to the novel,

---

[1] John 14.22. This and all subsequent Biblical quotations in this volume are from the *New English Bible*.

and were ready to dismiss it altogether. Apparently somewhat embarrassed by Wiebe's explicitly religious themes, reviewers failed generally to receive the novel on its own terms—as a serious attempt to deal aesthetically with a way of life dogmatically sustained by the Mennonite prairie settlers—and acknowledged the work simply as a token of a new author's "promise." Numerous influential members of the Mennonite community itself were unable to approach the book from a detached perspective, and so further obscured its merits with heated and prolonged controversy.

Critical consideration thus remains confined to these early reviews in which the novel is frequently perceived as flawed by undue moralizing. Reviewers remain oblivious to young Hal Wiens, who is both thematically and structurally a central figure. *Peace* is not primarily his story, yet Hal, whose name is an abbreviated form of Helmut (from the German: "bright spirit"), represents the positive force sustained throughout the novel which finally points toward a renewal of the life of the Wapiti community.

The story begins with Hal and Jackie Labret, one of the local Métis kids, looking for frogs' eggs while playing hooky from school on a spring morning:

> Brandishing his empty pail, the fair boy edged farther, eyes wild with the pushing life of spring.
> "The eggs should be out today—oogh!" he gasped, the water numbing his knees.
> "Yah!" The dark boy pushed gurgling by towards the sprouting grass of the slough-flats. The frogs were croaking loudly. (10)

It is significant that this young Mennonite boy should be exploring the countryside with one of the "half-breed" children, as the Mennonites call them. Friendly association with them is not condoned among the adults, a fact made evident with regard to the relationships between Herman Paetkau and Madeleine Moosomin, Elizabeth and Louis, Thom and the Indigenous children. Hal's attitude to his peers sets him apart from most other members of his community:

> You couldn't tell the difference between Jackie Labret and Johnny Lepp by the way Hal talked about them. (222)

"Half-breed" to Hal was merely a species of being that did certain things he himself was not allowed to do because they were "bad." (15)

Hal appears in three of the four lyrical preludes that define the cyclical structure of the novel. Spring, Summer, and Autumn. Significantly, he does not appear in the prelude to Winter, a season which the narrator himself indicates bears a direct relationship to the "spiritual winter" of humanity. It is only when the heart of Winter has passed that Hal's older brother, Thom, and other members of the community, begin to realize the folly of their life of avoidance and to reconcile themselves to a mode of acceptance already practised by this simple child who innocently embraces the world. Young Hal symbolically prefigures the state of inner peace, the reality and significance of which others are made to comprehend only at the end. He is the agent who announces in the last pages of the book that the community's isolation will end, by his denying the notion that the bush—which, as the central metaphor, represents the barrier between Wapiti and the world—defines its physical and spiritual borders.

As the world of Wapiti begins to disintegrate and the superficially-accepted formulae by which the people of the Mennonite community have structured their existence fail to sustain them, Thom Wiens comes to a fresh awareness. On Christmas eve he begins to perceive how Deacon Block's attempt to maintain an old, external order in a new land has strained the concept of Christian brotherhood and the pacifist stance so central to the early Anabaptist faith. Thom, whose call into military service is imminent, has already begun to question the working out of the beliefs of his forefathers against the demands of war. He is struck now by what meaning the Christmas pageant might have for him as a member of a traditionally non-resistant religious group. As he watches and listens, the barn adjacent to the Wapiti school becomes a grotesque parody of the scene of the nativity. The violence he witnesses makes him realize that he must consider the question of non-resistance in a context that extends far beyond the immediate conditions of the war:

> [A] long forgotten statement by Joseph rose to his memory. "We are spared war duty and possible death on the battlefield only because we are to be so much the better witnesses for

> Christ here at home." Comprehending suddenly a shade of those words' depth, he realized that two wars did not confront him; only one's own two faces. And he was felled before both.
>
> No. If in suppression and avoidance lay defeat, then victory beckoned in pushing ahead. Only a conquest by love unites the combatants. And in the heat of this battle lay God's peace. (238)

Thom, equipped with Joseph Dueck's knowledge about the meaning of peace, suddenly realizes the significance of the words boldly displayed at the front of the Wapiti school: "Peace on Earth, Goodwill towards Men." The discovery of peace as an inner state is central to the working out of Thom's mental and spiritual struggle. Similarly, in *The Blue Mountains of China*, the recognition that peace is not an outward condition allows David Epp and John Reimer to affirm their own unique responses to their world.

Because the theology of *Peace Shall Destroy Many* is consistent with that of *The Blue Mountains of China*, the first novel, which is mostly concerned with defining the nature of what Wiebe regards as the peace Jesus spoke of, serves as a valuable introduction to *The Blue Mountains*; the latter is concerned with the practical experience of this peace. Central to an understanding of the theology of both novels are Joseph Dueck's lengthy comments on the several meanings of the term "peace," comments making up a treatise rather too awkwardly presented within the context of *Peace* in the form of a letter from Dueck to Thom Wiens. Wiebe will not be misunderstood here. Dueck, who acts as the author's mouthpiece, delineates in a very straightforward manner several of the traditional ways of apprehending and applying the term "peace." He begins by saying:

> "peace" is often used in a general statement "to hold one's peace"—that is, a state of restfulness which includes silence. ... As long as everything goes smoothly and they themselves cannot be blamed, "peace" is being maintained. (162)

The "peace" Dueck speaks of here is, as he himself states, the form "frequently applied in our church meetings when a difficult point arises" (162). This is the quiescence Thom refers to when he speaks with his mother about Block: "he is Deacon; everyone's quiet and peaceful when he speaks" (218). Similarly, it is what the Deacon himself refers to when he approaches Herb Unger about the running of the latter's farm: "[W]e all want to live at peace together. That is best" (77).

By its very nature both superficial and threatening, it is a kind of whitewash that harbours decay underneath. Like the second use of the word "peace" which Dueck defines, its presence is a symptom of the impending destruction of the community: "As long as God gives us good crops and we don't have to fight in any war we are at peace. We can squabble with our neighbour as much as we please. Or we can neglect him entirely" (162). Not peace but meretricious good order is what the people of Wapiti experience in their relationship with their Indigenous neighbours, whom Dueck refers to at the *Gemeindestunde* [congregational meeting]: "They know that when war was declared, we all, on the instant, professed a love for our fellow man, men thousands of miles away whom we had never seen, a love which they, living beside us for fourteen years, had never felt" (61).

The overriding desire among the people of Wapiti for such a public tranquility makes Thom Wiens's thought that perhaps "it would be better living in a community with a man named Two Poles than with a man named Unger" strike him as the "strangest thought [he] could imagine" (39). The desire for the maintenance of this kind of peace provides an excuse for the fact that no one ever visits Herman Paetkau, the rationale for buying out all the English and Métis in the area and, finally, the grounds for Thom's question to his mother: "And why must we in Wapiti love only Mennonites?" (215).

Dueck defines near the end of this letter what he perceives to be the peace of which Jesus spoke; it is the peace that allows him to leave Wapiti.

> Peace is not a thing static and unchanging: rather a mighty inner river … that carries all outward circumstances before it as if they were driftwood. This was the peace Christ brought; he never compromised with a sham slothful peace, as we want to. He said, "Do not think that I have come to bring peace on earth; I have not come to bring peace, but a sword." He brought no outward quiet and comfort such as we are ever praying for. Rather, he brought inward peace that is in no way affected by outward war but quietly overcomes it on life's real battle-field: the soul of man. By personally living His peace, we are peacemakers. (162–163)

Dueck is responding here to Wapiti's avoidance of everything that does not relate directly to the wellbeing of the immediate community. For the

Mennonites here, apathy and retreat had become a vulgarized expression of the social and political passivity that had been adopted by the Anabaptists during and after their many years of persecution. Although they had originated as the forceful left wing of the Reformation, the Mennonites, driven relentlessly by their pursuers into the far corners of the continent, had been early forced to withdraw from all forms of public life. They came to be known, and to regard themselves, as *die Stille im Lande*; that is, "the quiet in the land." Their passivity was most obviously demonstrated in their doctrine of non-resistance, a belief initially respected by the governments of the countries in which they chose to settle. In his message to Thom, Dueck insists that the Mennonites must begin to express their pacifism not by turning away from the hatred and warfare in the world, but by combatting it with positive action. This idea is more insistently reiterated by the inwardly tormented Samuel U. Reimer when he replies to the psychiatrist in Chapter 12 of *The Blue Mountains of China*:

> "Maybe one man can't change the way the world runs. But can't he do something, anything, just some little thing maybe about what he thinks is worst? Can't he?"
> ...
> "You were in the big war and you say it's terrible. Okay, I wasn't. I was a Mennonite C.O. In 1943 the church worked it out for me and I worked in a camp, but that doesn't mean I'm not really a C.O."
> ...
> "I did, well, mighty little then—dirt jobs, that was the way to live for others in World War II; I guess. I'll never be sorry for planting a tree rather than shooting a man. Anyway that's the way I did, then, and less ever since. Nothing really. But now—now ... now such nothing isn't enough ... For me war, mutilation, starving people, that's the worst, now." (172–174)

Sam Reimer stands somewhere between those characters whom Wiebe presents as people able to move forward positively, enthusiastically embracing an existence to which a faith in God has given meaning, and those in whom irrepressible guilt has brought about a complete rejection of life. Beside Sam on the one hand is David Epp, "reckless of anything save his reckless faith" (137); on the other, Jacob Friesen V, so driven by fear of an omnipresent God that he can cope only temporarily with his existence by repeating mechanically the bedtime prayer common among Mennonite children: "*Lieber Heiland, mach mich fromm, dass ich in den Himmel komm*"—"Blessed Saviour make me pure that I may get to Heaven."

During the time that Sam encounters all the social obstacles that prevent him from going to Vietnam to "proclaim peace" he continually recalls the story of David Epp, of whom his brother John had told him. David had received God's call as abruptly as Sam had, but despite his misgivings he had responded at once: "David ... such a dreamer such a wonderful dreamer who even when they were in China already, over the border with their whole skin and not a communist in two hundred miles to touch them he still keeps right on dreaming" (55). On the other side of the blue mountains, David Epp suddenly had recalled with a troubled spirit what his father once had said about there being peace over every hilltop, and he had recognized that he had been deceived. Overwhelmed with the realization that his personal peace did not lie across the mountains, he had resolved to return to his Russian village and to those friends and relatives whom he and the others had betrayed. For Sam Reimer, however, the realization that he should have gone anyway, gone to Vietnam, somehow, despite all the obstacles that had been thrown in his way, came too late:

> "It was a mistake. When I heard the voice, I should of gone. Left a note and gone. When you know like that, are chosen, you shouldn't wait, talk. Go."
> "Sam," [Emily] said. "Sam, what would it have helped? What?"
> "Maybe not a thing, nothing. Like that Epp that went back." He thought a little. "Yes. It would have helped nothing. But do it, that's it. Some of it, just do it," he added heavily. (179)

David, "that Epp" to whom Sam alludes, is never heard of again after he crosses the mountains back into Russia, yet Wiebe makes it very clear that if David had to die, he would have done so as a man at peace with himself, free from the anguish Sam suffers for not knowing if he might indeed have been able to proclaim peace in Vietnam. The prose passage that expresses David's emotions when he arrives in Russia after crossing back alone over the blue mountains of China contains one of the most explicit allusions to the title of the novel and illuminates its thematic significance. The phrase "the blue line ... of the mountains" is interrupted by a significant short interior monologue—a narrative mode which, throughout the novel, renders the most personal responses of a character to his immediate condition—"*over every hilltop is peace now every treetop moves through you: every breath cease the nestlings hush in the wood now only wait you too will soon have peace*" (140). David realizes the multiple ironies that accompany his father's belief that peace can mean anything anywhere else but in a person's own soul.

The final scene of David's story shows him sitting at home before "the dishes from their last eating." The description is reminiscent of the last supper of Christ. David, a betrayer, has been unable to wrest his mind from the fact that "*the Lord Jesus the same night in which he was betrayed*" offered the first communion, and said "*but let a man examine himself and so let him eat of that bread and drink of that cup for he eats and drinks unworthily eats and drinks damnation to himself*" (126, 130). The only peace David Epp can finally experience—the peace that was denied Sam Reimer—is the peace of reconciliation with God, documented by Joseph Dueck in *Peace Shall Destroy Many*. While he sits in his deserted Russian home, David sees the mountains again, but recognizing the irony inherent in what the blue mountains of China had actually come to represent to him, he sees them in a significantly new light: "he thought he could see the blue line ... of the mountains far away, beautiful as they had ever been from there. But he knew now that was only his imagination. Or romantic nostalgia" (140).

As it is the language of a visionary dream (in Daniel 8.23–25) that provides the title for *Peace Shall Destroy Many*, so it is the action of a dreamer, David Epp, which becomes—indirectly at least—the inspiring force directing the peace missions of David Epp, Jr., and John Reimer, and the would-be pilgrimage of Samuel U. Reimer.

All these men demonstrate a principle already articulated by Thom Wiens in *Peace Shall Destroy Many*, that it was "not reasonable," for example, "for Menno Simons to give up a fat priesthood to become a hounded minister" (47). It is not "reasonable" for David Epp to cross back into Russia, nor for his son to live with Indigenous peoples in Paraguay, nor for Sam Reimer to want to go to Vietnam to proclaim peace, nor for his brother John to carry a cross from Winnipeg to Edmonton. "But Joseph keeps questioning," says Annamarie Lepp in *Peace*, "can a Christian cast off responsibility by mere refusal—by mere avoidance?" (46). Jesus says in Matthew 16.24–26, "If anyone wishes to be a follower of mine, he must leave self behind; he must take up his cross and come with me. Whoever cares for his own safety is lost; but if a man will let himself be lost for my sake, he will find his true self." The peace that Jesus brought, as Joseph defines it in *Peace*, is the peace John Reimer experiences, symbolized by his taking up an actual cross. Like David Epp, he finds the "inward peace" that "quietly overcomes" external disturbance on what Wiebe refers to as "life's real battle-field: the soul of man" (*Peace* 162–163).

Inspired by his brother Sam who, in turn, was inspired by David Epp, John Reimer takes a walking tour toward the mountains. He is a Mennonite Everyman, but he is not rushing from persecution nor toward the peace that his fathers so erroneously sought over and over again beyond mountain ranges. A boy from Nabachler,[2] John is just walking: "I am not going anywhere; at least not in Canada. That's the whole point, and I have to carry something that shows that … I am a human being, walking. That's all." When he reaches Calgary he perceives the mountains, as David Epp had observed the mountains of China after he had returned to Russia, in ideal terms: "sharp, beautiful, clean." But both men regard with irony any promise of peace on the other side. Like David, John realizes that "usually when you get over there's always more of what you climbed them to get away from." So he decides to go north instead of west, a decision affected primarily by his own interpretation of Jesus' teaching. John feels no need to cross over the mountains: "On the mountain Moses said, 'Go over that river, there's the land God has given you forever,' but Jesus just said, 'I'm going to make a place ready for you and then I'll come and get you. You wait'" (225–227).

The most prominent theme of *The Blue Mountains of China* is that Mennonites are New Testament Christians whose promised land "isn't anywhere on earth." Their role, according to Wiebe, is not to seek the peace that they variously and erroneously have interpreted as quiescence, good order, or public tranquility. Peace, Wiebe insists, is an inner state. Nor are they to become passive and apathetic at home, as Reimer says accusingly, "growing fat off the land." According to Wiebe's theology, Jesus came not to offer *Gemütlichkeit* [comfortableness], but, as John Reimer says, He came "to lead a revolution" for social justice. The new society John describes is composed of peacemakers like Joseph Dueck and David Epp, for example: those who choose first to live Christ's peace.

---

2 Wiebe derived the name Nabachler from the endings of the names of the three most prominent Mennonite settlements in Manitoba: Gretna, Steinbach, and Winkler.

Of all Wiebe's mature characters—that is, those who have passed beyond the time of childhood innocence and the accompanying "peacefulness" demonstrated by Hal Wiens in *Peace Shall Destroy Many*—it is Frieda Friesen who stands out as the one who expresses most completely that perfect state of being. Like Thom Wiens, Sam Reimer, and David Epp, Frieda is confronted quite abruptly with a crisis situation during which she chooses the way that leads to inner peace:

> It was a little later, November, 1906, when we already had two nice children, Johann and Esther, that God sent me great temptation and doubt. My nerves were very bad; I could not be alone. The devil stood right beside my bed with red horns and said, "Do it, do it!" though he never said what. Twice the elders had to come to pray. Then I learned to know our Lord Jesus. Through many prayers and sleepless nights and God's grace I found forgiveness of all my sins and came to the true quiet faith. I was teaching our little Johann the night-prayer I had learned as child, but I had to learn to pray it again then, like a grown-up who knows has to pray to God:
>
> *Tired am I, go to rest,*
> *Close my eyes, hands on my breast.*
> *Father, may your eye divine*
> *Watch above this bed of mine.*
> *Where I did some harm today,*
> *See it not dear God, I pray;*
> *For your grace and Christ's red blood*
> *Makes all of my evil good.* (*Blue Mountains* 46)

In John 16.33, Jesus says: "I have told you all this so that in me you may find peace. In the world you will have trouble. But courage! The victory is mine; I have conquered the world." Frieda, in her "true quiet faith," is satisfied that her life is in God's hands. In her gentle first-person narratives, which are effectively interspersed throughout *The Blue Mountains of China*, she emphasizes in her quiet way the value of her own experiences, and by implication, the ultimately coherent, meaningful nature of experience in general. While telling of her life she has counsel for her listeners, wisdom passed down to her from her own father. "'But think always like this,' he said, 'it does come all from God, strength and sickness, want and plenty'" (10).

Frieda bears a name that suits her most appropriately. "Frieda" is a derivative from the German word *Friede*, which means "peace." "When my father came to get us in the evening," she relates to her listeners, "I said right away that the teacher had said in school I was Frieda. My father laughed. 'Yes, yes. You aren't home now. You aren't Fritzchi like at home and just watch out that you're *friedlich* at school, like your name'" (8).

Frieda's *Friedlichkeit* is such that Wiebe is able to use her life as a fictional exploration of what it might mean for human beings to experience peace, such as the world cannot give, and trust in God that allows them to accept both the easy and the hard of life with goodwill and enthusiasm. Wiebe has created in Frieda a completely believable and engaging character living out an ideal freedom from that inner tension that has come to be called the existential angst, and thriving as a spiritual being regardless of the nature of external circumstances. Simply to affirm the truth of a promise of God is for many of Wiebe's characters the most significant gesture of their lives. To be able to live day by day in quiet faith, with the conscious knowledge of being at peace because, in the words of Frieda Friesen, "some things in this world only God has to understand," is the promise realized.

WORKS CITED

Toews, David. "Rudy Wiebe—The Blue Mountains…." *forum*, April 1971, pp. 4–5.
Wiebe, Rudy. "Passage by Land." *The Narrative Voice: Short Stories and Reflections by Canadian Authors*, ed. John Metcalf, McGraw-Hill Ryerson, 1972, pp. 257–260.
———. *Peace Shall Destroy Many*. McClelland & Stewart, 1962.
———. "Rudy Wiebe: The Moving Stream is Perfectly at Rest." *Conversations with Canadian Novelists*, ed. Donald Cameron. Macmillan, 1973, pp. 146–159.
———. *The Blue Mountains of China*. McClelland & Stewart, 1970.

Two

The Role of Art and Literature in Mennonite Self-Understanding*

IMPLICIT IN MANY modern definitions of art is the fully acceptable notion of art as an aesthetic device that serves to make the mundane—the everyday—seem strange, that interferes with our habitual, automatic way of seeing in order to force us to see with fresh eyes. Contemporary Mennonite writers and artists, insofar as they portray various forms of Mennonite experience in such a way as to distort and objectify the commonplace, effectively fragment their markedly diversified parochial audience. The experience of estrangement that art provides is intrusive and threatening for some (sometimes for disproportionately many); for others, precisely because art demands that readers or viewers reassess their experience, this estrangement is (in the broadest sense) liberating.

The artist has been described as one who "breaks through the crust of conditioning, of that which is accepted as 'normal' and sanctioned by unchallengeable 'order'" (Fischer 57). In the context of Mennonite art and literature this observation is applicable on several planes, for the Mennonite community's conditioning has included over the past 450 years not only

---

* First published as Hildi Froese Tiessen, "The Role of Art and Literature in Mennonite Self-Understanding." *Mennonite Identity: Historical and Contemporary Perspectives*, ed. Calvin Wall Redekop and Samuel J. Steiner, UP America, 1988, pp. 235–252.

traditional ways in which to perceive and embrace the world, but also a conventional resistance to narrative representational art in particular and to ornamentation in general.

Many contemporary Mennonite artists have provided for the spectator, in their aesthetic transformation of the conventional, a means of distance from the mundane. At the same time, by their propensity to aestheticize objects, customs, and modes of speech which have conventionally served to define Mennonite identity, they have (unwittingly and corporately) traced a route by which the fine arts could create for themselves a place within the Mennonite community. There is, as we shall see, in the emergent traditions of Mennonite art and literature a discernible movement toward an appreciation of the aesthetic unencumbered by the functional. A loose analogy might clarify this: just as Mennonite narrative fiction has tended to come the way of journal and memoir through historical fiction, to fiction no longer embedded in history, so too have Mennonite art and literature in general emerged progressively out of a growing awareness of the aesthetic quality of what were once commonplaces in the Mennonite community—commonplaces of speech (Low German, or *Plautdietsch*, for example) or functional artifact (most notably the quilt). In the progressive transformation of the familiar, Mennonite artists have at once embedded their art in Mennonite experience and released it from the imperatives of that experience. In this process they have stimulated the Mennonites in their audience to look at themselves and provided for them a means by which to assess their presents and their pasts.

I'd thought for some time that I'd like to begin this paper dramatically—with something like the following quotation from Sandra Birdsell's *Night Travellers*: "Being Mennonite," Lureen Lafrenière remarks, is "like having acne ... shameful, dreary. No one invited you out" (131). Lureen, the self-acknowledged black sheep of a Mennonite/Métis family, spurns the Mennonites, her mother's people: "I despised their fervent good works and their complete lack of adornment. It made them seem unnatural and grimly severe. They seldom smiled" (129). Certainly, to begin like that would have been to start to answer at least one of the questions implied by my subject: what have Mennonite writers and artists had to say about their community? And Birdsell is not, after all, alone among her colleagues in allowing the more vociferous of her characters to express anything from unqualified cynical disdain to a moderate sense of comfort as they reflect on their peculiar ethnic identities.

The longing for disconnectedness, for disassociation from enforced ethnic stereotypes that Birdsell's Lureen expresses is evident also in the interior monologue of the young narrator of "The Wedding," an unpublished story by Patrick Friesen. The teenaged narrator is surveying the gestures of a stranger his own age as both of them loiter in the parking lot of a church during a Mennonite wedding in the country:

> it was absolutely necessary that he know I was not part of all this; this church, this wedding, this white shirt, this singing, this German, these funereal cars, the chaff, the death you could hear in the buzzing of fat blue flies inside cars with their windows rolled up. I needed him to know I was something outside of all this, all this grain and Bible and black tires. Maybe I would tell him I was adopted.

Adopted? A similar notion—that one could extract oneself from the community by pretending one never belonged in the first place—prompted Rudy Wiebe, a few years ago, to publish in *The Camrose Review* a fantasy interview revealing how he came to be a Mennonite and why in deciding to join the group he had not, he thinks now, been as astute as he once had thought. Absurdly taking on the role of "the son of the Inspector General of the British Army" who deliberately took on a Mennonite persona in his youth, he wrote:

> I'm British, I'm English. I never had anything to do with Mennonites; that's a fiction I made up because of course in Western Canada there's much more point to being ethnic than to being English. Actually, a Canadian writer has an enormous disadvantage in being English, as you perfectly well know, rather than Ukrainian or Greek or Icelandic, or Mennonite. I had the races of the world to choose from and I made a really bad choice. ("Blindman" 40)

Wiebe directs some of his irony here at himself, but most of it at the Mennonite community that has revealed such ambivalence in its reception of both his work and his person.

Rudy Wiebe has created sympathetic characters who feel very comfortable within the Mennonite community (most notably, perhaps, Frieda Friesen in *The Blue Mountains of China*); others of his fictional people express the same resentment or disdain we've noted in Birdsell's and Friesen's characters. Liesel Driediger, for example, in *The Blue Mountains of China,* wants more than anything to escape her people with their "bulky shawls and fur caps," their "stupid old village [where they] just talked Low German and German that would sound like—like—she could think of nothing but the heavy felt boots some men still wore, so stinking when they shuffled by" (77, 81).

I would have liked to have begun with this sort of thing; with some of the explicit, unequivocal responses to the community; with Thom Wiens (in *Peace Shall Destroy Many*) provocatively questioning his mother, "And why must we in Wapiti love only Mennonites?" (215) or Aunt Lizzy in Barbara Smucker's *Days of Terror,* attempting to shake off the guilt of her class for the atrocities the Mennonites suffered during the revolution, muttering in retrospect, "Our terrible riches … It was so much more than most" (58). But there are problems with proceeding this way, even though remarking that characters in Mennonite fiction equate Mennonitism with having acne or with the presence of foul-smelling felt boots or inordinate wealth is interesting enough. Once we've catalogued and classified the various categories of response to Mennonites we find in Mennonite literature—then what? Moreover, doesn't the very notion of Mennonite arts beg the question? What, after all, are Mennonite art and literature? Let's begin again—with this.

I will not presume to define Mennonite literature (or art) in any absolute way. Instead, I will attempt to limit my use of the term to its fitting application here. For the purposes of this discussion, then, Mennonite literature and art consist of work produced by individuals who were nurtured within a Mennonite community, who—especially during their formative years—had access to the inside of the *Gemeinschaft.* Whether they chose later to withdraw in part or in whole from the Mennonites is—for my purposes here—irrelevant, as is the question of whether the subject matter of their work can be immediately identified as peculiarly reflective of Mennonite individual or corporate experience (even though, in most cases, it can be).

It is necessary to limit this working definition even further. I have restricted the authors and artists who appear in my discussion for the most part to those whose work has been acknowledged as creative literature or fine art—both inside and outside the community. This is work, in other words, that plays a discernible role in the broad mainstream of Canadian or American culture. Certain names come immediately to mind, especially in Canada where several Mennonite writers and artists are acknowledged as national literary and artistic figures. Rudy Wiebe, the winner of the Governor General's Award for Fiction and former Chair (1986–87) of the Writers' Union of Canada;

Andreas Schroeder, former Chair (1966–67) of the Writers' Union of Canada; Patrick Friesen, member of the executive of the League of Canadian Poets and founding president of the Manitoba Writers' Guild; children's author Barbara Smucker, winner in 1979 of the Canada Council Award for Children's Fiction (for *Days of Terror*, a novel about the Mennonite experience in Russia during the Revolution); Victor Enns, executive director of the Saskatchewan Writers' Guild, where his annual budget of close to half a million dollars is used to encourage new and established Saskatchewan writers, and to make Saskatchewan literature known and accessible across the province; Sandra Birdsell, selected in 1986 as one of the ten finest Canadian writers of fiction in the post-Atwood generation.

Of particular note in the visual arts are filmmaker Allan Kroeker, whose television dramas and dramatic features have won international distinctions at film festivals around the world, and sculptor-painter Gathie Falk, whose 1985-86 retrospective (on the West Coast and in Montreal) was the largest one-person show ever launched at the Vancouver Art Gallery.

There are, also, artists who do not have the high profile of those just listed but have nevertheless received attention for their work both inside and outside the Mennonite community. Cultural impresarios Jacob H. Janzen and Arnold Dyck; fiction writers Sara Stambaugh and Armin Wiebe (whose *I Hear the Reaper's Song* and *The Salvation of Yasch Siemens* were respectively shortlisted among the top first novels in Canada in 1984); poet David Waltner-Toews; writer Di Brandt; Ontario assemblage artist Susan Shantz and New Jersey painter Erma Martin Yost; Connecticut painter Woldemar Neufeld; Winnipeg artists Aganetha Dyck and Wanda Koop (both of whom have seen their work featured in major Canadian art periodicals).

This list is of course merely representative. Yet it provides a body of work by mainstream Mennonite artists and gives one the opportunity to begin to ask questions about the place of the arts in the Mennonite community. Not only, of course, questions like "are the Mennonites in general receptive to the arts?" and "what have Mennonite artists had to say about their people?" but also "what dominant motifs and themes are discernible in modern Mennonite literature and art?" (To this one could respond: the mythologizing of the past, especially of the Russian experience; the exploration of the role of language-as-weapon, cultural barrier, shibboleth, incantation; the dynamics of cultural assimilation and passage; sexual repression; the isolation of the community; the elevation of the mundane; the fall from innocence; and so on.)

Having defined for our present purposes the nature of Mennonite art and identified some mainstream artists, and having rejected the temptation to relate how Mennonite art reveals—simply, literally—ethnic identity, I'll return once more to the beginning, for we're interested here not so much in an exploration of art and literature as straightforward cultural reflection as in the arts as a powerful shaping force among a people—specifically in the arts' creating for themselves, perhaps since the turn of the century, but especially more recently, a legitimate place in the world of the Mennonites (and at the same time in their suggesting something about who the Mennonites are). I'll refer in the discussion that follows primarily but not exclusively to work produced in Canada, where the Russian Mennonites have been particularly heavily engaged in literature and the visual arts (not to mention music, which has played an enormous cultural role in the community, a role explored elsewhere by others). Why Canadian in particular? For several reasons, including the fact that the federal government's policy on multiculturalism (especially with its aggressive aid-to-publications program) has encouraged and supported in the last decade or so a significant body of Mennonite writing (including translations of almost-forgotten German works such as Hans Harder's *No Strangers in Exile*, and other works from the Mennonite Literary Society's series, as well as my own collection of Mennonite short fiction, *Liars and Rascals*).

The emergence of an aesthetic (a way of looking at art) has developed within the Mennonite community alongside (and in the context of) the discernible development of the artist figure—a figure with which Mennonites, as a community, remain relatively uncomfortable. We can see (since the publication of Arnold Dyck's *Lost in the Steppe* in the 1940s) an expressed desire in Mennonite literature for artists, dreamers, to find for themselves a place in the community, to be given a sense of integrity and worth. Hans Toews, in *Lost in the Steppe*, believes near the beginning of this *Bildungsroman* that his artistic sensibility is inevitably stifled on the steppe, where he is seen as valuable to the community only insofar as he demonstrates the efficiency of an industrious farm boy. Hans, however, is captivated by a world of story. The community's expectations of him, therefore, simply aggravate his frustrations when he awakes from his charmed dream world, his world of knights and dragons, to find himself once more "in Hochfeld, on the barn doorsill."

> Once more, as in Kronsweide, Hans quarrels with his fate.
> What is Hochfeld to him, this insipid village with its straight

lines and right angles, with its farmyards all formed after the same plan, houses with the same room arrangement, barns and sheds built after the same pattern, front gardens, back gardens, all the same. A mulberry hedge, running from one end of the village to the other, provides a border for all the gardens. Everything is a thirty-fold repetition of the same pattern. If one steps through the hedge into the open, one sees the endless grain fields, all of the same size, all planted with the same kind of grain, and beyond them the steppe, the pasture, more monotonous than everything else ... How poor and how lost Hans feels in this steppe desert, and how fortunate and rich seems the poorest charcoal burner's boy in those distant charmed forests where one can meet a bewitched princess, a proud knight or a daring highwayman at every step, if not even a fire-spewing dragon ... [Hans] lies there, until perhaps a raw voice asks mockingly: "Well, why does this one lie around here?" Enchanted princesses would not ask such stupid questions. Hans steals quietly home—and again reaches for his book. (131–132)

Despite his frustrated sensibility here, and his belittlement by the "raw voice" suggesting accusingly that the young dreamer is wasting time, Hans sustains his vision of an existence beyond the pragmatic, repetitive life of the farm. When he later does break through to an artistic vision by which he realizes his inner experience, he stumbles upon the necessary discovery celebrated in so much Mennonite art: that the mundane, the commonplace (for Hans in particular, the steppe and the little parochial village of Hochfeld) can be re-imagined as art and so revealed in its newly-acquired, aesthetically-framed complexity.

Patrick Friesen remarked, a few years ago, in an interview published in *Visions and Realities*, how he was liberated as an artist when he recognized in the commonplace the stuff of poetry:

I remember my big breakthrough was when I used the word "railroad" in a poem. You could use railroad? I read it in a poem by Betjeman, railroad. And I said "Wow, this guy's really a common person; he's really mundane and how could he get away with this?" (qtd. in Reimer and Tiessen 245)

Hans Toews's analogous discovery in *Lost in the Steppe* marks one of the first significant self-conscious moments in Mennonite literary culture when the artist figure recognizes that the mundane world he occupies can be comfortably discovered and embraced—indeed, reshaped—in the forge of his imagination.

About two thirds of the way through *Lost in the Steppe*, the book's sensitive young protagonist has an epiphany. During a trip to the city, he observes in a shop window an exhibit of large paintings of Russian seascapes and landscapes; and as these images clash in his mind with his own persistent view of "prosaic" village life, he muses:

> Pictures are always about something grand or something remote, never something seen here in the steppe, in Hochfeld, its people and houses, and its corn and grain fields. Why is that? May one not paint such things, isn't it feasible, or is it all so insignificant that it isn't worth painting? Maybe the reason is that none of all the artists knows that villages such as Hochfeld exist. That must be it, no one in the world knows anything about Hochfeld and its people, and that's why one never reads about them in a book. Whatever it may be, he is going to paint such a picture, the little Hochfeld farmboy in the corn field. (213–214)

We find in this minor incident not merely a poignant rendering of the awakening of an artistic sensibility (that is developed throughout the book). We find, rather, the young Mennonite boy projecting suddenly, upon a world he has consistently thought "insipid" and "monotonous," a new identity. He has forged in his mind a myth about the Mennonite village of Hochfeld, to say nothing about the little Mennonite urchin on the steppe.

Art is, of course, as Hans's experience implies, a great shaping force, not something that merely offers a rendering of reality, but something that gives form to what we experience, something that moulds and enriches life. It doesn't so much reproduce what we see as determine both what we see and how we see it. Hans is ambitious to interpret Hochfeld to the world; what is more important is that he would interpret Hochfeld to the Hochfelders. It was undoubtedly a tradition of recognizing this unqualified force of art in determining what and how we see even that which has become most familiar that accounts for the resistance to the arts (to realistic fiction in particular) in the Mennonite world.

The volume and tone of the letters that swamped the *Mennonite Brethren Herald* in response to the *Herald*'s positive review of Rudy Wiebe's *My Lovely Enemy* demonstrate the degree to which many members of the Mennonite community continue to regard the writer of fiction as an iconoclast, a heretic, or simply a rascal (Nickel 26–27). (It's worthwhile noting here that a significant number of Wiebe's most vociferous epistolary detractors declared—with pride—that they hadn't deigned to read the treacherous tome!)

A repressive vision vis-à-vis the arts can often be identified in Mennonite literature with a pious religiosity that is cast in opposition to the inevitably more liberal and more complex sensibility of the artist figure. The lack of ease with which the pious figure (inevitably the mother) greets the threatening world of art's alternative vision finds expression in *Lost in the Steppe*, where Mother is seen to disapprove of her son's reading. (Father, interestingly, is more readily receptive to literature.)

> [Father] sits and reads. Before he read in the Bible only, but with the years and as his sons grow up, he too has become more "worldly." He reads newspapers today, especially the *Messenger*, and also the *Voice of Peace* ... In addition the family calendar appears around Christmas, making for very welcome reading material. He often asks Hans for the *Children's Friend*. He has read all of it already, but likes to re-read this or that. And recently father has even started to read regular "story books," the same that Berend and Hans read. Now that is "useless stuff," but it's fun for him, and mother often must call two or three times before he puts away the book and comes to the dinner table. Mother in her quiet manner scolds at such book reading; it surely looked nice, for him, the father, to foster such a bad habit; it was enough not to be able to pry the boys loose from their books. Quite likely he would soon begin to read novels too. Thus mother scolds. —Novels—something worse, leading people directly to perdition, didn't exist for the sedate Hochfelders, at least as far as the older generation was concerned. Novels—ha!—Sure enough, one day father sits behind a novel; Berend didn't happen to have anything else. And, look, there, no earthquake! When the world continues to spin on its axis as usual, father continues with a second "love story." Berend, the rascal, laughs up

his sleeve for having seduced his father to sin, and because he now has "got his man" as far as the matter of books is concerned. (159)

In an analogous setting in *The Trail of the Conestoga* by Mabel Dunham (a descendant of the Swiss/Pennsylvania Mennonite settlers who founded the city of Kitchener), the mother figure Nancy Eby condemns, in a fit of righteous anger, her son's reading of *Pilgrim's Progress*:

> No sooner had the dishes been cleared from the table and replaced by the red tablecloth than Hannes took a book from his pocket, sat down at Christian's place and began to read.
>
> Immediately Nancy was concerned. She bustled about excitedly, and looked over her son's shoulder. Just as she expected. He was reading that useless story book of his. "He's at it again," she told her husband.
>
> "Ach, leave him be," said Christian, not in the least alarmed.
>
> "That's always the way," replied Nancy, in an aggrieved tone of voice. "You let me with all the trainin' to do. All them lies he is readin'! It'll ruin him body and soul!"
>
> Christian was sufficiently interested in his son's spiritual welfare to put on his spectacles and go and look over his shoulder to see what was the nature of this pernicious literature that Hannes was imbibing with such avidity. He was surprised to find his own name printed there. "Christian in the Slough of Despond," he read.
>
> "It's all a pack of lies," reiterated Nancy.
>
> But Christian was absorbed in this namesake of his who seemed to have fallen into a terrible pit. He was so anxious to know if he got out again that he could hardly wait until Hannes had turned the page.
>
> "You're readin' them lies, too," cried Nancy, consumed with that species of temper known as righteous indignation. She swooped down upon the table, seized the contaminating thing, and threw it into the fire. "There," she said with satisfaction. "Now it can't hurt either of you. Ain't the Bible good enough for you no more?"

> Hannes was amazed, but he said nothing. It was no use, he knew.
>
> "Where did you get it?" whispered Christian.
>
> "From Jake Brubacher," replied Hannes. "He fetched it from Lancaster last week already."
>
> Christian was keeping a watchful eye over Nancy's movements. At an opportune moment he drew out his purse, took out a number of coins, and said: "Tell him he can fetch you another one along over sometime when he goes again."
>
> "It's a story-book," said Hannes, unwilling to spend his father's money for riotous literature without his knowledge and consent.
>
> "A true story-book," replied Christian, shoving the money into the young man's pocket. "I read enough to know that. But you must hide it, Hannes, or it will come in the fire too." He glanced knowingly in Nancy's direction.
>
> So the secret bargain was sealed. (14–16)

(I'm tempted to digress here—to probe the implications of the small myth that has emerged from the constellation of texts just quoted: the Mennonite matriarch as subverter of the arts. But I'll resist the temptation.)

Nancy Eby's conviction that fiction leads to perdition because it's "a pack of lies" is not, of course, a peculiarly "Mennonite" one. The rejection of fiction on the basis of its departure from "objective truth" can be seen in various cultural traditions, including that of the Puritans of seventeenth-century England, who might very well have produced a whole school of poets along with Milton had they not regarded with suspicion the secular imagination that was capable of producing icons and statues and elaborate ecclesiastical rituals—all allurements of the sensual world, enticements that threatened to contaminate and diffuse the energies of the spirit. That the Mennonites shared the Puritans' suspicion of adornment and ornamentation is well known. And their lack of ease with "fiction" (a discomfort that extends, as I've already noted, into this decade) is an expression of a far-reaching conventional resistance to fabrication, to the very "lies" Nancy objects to in Dunham's novel.

Most certainly the resistance to literature and art among the Mennonites was not likely ever to have been all-encompassing, as the rather impressive catalogue of Mennonite writers in the *Mennonite Encyclopedia* suggests. Receptivity to the arts within the Mennonite community has been and remains inconsistently developed, as Jacob H. Janzen, a champion of the arts among his own people, revealed in the first issue of *Mennonite Life* (January 1946) where, in a short passage in his essay on "The Literature of the Russo-Canadian Mennonites," he recalled how he—a writer of fiction—was received by church officials upon his arrival in Canada in 1924:

> when I came to Canada and in my broken English tried to make plain to a Mennonite bishop that I was a "novelist," (that being the translation for "Schriftsteller" in my dictionary) he was much surprised. He then tried to make plain to me that "novelists" were fiction writers and that fiction was a lie. I surely would not want to represent myself to him as a professional liar. I admitted to myself, but not aloud to him, that I was just that kind of "liar" which had caused him such a shock. (22)

Janzen, along with Arnold Dyck, was to campaign vigorously for the acceptance and development of the arts among the Mennonites of Canada. Both perceived one of their most important roles to be the nurturing of the Mennonite audience that had, Janzen argued, developed by 1935 a favourable enough response to interesting narratives—whether they recorded the lives of the saints or the adventures of settlers and Indigenous peoples on the American frontier. But this same audience was decidedly unreceptive to work written about the Mennonites themselves, as Janzen observed:

> Mennonitism was regarded in certain respects as a "terra sancta" on which the jugglery of belle-lettres dared not appear. That Mennonites would write in this genre [fiction] was simply sin. After all, one could not treat Mennonitism that way. (22)

Janzen's self-conscious despair about the Mennonites' reception of the arts finds further expression in his observations, in the same essay, about Joost von den Vondel, the seventeenth-century Dutch author—indeed, the master of the Golden Age of Dutch Literature. Of Mennonite ancestry on both sides and for four years (1616-1620) a deacon in the Mennonite church, he left the Mennonites in 1641 to become a Roman Catholic. His transfer to Catholicism, Janzen suggests with regret, was not (as many have assumed) "founded in ungodliness or disloyalty to the brotherhood in which he was born," but rather occurred so that the Mennonites would no longer hinder his talents (22). Janzen laments openly when he wonders whether Fritz Senn (Gerhard Friesen), whom he calls "the Tschaikowsky of the Mennonite poets and novelists," left the church because—like von den Vondel—he found it "too narrow and complacent": "Oh, when will we finally realize that people that have been called to render a great service must also have the freedom and opportunity to render this service?" Janzen asks. "God be merciful to us!" he adds, as he despairs over the Mennonites' ungracious reception of the artists among them (Janzen 24).

In Arnold Dyck's *Mennonitische Volkswarte* of September 1935, a regular contributor on the arts, G. Loewen, echoes Janzen's sentiments:

> It often seems to me that, in general, we Mennonites belong to the most prosaic people in the world. We are much too materialistically minded, and so quickly and easily forget that there are things superior to money and goods, and everything that the body receives, that we also have a mind and soul which want to be satisfied… It is our duty to develop [our finest aesthetic sensibilities] and to further cultivate them. He who does not heed his physical gifts lets them waste away, so that they are of use to neither himself nor to others. The same also applies to the goods of our mind. (338)

Dyck's, Janzen's, and others' encouragement of the Mennonite community to acknowledge and develop the significant role art and literature can and should be allowed to play has, over the years, had an effect. Yet even today Mennonite artists are likely to feel constrained by a community that explicitly or implicitly denies them artistic autonomy. The role of artists among the Mennonites remains complex, unresolved, and they are likely to have to leave the community or—if they remain—be willing to adopt the role of the apostate.

The New Jersey painter Erma Martin Yost has observed that since being an artist meant working with her hands, her family felt comfortable with her vocation. But to major in art in college was frowned upon in her Indiana Mennonite environment: "people … were very discouraging. It was not 'service'" (Yost). In an interview in *Visions and Realities*, David Waltner-Toews has revealed something of his own perception of the Mennonites for whom he writes:

> When I was growing up it was a very closed world; you couldn't see beyond it. So when I write about Mennonites I often think I'm writing for my father's audience. Sometimes I give up on them and then the next minute I don't give up on them. If I have a responsibility to anybody in the world ... then it should be to those people in some way. In fact, it causes me to edit some things, just technical things, in terms of language and stuff, which I might otherwise leave in because they don't offend me, but I think they might offend those people. (qtd. in Reimer and Tiessen 248)

In the same joint interview, Patrick Friesen observes defensively: "I want to insist—at least speaking for myself—I'm a writer, I'm not a Mennonite writer. I'm a Mennonite and I'm a writer and you must differentiate" (253).

It is apparent that artists or writers among the Mennonites struggle to find a place—or, finding none, leave the community (insofar as they can leave, for their ethnic home will inevitably continue to inform their work). And this apparent leaving will, without a doubt, raise a sigh of relief in one quarter and a cry of regret in another. "When I was 12," Sandra Birdsell was quoted as remarking in a 1984 issue of the *Toronto Star*, "I decided I wasn't going to be a God-fearing Mennonite. There wasn't anything [my Mennonite mother] could do about it. The odd thing is that now the Mennonites are claiming me as one of them."

Birdsell, Friesen, Andreas Schroeder, and others who have deliberately adopted the stance of outsider have a freedom of expression vis-à-vis their Mennonite audience not available to insiders like Waltner-Toews and Rudy Wiebe. While Birdsell declares her surprise at being embraced by a community she thought she'd abandoned years ago, Wiebe struggles for autonomy, though not without having developed a sense of irony, evident in his closing statements in his mock interview in the *Camrose Review*:

> *Then why have the Mennonites laid claim to you? What's in it for them?*
>
> Oh well, heck, they're just glad to grab any publicity they can get. I mean they have so little artistic reputation, until

my generation they've never had a writer writing in English in this country worth reading twice.

Then how did they end up with you? Couldn't they have chosen someone else?

They've certainly thought so many times since, I assure you, but after my first book came out the die was cast. They couldn't do anything about it and they just have to put up with it, now. ("Blindman," 44)

    One can see in Mennonite literature and in the development of a Mennonite artistic tradition the emergence of an artist figure foregrounded against an ambivalent constituency. Similarly, one can perceive in the literary and other artifacts Mennonite artists have produced the blossoming of an aesthetic—not a self-conscious articulation of the clause: "this is art," or "this is aesthetically pleasing," but an ongoing, unselfconscious discovery of the possibility of the aesthetic in the commonplace. In the process of this discovery artists learn to distance themselves from their experience and so enable themselves—and those who willingly respond to their work and so effectively become co-producers and not merely consumers of art—to discover the new in the once familiar. Artists, that is (along with their responsive audience), in embracing their world aesthetically, allow it to be endlessly reshaped.

    When young Hans Toews realizes that he will return to the village of Hochfeld and paint it and so make it visible, his epiphany is not without context. Dyck has alerted us from the very beginning of this *Bildungsroman* to young Hans's artistic sensibility—specifically to his noting with surprise the occasional implicit acknowledgement of aesthetic pleasure by other members of the household. He notes with particular interest (and dismay) a family propensity to collect fragile keepsakes known as "sugarthings" which, he observes, "do not exist because of the sugar, but stand empty and unused decade after decade in the china cabinet of the great room because of their external splendor" (25). Why, Hans wonders, have certain household objects been singled out as valuable in spite of their function? He's never, after all, learned to appreciate adornment for its own sake, and it's not just the "sugarthings" that perplex him:

> There, over the door leading into the small room, a board has been attached with a wooden rod before it. The board

> and the rod serve as a support for the plates ranged behind the latter. They stand on their edges in such a manner that their inner sides with their decorations are turned toward the viewer. Five plates stand next to one another, extending over the whole breadth of the door. In notches made in the front edge of the board hang a dozen round pewter tablespoons with the handles down. Once Hanschen had thoroughly perceived the wallboard with the plates and the spoons, he often thought about it. He wasn't able to understand why mother would keep plates and spoons in this manner, a waste of space. "That's for looks," she explained to him. Now he understood the thing less than ever. Does he perhaps not understand because, aside from this plate shelf, another such in the great room, and the brightly embroidered show pillows on the guest bed, there is nothing, nothing at all, that serves the sole purpose of beautifying the home? (21)

By acknowledging that functional objects could have another, independent aesthetic value, the Mennonites can progressively develop (Dyck seems to suggest) an original artistic sensibility, a cast of mind that would allow their distinctly Mennonite arts to begin to flourish. For Arnold Dyck, the Mennonites' repressed aesthetic sense finds expression in the decorative glass and china that, as Hans observes, seem to belie the practised plainness of the typical Mennonite home. (This mode of response found expression also, Dyck suggested [with his inimitable wit], elsewhere: in the Canadian Mennonites' seemingly unqualified [and unrefined!] embrace of the Eaton's catalogue as artifact.) In *Mennonitische Volkswarte*, he wrote:

> Paintings, pictures! Don't we have the most beautiful wall calendars hanging in every room, with magnificently large pictures! Don't we have the newest Eaton's catalogue lying on the shelf, the book which (malicious tongues wish to claim) must be judged in this country as the second Bible, and which is actually worn out in some households before the Bible. Eaton's catalogue—how many of us that came into this country as foreigners didn't draw their first knowledge of English out of this book? The book with so many beautiful

pictures. An instructive book, a useful book. All evening long we sit around and enjoy it. ("Ernstes" 29)

It is in what Dyck here gently mocks as the Mennonites' being vulnerable to "pretty things"—whether they be plates or glass or pictures on a calendar or in a catalogue—that the Mennonite aesthetic sensibility seems to be based. The artist recognizes the aesthetic potential of the ordinary, but in distancing the commonplace object from its pragmatic function, by removing it from the context in which the community customarily sees it (the plate above the door rather than on the table), he alters its perceived value. Once the plate has been seen hanging above the door, it becomes something else. Out of a recognition of patterns of convention in Mennonite households such as the enshrining of the decorative plate emerges a receptive attitude toward art rooted in the Mennonite experience.

The plate above the door probably has a less forceful impact as art than, for example, the quilt on the wall. What is significant is that for an individual to accept the plate as art, its context must be seen to have altered. A significant problem emerges when this doesn't happen. Consider the widespread rejection by the Mennonite constituency of what we call realistic fiction, for example. This audience resistance is rooted quite simply in a sustained confusion of art and life. The Mennonites won't fully accept art until they acknowledge what it is.

Several artists among the Mennonites have played significant roles in gently demonstrating how art, while it borrows from life, simultaneously breaks itself away. Their art, by means of its combined subject and form, teaches its audience what art is. The work of Erma Martin Yost is of particular interest in revealing how the Mennonite arts provide—to a large degree—a readily discernible catalogue of their own development from the pragmatic to the aesthetic. The works in Yost's quilt series—made up of double-blocked panels with actual patchwork designs at the bottom and painted "transformations" at the top—doubly objectify the quilt as household object.

But Yost's transformation of the quilt is just one example. The fact that Merle and Phyllis Good—who have taken upon themselves the role of impresarios of Mennonite art, literature, and pop culture in the United States especially—have published a series of glossy illustrated quilt books over the past few years endorses this interpretation of Yost's transformations. The quilt, in other words, no longer exists for Yost or the editors of the Goods' books as a functional object. Separated from its function, it is transformed by paint or photograph into something else. The Goods' promotional material confirms this reading: "This gallery of over 200 antique quilts includes masterpieces from all the major Amish communities," it says, encouraging the reader to think of the quilts as art; or it suggests that the readers "recreate the charm and beauty of the antique masterpieces" by making quilts of their own.

Another transformer of the patchwork blanket is Canadian artist Gathie Falk, who describes her artistic intention as taking "commonplace items—recordings of unimportant events, throw away pieces of life, and ... making [of them] something singular, if not exotic"; her work has been referred to as "a veneration of the ordinary" (8). Falk, referring (presumably) to the well over 100 ceramic cabbages she molded, bisqued, fired, and painted leaf by leaf to exhibit (150 at once) suspended by string at eye level in a public gallery in 1978, and to her paintings of these rather common vegetables, declares, "I want to make cabbages precisely because they are not exotic." Falk is working in a tradition of mid-60s "funk," but her work, like Aganetha Dyck's domestic sculptures and assemblages, appropriately reveals the search for the acceptable aesthetic that finds parallels in so much other Mennonite art and literature. Like Yost's quilts, Falk's cabbages, and her shoes and chairs, Dyck's jars of preserves occupy two worlds at once; they remain (denotatively) what they were, yet are metamorphosed into objects of art. In essence, they evoke the world of everyday while occupying the world of art. They invite their audience to say: "This is familiar" or (colloquially) "I can relate to this" and at the same time to remark, "But I've never seen it quite this way" or "On the other hand, it's not familiar at all; it's something else." By their very familiarity the quilts, the cabbages, the jars of preserves deny the "otherness" of art and so diffuse the threatening claims that art has periodically made on the realm of the spiritual, the transcendent.

What we've observed here as a noticeable pattern in the visual arts of the Mennonites is revealed also in the fiction of several recent Mennonite writers who have enshrined Low German—the conventional "everyday" language of the Russian Mennonites—in their English fiction and in so framing it have effected the same sort of thing we see in Yost's quilts: function becomes a memory; the Low German words and phrases become ritual, incantation, shibboleth. The most recent example of Low German used in this way is Armin Wiebe's *The Salvation of Yasch Siemens* where folk expressions such as *heista kop* and *drankahma*, *fuschel* and *freumensch*, and nicknames like Penzel Panna, Laups Leeven, Hingst Heinrichs, and Pracha Platt are not only peppered throughout the work but in fact define the prose rhythms and tone of the entire novel (the book is neither technically nor functionally a novel, of course, but a collection of stories). The fact that the book—in spite of its linguistic acrobatics, or because of them—has a wide and enthusiastic English-speaking audience confirms the role of the Low German as sound and ornament rather than conventional communicative expression.

Armin Wiebe is not alone among the Mennonites to embrace and aestheticize the mundane in the form of language. The poet David Waltner-Toews similarly packages in his "Tante Tina" poems clichés referring to ethnic food and transforms them into shibboleths, passwords that can confirm or deny community membership on the one hand and serve as ritual sound on the other. Tante Tina speaks of Hanschen, her son, in Waltner-Toews's collection *Good Housekeeping*:

> He wants to be rich, like the English,
> and save us all from Mannagruetze.
> His heart is tight as a peppernut.
> His head is a piroshki
> stuffed with fruit.
> ...
> Oh my son
> my heart is heavy,
> thick as glums.
> If you come home
> it will rise, light and sweet.
> I will make you porzelky for breakfast
> and we will celebrate the New Year
> every morning. ("Tante" 80–81)

A similar packaging of words and phrases is cleverly executed by American writer Warren Kliewer. In his collection of stories entitled *The Violators*, Kliewer enshrines and preserves (crystallizes? mummifies?) pietistic phrases as surely as Gathie Falk preserves shoes in cabinets or Plexiglas or as Aganetha Dyck preserves (mock) fruit in jars. What follows (from Kliewer) is a conversation, ostensibly among three men, although the third man—the "young man" of the first sentence—isn't heard.

> "Young man," Ezra said, "we all thought you would turn wicked in the big city. What do you do in your evenings?"

> "Let me beseech you," the pastor replied, "if you have sinned, to fall down on your knees and pray for forgiveness."
>
> "Do you run around with wicked women?"
>
> "Amen, my brother. The Lord will forgive."
>
> "What does the school board in Winnipeg say about what you do? Don't they ever check up on you?"
>
> "The Lord will be a protection to his children, even unto the wicked and the unworthy." The minister's red face smiled.
>
> "What'll you do if they catch you sometime?"
>
> "My brother, fly to the strong and gentle wings of the Lord, and he will uphold you."
>
> "Or maybe you'll tell me now that schoolteachers don't do things like that. Schoolteachers are better than us farmers."
>
> "Even the best of us, aye, the saint and sinner alike, need the comfort and solace which God has given us for the hour of need." (89–90)

The pastor's canned words of wisdom operate here on the level of camp. What these phrases once meant and the appropriate occasion for their use has been forgotten, Kliewer suggests, even by the speaker himself. Like the German and Low German words and phrases of Armin Wiebe and Waltner-Toews, Kliewer's pastoral cliches no longer function by denotation, but by connotation and evocation alone. These commonplace phrases, absurdly stripped of context and function, have become the elements of a verbal pop culture.

Very near the beginning of *Lost in the Steppe* Arnold Dyck provides an analogue for the crystallizing and enshrining of the mundane that occupies so many contemporary Mennonite artists and writers. He describes the inner workings of young Hans Toews's mind, his ability to make commonplace objects perform.

> His mind and soul have to cope with pretty insipid surroundings, far too insipid for the now six-year-old, whose natural tendencies are hardly toward the prosaic. If they were, he would certainly not see things in these surroundings which others didn't see. For Hanschen is the kind for whom, as he sits reclined in a corner of the sleeping bench in the gathering dusk, things become alive and who, no matter where he looks, sees the most curious pictures.

On the table leg, where the yellow paint begins to peel and the ground colour is revealed, in the maze of intertwining lines formed by the persistent cracking of the whitewash on the oven wall, in the grain of the beams and boards of the ceiling, browned by age, on the befogged window on which one drop joins another until they suddenly fall, leaving clearly marked zigzag lines on the glass—everywhere lurk the strangest things and figures, that is, for someone who sees them, someone who looks at the world with Hanschen's eyes. (14)

The impulse to transform, by means of the creative imagination (as Hans does here)—not cracks and peeling paint into fish and dogs, but the commonplace into the aesthetic—finds expression in much of the art and literature of the Mennonites, and where we find it, it catalogues and documents the development of an aesthetic. Consider the action or process of Allan Kroeker's film *Capital*, a half-hour drama the director has described as his most Mennonite film. "You can always tell a good car by the sound of its radio," says the film's middle-aged protagonist, who, along with his son makes a meagre living by beautifying (and selling) old cars. Note: he makes them appealing, not functional. And what about Andreas Schroeder, whose latest novel *Dustship Glory* is about a man who builds an ocean-going vessel in the middle of the flat Saskatchewan prairie? The real-life shipbuilder on whose life the tale is based died leaving his ship marooned on land miles from the closest river and over 1000 miles from the nearest sea. It makes sense that Schroeder and Kroeker should be enamoured of these men who reveal the impulse of so many Mennonite artists: to foreground the pragmatically familiar deprived of its one function.

In stripping the commonplace of its conventional use and context, the Mennonite writer or artist sets it apart, leaves it open to examination. By disarming, dislocating the functional, many contemporary Mennonite artists force themselves and their community to take a fresh look at the most ordinary signs of their ethnic identity and to question their significance. Everything from German and Low German to quilts and *Rollkuchen* is redefined connotatively. Implicit in this redefinition, this metamorphosis through art, is an evocation of the complexity of these familiar cultural signs.

What do Mennonite arts have to say about the nature of being a Mennonite? Perhaps sometimes, directly, that in some sense at least being a Mennonite is, as Lureen Lafrenière observes, like having acne. But there is more. The ultimate paradox of coming of age as an artist (or as a people) is, a literary critic has remarked, "to humanize one's heritage by exposing it; to create one's existence by making it into fiction; to escape one's fate by embracing it aesthetically" (A.P. Dawson, qtd. in Hillis 3). Mennonite artists and writers, by isolating and transforming the artifacts and languages of their people's past and present, are forcing new perspectives from which they can perceive who they and their people are and in the process are grinding for all new lenses with which to see.

WORKS CITED

Birdsell, Sandra. *Night Travellers*. Turnstone Press, 1982.
Dunham, Mabel. *The Trail of the Conestoga*. McClelland & Stewart, 1942.
Dyck, Arnold. *Lost in the Steppe*. Trans. Al Reimer, Steinbach, Derksen Printers, 1974.
———. [Writing as Fritz Walden]. "Ernstes und Heiteres." *Mennonitische Volkswarte*, vol. 1, no. 2, 1935, p. 29. [Trans. Wendy Gray.]
Falk, Gathie. *Gathie Falk Retrospective*. Vancouver Art Gallery, 1985.
Fischer, Ernst. *Art Against Ideology*. Trans. Anna Bostock, Penguin, 1969.
Friesen, Patrick. "The Wedding." Unpublished story. Patrick Friesen Fonds, Library and Archives Canada, Ottawa.
Good Books. "Educational Books about Amish and Mennonite Life and Thought." www.goodbooks.com. Accessed 1988.
Harder, Hans. *No Strangers in Exile*. Trans. Al Reimer, Hyperion Press, 1979.
Hillis, Doris. "Shaping a Vision." Profile of Patrick Friesen. *Canadian Author & Bookman*, vol 59, no.1, 1983.
Janzen, Jacob H. "The Literature of the Russo-Canadian Mennonites." *Mennonite Life*, vol. 1, January 1946, pp. 22–25, 28.
Kliewer, Warren. *The Violators*. Marshall Jones, 1964.
Kroeker, Allan. (Director.) *Capital*. National Film Board, 1981.
Loewen, G. "Harmless Small Talk about Poetry and Related Topics." *Mennonitische Volkswarte*, Trans. Wendy Gray, vol. 1, no. 9, 1935, p. 338.
Nickel, Gordon. "When Fantasy and Imagination are Enemies." Review of *My Lovely Enemy* by Rudy Wiebe. *Mennonite Brethren Herald*, vol. 23, no. 5, 1984, pp. 26–27.
Reimer, Margaret Loewen, and Paul Tiessen. "The Poetry and Distemper of Patrick

Friesen and David Waltner-Toews." *Visions and Realities*, ed. Harry Loewen and Al Reimer, Hyperion Press, 1985, pp. 243–253.

Smucker, Barbara. *Days of Terror.* Clarke, Irwin, 1979.

Stambaugh, Sarah. *I Hear the Reaper's Song.* Good Books, 1984.

Waltner-Toews, David. *Good Housekeeping.* Turnstone Press, 1983.

Wiebe, Armin. *The Salvation of Yasch Siemens.* Turnstone Press, 1984.

Wiebe, Rudy. *Peace Shall Destroy Many.* McClelland & Stewart, 1962.

———. *The Blue Mountains of China.* McClelland & Stewart, 1970.

———. "The Blindman River Contradictions." *The Camrose Review*, vol. 5, 1984, pp. 40–44.

Yost, Erma Martin. MS fragment mailed to author, n.d.

Three

Mother Tongue as Shibboleth in the Literature of Canadian Mennonites[*]

F EW DISCERNIBLE BRANCHES of contemporary Canadian literature have, over the past decade or so, received as much critical attention as the collective work of the country's ethnic writers, among whom few are presently as productive as the Mennonites. Yet Mennonite writers like Rudy Wiebe, Armin Wiebe, Patrick Friesen, Sandra Birdsell, David Waltner-Toews, Di Brandt and others, while they persist in writing out of, about, and—at least in part—for their minority-culture community, function, in relation to the Mennonites, as outsiders: like the ubiquitous and threatening figure of the stranger in their own literary creations, they individually and collectively tend to objectify their people's peculiar social and spiritual modes of discourse and so in effect contribute significantly to the dismantling of the traditional barriers of ethos, language, and belief that have, for some 400 years, kept the Mennonites a community palpably and self-consciously separate from worldly society.

However, even as these writers objectify (and so appear to threaten, and even subvert) the conventions and rituals that sustain the Mennonites'

---

[*] First published as Hildi Froese Tiessen, "Mother Tongue as Shibboleth in the Literature of Canadian Mennonites." *Studies in Canadian Literature*, vol. 13, no. 2, 1988, pp. 175–183.

centuries-old identity as "a people apart," many of them employ linguistic devices that function to endorse and support the Mennonites' exclusivistic culture—characterized by the affirmation of the insider and suspicion of the outsider. Indeed, through the persistent (in fact, increasingly prominent) use of a linguistic discourse that often only "insiders" can understand—by their use, that is, of mother tongue (German, and more particularly, Low German)—these writers maintain and perhaps even extend the barriers that separate the Mennonites' minority culture from the contemporary social order.

It is worthwhile, I think, to begin a discussion of mother tongue as shibboleth—as a test word or catchword distinguishing one group of people from another—by referring briefly to the theological notions underlying the Mennonites' commitment to separateness or nonconformity, and by remarking on the role of Low German and German as conventional means of confirming and preserving the community's separation from the world.

The place to begin is the sixteenth century, a decade after the publication of Martin Luther's Ninety-five Theses, in the early years of Protestant reform. In 1527, at Schleitheim, Switzerland, leaders of Anabaptism, the radical wing of the Reformation, reached a consensus on "seven points of faith" that "brought structure and focus" to their movement (Gross 3–4). The fourth of these points concerned the separation of the fellowship of believers from the world:

> everything which has not been united with our God in Christ is nothing but an abomination which we should shun … From all this we shall be separated … (qtd. in Gross 12)

The Anabaptists' belief in separation from the world was reflected in their theology of two kingdoms: their belief in a radical dualism "between the community of the redeemed and the larger society" (Toews 14–15). The Mennonite historian Harold S. Bender aptly summarizes this aspect of what he has named the Anabaptist vision:

> An inevitable corollary of the concept of the church as a body of committed and practicing Christians pledged to the highest standard of New Testament living was the insistence on the separation of the church from the world, that is nonconformity of the Christian to the worldly way of life. The world would not tolerate the practice of true Christian principles in society, and the church could not

tolerate the practice of worldly ways among its membership. Hence, the only way out was separation (*Absonderung*), the gathering of true Christians into their own Christian society where Christ's way could and would be practiced ... In a sense, this principle of nonconformity to the world is merely a negative expression of the positive requirement of discipleship, but it goes further in the sense that it represents a judgement on the contemporary social order, which the Anabaptists called "the world," as non-Christian, and sets up a line of demarcation between the Christian community and worldly society. (27–28)

The belief in separation from the world formulated in the first years of the Reformation continued to shape Anabaptist experience and self-definition as the movement grew over the next four centuries and its adherents spread out geographically, fleeing from persecution, attracted by prospective new homelands that would promise religious liberties. That faction of the Anabaptist reformers known as the Mennonites (after one of their leaders, the former Dutch priest Menno Simons) were themselves represented by two major streams of adherents—one South German-Swiss in origin and the other (the one that concerns us here) North German-Dutch. The descendants of the Dutch Mennonites, in their attempts to escape persecution in the Netherlands in the sixteenth century, fled to Prussia (where they began to settle in the Vistula Delta around the mid-1500s, and developed their use of a Lower-Prussian dialect, *Plautdietsch*, for day-to-day discourse). At the same time they continued to employ the Dutch of their former homeland "as the language of worship, of record-keeping and ... written communication" until well into the eighteenth century, "when Dutch gave way to High German" (Epp 65). The history of Mennonite migrations and the inevitable shifts of mother tongue that accompanied them is, as we shall see, central to the Mennonite experience. What, after all, could more effectively secure the separation of the Mennonites (and, incidentally, retard the possibilities of their developing a sophisticated book culture) than their persistent use of languages foreign to the cultures that surrounded them?

The Mennonite ancestors of the Rudy Wiebes and Patrick Friesens of the contemporary Canadian literary mainstream, typically, it seems, did not remain in the Vistula Delta (in the general region of what was then the Prussian city of Danzig), but began, near the end of the eighteenth century, to migrate once again. At the invitation of the Russian Empress Catherine II they established a prosperous agrarian commonwealth (composed of some 400 villages with a total population around 100,000) on the steppes of Ukraine. Here their separate way of life (where the languages of discourse remained Low German and German) allowed them to live comfortably, indeed to prosper, until their isolated and vulnerable settlements were threatened, first by the Russification of the 1870s and then by the violence of the Revolution and by the personal and community chaos effected by the collectivization of the new communist state in the 1920s. Once more fleeing their adopted homeland, many sought refuge in North America where a large contingent of Mennonite immigrants settled in two waves of immigration on the Canadian prairies, in the 1870s and the 1920s. Of the 600,000 practising Mennonites in the world today, some 60,000 live in Manitoba. "Of these at least 26,000 live in Winnipeg, making it the largest concentration of Mennonites in the world" (Reimer 13).

The present high level of literary activity among Canadian Mennonites follows centuries during which these people had virtually no literature of their own. Their history of migration, as well as their Puritan disposition towards the arts (indeed, toward any form of embellishment or ornamentation), their suspicion of fiction (which consisted, after all, of the unacceptable activity of telling lies) and their state of isolation from the cultural activities of other Europeans precluded the emergence of any kind of sophisticated artistic tradition among these people—until the mid-1800s, when the Mennonites in Russia experienced a marked increase in the level of education and cultural sophistication in their own settlements. (This "cultural awakening" resulted to a large degree from the prosperity that allowed some of the intellectually gifted males among the German speaking Russian Mennonites to study abroad and so to escape their own culturally restrictive environment and, in effect, to appropriate for their people, upon their return to the colonies, some of the cultural practices and concerns of mainstream Europeans.)

What we would identify today as the literature of the Canadian Mennonites began in the Russian colonies at the turn of the century, during what has been called the "Golden Age" of the Russian Mennonite commonwealth. Courting a potential, but as yet largely untutored, Russian Mennonite audience, Jacob H. Janzen (who would settle in Canada in 1924 and continue to write), along with some of his similarly literarily-disposed colleagues, began to compose and publish distinctly Mennonite poetry, prose, and drama (in either or both of the Mennonites' two mother tongues) in the years before the Revolution. Another Russian-born Canadian Mennonite immigrant, initially inspired by Janzen and later influential as a kind of Canadian Mennonite man of letters and cultural impresario, Arnold Dyck, worked indefatigably during the 1940s to nurture in Canada a Mennonite audience for literary and cultural endeavours. Both Janzen and Dyck composed in their mother tongues: German (the Mennonites' formal language of religion and education) and Low German (the language of work and village life, the intimate language of family and friendship).

Privately printed chapbooks such as those Janzen and Dyck produced found virtually no Canadian audience outside the Mennonite community where their works of gentle good humour were regarded as interesting by some, frivolous by others, and threatening by few. These intimate expressions of Mennonite community life, written in either mother tongue, tended to assert the cohesiveness and unique identity of the Canadian Mennonite community which, settled then mostly in villages on large tracts of prairie farmland in the pattern of the Russian colonies, still valued its separation from the dominant "English" culture. So mother tongue continued to mark and sustain the separation of the Canadian Mennonites from the dominant culture of their adopted homeland. In fact, Mennonite leaders here in Canada (as Rudy Wiebe so forcefully observed in his first novel, *Peace Shall Destroy Many*) continued to exploit language "to perpetuate apartness" (James R. Jaquith, qtd. in Loewen 13) as they had for at least 400 years:

> First they [had] used Dutch as the barrier in Low German Prussia, then they used Prussian Low German as the barrier in High German-speaking Danzig and finally they used Low German and High German as the barrier against the national languages in Russia and in [North] America. (Loewen 24)

German and Low German remained the languages of Mennonite literature in Canada well into the 1940s. It was not until 1962, with the momentous publication by McClelland & Stewart of *Peace Shall Destroy Many*, that a Canadian Mennonite work of fiction appeared in English. The furor that followed its publication (resulting in Wiebe's informal, but nevertheless brutal, disenfranchisement from the community and his subsequent move to a temporary sanctuary in the USA) demonstrated the degree to which the Mennonites wished to remain—even in Canada in the 1960s, where many of them already held prominent positions in business, education, and the professions—a people set apart from the dominant Canadian culture. That Wiebe would be critical of his own people in fiction was bad enough; that he would write in English and publish with the country's most prominent publisher—and so expose this private people's private affairs to public scrutiny—was nothing less than a scandalous breach of trust.

One of the themes of this watershed publication, *Peace Shall Destroy Many*, is, significantly, the "language problem" (a subject, that has, deservedly, an entry of its own in the *Mennonite Encyclopedia*):

> Problems caused by language have repeatedly arisen among the Mennonites because of their migrations from one language-and-culture area to another ... The maintenance of the language of the motherland has aided in maintaining separation from the surrounding culture in the new homeland and thus strengthened the sense of nonconformity to the world. (Bender, "Language")

Through his protagonist Thom ("the doubter"), Wiebe questions the notion of separation as it was practised in Wapiti, a fictional Mennonite settlement on the Canadian prairie. Finding untenable the dominant ethos of the community that obliged the Mennonites to retain German as the exclusive language of religious fellowship and in effect to ostracize their Métis neighbours, Thom provocatively asks his mother, "'And why must we in Wapiti love only Mennonites?'" (215). Echoes of Thom's question, and the challenge it represents to what had, over centuries, become the standard convention of using language as a means by which to preserve the coherence and identity of the Mennonite world, reverberate throughout Canadian Mennonite literature. Arnold Dyck explicitly anticipated the question in *Lost in the Steppe* and David Waltner-Toews, Patrick Friesen, Rudy Wiebe in his later works, and others, have uttered it explicitly or implicitly, over and over again.

Insofar as these writers compose in English, they have ostensibly already displaced or rejected the language barrier that had for so long been absolutely integral to the dominant ethos of their people. Yet in their progressively less reticent embrace of mother tongue as linguistic technique or embellishment over the last decade in particular, they have revealed their ambivalence towards "the language problem." The dynamic conflicts in the mind of the artist who throws the patterns of his culture up onto the screen and finds them wanting, yet who feels the desire to evoke (not always nostalgically) a fading ethos is focussed in the powerful image of ambivalence in Patrick Friesen's "end poem" in *Unearthly Horses*:

ich stehe
zwischen nein
ein fusz im feuer
ja. (75) [1]

It has already been suggested here that few Canadian ethnic groups have established themselves as prominently in the mainstream of Canadian literature as have the Mennonites. Both Andreas Schroeder and Rudy Wiebe have chaired the Writers' Union of Canada; Sandra Birdsell, Patrick Friesen, Armin Wiebe, and Victor Enns were founding executive members of the Manitoba Writers' Guild (Enns went on to become Executive Director of the Saskatchewan Writers' Guild); Patrick Friesen and Di Brandt have been executive members of the League of Canadian Poets; Rudy Wiebe has won the Governor General's Award (Lois Braun was shortlisted for the award in 1987, Di Brandt in 1988); Sandra Birdsell has been selected by a national panel as one of the ten best Canadian writers of the post-Atwood generation, etc. As they have moved relentlessly into the mainstream, many of these Mennonite writers have incorporated mother tongue into their work in such a way that it functions as shibboleth, re-delineating the very barriers between insider and outsider many of them have railed against in their work.

The use of German and Low German in contemporary Canadian Mennonite literature is extensive. Rudy Wiebe uses German phrases to evoke the repressive piety of Jacob Friesen V in *The Blue Mountains of China*, for example, or to evoke the irrepressible romanticism of David Epp. Armin Wiebe uses Low German words, phrases, epithets, and syntax throughout his humorous novel *The Salvation of Yasch Siemens* to evoke the primal, sometimes coarse personal life of Yasch, a village bumpkin. Patrick Friesen and David Waltner-Toews use German liberally in their poetry, as does Audrey Poetker, who borrows from both the Mennonites' mother tongues to enrich the texture of her work.

Patrick Friesen quotes, at the end of *The Shunning*, "*O dass ich tausend Zungen hätte*" ["Oh, that I had a thousand tongues"]—the opening words of one of the Mennonites' most widely-used invocational hymns. With this resonant phrase, Friesen embraces his (implied) Mennonite audience by stimulating it to recall a seemingly lost world where the coherence of community was assured by the resonating, integrating power of familiar verbal ritual.

---

1 "*I* stand / between no / one foot in fire / yes."

Audrey Poetker, in her collection of poems aptly named *i sing for my dead in german*, both evokes and laments the loss of the mother tongue that once confirmed the common identity of individuals who were otherwise generations—even worlds—apart:[2]

> i tell *grosmama* the line in armin wiebe's book
> about *himmelfahrt* being the day
> when jesus goes to heaven & mennonites
> to winnipeg
> & she laughs until she almost *fuschlucks* herself
> *en vieb dann noch*
> yes but no relation
> *grosmama* i say *grosmama*
> but can't remember the low german word
> for love. (21)

It is not, of course, unusual for writers of ethnic background to employ some of the words of their mother tongue in their literary compositions. But this practice has particular significance among the Mennonites where language has been used conventionally to effect separation from and nonconformity to the world. Because of the rapid disintegration of the ethos of the traditional Canadian Mennonite community and the accompanying loss of the use of German and Low German, mother tongue in English Mennonite literature functions inevitably as shibboleth, as a byword defining the limits of Canadian Mennonite experience. What the "insider," the Mennonite raised in the rapidly disappearing, traditional Mennonite world, recognizes in a work like David Waltner-Toews's poem "Tante Tina's Lament" is a kind of exclusive intertextuality that probes poignantly beyond the gently ironic humour of the poem into the last records of a people's fading means of common (and exclusive) discourse:

> Oh my son
> my heart is heavy,
> thick as glums.
> If you come home
> it will rise, light and sweet.

---

[2] Translations for the Low German in this poem: *grosmama* [grandmother]; *himmelfahrt* [Ascension Day]; *fuschlucks* [cough; choke on water]; *en vieb dann noch* ["and, on top of all that, a Wiebe!"].

> I will make you porzelky for breakfast
> and we will celebrate the New Year
> every morning. (81)

Mother tongue as a source of resonance for the insider is used by many contemporary Mennonite writers to restructure ritualistically the ethos, the cultural and spiritual texture of a Mennonite world that no longer exists as an entity separate from the society around it. For over 400 years mother tongue functioned as shelter for the Mennonites committed to existing as a people apart. Now, as the Mennonite world becomes ever more dispersed, its literary artists are evoking a past world in the words and syntax of German and Low German. Whatever these authors hope to accomplish through their use of mother tongue, the result of their technique is to divide their audience into insider and outsider and so, in effect, to re-establish barriers separating the traditional Mennonites' experience from the world's.

The use of German and Low German in Mennonite writing intended for the mainstream Canadian audience (and not at all for an exclusively Mennonite audience) evokes an ethos that was defined by no thing as much as it was by language. To allow mother tongue to find its place within a predominantly English discourse is for Mennonite authors to affirm the very exclusivistic culture so many of them rail against. It's almost as if, having gained unlimited access to the coveted Canadian literary mainstream, the Mennonite writers who use their mother tongue want to assert that they are different, after all.

WORKS CITED

Bender, Harold S. *The Anabaptist Vision*. Herald Press, 1944.

———. "Language problem." *Global Anabaptist Mennonite Encyclopedia Online*. 1957, www.gameo.org.

Epp, Reuben. "Plautdietsch: Origins, Development and State of the Mennonite Low German Language." *Journal of Mennonite Studies*, 5, 1987, pp. 61–72.

Friesen, Patrick. *Unearthly Horses*. Turnstone Press, 1984.

Gross, Leonard. Introduction. *The Schleitheim Confession*, ed. and trans. John H. Yoder, Herald Press, 1973.

Loewen, Jacob A. "The German Language, Culture and the Faith." Symposium on

Dynamics of Faith and Culture in Mennonite Brethren History, 14–15 November 1986, Winnipeg. Unpublished typescript.

Poetker, Audrey. *i sing for my dead in german*. Turnstone Press, 1986.

Reimer, Al, Anne Reimer, and Jack Thiessen. *A Sackful of Plautdietsch: A Collection of Mennonite Low German Stories and Poems*. Hyperion Press, 1983.

Toews, Paul. "Faith in Culture and Culture in Faith: Mennonite Brethren Entertaining Expansive Separative and Assimilative Views about the Relationship." Symposium on Dynamics of Faith and Culture in Mennonite Brethren History, 14–15 November 1986, Winnipeg. Unpublished typescript.

Waltner-Toews, David. *Good Housekeeping*. Turnstone Press, 1983.

Wiebe, Rudy. *Peace Shall Destroy Many*. McClelland & Stewart, 1962.

Four

Mennonite Writing and the Post-Colonial Condition[*]

Someone asked me about being on the edge or the periphery, and I really don't feel that way. I see myself as being at the centre, but I don't know where that centre is. Maybe it's writing.

Sandra Birdsell

IN THE CLOSING panel of the 1990 Waterloo conference on Mennonite/s Writing in Canada, Robert Kroetsch remarked that "Mennonite writing has come to its maturity at a time of extreme self-consciousness about what writing is" (225). Few critics in this country have speculated more prolifically on "what writing is"—particularly in the Canadian context—than Kroetsch. "How do you write in a new country?" (5) he asks in the first of his essays collected in *The Lovely Treachery of Words*; how do you make a part of the Canadian experience "available ... for literary purposes" (7)? In another essay he laments the fact that Canadian writers who write in English are compelled to use words in which unfamiliar experiences—sometimes British, sometimes American—are embedded, concealed. The language available for their use, that appears to be their own, is borrowed from other English-speaking cultures. One

---

[*] First published as Hildi Froese Tiessen, "Mennonite Writing and the Post-Colonial Condition." *Acts of Concealment: Mennonite/s Writing in Canada*, ed. Hildi Froese Tiessen and Peter Hinchcliffe, U Waterloo P, 1992, pp. 11–21.

could assume that if Canadian writers raised with English as their mother tongue could be said to be a level removed from an authorizing linguistic and cultural centre (the English of Wordsworth's daffodils, for example), writers raised in the context of one of Canada's minority cultures would be several times removed, and so would find even more challenging the process of "demythologizing the systems that threaten to define them," as Kroetsch has put it, in order to posit their own authentic identity (*Lovely* 58).

Writing in a language not entirely one's own is an activity familiar enough to Canadian Mennonites, particularly those of North-German/Dutch ancestry, who when they started producing works of drama and fiction in Russia in the late-nineteenth century found themselves in a peculiarly difficult situation: the Low German they used to express themselves in everyday settings (in casual social discourse with family and friends)—their language of humour and intimacy—had no standard orthography. High German, the language they employed in religion and education, was the only written language readily available to them, but its use implied a formality reserved for church and school (see Toews 157–158). Raised in a Low German culture on the steppes of Russia, this earlier generation of Mennonites wrote in German (or an unstandardized, phonetic Low German); raised mostly in Low German- and German-speaking rural communities in Canada, the current generation writes in English, with a sprinkling of German and Low German words and syntax that, as Bill Ashcroft and his colleagues, in their study of theory and practice in post-colonial literatures, have suggested, function as signs of cultural distinctiveness and "stand for the latent presence" (62) of another culture.

Post-colonial literary theory might well prove to be instructive in any future study of the development and place of the literature of the Mennonites in Canada in so far as it has focused on how language and writing in post-colonial cultures have been appropriated for use away from a "privileged norm" or dominant cultural centre (such as Britain has been for the English-speaking world). There has been in the literatures of Africa, Australia, Canada, the Caribbean, India, New Zealand, Pakistan, and other former British colonies a concerted effort to "escape from the implicit body of assumptions to which English was attached, … the oppressive political and cultural assertion of metropolitan dominance, of centre over margin" (Ashcroft et al. 11, citing Ngũgĩ wa Thiong'o). All of this has been taking place, of course, in an era in which the exclusive claims of "the centre" are questioned on every front, including that of literary discourse, where innovative, pluralistic, post-colonial, and "ethnic" literatures are championed as never before.

Attention to the cultural distinctiveness of any particular literary tradition in Canada has evoked a mixed response from critics and writers alike. In an effort to be identified with what has been seen as a validating centre, many writers who have emerged out of Canada's several minority literary cultures have, over the past few decades, registered responses to the notion of a diversity of Canadian literatures in English in a manner similar to Janice Kulyk Keefer's recent remark:

> I think I've always been quite definite on the fact that I wanted to get published simply as a writer, a Canadian writer, rather than as an "ethnic" writer, because I think it's the unfortunate tendency still to marginalize the ethnic, to see it as something colourful and peripheral. (291)

This, Keefer says as a qualification, is how, some five years ago, she would have assessed her situation as a writer raised in a minority culture in Canada. This is how she would have thought about herself as a writer then, before she had begun to value the degree to which her writing "has been directly fed" and "inspired" by her "ethnicity" (Keefer 295–296).

"Ethnicity," a term no longer acceptable in literary criticism because it connotes the very exclusionary cultural politics to which the post-colonial critic would object, has not, of course, evoked a uniform response from Canadian writers. "No writer ever thinks about whether he's ethnic or not ethnic," Mordecai Richler says dismissively in an interview. "He writes about what he knows" (43). Multicultural literature has only relatively recently found a legitimate place in the consciousness of this country's literary world, where concerns about the definition and advancement of a "national" literature have been paramount. Bill Ashcroft and his colleagues rightly observe that until well into the last decade "Canadian literature, perceived internally as a mosaic, [has remained] generally monolithic in its assertion of Canadian difference from the canonical British or the more recently threatening neo-colonialism of American culture" (35). Canadians have distinguished themselves, Ashcroft et al. argue, "by retreating from the dynamics of difference into the neo-universalist internationalist stance," but in the process have missed, in large measure, the opportunity to privilege work that has arisen so richly out of Canada's cultural complexity (36).

Black Canadian author Dionne Brand records something of the shift in sensibility we have begun to experience in this country when she observes that "'Twenty years ago there was a national wave of Canadian writing which set itself up against American writing and the deluge of American culture in

Canada. We are the new wave of Canadian writing. We will write about the internal contradictions" (277). With the celebration of our cultural diversity (in the context of a sensibility that challenges the centrality of the very concept of "norm") has come the dismantling of the notion of a privileged "standard" of Canadian literature. "The margin, the periphery, the edge, now, is the exciting and dangerous boundary where silence and sound meet," the postmodern Kroetsch asserts. "In our happier moments we delight in the energy of the local, in the abundance that is diversity and difference, in the variety and life that exist on any coastline of the human experience" (23). The periphery is "the place of possibility," Linda Hutcheon agrees (3). She goes on to contextualize:

> The 1960s saw the "inscription" into history of those previously silenced ex-centrics: those defined by differences in class, gender, race, ethnic group, and sexual preference ... Female, gay, and various ethnic voices can now be heard, and the postmodern interest in the ex-centric has, I think, contributed both to this new valuing and to the challenging of all kinds of "-centrism." (11)

That there is no authorizing centre, or "mainstream" in Canadian literature in the closing decade of this century has been variously announced and celebrated by critics and writers alike. Although Rudy Wiebe asserts that "the strongest strand in Canadian writing" is what he calls "the English tradition: Findley, Atwood, Munro, Davies, Birney, David Adams Richards," he asserts that these well-known Canadians comprise but one, albeit dominant, "ethnic writing strand" among the numerous traditions that feed the stream of Canadian literature (86).

Matt Cohen, asked as representative of another dominant strand of writing in English Canada, the Jewish tradition, to comment on the role of the "ethnic" writer, observed:

> As Canada fragments into regions, writers have to find their voices not simply in terms of some pan-Canadian identity, but also in terms of their own history and their current interests. In that sense "ethnic writing"—writing from outside the boundaries of what has been considered Canadian—is now more and more interesting. Because the mainstream—both in terms of politics and literature—is now so weak and fragmented, it's an excellent time for writers of different

backgrounds who bring different ideas about language and books. (174)

The postmodern shift away from the central, the normative, or the universal towards the peripheral, the distinctive, and the particular has cleared a place for the literature of minorities in Canada, where one of the principal activities of a growing number of people is negotiating the gap between cultures, between worlds of experience, exercising what Michael Ondaatje has called "the migrant's double perspective" (197).

The move to shake hegemonic assumptions about the inalienable centrality of certain sites of experience has had unmistakable effects on the literature of English Canada, which was once clearly dominated by a centre with a distinct "Anglo-Saxon complexion" (Tapping 92). More specifically, the themes and manifestations critics have identified as being characteristic of postmodern and post-colonial writing would seem to have a singular relevance for the Mennonites writing in Canada during this period of transition, for the Mennonites' theology and lived experience since the 1500s could readily be expressed in terms of the categories that are pre-eminent in the current discussion. These categories include, for example, cultural distinctiveness and the negotiation between worlds of experience (consider in this context the Mennonites' centuries of geographical and linguistic displacement, and their fundamental belief that they should be "in the world, but not of it"). They include the validation of the periphery (consider the Mennonites' doctrine of nonconformity, their egalitarian ecclesiology—the "priesthood of all believers"—their commitment to minority positions such as, for example, the doctrine of non-resistance). The categories upon which the post-colonial discussion focuses include, also, the central role of language in the exercise of power and the determination of identity (consider in this context the Mennonites' non-conformist appropriation, during the Reformation and since, of the language of the Bible—which they consider the reliable and authoritative word of God—and their exploitation of language to affirm identity and sustain "apartness" for some four hundred years).[1]

Although the terms of reference I've raised here did not at any point become the explicit focus of the 1990 conference on Mennonite/s writing in Canada, many of the issues suggested by our postmodern, post-colonial condition did emerge there, implicitly at least, as questions were raised, for example, about established patterns of authority in Mennonite culture. Magdalene Redekop's powerful lament for the Mennonite mother would seem to have glossed and

---

1 See "Mother Tongue as Shibboleth" elsewhere in this volume.

challenged Victor Doerksen's account of the Mennonite writers' gradual, ambivalent dismantling of the patriarchy. Redekop passionately derides the phenomenon of the Mennonite mother's having been universalized and essentialized out of existence by authors who, after the established patterns of Mennonite social discourse, have in text after text registered and perpetuated her absence and powerlessness.

Harry Loewen, in his engaging and informative survey of the career of the poet Gerhard Loewen, suggests tentatively that there might be a coherent association between this follower of German classical and romantic models and Canadian writers like Rudy Wiebe. One might note, however, that Loewen's suggestion was implicitly questioned at the conference when a number of people challenged the generally accepted notion that Rudy Wiebe himself must have been a formative influence on a whole generation of younger Mennonite writers. In fact, questions of continuity and coherence in the literary world of Canadian Mennonites arose in various contexts, fully in keeping, it would seem, with the currents of the day. Nancy Lou Patterson's instructive illustrated lecture on Mennonite folk art reminded the audience that the artistic sensibility of the Swiss Mennonites of whom she spoke seems to bear little relation to the less communal, more self-conscious, literary sensibility of the North-German/Dutch/"Russian" Mennonites who so obviously dominate the Canadian Mennonite literary world. Furthermore, what emerged explicitly in the context of David Arnason's talk, and seemed palpable enough as an undercurrent throughout the conference, was the question of whether the descendants of the two principal "Russian" Mennonite migrations to Canada (1870s and 1920s) were themselves writing in the same vein. There was evidence in the discussion of a growing sense of urgency for Mennonite writers to "decreate," in Kroetsch's words, literary traditions that would tend to bind them "into not speaking the truth" (*Lovely* 62).

Conference participants used a variety of critical approaches to probe the character and impact of the literature of the Mennonites. W.J. Keith's observation that the elusive Low German words peppered throughout the first chapter of *The Blue Mountains of China* serve simply to establish "a sense of distinct cultural atmosphere" and do "not need to be understood" (96) by the reader ("Its meaning doesn't matter; what does matter is the non-verbal message that it conveys") would seem to assert a kind of universalization of the text that dismisses the inscription of difference the language would suggest (see Ashcroft et al. 41–57). Thus, even as he creates an argument for the broadest possible readership for Wiebe's fiction, Keith would seem to undercut the validity of the text's warning (in those elusive words) that Wiebe's novel is, as

Ashcroft asserts of many post-colonial texts, "not the site of a shared mental experience, and should not be seen as such" (59). Keith's very interesting suggestion that Rudy Wiebe's Mennonite fiction is equally accessible to a broad spectrum of Mennonite and non-Mennonite readers alike is, to some extent, offset in this volume by Clara Thomas's assertion that while she can "agree with Bill Keith that *The Blue Mountains of China* is a magnificent epic and religious novel ... it does not and cannot identify me to myself as does, for instance, *The Stone Angel* or *The Diviners*." Both of those works, she says, were "written from a background so close to my own that Hagar is my mother, myself, as Morag is my sister, myself." Thomas remarks, "I hope I understand something of the duality of culture and religion which Mennonites possess and are possessed by," but "I don't have and can never fully know the searing experience of generations of marginality and oppression ground into my bones, blood and spirit" (130).

Andrew Stubbs, who, drawing upon the discourses of feminism and deconstruction, examines the degree to which Sandra Birdsell's fiction evokes in him a "feeling of exclusion, verging on uncanniness" (174), speaks also to questions of difference and distance implied in other papers, including those of Keith and Thomas. He quotes feminist critic Lorraine Weir: "Full visibility and accessibility constitute an inherent danger for the colonized, the underground ones, the ex/centrics" (qtd. in Stubbs 175). Stubbs's assertion that the writing of women and minorities tends to make use of structural ellipsis or distinctive cultural codes (including language) to subvert the constructed imperatives of the dominant culture and avoid being appropriated by it could richly inform our reading of texts by Mennonite writers like Birdsell and others.

Wayne Tefs, in his provocative paper on the forbidden discourse of violence in writing by Mennonites, pointedly demonstrates how critical theory can illumine the centre/margin relationship that Mennonite writers have had within their own communities, as they have challenged the dominant myths of their own culture by occasionally foregrounding "a culturally specific 'terrain of the unspeakable'" in their work.[2] Tefs' paper focusses on expressions of violence in Mennonite writing that challenge the Mennonites' traditional commitment to a pacifist ideal. Patrick Friesen's observation in the closing panel about the "true" meaning of pacifism probes the implications of Tefs' remarks:

> Where I grew up, I rarely thought of pacifism as meaning that you didn't fight; I knew that was true. Pacifism meant

---

2 The phrase belongs to Stephen Slemon and Helen Tiffin, xvii.

>that you didn't argue or confront each other very often either, and so you found all kinds of other subtle ways of getting around that. And I think that's actually where a lot of Mennonites learned how to write. ("Closing" 236)

Writing around an issue, or speaking around it, as Al Reimer observes in his reference to Arnold Dyck's expression *derjche Bloom räde*—"speaking through the flower"—is a means by which the margins write back to the centre, to subvert or dismantle it while protecting themselves in the process by acts of discursive concealment (Reimer 34).

"Acts of Concealment," the title of the collection of work by and about Mennonite writers published following the 1990 conference, derives from a phrase that comes out of Robert Kroetsch's remarks in the concluding panel of the conference, a phrase he had used at least once before, in an essay called "The Veil of Knowing," which begins like this:

>To reveal all is to end the story. To conceal all is to fail to begin the story. Individuals, communities, religions, even nations, narrate themselves into existence by selecting out, by working variations upon, a few of the possible strategies that lie between these two extremes. (*Lovely* 179)

The essays, poems and stories included in *Acts of Concealment*, as they chronicle and exploit the productive tension between revelation and concealment that lies at the heart of writing, examine and contribute to a communal narrating into existence of one of the most energetic and successful strands of Canadian literature. Somewhere in the gaps and omissions scattered among the readings, papers and conversations—among the apparent gestures of disclosure—are stories yet to be uncovered.

Reflecting during the panel discussion on the direction Mennonite writers are likely to take in the coming decades, Kroetsch remarked that a feature likely to be dominant in their work is "that question of the narrative of self in relationship to the *other*, whatever that *other* might be" (226). Presumably, then, Mennonites are likely to go on writing in the mode to which they are accustomed. There is hardly a motif more readily identified with the belief systems and experiences of these followers of the radical reformers of the sixteenth century. A heightened sense of "self in relationship to the *other*" is commonplace for a people with so long a history of persecution and sojourning in foreign lands. At the same time, of course, writers such as these might move in altogether different directions and not necessarily as any discernible group within Canadian culture.

Still, it is an interesting coincidence that Mennonite writing in Canada should flourish at a time when notions of difference, otherness, marginality are predominant in literary discourse. Like representatives of other minority cultures in this country, the Mennonites have lived in a world defined by terms such as these for a long time. Questions of identity relative to a variety of centres—cultural, political, ecclesiastical, theological, familial—are pervasive indeed in the literary texts of these people, from Rudy Wiebe to Di Brandt.

The 1990 conference of Mennonite/s Writing in Canada drew together a group of over a hundred people who acknowledged by their attendance and involvement that to speak of writing by Canadian Mennonites is to speak of a tangible literary force in this country. Yet, for every word or gesture that spoke of something that one could call a coherent "tradition" of Mennonite writing, another denied that any such thing does—or should—exist. Implicitly countering vocal protests against the very idea of conferences such as this was the intellectual and emotional intensity of the broadly-based involvement. Questions of influence and continuity, of familiar and forbidden discourses, of identity and homelessness, of self and *other*, of accessibility and concealment— all were raised in the course of the discussion and left unresolved, so that no masquerade of coherence, no overriding act of concealment obscured the rich play of fragments that emerged over several days to confirm a space for this distinctive, self-defining Canadian literary voice.

WORKS CITED

Ashcroft, Bill, Gareth Griffiths, and Helen Tiffin. *The Empire Writes Back: Theory and Practice in Post-Colonial Literatures*. Routledge, 1989.

Birdsell, Sandra. "Interview." *Prairie Bookworld*, vol. 2, no.1, Summer 1991, p. 11.

Brand, Dionne. "Interview by Dagmar Novak." Hutcheon and Richmond, pp. 271–277.

Cohen, Matt. "Interview by Mervin Butovsky." Hutcheon and Richmond, pp. 172–178.

Doerksen, Victor G. "The Role of Arnold Dyck in Canadian Mennonite Writing." Tiessen and Hinchcliffe, pp. 39–51.

Friesen, Patrick. "Closing Panel." Tiessen and Hinchcliffe, pp. 223–242.

Hutcheon, Linda. *The Canadian Postmodern. A Study of Contemporary English-Canadian*

Fiction. Oxford UP, 1988.

———. and Marion Richmond, eds. *Other Solitudes: Canadian Multicultural Fictions.* Oxford UP, 1990.

Keefer, Janice Kulyk. "Interview by Jars Balan." Hutcheon and Richmond, pp. 290–296.

Keith, W.J. "Where is the Voice Going To? Rudy Wiebe and his Readers." Tiessen and Hinchcliffe, pp. 85–99.

Kroetsch, Robert. *The Lovely Treachery of Words: Essays Selected and New.* Oxford UP, 1989.

———. "Closing Panel." Tiessen and Hinchcliffe, pp. 223–242.

Ondaatje, Michael. "Interview by Linda Hutcheon." Hutcheon and Richmond, pp. 196–202.

Reimer, Al. "The Role of Arnold Dyck in Canadian Mennonite Writing." Tiessen and Hinchcliffe, pp. 29–38.

Richler, Mordecai. "Interview by Marlene Kadar." Hutcheon and Richmond, pp. 40–48.

Slemon, Stephen, and Helen Tiffin. "Introduction." *Kunapipi,* vol. xi, no.1, 1989, pp. ix–xxiii.

Stubbs, Andrew. "The Rhetoric of Narration in Sandra Birdsell's Fiction." Tiessen and Hinchcliffe, pp. 174–192.

Tapping, Craig. "Oral Cultures and the Empire of Literature." *Kunapipi,* vol. xi, no.1, 1989, pp. 86–96.

Tefs, Wayne. "Rage in Some Recent Mennonite Poetry." Tiessen and Hinchcliffe, pp. 193–205.

Thomas, Clara. "Western Women's Writing of 'The Childhood' and Anne Konrad's *The Blue Jar.*" Tiessen and Hinchcliffe, pp. 129–142.

Tiessen, Hildi Froese. "Mother Tongue as Shibboleth in the Literature of Canadian Mennonites." *Studies in Canadian Literature,* vol. 13, no. 2, 1988, pp. 175–183.

———, and Peter Hinchcliffe, eds. *Acts of Concealment: Mennonite/s Writing in Canada.* U Waterloo P, 1992.

Toews, John B. "Cultural and Intellectual Aspects of the Mennonite Experience in Russia." *Mennonite Quarterly Review,* vol. 53, April 1979, pp. 137–159.

Wiebe, Rudy. "Interview by Linda Hutcheon." Hutcheon and Richmond, pp. 80–86.

Five

Beyond the Binary: Re-Inscribing Cultural Identity in the Literature of Mennonites*

IN A COMPELLING article published in 1997, poet Julia Kasdorf quotes the closing lines of a prose poem by her Canadian Mennonite literary colleague Di Brandt: "i hate having to choose between my inherited identity & my life: traditional Mennonite *versus* contemporary Canadian woman writer, yet how can i be both & not fly apart?"[1] Commenting, some years earlier, in 1992, on the imminent publication of her own first book of poetry, *Sleeping Preacher*, Kasdorf observed that many of the poems in that collection had been "written from the perspective of an outsider—either a Mennonite outside American culture, or a critical sheep in the Mennonite fold.[2] I've had it both ways," she said, "to be in the community and in the world—which, of course, means to have it neither way. Alienating as it sometimes feels, this non-home is my home" ("Bringing" 10). Writers like Kasdorf and Brandt, and others who in recent decades have chosen to write both creatively and critically about Mennonite experience from a Mennonite perspective, have

---

* First published as Hildi Froese Tiessen, "Beyond the Binary: Re-inscribing Cultural Identity in the Literature of Mennonites." *Mennonite Quarterly Review*, vol. 72, 1998, pp. 491–501.

1 Brandt, qtd. in Kasdorf's "Bakhtin," 185.

2 Note Kasdorf's unselfconscious use of the term "outsider" in this piece.

given a good deal of attention to the question of what it means to be "inside" or "outside" a community that once represented for them a fairly unqualified "home."³ In the process, they have tended to foreground general questions of Mennonite cultural identity and to probe, more specifically, questions about how their writing might be regarded as a means of "locating" themselves (and, presumably, other contemporary North American Mennonites) relative to the two monoliths Brandt once referred to as "the Mennonite world" and "the worldly world out there" ("how" 27).

Of course, neither Mennonite writers nor Mennonites in general have a sole claim to the tensions involved in an individual's trying "to be true to two worlds" (to quote the University of Pittsburgh Press's promotional material announcing Kasdorf's *Sleeping Preacher*) or to more general experiences of displacement or deterritorialization in the closing years of this century. "The migrant's sense of being rootless, of living between worlds, between a lost past and a non-integrated present," cultural studies critic Iain Chambers has observed, is, after all, "perhaps the most fitting metaphor of [our] (post)modern condition" (27).⁴ It is not surprising, then, that a good many contemporary theorists should attempt to come to terms with, and to theorize, what novelist Michael Ondaatje and others have referred to as "the migrant's double perspective" (qtd. in Hutcheon 197). As writers and critics have struggled to make sense of what it means to live between cultures, they often have revealed the human tendency to try to understand the complexly intertwined several contexts they occupy in simple, binary terms: centre/margin, home/exile, community/individual, insiders/outsiders, and so on.

Such a tendency to perceive one's contexts—or, one might say, the locations of one's personal or cultural existence—in binary terms has contributed to the emergence of a monolith Mennonites conventionally refer to as "the

---

3 This paper is concerned with Mennonite "cultural identity," a category not restricted to, and not to be confused with, Mennonite "ethnic" identity, which we have come to understand as generally either "Russian" or "Swiss." I happen to have in mind here the critical observations and creative work of "Swiss" writers like Julia Kasdorf and Jeff Gundy. Their exploration of issues of cultural identity tend to be particular to their personal circumstances; the questions to which they give voice are not, however, unique to them. Mennonite writers who move among two or more cultural subject positions, no matter what their ethnicity, would presumably share with Kasdorf, Gundy, and other writers questions about how they might locate themselves relative to the several cultural sites on their lives' itinerary.

4 Contemporary literary critics, cultural theorists, anthropologists, and other commentators on the worlds we live in observe that displacement—migration between cultures through physical dislocation "as refugees, immigrants, migrants, exiles or expatriates" or by colonization—is, indeed, as literary critic Angelika Bammer has observed, "one of the most formative experiences of our century" (xi).

Mennonite community." In fact, such a monolith has been projected in numerous commentaries on Mennonite writing, at least since John Ruth's landmark lectures on "Mennonite Identity and Literary Art" in 1976. Moreover, "the Mennonite community" (or "the Mennonite world") has, in recent decades at least, become a powerful trope that has dominated both critics' and writers' thinking about the role of the writer among Mennonites.[5] This trope of the essentialist, monolithic centre has had a significant function in the provisional resolution of issues related to Mennonite cultural identity. In Mennonite literary circles at least, the trope of "the Mennonite community" has in fact come to represent an unproblematized cultural identity that, to borrow the words of theorist Stuart Hall, is suggestive of "a sort of collective 'one true self' ... which people with a shared history and ancestry hold in common." As a trope, Hall continues, "the community" reflects

> the common historical experiences and shared cultural codes which provide us, as "one people," with stable, unchanging and continuous frames of reference and meaning, beneath the shifting divisions and vicissitudes of our actual history.

---

5 The trope of "the Mennonite community" has been developed and sustained in literary circles by what Jeff Gundy has referred to as the Mennonites' "seemingly endless preoccupation with individual/community relations." See Jeff Gundy, "U.S. Mennonite Poetry and Poets: Beyond Dr. Johnson's Dog," *Mennonite Quarterly Review*, vol. 71, 1997, pp. 5–41; Warren Kliewer's essay on art and artists, "Controversy and the Religious Arts," *Mennonite Life*, vol. 20, 1965, pp. 8–11; John Ruth's Menno Simons Lectures on "Mennonite Identity and Literary Art" in 1976, published with the same title in *Mennonite Life*, vol. 32, 1977, pp. 4–25, and in *Mennonite Identity and Literary Art*. Herald Press, 1978; my own "The Role of Art and Literature in Mennonite Self-Understanding," in *Mennonite Identity: Historical and Contemporary Perspectives*, ed. Calvin Redekop and Samuel J. Steiner. UP of America, 1988, pp. 235–52; Jeff Gundy's "Humility in Mennonite Literature," *Mennonite Quarterly Review*, vol. 63, 1989, 5–21; my introductions to *Liars and Rascals: Mennonite Short Stories*. U Waterloo P, 1989, pp. xi–xiii, and to *The New Quarterly* [special issue on Mennonite/s Writing in Canada] vol. 10, 1990, pp. 9–12, and to *Prairie Fire* [a special issue on Canadian Mennonite Writing], vol. 11, 1990, pp. 8–11; Al Reimer's *Mennonite Literary Voices: Past and Present*. Bethel College, 1993; Elmer Suderman's "Mennonites, the Mennonite Community, and Mennonite Writers," *Mennonite Life*, vol. 47, 1992, pp. 21–26; Julia Kasdorf's musings anticipating the publication of her first collection of poetry, "Bringing Home the Work: Thoughts on Publishing a First Book," *Festival Quarterly*, vol. 19, 1992, pp. 7–10; Jeff Gundy's "Some Words on Poetry, Band Camps, Guitars, Gifts, Transgression, Community, Mennonite Art, Etc.," *Mennonite Life*, vol. 48, 1993, pp. 15–16; and the epigraph chosen for the web page announcing the 1997 conference at Goshen College on Mennonite/s Writing in the U.S.—a quotation taken from the closing paragraph of Julia Kasdorf's essay on the *Martyrs Mirror* titled "'Work and Hope': Tradition and Translation of an Anabaptist Adam," *Mennonite Quarterly Review*, vol. 69, 1995, pp. 178–204. All these critical reflections, each of them a signpost along the trail of Mennonite literary history, speak of "the tension between the artist and community" in Mennonite literature.

> This "oneness" underlying all the other, more superficial differences [has been perceived as] the truth, the essence [of the given community] (69)

—in this case, presumably, of Mennonitism.

This way of defining ourselves in terms of monolithic and binary categories is, of course, reflected in identity politics as we find it expressed around the world. It is central to the kind of "imaginative re-discovery" (Hall 69) advocated by commentators like John Ruth in his 1976 lectures on Mennonite identity and in his review of *Liars and Rascals* in the *Mennonite Reporter* in 1989—a review for which, Julia Kasdorf remarked in 1992, Ruth "had read [the collection of stories by Mennonite writers] searching for a single expression of the 'communal soul' that would somehow offer a standard interpretation of our collective experience" ("Bringing" 10). The imposition of such an "imaginary coherence" (Hall 70) onto Mennonite identity results in the emergence of a master narrative (rooted in binary thinking) that has, in fact, become a principal resource of resistance for dissenting voices. That is, John Ruth's "unique center of covenant-conviction" or what he has called the "very soul-drama" of the "covenant community" of the Mennonites ("Mennonite Identity" 5, 25) becomes the ground *against* which the "outsider-prophet" or "iconoclast of the imagination"—Al Reimer's terms for the Mennonite artist—speaks (59). In such a typically hierarchical binary opposition, one party is seen to be ascendant: for Ruth, the "covenant-community"; for Reimer, "the new Mennonite literary prophet."

This kind of dualistic thinking, in which one dynamic is privileged, the other diminished by implication, is familiar enough to those individuals who grew up among North American Mennonites in the years on either side of World War II: those who were nurtured in a Mennonite world where the lines between "insiders" and "outsiders" were fairly clearly drawn and the categories of identity, as they experienced them, rigid and relatively stable.[6] But in late twentieth-century North America, urbanism, evangelicalism, and easy access to travel and information have precluded the sustaining of this kind of "oneness." Nevertheless, still compelled by the paradigm of binary opposites, Mennonites insist on referring to something they call "the

---

6 The categories were stable, although with occasional, jarring exceptions here and there where stratification along lines of class—a category conveniently obscured by other predominant paradigms—provided "insider" status to some who would otherwise be cast out. Much work needs to be done on the operation of class in the Mennonite communities in North America.

Mennonite community" and persist also in accepting the notion that any voices that do not emerge from what they have conventionally regarded as "the centre" must be perceived as "marginal" at best.

In the 1960s Rudy Wiebe, Warren Kliewer, Dallas Wiebe, and a few others were representing in fiction analogues for the Mennonite communities they had come to observe. These communities were, in the imaginations of these writers at least, dominated (and defined) by a relatively stable religious and cultural orthodoxy. Rudy Wiebe's *Peace Shall Destroy Many* suggests something of the inherent destructiveness of such monoliths. In 1962 Wiebe found no recourse for Joseph Dueck (the compelling dissenter in Wiebe's first novel) but for this insightful man to abandon the community that had been the object merely of his good will. The most significant difference between Joseph Dueck and today's "Mennos on the margins" or Mennonots—so christened in this decade by poet and editor Sheri Hostetler—is that Dueck had no recourse but to leave his communal home once he had given voice to his dissent. The *Mennonots* (or Mennonites who want to lay claim to their heritage, even though they might be ambivalent about much that it represents), as Hostetler declared at the "Quiet in the Land?" conference in Millersville in 1995, have no intention of going away. In her editorial comments in the first issue of the magazine *Mennonot: For Mennos on the Margins* (Fall 1993), Hostetler wrote: "perhaps *Mennonot* can ... help articulate what it means to be a biworldly Mennonite, for those of us still claiming that name for ourselves" (2). In effect echoing Brandt and Kasdorf, she declares: "I found myself in that crevice between worlds I've fallen into many a time since leaving home 10 years ago. I sometimes felt that I'd taken the Mennonite dictum to 'be in the world but be not of it' one better: I was living in two worlds and wasn't a part of either of them" (1).

Hostetler's comments speak to particular, contemporary identity issues. But they also reveal the degree to which she and other self-defined Mennonots have come to perceive their community of origin in terms of a binary logic that identifies insiders and outsiders, home and exile, centre and margin—Mennonites and Mennonots—and sustains these categories in a posture of opposition. It is true that in *Mennonot* Hostetler, like other writers who have situated themselves "in the margins," has cleared a space for herself and others to speak. But there is an inherent weakness in her "marginal" position as she defines it, a weakness rooted in the very binary assumption underlying her work and the title of her magazine.

As long as Mennonite literary critics and writers continue to accept the limiting, inherently hierarchical binary paradigms of centre and margin, insider and outsider we are examining here, they give credence to the persistent and prevailing notion that the territory the writers nurtured among the Mennonites occupy is, well, marginal. Margins consist, of course, of peripheral space, of that which is allowed beyond what is necessary. Texts of the margin, although they might offer illuminations and/or annotations, tend to be determined and limited by the primary texts—the master narratives, if you will—to which they refer.[7]

The point I am making here is this: the critics of Mennonite writing—and several of the writers who themselves comment critically on various aspects of the creative process and/or the creative condition—have tended to place the Mennonite writer in the context of a binary paradigm, with its inherent hierarchical structure. That is, they have accepted that those writers who have offered alternative readings of Mennonite cultural identity are appropriately perceived as marginal (and they have, in large measure, presented themselves that way). To be sure, Julia Kasdorf has argued in "Bakhtin, Boundaries, and Bodies" for a corrective dialogic paradigm for the interaction of all Mennonite voices (and, specifically, for the integration of the voice of the creative artist)—a paradigm based on the work of Bakhtin, which ideologically eschews the hierarchies binary paradigms imply and allows both sides of a dualistic model to be given equal weight. But her model (in true Bakhtinian fashion) merely inverts previously held hierarchical assumptions about the community and the artist. In Kasdorf's dialogic universe, that is, the world remains divided along binary lines, and the writer simply takes the place of the community in subsuming and embodying all contradictions.[8] Kasdorf's thoughtful essay is extraordinarily valuable in that it suggests a way for all who identify themselves as Mennonite to interact in "form-giving conversation" (Bakhtin, qtd. in Kasdorf, 188). But it leaves intact the persistent, problematic binary categories that have governed Mennonite identity politics (inclusive of centre and margin, insiders and outsiders). Her views, like the views of other writers and critics who have spoken about the role of the writer relative to the Mennonites, have been shaped, first of all, by binary hierarchies that have tended to oversimplify

---

7 See Anzaldúa, especially p. 78.

8 In Kasdorf's model the individual would, in effect, embody the community. "The point is not how we remain part of the Body of Christ—or of the Mennonite community—," Kasdorf observes, "but how the Body remains part of us and acts through us in the world" ("Bakhtin" 185). She concludes: "Outsiders or those who inhabit the margins of the community would be valued for their ability to offer consummating images of the Body in relation to its context, views impossible to grasp from an interior perspective" (188). The binary paradigm of outsider/insider (with its implied limiting essentialism) persists in Kasdorf's otherwise valuable model.

the nature of the "precarious discursive construction"(Gilroy, qtd. in Chambers 86) so often referred to as "the Mennonite community."

The overwhelming power of the centre, as Mennonites have acknowledged it, has been usefully interrogated or challenged by some Mennonite writers who have argued from the margins, as it were. However, it is in Mennonite writers' creative work—not in their own and others' critical observations—that they have in fact escaped not only the binary categories that support the assumption that the centre is fixed and unified but also the politics of the margins. It is in their poems and stories that writers like Julia Kasdorf and Jeff Gundy, for example, have been able to move us into the productive territory of what might be described as "the politics of difference"(Chambers 86), for it is in their creative writing that they confront their readers with what Iain Chambers refers to as "a continuous disbanding and dispersal of the terms that claim to represent us, them, and reality" (86). In their creative work, these writers have been prepared to trust to fragments, as Canadian postmodernist literary critic Robert Kroetsch would say, "letting them speak their incompleteness" (24). Here the fixed construction we have come to designate as the centre defers to that which is unstable and diverse, and issues of identity that were once invariably controlled by limiting binary categories are allowed some flexibility.

"Identity," British author Jeffrey Weeks has observed, "is about belonging, about what you have in common with some people. . . . At its most basic it gives you a sense of personal location"(88). Identity, Stuart Hall says, with acuity, is formed "at the unstable point where the 'unspeakable' stories of subjectivity meet the narratives of history, of a culture" (qtd. in Schwarz 157). This "unstable" intersection where identity comes into being—or, more accurately, this series of intersections—is what Homi Bhabha calls "a contingent 'in-between' space," an "intervening space" (7).[9] Post-colonial and postmodern theorists like Bhabha and Hall eschew the notion that centre and margin or insider and outsider might be acceptable as absolute categories. On the contrary, identity—or a sense of cultural and/or personal location—tends to be found in what Gloria Anzaldúa refers to as a "place of contradictions" (n.p.), a "wholly new and separate territory" (79). Moreover,

---

9 Bhabha states that "the borderline work of culture demands an encounter with 'newness' that is not part of the continuum of past and present. It creates a sense of the new as an insurgent act of cultural translation. Such art does not merely recall the past as social cause or aesthetic precedent; it renews the past, refiguring it as a contingent 'in-between' space, that innovates and interrupts the performance of the present. The 'past-present' becomes part of the necessity, not the nostalgia, of living" (7).

the site of identity is "in a constant state of transition" (3).[10] Anzaldúa refers to it as a borderland and speaks of it as a place of empowering hybridity. This is a place "that has to be engaged," Homi Bhabha argues, paraphrasing Salman Rushdie, "in creating the conditions through which 'newness comes into the world'" (227).

During a time when cultural boundaries are generally acknowledged as fluid rather than fixed, identity—this place of "perpetual transition," as Stuart Hall has observed—undergoes "constant transformation." Identity, Hall argues, "[f]ar from being eternally fixed in some essentialized past," is "subject to the continuous 'play' of history, culture, and power":

> Far from being grounded in a mere "recovery" of the past, which is waiting to be found, and which, when found, will secure our sense of ourselves into eternity, identities are the names we give to the different ways we are positioned by, and position ourselves within, the narratives of the past. (70)

Surely this speaks to the heart of what Mennonite writers like Jeff Gundy and Julia Kasdorf and others are doing in their creative work. Gundy has remarked that many writers find their art "in the difficult space where faith, doubt and real, lived experience cohabit or collide" ("U.S." 8). This is not unlike the "in-between space" of which Bhabha speaks, the contingent, provisional space from which the occupant can apprehend the continual, ultimately arbitrary re-positioning or re-siting of the border itself. This is the place of cultural hybridity that "resists unitary paradigms and dualistic thinking" (Boyce Davies 16), a place where transient, versatile, multiple, and unstable boundaries of difference are "re-mapped" and "re-named" (qtd. in Boyce Davies 10).[11] The act of writing in this interstitial space consists, as Julia Kasdorf has observed, of an attempt to

---

10 Anzaldúa, who writes about the US-Mexico border "where the Third World grates against the first and bleeds," speaks of a border culture as a site where "the lifeblood of two worlds [merge] to form a third country—a border culture." She continues: "Borders are set up to define the places that are safe and unsafe, to distinguish us from them" (3). This paper borrows from a number of critical paradigms, including Anzaldúa's; the "border cultures" posited here that Mennonites might encounter tend to be cultural and/or chronological.

11 I take these terms from Juan Flores and George Yúdice, cited in Boyce Davies (10): "The view from the border enables us to apprehend the ultimate arbitrariness of the border itself, of forced separations and inferiorizations ..." Flores and Yúdice speak of an inclusive society that "has to do with nothing less than the imaginative ethos of remapping and re-naming in the service [of] ... all claimants."

locate herself relative to the dislocations of contemporary life.[12] And as writers negotiate this indeterminate middlespace and construct ways to make sense of the complex worlds we occupy, they offer those constructions to others "as one possible form of existence" (Alcoff 109). It is liberating to recognize that movement within that space, as Paul Carter has observed, might be regarded not as "an awkward interval between fixed points of departure and arrival, but as a mode of being in the world" (qtd. in Chambers 42).[13]

The fixed categories of identity that Mennonites once believed they could slip into unproblematically are no longer useful. The binary oppositions inscribed in their literary-critical writing and thinking over the past half century serve them ill. Those who talk about Mennonite cultural identity must now learn to read the expanded text (or "assemblage of texts" [Clifford 41]), that creative writers have begun to inscribe.[14] The place that Mennonite writers are writing from, like the place most of us occupy, is not eternally fixed but is "somewhere in motion" (Rutherford 13)—between the early twentieth-century world of George and Clara in Jeff Gundy's *A Community of Memory* and the world of Gundy's self-conscious, sometimes postmodern narrator, for example; or between the modest sensibility of conservative Mennonite market vendor Emma Peachey and the ambivalently urban/e consciousness of the speaker in Julia Kasdorf's "Green Market, New York," the opening poem in *Sleeping Preacher*. Poems, Jeff Gundy has observed, "probe areas that the credos leave untouched, they insist that all experience and all feeling deserve attention, they work toward the messy inclusiveness of life itself" ("U.S." 8). Creative works like Gundy's and Kasdorf's are compelling explorations of that "in-between" world the Mennonites' binary understandings have not allowed them to name or claim: a place of re-territorialization, reconnection, re-inscription, re-membering.

---

12 In "Bringing Home the Work: Thoughts on Publishing a First Book," Kasdorf observed that "Paradoxically, a precarious sense of location is exactly what has fueled much of my writing so far" (10).

13 The paragraph containing this statement, from Paul Carter's 1992 *Living in a New Country: History, Travelling and Language*, is instructive here: "An authentically migrant perspective would, perhaps, be based on an intuition that the opposition between here and there is itself a cultural construction, a consequence of thinking in terms of fixed entities and defining them oppositionally. It might begin by regarding movement, not as an awkward interval between fixed points of departure and arrival, but as a mode of being in the world. The question would be, then, not how to arrive, but how to move, how to identify convergent and divergent movements; and the challenge would be how to notate such events, how to give them a historical and social value" (qtd. in Chambers 42).

14 Clifford refers to culture as an assemblage of texts, loosely and sometimes contradictorily united (41).

In their critical work writers like Gundy, Kasdorf, and others have not entirely escaped the fixed, oppositional essentialisms that have, for decades, confined the Mennonites and their writers; but literature, by its very nature, eschews the fixity and essentialism that binary propositions imply. In their poetry and stories, Mennonite writers have demonstrated that the conventionally bounded and hierarchical binary categories of insider and outsider, home and exile reveal little about the complex personal and cultural situations in which contemporary Mennonites live. By exploring and re-mapping the "postmodern world of indeterminacy and undecidability" in their creative work (Gundy, "U.S." 30), Mennonite writers have begun to inscribe the diverse, multiple, and unfixed "locations of culture"[15] where contemporary Mennonites inevitably find themselves, and hence to re-inscribe the Mennonites' cultural identity. "I believe that we will benefit from listening to our poets," Jeff Gundy remarked recently. "I doubt that they will save us," he continued modestly, "but I believe they can make us a little less lost" ("U.S." 39).

WORKS CITED

Alcoff, Linda Martin. "The Problem of Speaking for Others." *Who Can Speak? Authority and Critical Identity*, ed. Judith Roof and Robyn Wiegman, U Illinois P, 1995, pp. 97–119.

Anzaldúa, Gloria. *Borderlines/La Frontera: The New Mestiza*. Aunt Lute Books, 1987.

Bammer, Angelika. *Displacements: Cultural Identities in Question*. Indiana UP, 1994.

Bhabha, Homi K. *The Location of Culture*. Routledge, 1994.

Boyce Davies, Carole. *Black Women, Writing and Identity: Migrations of the Subject*. Routledge, 1994.

Brandt, Di. "how i got saved." *Why I Am a Mennonite: Essays on Mennonite Identity*, ed. Harry Loewen, Herald Press, 1988, pp. 26–33.

Carter, Paul. *Living in a New Country: History, Travelling, and Language*. Faber, 1992.

Chambers, Iain. *Migrancy, Culture, Identity*. Routledge, 1994.

Clifford, James. *The Predicament of Culture: Twentieth-Century Ethnography, Literature, and Art*. Harvard UP, 1988.

---

15 I borrow the phrase from Homi K. Bhabha's collection of essays by the same name, *The Location of Culture*.

Gundy, Jeff. "Humility in Mennonite Literature." *Mennonite Quarterly Review*, vol. 63, January 1989, pp. 5–21.

———. "Some Words on Poetry, Band Camps, Guitars, Gifts, Transgression, Community, Mennonite Art, etc." *Mennonite Life*, vol. 48, December 1993, pp. 15–16.

———. *A Community of Memory: My Days with George and Clara*. U Illinois P, 1995.

———. "U.S. Mennonite Poetry and Poets: Beyond Dr. Johnson's Dog." *Mennonite Quarterly Review*, vol. 71, January 1997, pp. 5–41.

Hall, Stuart. "Cultural Identity and Cinematic Representation." *Framework*, vol. 36, 1989, pp. 68–81.

Hostetler, Sheri. "The Story of *Mennonot*." *Mennonot: A Zine for Mennos on the Margins*, Fall 1993, p. 2.

Hutcheon, Linda, and Marion Richmond, eds. *Other Solitudes: Canadian Multicultural Fictions*. Oxford UP, 1990.

Kasdorf, Julia. "Bakhtin, Boundaries, and Bodies." *Mennonite Quarterly Review*, vol. 71, April 1997, pp. 169–188.

———. *Sleeping Preacher*. U Pittsburgh P, 1992.

———. "Bringing Home the Work: Thoughts on Publishing a First Book." *Festival Quarterly*, vol. 19, Spring 1992, pp. 7–10.

———. "'Work and Hope': Tradition and Translation of an Anabaptist Adam." *Mennonite Quarterly Review*, vol. 69, April 1995, pp. 178–204.

Kliewer, Warren. "Controversy and the Religious Arts." *Mennonite Life*, vol. 20, January 1965, pp. 8–11.

Kroetsch, Robert. *The Lovely Treachery of Words: Essays Selected and New*. Oxford UP, 1989.

Reimer, Al. *Mennonite Literary Voices: Past and Present*. Bethel College, 1993.

Ruth, John L. "Mennonite Identity and Literary Art." *Mennonite Life*, vol. 32, March 1977, pp. 4–25.

———. "Stories reveal individual psyches offended by stingy heritage" [Review of *Liars and Rascals: Mennonite Short Stories* edited by Hildi Froese Tiessen]. *Mennonite Reporter*, 26 June 1989, p. 11.

Rutherford, Jonathan. "A Place to Call Home." *Identity: Community, Culture, Difference*, ed. Jonathan Rutherford, Lawrence Wishart, 1990, pp. 9–27.

Schwarz, Bill. "Memories of Empire." *Displacements: Cultural Identities in Question*, ed. Angelica Bammer, Indiana UP, 1994, pp. 156–171.

Suderman, Elmer. "Mennonites, the Mennonite Community, and Mennonite Writers." *Mennonite Life*, vol. 47, September 1992, pp. 21–26.

Weeks, Jeffrey. "The Value of Difference." *Identity: Community, Culture, Difference*, ed. Jonathan Rutherford, Lawrence Wishart, 1990, pp. 88–100.

Six

Mennonite Literature and Postmodernism:
Writing the "In-Between" Space*

> *But still the crossroads does have a certain dangerous potency; dangerous because a man might perish there wrestling with multi-headed spirits, but also he might be lucky and return to his people with the boon of prophetic vision.*
>
> Chinua Achebe, "Named for Victoria, Queen of England"

IT SEEMS TO me it is best to temper a project like the one I embark on here with self-reflexive humor. Cultural studies theorist Dick Hebdige has offered this observation on what we seem to be involved in when we speak of postmodernism:

> When it becomes possible for people to describe as "postmodern" the decor of a room, the design of a building, ... the collective chagrin and morbid projections of a post-war generation of Baby Boomers confronting disillusioned middle age, the "predicament" of reflexivity, a group of rhetorical tropes, ... a process of cultural, political or existential fragmentation and/or crisis, the "de-centring"

---

* First published as Hildi Froese Tiessen, "Mennonite Literature and Postmodernism: Writing the 'In-Between' Space." *Mennonites and Postmodernism*, eds. Susan Biesecker-Mast and Gerald Biesecker-Mast. Pandora Press U.S., 2000, pp. 160–174.

of the subject, an "incredulity toward meta-narratives," the replacement of unitary power axes by a pluralism of power/discourse formations, the "implosion of meaning," the collapse of cultural hierarchies, ... the decline of the university, ... broad societal and economic shifts into a "media," "consumer" or "multinational" phase, a sense ... of "placelessness" or the abandonment of placelessness ... or (even) a generalized substitution of spatial for temporal co-ordinates—when it becomes possible to describe all those things as "postmodern" (or more simply, ... as "post" or "very post") then it's clear we are in the presence of a buzzword. (174-175)

Where to begin?

Clearly, my first challenge is to focus on something. To establish a context for that focusing, I will offer a general observation from Andreas Huyssen: "No matter how troubling it may be, the landscape of the postmodern surrounds us. It simultaneously delimits and opens our horizons. It's our problem and our hope" (221). To begin to focus on the literary, we could add to these words a remark by literary critic Robert Wilson, who has observed that postmodernism "bears in itself a nebulous frontier, an unmapped zone of bogs and tangled bush, between its uses as a period, and as an analytic-descriptive, term" (111). With these words, Wilson actually begins to bring order to the plethora of perspectives the discourse of postmodernism offers the literary scholar. Wilson speaks of two "archives" of postmodernism that "overlap and coincide" but nevertheless demonstrate two principal ways in which the postmodern finds expression in the literary world. And it is the world of literature that interests me here, and some of the various ways the literary and the postmodern have engaged each other, and how we might look at that engagement relative to the work of some writers who continue to write out of their Mennonite experience.

Postmodernism interests the literary scholar, first of all, as a historical condition that draws our attention, as cultural theorist Stuart Hall puts it, to "some of the deeply contradictory tendencies in modern culture" (qtd. in Grossberg 131). *As a historical condition or period*, postmodernism challenges notions of stability, coherence, unity; it throws into question any certainties; it demands to see all sides, to defer judgment, to make all that once went without saying subject to interrogation. Such challenges cannot help but affect the ways we write and read literary texts or see history, narrative, trope, convention. As a *literary style* the postmodern prefers discontinuity and multiplicity over order and unity; it favors the playful, the ironic, the derivative, the subversive, the self-reflexive. The character of a literary work we speak of as postmodern tends to be provisional, decentred, fragmented, eclectic; it tends to focus on the local and the particular. It blurs boundaries, breaks rules, mixes codes, subverts convention.

Where the period and the style we have come to speak of as postmodern perhaps converge most notably in the literary world, as elsewhere, is in challenging all "givens," the givens by which we live and the givens by which we express that living. That is, postmodernism challenges the legitimizing master narratives of history—what Linda Hutcheon, citing Lyotard, refers to as "the received wisdom or the grand narrative systems that once made sense of things for us" (*Canadian Postmodern* 15). In the arts, postmodernism challenges the presumed imperatives of style we refer to as convention.

The postmodern impulses to question, to problematize the givens, to challenge their authority, is evident in the work of a number of writers writing among Mennonites today. "I don't pretend to have answers," Rudy Wiebe's good friend, postmodernist Robert Kroetsch, has remarked with some degree of earnestness; "I am much more interested in the questions we ask ourselves than in the answers we hide behind" (*Likely* 131). Mennonite writers like Rudy Wiebe and Di Brandt, for example, would tend to agree with him.

In this paper I hope to demonstrate that one way postmodernism has informed the literature we refer to as "Mennonite" is in offering, in the model of the dismantling of the master narrative, a means by which Mennonites can productively interrogate their culture. A useful strategy for this interrogation is a rhetorical device Linda Hutcheon has named "postmodern irony." By means of postmodern irony a number of Mennonite writers have challenged the givens of Mennonite culture without being utterly dismissive of that culture. They have rather, in fact, begun to demonstrate a way for Mennonites to move beyond the monolithic and dualistic categories in terms of which they have tended to function. They have created the possibility for members of the Mennonite community to begin, in the words of cultural studies theorist Iain Chambers, to "break with the silent authority of certain inheritances," to rework the past "from another vantage point," and to create new anti-monolithic models of discourse by means of which to engage the postmodern world and to initiate continuing transformations within it ("Waiting" 206).

I am interested in how contemporary critical thinking can inform our understanding of the place of literature in Mennonite culture and thought. Like many Canadianists (who live with an awareness of Canada's marginal position internationally and its marked discontinuities domestically), I have taken a particular interest, in recent years, in the critical language of post-colonialism. My interest in postmodernism lies in areas where the concerns of these two contemporary critical discourses overlap: in their foregrounding of the marginal, the particular, the local over any version of a totalizing centre, for example; in their often-productive challenging of the "givens" by which we have tended to live. Both post-colonialism and postmodernism, as Linda Hutcheon has remarked, have been "embroiled in debates and dialogues with the past" ("Circling" 168).[1]

It is this sort of dialogue, or this type of confrontation, with inherited narratives—what poet Di Brandt calls "the official story" and perceives as a religiously infused discourse, with its own imperialist centralism—that finds expression in some of the work of Mennonites writing today (*Dancing* 36). "I doubt the *official* given history," Rudy Wiebe remarked in an interview conducted by Shirley Neuman in 1980. "You know there is another side to the story and maybe that's the more interesting side. Maybe even truer?" (qtd. in Neuman 230). Di Brandt is more strident, less tentative than Wiebe, when she speaks of "taking off the clothes of the official story, layer by layer, stripping away the codes we have lived by to get to the stories underneath of our real, aching bodies in the world" (*Dancing* 36).

Challenging the Official Story, Productively

> *At this point postmodernism, like any–ism, is not, of course, the answer. But its disruptive presence, which is certainly both theoretical, irreverent, and sometimes simply modish, has produced a space in the West in which to explicitly evaluate the adequacy of our accounts. ... Put in other terms, the world we inherit and inhabit can still be transformed.*
>
> Iain Chambers, "Waiting for the End of the World"

---

1 Hutcheon remarks that, unlike the postmodern, which tends to be politically ambivalent, the post-colonial possesses "a strong political motivation that is intrinsic to its oppositionality" (168).

Of course, the challenging of "the official story" or, to employ the language Rudy Wiebe uses in his first novel, *Peace Shall Destroy Many*, the questioning of "the ways of the fathers," began in Mennonite literature some decades ago. When Wiebe's novel first appeared in 1962, many Mennonites did not take easily to the fact that it challenged the idealized projects of community leadership, and, by implication, questioned the fixed set of protocols by which at least some Mennonites had come to live.[2] Joseph Dueck is the character most relentless in his refusal to accept the givens by which the patriarch in the novel, Deacon Block, maintains control of everything that happens in this isolated sectarian community. Dueck has no recourse but to leave after laying open to question the community's metanarrative and its tyrannies.

I do not mean to suggest that *Peace Shall Destroy Many* is a postmodern work, either in sensibility or style. In fact, Wiebe's modernist temperament is revealed when in the end he resolves the contradictions at the core of the novel by ridding the community of the forces that once denied or concealed all disorder, fragmentation, and contradiction. But Wiebe's work is prophetic. Over the past 20 years or so, while voices of creative writers among Mennonites have grown in number and intensity, questions such as Wiebe raised, about what lies at the heart of Mennonite culture as lived in communities scattered throughout North America, persist.

However, unlike Wiebe's own Joseph Dueck, those who insist on asking the questions now do not go away anymore. That is, even the voices of those who in effect spiritually leave the community of Mennonites—which nevertheless seems to remain a kind of monolithic force shaping the way many of these writers encounter and interpret the world—continue to speak and to be heard, both in the community and out. The questions that impel such Mennonites to give expression to their experience of the religious and cultural communities in which they grew up readily find a place in the postmodern world, which is particularly hospitable to discontinuities of experience and identity. In fact, one of the most compelling questions for Mennonite writers, if one is to judge from a fairly comprehensive survey of the work they have produced over the past two decades or so, concerns the apparent contradictions that have become so palpable in the Mennonite ethos itself, where the codes that once gave shape and coherence and meaning to the members of a community seem to function, if at all, only in fragmented ways.

A question implicit in many of the stories and poems produced by writers who have been nurtured in Mennonite communities in Canada, especially in

---

2 See Wiebe's "The Skull in the Swamp." *Journal of Mennonite Studies*, vol. 5, 1987, pp. 8–20.

the second half of this century, is what to make of a world that once seemed to so many to be whole. That is the world Di Brandt, mixing irony and nostalgia, calls "not the worldly world out there full of complacency and sin but the Mennonite world the real world of flower gardens & apple trees & green villages with names like Blumenort & Rosengart & Schoenwiese both gentle & proud"—a world which, on closer examination, appears to have had little real coherence at all ("how" 27).

Like pretty well everyone in my generation, I was trained in literature to read texts as a New Critic. We began with the assumption that every work of art was a coherent whole, and our analysis followed. Every literary trope and stylistic flourish was made to offer its unique and necessary contribution to the whole. Whatever did not fit we skillfully ignored. If we literary critics were to explore self-consciously our migration from the New Criticism to our eventual embrace of other ways of receiving texts, if we were to document our abandonment of the ruse of unity and order and coherence, and our discovery of how to engage the silence, the fragment, and the gap, we might provide, in that documentation, an analogue for how many Mennonite writers have come to see the Mennonite world.

And we might, in the best of circumstances, begin to feel comfortable "trusting," in the words of Robert Kroetsch, "to fragments of story, letting them speak their incompleteness" (*Lovely* 24). What else is the New Critic's coherent text than a paradigm for the master narrative that validates certain modes of being even as it silences or consigns to the margins whatever does not seem to fit the substance and momentum of the complete One?

Postmodern Irony: A Discourse of Complicity and Critique

> *Postmodern theory with its crazy affinities for contradictions and split identities and discontinuous narratives . . . gave permission for my own crazy, contradictory story.*
>
> Di Brandt, *Dancing Naked*

Mennonites are "trying always to keep the story the same," Di Brandt observed at a literary conference in Ottawa in spring 1998. Brandt speaks of "having to recognize" in herself "the 'rebel traitor thief,' willing to sell out, blow up, throw away the family stories and the official narratives of the culture, for art" (10). She regards her writing as a transgressive act, "transgressive and dangerous" ("questioning" 46). This is writing, she observes, that "breaks apart the official story, the inherited Mennonite narrative" (*Dancing* 36) that challenges what Hutcheon refers to as the "total explanatory system" of a culture (*Splitting* 2). Some of Brandt's work can indeed be seen as transgressive. Some registers a lament for undelivered promises and lost souls, sorrow for a fractured world. Thus her work reflects the split between an idealized world sustained by codes and conventions and "real" lived experience—a split, in the words of critic Coral Ann Howells, that tends to reveal "the incompleteness or falsity of tradition" (qtd. in Hutcheon, *Splitting* 97).

at Basil's

> Menno's sons meet every Wednesday
> evening at Basil's for beer they
> pretend they've gone worldly eat
> chicken fingers with honey dip
> burn each other's cigarettes but
> the room is made of mirrors & if
> you look past their jokes & their
> bland faces you can see the backs
> of their heads through the smoke
> beginning to crack open & Menno's
> guts spilling out Jake wears his
> baseball cap everywhere even to bed
> so he won't have to think about the
> split in his skull getting wider each
> year his mother worries about him
> Pete figured out long ago how to
> make the room dance he doesn't mind
> the numbness in his chest after the
> third or so it reminds him strangely
> of home though he will cry someday
> Pete will for another chance & where
> will Menno's promises be then & where
> was God when all these young men
> felt their souls crumble to dust &
> where is he now when all i can see
> in the mirror is the vines & tendrils
> of something wild growing in their

> brains & where's my long lost brother
> Mike who might have inherited the
> earth with me Menno where's Mike. (Brandt, *Agnes* 11)

This poem, which reveals something of the poignant sense of loss Brandt's transgressive voice occasionally allows, can be found soon after an unnamed poem, a fragment of which follows here, also from Brandt's second collection, *Agnes in the sky*:

> the man in the pulpit quotes Jesus
> & Shakespeare to prove the world
> is still round a perfect circle in
> God's eye despite acid rain & the
> hole above Antarctica ripping the sky
> apart ... (5)

Brandt's work, as this short excerpt of an untitled poem suggests, challenges defining narratives that are not restricted to the narratives of the Mennonites. Brandt, richly informed by and involved with other Canadian literary feminists, refers, in her allusion to Shakespeare, for example, to the Great Tradition that has for centuries defined the nature of English (and, of course, Canadian) literary history. With Robert Kroetsch, Brandt would agree that "one of the tasks of writers [is] to say, once we adopt a certain story which we all tell and retell, what is being left out, what is being concealed, what is being hidden, what is being ignored?" ("Closing" 225).

Like Di Brandt, Rudy Wiebe expresses in his work a distrust of grand narrative systems. But Wiebe tends to direct his skepticism at the dominant eastern Canadian and Eurocentric interpretations of the history of the Canadian West more often than at any Mennonite narratives. (When Wiebe has challenged the latter, as in *Peace Shall Destroy Many* in 1962 and *My Lovely Enemy* in 1983, community response to his work has tended to be swift and negative and fairly fierce.) Like Brandt, Wiebe is tenacious about exploring what the master narratives of our culture have left out. Like her, he is committed to telling the minority story from the minority perspective. One of his most recent projects was writing the script for a four-hour, two-part adaptation for television of his award-winning 1973 novel, *The Temptations of Big Bear*. The film was shown on the national network CBC in early winter 1999.

Wiebe has taken great delight in the fact that the Indigenous characters in the film of his novel spoke English, the language English-Canadian television audiences of course most readily understand. Their English colonizers spoke in a language Wiebe constructed for them. Wiebe calls it jabberwocky. Its roots are distinctly Low German, he explains with a sly grin. He wanted consistency in the language he developed for the British invaders and, after all, Low German, Wiebe's mother tongue, occurs in the same family of languages as Old English. So Queen Victoria was referred to on national television as *de Fruh* and Russian Mennonites in Canada were presumably able to pick up other echoes and nuances in Wiebe's distinctly postmodern exercise. As for the rest of the country, translations of what the British were saying were provided by subtitle. One assumes the Canadian audience at large got the post-colonial message of the film. Meanwhile, Mennonites had the added opportunity to ponder several layers of irony.

The playfulness of Wiebe's approach in his film script was, of course, evident in the text of *Big Bear* itself, where the English invaders' attempts to impose their inflexible way of seeing the world was shown, over and over again, to amount to utter foolishness. Wiebe has commented on his own method of dismantling the ways of the English in their colonization of the Canadian West, and the subsequent historical rendering of that colonization in the neatly ordered, Eurocentric histories that emerged—full of absences and elisions—out of eastern Canada. In an interview he said that "once you have taken this angle, this attitude of telling the minority story, then you drop in the majority documents and see how stupid they sound or what kinds of ironic changes you can ring on them. It's amazing how ironic it sometimes becomes" (qtd. in Neuman 230).

Rudy Wiebe has discovered in irony what Linda Hutcheon calls "a popular strategy for working in existing discourses and contesting them at the same time" ("Circling" 170-171). Hutcheon, who, as I have observed, has written a great deal on the subject of postmodern irony, speaks of it as one of the "major strategic rhetorical practices of postmodern art" (*Splitting* 39). It allows writers, she notes, "to address a dominant culture from within its own structures of understanding, while still contesting and resisting those structures" (31).

Rudy Wiebe's use, on the page immediately inside the front cover of *Playing Dead*, of a map of the Canadian North with south at the top of the page, is a perfect example of the strategy Hutcheon has in mind here: the inversion "at once inscribes and subverts the conventions and ideologies" of the dominant order (*Politics* 11). We all recognize the map and have no reason to doubt its dimensions, but the fact that it is upside-down (from our conventional perspective) objectifies it and causes us to raise questions about why it has always seemed "natural" to us for it to be the other way around. With south to the north, the upside-down map both acknowledges and contests the force of the dominant culture. The map is not wrong; it is problematized, shown to be subject to interrogation.

Wiebe manipulates the language of the dominant order in such a way as to make it, in effect, the base of the very disruption he undertakes. Similarly, in some of Di Brandt's most transgressive poetry she too throws into question the fairly evangelical discourse that shaped her religious sensibility. The trope of Jesus as lover sits at the base of her "missionary position" poems in her first collection, *questions i asked my mother*.

> *missionary position (1)*
>
> let me tell you what it's like
> having God for a father & jesus
> for a lover on this old mother
> earth you who no longer know
> the old story the part about the
> Virgin being of course a myth
> made up by Catholics for an easy
> way out it's not that easy i can
> tell you right off … (28)

The series of six poems, of which this is the beginning of the first, ends with one in which the speaker takes a dozen lovers—for God "made twelve a / good number for mates." This last poem in the series is followed by a page that has on it only three words: "just kidding ma" (34).

Brandt's work depends on irony, on the often playful treatment of a contradiction, a doubleness; on a "parodic recall" or "critical revisiting" of some element of past experience (see Hutcheon, *Canadian* 10). Her treatment of an evangelical Mennonite camp experience in a short prose piece ironically entitled "how i got saved" works in the same way.

> the Talk with the counselor this caught me by complete
> surprise i was sitting at the blue picnic table under the trees
> one afternoon with my counsellor Miss Krahn i had just
> finished reciting the entire lot of verses from Abraham &
> Isaac to *In the beginning was the Word* feeling relieved &
> not a little proud when she asked me quite suddenly was i

> a Christian yes i answered quickly startled at the question & when did you become one she asked   i don't know i said i can't remember   but you're sure you're saved she said doubtfully pencil poised above my card   God they're keeping a file on us i thought & i don't have a date   from that day for many years i worried about the problem of my conversion which came to a head every summer at Bible camp some years i felt miserable & dark despair about my inevitable damnation other years i cited some up lifting religious experience or another & thus located my salvation temporarily on the calendar i'm wondering now if it was a cumulative file & whether they did graphs on the fluctuation of our spirits from one year to the next every summer i wanted desperately to say no i'm not saved to see what they'd do to me how they'd snare me 'n make me a Christian but i never quite trusted them to meet the demand of the moment they would see me slipping into hell i thought & they wouldn't be strong enough to pull me out so i let it pass. (30)

The kind of dismantling Brandt undertakes, to objectify an aspect of what for years went without saying in her own Mennonite culture, occurs as a more humorous—but no less probing—episode in a recently published short story by Rosemary Nixon, entitled "Mennonite Your Way." This story, by one of the few Swiss Mennonites among the many Mennonite writers in Canada, provides a commentary on how conservative Mennonite women have been encouraged to see themselves:

> For years [grandmother] Beulah [Gingrich] has had their name in the Mennonite Your Way travel directory. The Floyd Gingriches. They've entertained guests from all over the States, from Niagara Falls, Ontario; Attica, Saskatchewan; Antwerp, Belgium; Iceland. When Winnie and Roy reached high school, sixteen years ago, Floyd encouraged her to enter the directory.
>
> It's a way to serve, he said. Floyd's name. Her work. Floyd believes only women who work endlessly in the service of the Lord keep out of trouble. After sixteen years, here they are, at last on the other side, Mennoniting *their way* across the country. (141–142)

Beulah and Floyd, Swiss Mennonites from Pennsylvania on their way through Saskatchewan, stumble on Queenie McClancy, a rough-and-tumble, worldly woman familiar to Nixon's readers for her outrageous ways. Queenie wears shorts, cooks out of tins and boxes, and casually uses the Lord's name in vain. Over the course of an afternoon she comes to represent a kind of freedom to Beulah, who begins to rethink the nature of her own existence as a woman:

> [Beulah] stares at Queenie's knees, and Queenie stares back at Beulah's covering. Up to now she has seen herself always as a representative of something—a Mennonite, a Christian, a mother, a grandmother. At Queenie's table Beulah fantasizes her history, her tie to Mennonite blood, Anabaptist blood.
>
> [Queenie talks, while they sit around her kitchen table, and Beulah muses.]
>
> Those treasured childhood stories of people fried in frying pans for their faith, drowned in Swiss lakes, burned in fires. Generations of women sacrificing, of women serving. This woman Queenie is snatching from Beulah her picture of the world. Beulah knows what good women, Christian women, don't do. They don't wear jewelry. They don't dress immodestly. They don't cut their hair.
>
> [Queenie keeps talking, and grandmother Beulah begins to fantasize.]
>
> She feels noise rise in her chest and coughs to quell it. Lift up your heart. Lift up your voice. Rejoice. How can she claim such freedom? She longs for adventure. For a drugstore romance. For another planet. She looks down at herself, doubtful, betrayed into this future, while Floyd slurps his tea. Her body's a disguise. Has been so since the birth of her first child thirty-five years ago. Beulah imagines herself her own woman. Hitched to nothing. Donning shorts to dig in her Pennsylvania garden. Serving canned soup. Making lewd remarks. Making advances. Floyd resisting.
> "It's not natural," he says, snapping his false teeth. "You're fifty-seven. Act like a natural woman." (141–142)

Postmodern irony functions similarly in these pieces by Brandt and Nixon, to reveal the contrary—ultimately irreconcilable—elements in each case.[3] Postmodern irony, Hutcheon remarks, "allows a text to work in the constraints of the dominant while placing those constraints *as constraints* in the foreground and thus undermining their power" ("Circling" 177). The tension in these stories remains unresolved for the reader, especially for the "insider"—the member of the community in which these sorts of episodes occur, the person who understands the irony, the one who "gets it." The postmodern irony of these stories is not utterly dismissive of the thing mimicked or displaced. Nor does it result in any glib resolution. In the best of circumstances, it "opens up new space, literally between opposing meanings, where new things can happen" (Hutcheon, *Splitting* 17) or, to borrow words from Iain Chambers, it "reveals an opening, not a conclusion: it always marks the moment of departure, never a homecoming" (*Migrancy* 122).

Negotiating that Space

The Mennonite writers who employ postmodern irony use it as a means by which to negotiate a space that lies somewhere between what we might call an idealized world of tradition and the postmodern world of contingency and fragmentation in which all of us find ourselves. Postmodern irony lends a kind of authenticity to both those places but ultimately authorizes neither. Neither pole of the tension is finally satisfying; each is problematic. And there is no resolution. "Trust me," David Waltner-Toews has observed, "the truth lies / somewhere in between" (128). Postmodern irony begins to name, to give form to, that in-between space. By its mode of operation it rejects the simple structure of closed dualistic systems and allows for both ambiguity and new possibility. It helps us, in the words of Chambers, "as we attempt to transform our histories, languages and recollections from a point of arrival into a point of departure" (*Migrancy* 7).

The person who negotiates the undefined territory of the postmodern is, as Stuart Hall has suggested, a kind of nomad, traveling "in a world in which

---

3 Hutcheon's "postmodern irony" is another variant of the several kinds of irony that have acquired currency throughout the ages. Postmodern irony, as Hutcheon describes it, is not to be confused with the sort of irony that drew praise from the New Critics: a rhetorical device that synthesizes and reconciles opposites into a whole, and hence serves to resolve dissonance in a work. Hutcheon's irony offers not resolution, but a kind of ongoing creative tension. It serves to probe and problematize rather than to resolve the issue at hand.

the authority of previous guides has apparently crumbled" (qtd. in Chambers, *Border* 81). The question that remains is how to occupy, name, negotiate the middle space that has come to represent the complexity and contingency—and the opportunity—of our lived experience. Through the use of postmodern irony, a number of Mennonite writers have discovered a way to gather up traces of Mennonite culture in order to arrange them in new patterns that enable us to see in and among them things we have not seen before. These writers pick over and put together fragments of memory and lived experience and, in the process, create stories that confer sense and elaborate what Chambers calls "a poetics of the possible" (*Border* 111).[4]

In the best of their work some contemporary Mennonite writers break up what Chambers refers to as a "particular language of tradition and truth" and invoke "a different vision of meaning, another language in which the repressed and displaced reappear and begin to speak." By their action, they produce "another sense of the past, and with it the future" (*Border* 111). In the re-inscribing of voices, stories, and events, they give expression to the hopes and disappointments, passions and fears of our lived experience. They provide windows through which we can see a new realm of the possible. The postmodern condition and the postmodern gesture, then, serve, in some Mennonite literature at least, to create "a space of transformation" in a cultural landscape that might otherwise seem to offer merely "the scene of a cheerless destiny" (*Border* 112).

WORKS CITED

Brandt, Di. *Agnes in the sky*. Turnstone Press, 1990.

———. *Dancing Naked: Narrative Strategies for Writing Across Centuries*. The Mercury Press, 1996.

———. "how i got saved." *Why I Am a Mennonite: Essays on Mennonite Identity*, ed. Harry Loewen, Herald Press, 1988, pp. 26–33.

---

4 Chambers' chapter in *Border Dialogues* entitled "Voices, traces, horizons" is an evocative exploration of the condition of "homelessness" in a postmodern world; he attempts to articulate something of "the vital network of voices, traces and horizons in and through which we grasp and construct our historical, that is, complex and lived, sense of the world we inhabit" (111).

———. "'that questioning self.'" *Sounding Differences: Conversations with Seventeen Canadian Women Writers*, ed. Janice Williamson, U Toronto Press, 1993, pp. 45–56.

———. *questions i asked my mother.* Turnstone Press, 1987.

Chambers, Iain. *Border Dialogues: Journeys in Postmodernity.* Routledge, 1990.

———. *Migrancy, Culture, Identity.* Routledge, 1994.

———. "Waiting on the End of the World?" Morley and Chen, pp. 201–211.

Grossberg, Lawrence. "On Postmodernism and Articulation: An Interview with Stuart Hall." Morley and Chen, pp. 131–150.

Hebdige, Dick. "Postmodernism and 'The Other Side.'" Morley and Chen, pp. 174–200.

Hutcheon, Linda. *The Canadian Postmodern: A Study of Contemporary English-Canadian Fiction.* Oxford UP, 1988.

———. "'Circling the Downspout of Empire.'" *Past the Last Post: Theorizing Post-Colonialism and Post-Modernism*, ed. Ian Adam and Helen Tiffin, U Calgary P, 1990, pp. 167–190.

———. *Splitting Images: Contemporary Canadian Ironies.* Oxford UP, 1991.

———. *The Politics of Postmodernism.* Routledge, 1989.

Huyssen, Andreas. *After the Great Divide: Modernism, Mass Culture, Postmodernism.* Indiana UP, 1986.

Kroetsch, Robert. *A Likely Story: The Writing Life.* Red Deer College P, 1995.

———. "Closing Panel." Tiessen and Hinchcliffe, pp. 223–242.

———. *The Lovely Treachery of Words: Essays Selected and New.* Oxford UP, 1989.

Morley, David, and Kuan-Hsing Chen, eds. *Stuart Hall: Critical Dialogues in Cultural Studies.* Routledge, 1996.

Neuman, Shirley. "Unearthing Language: An Interview with Rudy Wiebe and Robert Kroetsch." *A Voice in the Land: Essays by and About Rudy Wiebe*, ed. W.J. Keith, NeWest Press, 1981, pp. 226–248.

Nixon, Rosemary. "Mennonite Your Way." *Conrad Grebel Review*, vol. 1, no. 2 (Winter–Spring 1997), pp. 136–144.

Tiessen, Hildi Froese and Peter Hinchcliffe, eds. *Acts of Concealment: Mennonite/s Writing in Canada.* U Waterloo P, 1992.

Waltner-Toews, David. *The Impossible Uprooting.* McClelland & Stewart, 1995.

Wiebe, Rudy. *Playing Dead: A Contemplation Concerning the Arctic.* NeWest Press, 1989.

Wilson, Robert Rawdon. "SLIP PAGE: Angela Carter, In/Out/In the Postmodern nexus." *Past the Last Post: Theorizing Post-Colonialism and Post-Modernism*, ed. Ian Adam and Helen Tiffin, U Calgary P, 1990, pp. 109–124.

Seven

Between Memory and Longing:
Rudy Wiebe's *Sweeter Than All the World*[*]

There are many ways to see us.
We can look elsewhere; there are mirrors
all around: let us begin with the Old Country.

David Waltner-Toews, "A Word in the Nest"

We believed
it would be always summer
always Sunday. On Khortiza Island
we fell on our knees
searching reluctant undergrowth
for evidence of our having been there.
Our fingers trace names
once chiselled deep
in weathered stone.

Sarah Klassen, "Origins"

---

[*] First published as Hildi Froese Tiessen, "Between Memory and Longing: Rudy Wiebe's *Sweeter Than All the World.*" *Mennonite Quarterly Review*, vol. 77, 2003, pp. 619–636.

> *Presumably all the parts of the story are themselves available. A difficulty is that they are, as always, available only in bits and pieces.*
>
> Rudy Wiebe, "Where Is the Voice Coming From?"

Collective memory and the allure of imaginary wholeness

Actual photographs—testimonies to historical circumstance—inform some of the narratives of Rudy Wiebe's *Sweeter Than All the World*. The following passage from the novel, and the accompanying photograph, illustrate what I mean [Plate #1]:

> Father, show me a picture.
> Which one, sweetheart?
> You know, you know.
> You made me laugh, he says, laughing. So hard I shook the camera under the hood. You and Greta Isaak were perfect slender young men in trousers and tied cravats, flat-brimmed hats, pince-nez and twirled moustaches, superb, she in black, stood leaning towards you in grey, seated in the round-backed chair with your left leg perched at the ankle on your right knee, each of you with a long cigarette elegantly between your fingers, rolled paper actually, such beautiful young men. (282)[1]

This essay investigates the relationship between literary fiction and the photograph. It probes the nature of collective memory. It suggests that

---

1 In contrast to other Peter Gerhard Rempel photographs that Wiebe invokes narratively in the text of his novel, this re-inscription of Plate 74 of *Forever Summer, Forever Sunday* is narrated as a personal historic event, not described as an artifact. The narrator here (photographer Alexander Wiebe) takes pleasure in the role-playing his subjects enact in his studio during their photographic encounter with him, and makes no reference to the ambiguity and subversion implied in their cross-dressing performance. That is, he does not seem to regard the tableau he describes as evocative of any state beyond itself, and so, in effect, makes all the more poignant the inscription of longing so palpably expressed, as we shall see, in other descriptive evocations of other photographic texts in the novel. All images from John D. Rempel and Paul Tiessen, *Forever Summer, Forever Sunday: Peter Gerhard Rempel's Photographs of Mennonites in Russia, 1890–1919* (Sand Hills Books, 1981) reproduced in this article are used with permission.

Between Memory and Longing

PLATE #1

sometimes cultural artifacts can engage our consciousness, invade our imagination and lead us "home."

Members of my own generation of "Russian Mennonites," children and grandchildren of 1920s German-speaking immigrants to Canada from the Mennonite colonies of southern Ukraine (our parents called it Russia),[2] are cognizant of how far we have travelled from the richly layered religious and social ethos our parents occupied, once, and of how little material culture we can gather around us to give us a palpable sense of how *they* lived and who *we* are relative to *their* past—our heritage. We find ourselves pondering the limited material inheritances our forebears have passed on to us (primarily photographs, that are evocative and in some sense, presumably, reliable). And we wonder whether these mementoes—these minor monuments—can offer us any meaningful access to a cultural and spiritual heritage we have come to know only second-hand.

In a very real sense people of my generation are engaging in what Marianne Hirsch calls "post memory"—a "'second generation' memory characterized by belatedness, secondariness, and displacements" (qtd. in Bal xii).[3] The personal memories of our parents and grandparents are being "crowded out," Hirsch would observe, by the "cultural memories" that have taken their place and now tend to dominate. Such cultural memories are both enlarged and subverted when they are extravagantly reconstructed by Mennonite writers of historical fiction and metafiction like Sandra Birdsell and Rudy Wiebe.

---

2 "Russian Mennonites" is a descriptor used to identify Mennonites whose ancestors come from the northern regions of Germany and Holland; the term "Swiss Mennonites," on the other hand, identifies those whose ancestors come from Switzerland or the southern regions of Germany. "Russian Mennonites," who sojourned in Prussia before migrating farther east, came to Canada by way of southern Ukraine; "Swiss Mennonites" came to Canada by way of the United States. "Russian Mennonites" tend to be categorized as either *Kanadier* (those who came to Canada in the first wave of migration in the 1870s) or *Russländer* (those who migrated to Canada in the second wave, the 1920s).

3 See also Marianne Hirsch, "Projected Memory: Holocaust Photographs in Personal and Public Fantasy," ed. Mieke Bal et al., *Acts of Memory: Cultural Recall in the Present*, UP New England, 1999, pp. 3–23.

"Cultural memory," Mieke Bal has remarked, "can be located in literary texts because the latter are continuous with the communal fictionalizing, idealizing, monumentalizing impulses thriving in a conflicted culture" (xiii). Historical fiction informed by the photograph—like Rudy Wiebe's *Sweeter Than All the World*—has the capacity to posit at once the allure of "imaginary wholeness" that collective memory would promise, as well as the unreliability of all the material means that would seem poised to deliver that wholeness (Huyssen 198). That is because the photograph—like the historical fiction itself—is essentially an unstable artifact, subject to diverse and contradictory interpretations.

In fact, both literary fiction and the photograph offer incomplete and unstable renderings of what was and what might have been—of both memory and longing. Historical novelists gather the fragments of what was in order to construct a rendering of what might have been. And they know, as they do this, that any material residue of the past—including the photograph—can invoke and represent a forgetting as much as a remembering. Andreas Huyssen, recalling an observation by Robert Musil, has suggested that "the more monuments there are, the more the past becomes invisible, the easier it is to forget" (184). Paradoxes like the one Huyssen identifies here speak to both the possibilities and the limitations inherent in the novelist's monumentalizing impulse. For the novelist knows—as Anthony Vidler has remarked—that "despite a yearning for a concrete place and time, the object of desire is neither here nor there, present or absent, now or then" (66). And so the novelist inscribes the gap—and invites his reader to inscribe the gap—between the historical evidence he has before him and the condition for which he longs. Sometimes that act of inscription—as Rudy Wiebe has so stunningly demonstrated in his powerful and much anthologized short story "Where Is the Voice Coming From?"—serves to transport both writer and reader beyond the artifact, beyond the text and, in an instant of transcendence, to deliver them to the location of their desire.

Among the facts and artifacts of history

Today we are experiencing, Svetlana Boym remarked in 2001, a "global epidemic of nostalgia, an affective yearning for a community with a collective memory, a longing for continuity in a fragmented world" (xiv). In the absence of "space which we [can] authentically occupy," Christopher Shaw and Malcolm Chase have written, we "fill the gap by manufacturing images of home and rootedness" (15). We might do well to take a cautious approach to nostalgia, as Mieke Bal has remarked. For nostalgia, Bal cautions, is "unproductive, escapist, and sentimental. It is ... the temporal equivalent of tourism ... It has also been conceived as longing for an idyllic past that never was" (xi).

It could be argued that parts of both Wiebe's *Sweeter Than All the World* and Sandra Birdsell's *The Russländer*, another novel dealing with the history of the Mennonites and also published in 2001, are, at least in part, expressions of nostalgia (even though, at the same time, they work to subvert that impulse). Certainly both novels offer investigations of an elusive past, expressions of "poignant yearning" for a world that can never be recovered in its entirety and yet is presented, in the very memorial artifacts constructed to invoke it, as more complete, more coherent than our own (Dames 121).

But these works reach beyond the romantic sentimentalism in which nostalgia trades. Questions about how the individual can gain access to the historical past—insert oneself within it—lie at the heart of Wiebe's work in particular. The search for the past that would confirm, say, Adam Wiebe's identity in *Sweeter Than All the World* becomes for Rudy Wiebe an analogue for any secular Mennonite's questions about what it means to make sense of or lay claim to a heritage from which one has become several steps removed. Adam's search, that is, becomes an analogue for the experience of many members of my own generation of Mennonites—people who know that the cultural and religious discourses that were, in another context, apparently sufficient for our parents' generation are not sufficient for us.

The structure of the novel itself, with Adam's quest complexly and unequivocally embedded in some seminal narratives of Russian Mennonite history, reinforces a central idea Wiebe seems to propose here: that in the very act of placing ourselves among the facts and artifacts that comprise our past, our personal history, we can make meaningful discoveries. In *Sweeter Than All the World* Wiebe returns to the issues he outlines in his great short metafiction "Where Is the Voice Coming From?" where, at the outset, he provocatively quotes Teilhard de Chardin: "We are continually inclined to isolate ourselves from things and events which surround us ... as though we were spectators, not elements, in what goes on" (135). As spectators, that is—and through the mediating force of what Wiebe (quoting Arnold Toynbee) speaks of as "the undifferentiated unity of the mystical experience"—we, as readers and seekers, can become elements in what goes on (135).

From rupture and dislocation to collective memory

The tone of *Sweeter Than All the World* is markedly different from the often more astringent tone common to many of the Mennonite literary texts that preceded it.[4] The early works of Mennonite fiction and poetry published mostly in the 1970s and 1980s documented the disintegration of various elements of what some had hoped would become a Mennonite commonwealth in Canada. They revealed that the social, cultural, and religious practices and traditions that would once have allowed the Mennonites of any particular region of Canada (the prairies, for example) to refer to themselves as a community—or a "people"—no longer had coherence or sustaining power. For most of the early wave of Mennonite writers in Canada, that is, the coherent community came to be recognized as a deception, and the disintegrating cultural and religious ethos, as a trap. As the writers looked back on their own experience among their people, they saw themselves moving outward and away, while the urgent, but finally ineffectual, words of the Mennonites' ubiquitous, dominant patriarchs echoed in a hollow landscape.

The Mennonite community, its writers observed, had become a place where those who raised questions were shut out: "You criticized the church before *that* group?" Deacon Block, in Rudy Wiebe's *Peace Shall Destroy Many*, demands of the author's primary spokesman Joseph Dueck (as if anticipating the harsh treatment the 28-year-old author, Wiebe himself, would experience at the hands of powerful forces in his own community): "You took pains to speak a language [outsiders could] understand to slander our church?"(60).

This first wave of Canadian Mennonite literature reflected the disillusionment of a younger, Canadian-born generation, reluctantly released by their communities into the world. Some among them eventually recognized the extent of their growing detachment from Mennonite traditions and undertook the search for what George Lipsitz calls a "precious and communicable past" (36). Like Rudy Wiebe's Adam in *Sweeter Than All the World*, they began to explore, in collective memory, for example, the shared identity that might

---

4 Wiebe's earliest novels about Mennonites, *Peace Shall Destroy Many* (1962) and *The Blue Mountains of China* (1970), and subsequent writers' major early works dealing with the experience of Mennonites in Canada—Patrick Friesen's *The Shunning* (1980), David Waltner-Toews' *Good Housekeeping* (1983), Armin Wiebe's *The Salvation of Yasch Siemens*, Sandra Birdsell's *Night Travellers* (1984), Di Brandt's *questions i asked my mother* (1987) and Sarah Klassen's *Journey to Yalta* (1988)—tended to probe the ongoing value of rigid doctrines and patterns of patriarchal dominance that old world Mennonite immigrants from Russia had tried to transplant in their substantial settlements on the Canadian prairie.

modify their sense of cultural alienation. Like Adam, authors such as Wiebe and Birdsell and others have now begun to probe their relationship to the history and ethos of Mennonite religion and culture in the decades and centuries prior to the Mennonites' immigration to Canada.

Sites of inscription

Two books lie at the heart of this essay. The first is Rudy Wiebe's novel *Sweeter Than All the World*. The second is a collection of black and white photographs published in 1981 as *Forever Summer, Forever Sunday: Peter Gerhard Rempel's Photographs of Mennonites in Russia, 1890-1917*, edited by John D. Rempel, the photographer's grandson, and Paul Tiessen, husband to Hildegard E. Tiessen (Hildi Froese Tiessen), translator of the book's epistolary text and author of this essay.[5] The book was known to most of the writers who maintained contact with members of the Mennonite community, especially writers like Rudy Wiebe and Sandra Birdsell, each of whom also had a professional relationship with its publishers. As one of the primary collaborators on the volume and as an avid observer of the field of Mennonite literature, I took notice when references to *Forever Summer, Forever Sunday* began to appear in Mennonite literary texts. This essay represents my first formal response to the emergence in that body of literature of the trope that I prefer to call "forever summer, forever Sunday," a trope that has found

---

5 *Forever Summer, Forever Sunday* was some eight years in the making. Although it was not the first book published by Sand Hills Books (a small press of which the Tiessens are principals), the book was, in a very real sense, the reason for Sand Hills' existence. After John Rempel and Paul Tiessen, both young academics, had begun to talk about the glass plate negatives Peter Gerhard Rempel had brought from Russia to Canada, they could not imagine *not* placing the rich visual archive of photographs in the public domain. Rempel and Tiessen found in these photographs, as their introduction reveals, the projection of a Russian Mennonite worldview later seemingly largely forgotten or actively suppressed. The editors spoke of the book as having community value as a documentary record of the dreams and achievements of the Russian Mennonites at the apex of their cultural and material development. The book was published (with material support from the Multiculturalism Program of the Government of Canada and the Ontario Arts Council) in fall 1981 in an edition of 950 copies. It was sold out in January 1982. Its primary audience turned out to be Mennonites in Canada, among whom the book was favourably reviewed in such prominent periodicals as *Mennonite Reporter* (7 December 1981), *Mennonite Brethren Herald* (18 December 1981), *Mennonite Mirror* (January 1982) and (in the USA) *Festival Quarterly* (Spring 1982). Reviews tended to be descriptive and positive. On the one hand they praised the photographer and editors for avoiding sentimentality and, on the other, cautioned readers not to take the lifestyle reflected in the photographs as broadly representative of village life in the Mennonite colonies of Russia.

expression in numerous Mennonite literary texts. *Forever Summer, Forever Sunday* was published by a small independent publisher, Sand Hills Books, in St. Jacobs, Ontario, in 1981. Photographs from the book have appeared in various Mennonite texts, as well as in an etching that forms part of a large metal sculpture depicting the history of the Mennonites, installed on the wall of the atrium of Conrad Grebel University College, the Mennonite college at the University of Waterloo.[6]

Photographs or details of photographs from the book have graced the covers of two major Mennonite literary works within the past decade: David Waltner-Toews's collection of poetry *The Impossible Uprooting* (1995) [Plate #2] as well as Sandra Birdsell's work of historical fiction *The Russländer* [Plate #3]. *Forever Summer, Forever Sunday* found its way, over the years, into various other *Russländer* texts as well, where its title evoked a contradictory landscape: a kind of palimpsest in which a utopian dream was overwritten by the shattering reality of revolution, disorder, plunder, and rape.[7] As monuments, photographs like Rempel's do not provide final, fixed meanings, of course. A photograph is always open to interpretation. Thus, the photographs do not so much transport their audience into particular narratives as provide sites of emblematic inscription: places where longing can be both observed and registered, perhaps even mystically realized; places where questions can be framed.

In *Sweeter Than All the World*, for example, the descriptions of specific photographs simultaneously evoke and erase the complex world of the Mennonite colonies of Russia as they seem to have existed in the early years of the last century. The world these photographs represented was finally not so much a particular time and place as an abstract and evocative landscape, an ethos in which, it would seem, individuals could find—or project—meaning and share it with others. Rudy Wiebe's Adam (along with the author himself)

---

6 "Ties That Bind," a multilayered sculpture of 41 copper panels, by metal artist Jo-Anne Harder.

7 Photographs from the book figured prominently in David Dueck's documentary film entitled *And When They Shall Ask* (Dueck Films, 1983), which was widely distributed among Mennonite audiences in a campaign of special screenings. The photographs were also featured in Volume 2 of Norma Jost Voth's *Mennonite Foods & Folkways from South Russia* (Good Books, 1991). The narrative and visual images of the film allude to Rempel's photographs but, in parts of the film at least, the trope of "forever summer" is inverted. In Dueck's film the Mennonites' aspirations to material success and cultural refinement that are fairly innocently foregrounded in Rempel's photographs tend to be debunked and devalued, as signs of moral degeneracy. That is, Dueck offers a fairly straightforward moralistic interpretation of the world Rempel's photographs evoke, unlike Wiebe, for whom the photographic images invoke aspiration and longing and remain more open to interpretation.

Between Memory and Longing

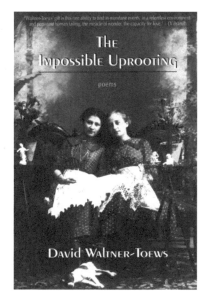

PLATE #2

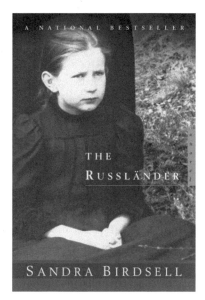

PLATE #3

is asking, "How can one insert oneself into such a cultural landscape? Such an ethos, a community? If those were my people, how might I find my way back to them?" As metanarrative, *Sweeter Than All the World* foregrounds questions like: "What access do secular Mennonites have to their ancestral past? What form might acts of cultural reclamation take, and what might they reveal? Is it possible to gain entry to the world beyond the cultural artifact? How might I appropriate that world—or it me? What would be the cost of attempting its recovery?"

It is not surprising that a great Canadian historical meta-fictionist like Rudy Wiebe should explore in a historical novel—a rich memorializing artifact in its own right—how difficult it is to engage the past in a meaningful way. How fact and artifact fail to provide a secure and reliable entry into an ancestral past; how they suggest something about what the past might have been, but fall short of conveying what it was and what it meant. How every monument—from the photograph to the work of literary fiction—is an expression of longing towards that place beyond the image, beyond the text. How sometimes miraculously, in a moment of epiphany as readers, we realize what we've longed for and sneak beyond the artifact in an instant of transcendence. How that epiphany we experience might stretch well beyond any actual lived history—any facts of existence—and how that doesn't matter.

Everyday mental property

It was some years after *Forever Summer, Forever Sunday* appeared that the compelling trope the title evoked[8] gradually began to capture the Mennonite imagination. The photographer's daughter, Tina Rempel, recalling with immense pleasure around 1980 the early twentieth-century period of her own life, pronounced that era a wonderful, idyllic time when every season seemed like summer, every day like Sunday. "*Bei uns war es immer Sommer, immer Sonntag,*" she declared. Tina Rempel's words, which—along with the idealizing photographs themselves—came five decades after her family's immigration into Canada from Russia, were deftly adapted by a number of Mennonite writers who made of the compelling phrase "forever summer, forever Sunday"—a trope suggestive of a time and place when the cares of the world seemed remote from the everyday life of the Mennonite colonists, an era that seemed now almost a fantasy, a period that ended when the Mennonite commonwealth was shattered by the violence of revolution and anarchy. The trope "forever summer, forever Sunday," that is, eventually became a kind of hinge connecting the all-too-present discomforting complexities of twentieth-century Mennonite immigrant experience in Canada with the apparently more stable and more coherent culture of the late nineteenth- and early twentieth-century, pre-Revolution Russian Mennonite commonwealth. Gradually it began to capture the Mennonite imagination. Indeed, these photographs, suggestive of harmonious and—to be sure—idealized variants upon a way of life, played a part in helping to construct among the Russian Mennonites of Canada what Alon Confino, in his study of collective memory, refers to as "common denominators" that function "to create an imagined community" (1399). The photographs allowed or stimulated Mennonites in general—and eventually writers of historical fiction like Birdsell and Wiebe in particular—to "construct a past through a process of appropriation and contestation" (Confino 1402).

During the 1980s and 1990s the trope emerged in the larger Mennonite consciousness as a kind of cultural icon. For many, it became what Confino calls "everyday mental property" (1402). Most Mennonites knew what it meant. It functioned, furthermore, to construct for many members of the *Russländer* audience—no matter how disenfranchised from their cultural and

---

8 This volume of pictures, reproduced from glass plates made in Russia by Peter Gerhard Rempel (who lived from 1872 to 1933), projects, in studio portraits and the adjacent text, a seemingly untroubled world of languor and luxury in the Mennonite colonies of pre-revolutionary Russia.

religious heritage they had come to feel—the possibility of realizing themselves "as historical subjects with a common past" (Lipsitz 32). Hence, a complex historical and cultural construct was evoked for Russian Mennonite readers when they read, in Sarah Klassen's collection of poetry *Journey to Yalta* (1988):

> Mennonites
> having come a long way
> like to return
> in herds like lemmings
> to places of death.
> Frozen forests declared out of bounds
> we surround the old oak tree we owned
> once. We stretched warm limbs
> along its rough-ridged branches,
> its roots
> loved the same rivers we loved. We believed
> it would be always Summer
> always Sunday ... (3)

Or in David Waltner-Toews's sixteen-page poem "A Word in the Nest," which begins:

> Rummaging through an old
> trunk in the attic
> I pulled out yellowed, crinkled
> pictures; My five-year-old mother with a cow,
> my four-year-old father on a horse,
> the long, warm day before the Revolution,
> forever Summer, forever Sunday,
> forever seen through the sepia of suffering. (37)

Birdsell and Wiebe, through their fictional reconstruction of cultural history in their most recent work, play self-consciously both within and against the trope of "forever summer, forever Sunday." In Birdsell's case, the central character Katherine (Katya) Vogt is featured on the dust jacket and paper covers of the novel, her image a detail of a larger photograph that evocatively informs her character[9] [Plate #4]. As for Rudy Wiebe, in *Sweeter Than All the World* he, too, "quotes" (if I may use that term figuratively and suggestively) Rempel's photographs. For him, a photograph from Rempel's volume has the power to evoke the gestures and tone of another age [Plate #5]. More than this, when Elizabeth Katerina Wiebe speaks, her words invoke the vast realm of longing and emotion beyond the photographic (and narrative) text:

> I remember my mother always slender, and pale.... In the finest portrait [my father, Alexander Wiebe] ever took with his large studio camera, she is half turned, half kneeling on a chair, her left leg almost doubling her long skirt under her and her arms crossed on the chairback; strands of her hair stray back down to her waist, and forward over the lace-trimmed blouse on her breast. She is looking right, serene as glass with the painted studio backdrop behind

PLATE #4

PLATE #5

---

9 I refer here to Plate 40 among Peter Gerhard Rempel's photographs in *Forever Summer, Forever Sunday* (Plate 4, here). Birdsell (to allude to her only in passing here) has on several occasions also identified other central characters in her novel (for example, Lydia and Greta) with the figures in Rempel's Plate 40 and has suggested the presence of a rich texture of relationship between Rempel's photographs (and by implication the utopian—and ironic—trope they represent) and various of the characters in her novel.

> her, her eyes raised as if anticipating a vision from heaven; it is coming, yes. Her lips will open in adoration. (261, 262)

Peter Gerhard Rempel's photographs function for both Birdsell and Wiebe as what David Lowenthal calls "emblems of communal identity, continuity" (xvi). They simultaneously draw upon and serve to shape collective memory; they unite these writers' present-day audience by alluding with some degree of literalness to self-representing artifacts from the past. This is how it was. This is what we knew. This is who we were.

The transformative power of individual recollection

One of the epigraphs to Wiebe's novel is taken from the Russian poet Joseph Brodsky: "You're coming home again. What does that mean?" *Sweeter Than All the World* explores, among other things, what it might mean for a secular Mennonite to probe his ancestral past, to come home. It begins with a mother "calling into the long northern evening. 'Where a-a-re you?'" (7). Adam Wiebe's life begins in a kind of garden, and the novel proceeds to document his attempt to recover some variant of paradise lost, an imagined community. The language describing worlds imagined, lost, and yearned for evokes the "forever summer" trope:

> And then, ahh then! Adam and Eve lived together in the most beautiful garden on earth, eating fresh fruit and playing with the gold and sweet gum and pearls and onyx stones that were in the four rivers that flowed out of Eden, and bathing in them too. It was always the perfect seventh day of creation, forever rest, forever summer. (9)

In the hands of Rudy Wiebe, the photographs of Peter Gerhard Rempel are narrativized. By incorporating the photographic images into the text as narratives that inscribe home and family and loss, Wiebe reveals how, when we take the material culture of history into the present, we must take possession of it in a very personal way. The monument (be it photograph or story), although it both shapes and reflects collective memory, is available to be inscribed—or have its meaning established—by every individual who encounters it.

Yes, Papa. Now, please, can I see a picture?

Which one?

Of Enoch and Abel, my beautiful brothers. Not where they are four and six and looking from under broad, black-brimmed hats, their small hands clutching the railing of a fake bridge set over a stream that does not exist on your sunny studio floor [Plate #6]; not the picture where they sit in a cardboard boat with sailor hats to sail across a paper-painted sea [Plate #7], no, show me the sweetest portrait of all, the one I watched you and mother arrange so carefully, together. There is a background of bushy shadow on the right, and wide scrolled and flowered steps leading upwards, left. Enoch, aged three, stands in his striped summer shirt and shorts looking into the distance while he holds the large china family chamberpot at his side. And just under his gaze, facing into the camera and bare to the waist, beautiful Abel, aged one, sits with his chubby legs bent, on the smaller, rounder chamberpot that was first mine, then Enoch's and now his, Abel's eyes so enormous and his face as blank and perfectly sad as any small animal's—O my brothers, O Enoch, O Abel, Abel, my lost brother Abel.... (278-279) [Plate #8]

Peter Gerhard Rempel's photographs seem to partake of the very world they represent in those early years of the twentieth century. Yet they are, from their inception, contrived and ultimately unstable, unreliable. Like all the facts and artifacts of history, they might lie strewn at the threshold of the past,

PLATE #6

PLATE #7

PLATE #8

but we cannot apprehend them as though they were the past itself. We can only place ourselves among them (as Wiebe's characters do) and inscribe them with narratives of our own. Sometimes when we do that, we find ourselves transported both into and beyond these fragments of history.

The mystical experience or aesthetic insight that might ensue is parallel to what happens at the end of Wiebe's "Where Is the Voice Coming From?" In a manner reminiscent of that story, *Sweeter Than All the World* explores the relationship between cultural artifact, memory, and longing. For Wiebe, the photographs of Peter Gerhard Rempel serve as representations (however unreliable in any literal sense) of a lost era. At the same time they are expressions of desire, icons that invoke the coherent community of Mennonite life and culture for which characters like Adam Wiebe yearn—along with so many of us, members of his generation, Mennonites dislodged from an ethos and a tradition that once seemed to hold together our world. Like Wiebe's character Elizabeth Katerina, we look to the artifact, the photograph, the novel. We seek refuge in it and, even more, in the depths beyond its dazzling surfaces between memory and longing, hope it will have the capacity to transport us home [Plate #9].

> Father, show me a picture.
> The summer picnic on the banks of the Dnieper River. Mother, on the right in her broad hat and long white dress, leans back against the cliff; your five friends lounge on the grass and against the rocks between you; and you sit on the left by the basket, the picnic blanket, and the samovar. Everyone except you holds a glass, lifting them towards you as if in a toast. Father, why are you holding a guitar, the fingers of your right hand curled as if you were playing it? Did you, could you ever, play the guitar? Sing?
> But he does not answer me. Finally I must continue for myself. I tell him: I am in the picture too, even if no one—not you, perhaps not even Mama—knows it. I am there below her heart, hidden, untouchable, safe. (287)

PLATE #9

In "Where Is the Voice Coming From?" the narrator surrounds himself with cultural artifacts that contradict each other and would seem to lead to no one place. When he finally gives in to the incompleteness of the fragments of history he uncovers, he is transported, by an embracing act of the imagination, into the realm of his own desire. He hears a voice emerging from the ruins—a voice as incomprehensible as it is compelling, a voice at once mysteriously intangible and deeply satisfying. In the above passage from *Sweeter Than All the World* Elizabeth Katerina seeks shelter in the shards of memory represented by her father's album of photographs. Like the narrator in "Where Is the Voice Coming From?" she finds herself submerged among the artifacts she ponders. She is as insistent as the narrator in "Where Is the Voice Coming From?" in declaring that she is *there*—where the actions of history take place. She is, at the same time, aware that she cannot, by any conventional means, communicate to others the essence of her experience. She simply declares it, and through Wiebe's skilful rendering of her personal narrative the fortunate reader is transported with her to that other realm.

Sweeter Than All the World is not an exercise in simple nostalgia, which tends, as Nicholas Dames has observed, to replace "stubbornly individual pasts with communal pasts" (131). Instead, the novelist (who is palpably present as a structuring force behind the novel's multiple narratives) celebrates the insertion of personal memory into history. Wiebe, that is, reclaims, recovers collective memory that has, in large measure, been "besieged, deformed and transformed by history," and gathers it into the realm of literary fiction, of art (Crane 1375, 1379). In *Sweeter Than All the World* he celebrates the transformative power of individual recollection (literally, re-collection: the taking up of the artifacts of the past one more time) and so, also, the power of the individual imagination. At the same time he recognizes that it is the collective (the community and the commonly held stories and other representations of the past) that makes the personal articulation of longing—and the realization of desire—possible.

In *Sweeter Than All the World* Wiebe embraces the historical photograph, with all its inherent indeterminacies, along with the imaginative narratives of the past, and posits an inclusive vision which holds that any one individual might place herself among the artifacts and narratives that would give testimony to her heritage and find among them a place sufficient to be called home.

WORKS CITED

Bal, Mieke. "Introduction". *Acts of Memory: Cultural Recall in the Present*. Eds. Bal et al. UP of New England, 1999, pp. vii–xvii.

Birdsell, Sarah. *The Russländer*. McClelland & Stewart, 2001.

Boym, Svetlana. *The Future of Nostalgia*. Basic Books, 2001.

Confino, Alon. "Collective Memory and Cultural History: Problems of Method." *American Historical Review*, vol. 102, no. 5, December 1997, pp. 1386–1403.

Crane, Susan A. "Writing the Individual Back into Collective Memory." *American Historical Review*, vol. 102, no. 5, December 1997, pp. 1372–1385.

Dames, Nicholas. "Austen's Nostalgics." *Representations*, no. 73, 2001, pp. 117–143.

Huyssen, Andreas. "Monumental Seduction." *New German Critique*, No. 69 (Autumn 1996) pp. 181–200.

Klassen, Sarah. *Journey to Yalta*. Turnstone Press, 1988.

Lipsitz, George. *Time Passages: Collective Memory and American Popular Culture*. U Minnesota P, 1990.

Lowenthal, David. *The Past is a Foreign Country*. Cambridge UP, 1985.

Rempel, John D., and Paul Tiessen. *Forever Summer, Forever Sunday: Peter Gerhard Rempel's Photographs of Mennonites in Russia, 1890–1919*. Sand Hills Books, 1981.

Shaw, Christopher, and Malcolm Chase. *The Imagined Past: History and Nostalgia*. Manchester UP, 1989.

Vidler, Anthony. *The Architectural Uncanny: Essays in the Modern Unhomely*. MIT Press, 1992.

Waltner-Toews, David. *The Impossible Uprooting*. McClelland & Stewart, 1995.

Wiebe, Rudy. *Peace Shall Destroy Many*. McClelland & Stewart, 1962.

———. *Sweeter Than All the World*. Alfred A. Knopf, 2001.

———. "Where is the Voice Coming From?" *Where Is the Voice Coming From? Stories by Rudy Wiebe*. McClelland & Stewart, 1974, pp. 135–143.

Eight

Critical Thought and Mennonite Literature:
Mennonite Studies Engages the Mennonite
Literary Voice*

THIS PAPER WAS given its initial generic title—"Critical Thought and Mennonite Literature"—when Royden Loewen invited me to participate in this symposium, "Mennonites and the Challenge of Multiculturalism: A 25 Year Retrospective," months ago.[1] I rather like the implied conflation of critical thinking and literature that such a title suggests, especially when we consider "literature" as we find it among Mennonites, where the "critical thinking" of creative writers has not always been welcome. I recall, in this context, the fact that when my colleague Jim Reimer, a few years ago, developed a new course on twentieth century Mennonite theology at Conrad Grebel University College in Waterloo, Ontario, he unselfconsciously named the course "Contemporary Mennonite Thought," as if to claim all serious Mennonite thinking for theology alone. Indeed, there was a time when any Mennonite critical thinking that

---

* First published as Hildi Froese Tiessen, "Critical Thought and Mennonite Literature: Mennonite Studies Engages the Mennonite Literary Voice." *Journal of Mennonite Studies*, vol. 22, 2004, pp. 237–246.

1 The symposium—a celebration of the founding of the Chair in Mennonite Studies—was held on 18 October 2003, at the University of Winnipeg.

attracted serious attention, within the community or without, did originate in conventionally masculinist disciplines like theology, for example, or history. Well, thanks to such forces as the literature courses offered by the Chair of Mennonite Studies and publications focussing on Mennonite literature published in the *Journal of Mennonite Studies*, Canadian Mennonites, over the past 20 years or so, have devoted a great deal of attention to the critical—and imaginative—thinking of Mennonite creative writers, whose voices are now possibly more widely listened to than those of any other thinkers to whom the Mennonite community might lay claim. One need only consider the immense popularity of the two great Mennonite novels of 2001—Rudy Wiebe's *Sweeter Than All the World* and Sandra Birdsell's *The Russländer*—to realize that this is so.

In 1987, early in her career, Mennonite poet Di Brandt summarized in an interview something of the trepidation she and other writers experienced in their encounters—and imagined encounters—with a Mennonite audience: "I have a sense that there is a real Mennonite audience out there," Brandt observed then, "a large, very hungry audience starved for Mennonite poetry … On the other hand, I'm also still very scared of the Mennonite community because my [poetry] probably asks for a bigger opportunity than most of them will be willing to give" (31). The opportunity for writers of Mennonite heritage to speak and be heard by their own people developed, to be sure, out of an array of social, political, and religious dynamics in Canada over the past several decades, but there can be no denying that the space that the founding Chair of Mennonite Studies, Harry Loewen, and his colleagues created for these voices had a discernible positive impact on the development of both Mennonite literature and a receptive Mennonite audience for this literature in Canada.

I was intrigued when I heard, in 1978, of the inauguration of a Chair in Mennonite Studies at the University of Winnipeg. I was familiar enough, at the time, with the initiatives of the federal government's program for multiculturalism, and would myself draw on its resources for some publishing ventures in years to come. I did not know Dr. David Friesen,[2] though I had become acquainted with his daughters, Ruth and Vicki, when the three of us briefly overlapped at the Mennonite Brethren Collegiate Institute some 20

---

2 Founder of the Chair in Mennonite Studies.

years before. Most intriguing for me was the identity of the Chair himself: Harry Loewen, whom I had first encountered in those years at Mennonite Brethren Collegiate Institute in Winnipeg, when I was just 15 and he something over 30. Harry was a great favourite among us students, displaying already then the wonderful mix of enthusiasm and earnestness, energy and empathy that would later make him a thoroughly engaging professor, an influential—if somewhat eccentric—churchman, and a creative and effective Chair of the program the success of which we celebrate today.

By the time Harry was appointed to the Chair, both he and I had moved east. In fact, we had become friends and colleagues at Wilfrid Laurier University in Waterloo, where Harry taught German literature and I (then the mother of two infant sons), English. I remember having several occasions, then, to introduce Harry to friends. When I spoke of him as I did then (perhaps awkwardly) as "my old teacher," he would demur and say, "Oh, Hildi, not so old!" Well, maybe not. That was a quarter of a century ago, and Harry still isn't old! As Al Reimer, in a tribute written on the occasion of Harry's retirement, declared in 1996: "Harry Loewen retiring? Impossible. He's not old enough.... To picture Harry in a permanent state of rest is as preposterous as to imagine Niagara Falls drying up, Mt. Vesuvius collapsing in ashes, prairie grain crops blighted by frost in midsummer" (Reimer 7). Niagara Falls? Mt. Vesuvius? Well, Al Reimer was never one to back away from hyperbole.

Ah, Al Reimer. His own efforts on behalf of numerous agencies committed to the nurture of Mennonite Studies (including his several years as co-editor of the *Journal of Mennonite Studies*) are prodigious. He was one of the more memorable profs I encountered at the University of Winnipeg. (I graduated in the first class after the new charter, in 1968.) The University of Winnipeg English Department taught little Canadian literature then, if at all. And certainly no literature by Mennonites. In a way Al made up for that when he regularly regaled our fourth-year literary criticism seminar with stories of his wayward youth. Reimer usually devoted the first good chunk of the class to recounting the dubious pleasures of growing up male and Mennonite in a small prairie town. I'm sure he reasoned, then, that his stories of Steinbach would smooth our way to the drier stuff that was the cause of our gathering in the first place: that is, to study literary theory of the likes of I.A. Richards and Northrop Frye. I remember arriving late for class one day with fellow student Naomi Levine, now a prominent Winnipeg litigator. I was a rather demure Mennonite girl then, unlike Naomi, who, finding Reimer in full flight over Steinbach 20 minutes after the hour, put her hands on her hips and demanded: "Aren't you finished yet?" Al Reimer, it seems, was already then testing his voice before a captive audience, in anticipation of his later, much more serious work in the field of Mennonite letters, as translator, editor, critic, and novelist.

Our official curriculum at the University of Winnipeg, like any English curriculum in the country in the late 1960s, included no Mennonite texts. But I enjoyed the next best thing: Mennonite profs. Not one or two or three, but four in the English Department alone, including Professors Reimer, Unruh, Siemens, and Pauls. What a great texture of conversation we could have enjoyed in those days, had our curriculum included the study of the (albeit then sparse) literature of our people.

Over the next decade, especially during and following my years of graduate study at the University of Alberta (1969-1973), Mennonite studies (that is, Mennonite literature) became a particular interest of mine. I had come to know Rudy Wiebe (also at University of Alberta) and his work. In 1970 Wiebe's compelling Mennonite epic, *The Blue Mountains of China*, appeared. If Wiebe's *Peace Shall Destroy Many*, published in 1962, had left any doubt in our minds about whether Mennonite experience was suitable stuff for literature, *The Blue Mountains of China* dispelled those doubts forever. And Wiebe wasn't just writing for us, as those three important words that graced the title pages of his fiction, then, announced: McClelland & Stewart. Canada's premier literary publisher. *Canada* was listening to what Wiebe had to say. About us. Our people. My people. Like Wiebe's parents, mine came to Canada among the relatively few who, late in 1929, were allowed to leave Stalin's Russia only after waiting anxiously at the gates of Moscow in full sight of the western world. Chapter Four of *The Blue Mountains* tells their story.

At the conference "Mennonite/s Writing in Canada" held at the University of Waterloo in 1990, the prominent Canadianist Clara Thomas (official biographer of Manitoba's own Margaret Laurence) declared that while she admired the work of Rudy Wiebe, his characters would never be able to reveal her to herself as Laurence's Hagar Shipley had done. And I thought then, "Oh yes, Professor Thomas. I am sure that is so. Go ahead and lay claim to Margaret Laurence and all the other Anglo-Presbyterian writers in Canada. Rudy Wiebe is ours!" (And, I would add, Patrick Friesen and David Waltner-Toews and Di Brandt and Armin Wiebe and Sarah Klassen and Sandra Birdsell and Andreas Schroeder and Victor Enns and John Weier and Ed Dyck and Maurice Mierau and Jack Thiessen and Al Reimer and

David Elias and David Bergen and Barbara Nickel and Miriam Toews and …). I recognize myself and the people among whom I was nurtured in these authors' stories and poems. I believe that I share with these writers a greater than usual understanding of certain subtexts. The tastes, smells, sounds of extended family gatherings, the inimitable rhythm of Low German and the tug of certain High German expressions of piety, the powerful force of four-part congregational singing, the paradoxical sense of belonging—while living self-consciously on the margin of the dominant culture, the ambivalence about matters relating to faith and salvation, the memories of fragments of Bible stories, the compelling revelations of Mennonite history from the martyrs to the arrival in Canada of the poor post-World War II refugees—all of these things, among others, the writers and so many of us hold in common.

Oh yes, I took an interest in the inauguration of the Chair of Mennonite Studies because of Harry Loewen and Winnipeg—and because the Chair promised to enlarge the spaces emerging then in Canada for Mennonite literary voices—voices that told our story for us and all to hear. Just a little over a decade earlier we could not have anticipated the breakthrough the Chair represented. I remember well the early 1970s visit to Alberta of the prominent eastern-Canadian literary critic Ronald Sutherland, for example, who had the temerity then to declare to us in the west that no literature that failed to address the issue of Canada's two founding peoples, the English and the French, could be called Canadian. I heard Sutherland in Edmonton and was appalled. His message might have had some resonance in the east, I thought then (though I know better now), but surely not in the west, where Mennonites and Poles, Ukrainians and Icelanders (never mind the people of the First Nations themselves) had a presence in regions of the country more coherent and more palpable than the English or the French would ever dream of.

Harry Loewen, in his introductory survey article on Mennonite literature in the first volume of the *Journal of Mennonite Studies* (1983), makes reference to Canadian Mennonite writers who wrote—in German—in the first half of the twentieth century. Among these Arnold Dyck and Fritz Senn would receive considerable attention from scholars in the journal issues to follow. Among English-language Mennonite writers, Loewen, in that earliest article, cited not only Rudy Wiebe but also children's author Barbara Smucker and poets Patrick Friesen and David Waltner-Toews—all of whom had by then published a number of works. He did not mention Sandra Birdsell, whose *Night Travellers* had just appeared months before, nor—of course—the many, mostly debut volumes of Mennonite writing that would, over the next decade or so, herald an awakening of the Mennonite literary voice: Armin Wiebe's *The Salvation of Yasch Siemens* in 1984; Al Reimer's *My Harp Has Turned to Mourning* and Anne Konrad's *The Blue Jar*, 1985; Audrey Poetker's *i sing for my dead in german*, 1986; Di Brandt's *questions i asked my mother*, 1987; Sarah Klassen's *Journey to Yalta*, 1988; Doug Reimer's *Older Than Ravens*, 1989; Jack Thiessen and Andreas Schroeder's *The Eleventh Commandment*, 1990; Rosemary Deckert Nixon's *Mostly Country*, 1991; David Elias's *Crossing the Line* and Lynette Dueck's *Sing Me No More*, 1992; David Bergen's *Sitting Opposite My Brother*, 1993; John Weier's *Steppe: A Novel*, 1995; and Miriam Toews's *Summer of My Amazing Luck*, 1996. And there were more—both along the way and later. The major Mennonite historical novels of Rudy Wiebe and Sandra Birdsell (already mentioned) were followed—perhaps most notably, if we speak of recent work—by David Bergen's national bestseller: *The Case of Lena S.*, 2002.

In his tribute to Harry Loewen's productive service as Chair of Mennonite Studies, Al Reimer remarked on what a fortuitous choice this first Chair represented. Perhaps the positive impact of that choice was nowhere as thankfully received as among Mennonite literary scholars. Sure, Harry was an historian. But we had a long tradition of these in our Mennonite past. No question that their voices were being heard. Harry was a theologian, too. Another familiar enough voice. No question that Harry's historian and theologian colleagues would be welcome to express their discoveries and opinions in the new journal. What was truly special and timely was Harry Loewen's interest in literature. The troubled and troubling reception Rudy Wiebe's first novel had received—and the lesser but nevertheless notable discomfort registered when Patrick Friesen's *The Shunning* was published in 1980 and Di Brandt's *questions i asked my mother* seven years later—demonstrated clearly that questions related to who could speak in the Mennonite community persisted.

Harry's writing and teaching created space for creative writers, particularly for those whose early, tentative forays into the liberal arts during the 1920s, 30s, and 40s had marked a territory in German that the new generation of Mennonite writers would cultivate in the language of English Canada. Like the scholars who accompanied feminism's second wave in the last century—feminist critics who sought their antecedents in history and brought early women writers into the spotlight as if to say "Women were there all the time; it's just that their voices were consistently muted"—the editors of the *Journal of Mennonite Studies* laid the base structure upon which the role of the creative writer within the Mennonite community could begin to be understood. To be sure, German-speaking Arnold Dyck and Fritz Senn had no noticeable direct impact on the Mennonite writers we read now in English, but the fact that they were there, struggling to express what lay in the hearts of their people, serves to objectify and illumine the role of the Mennonite literary artist today.

The *Journal of Mennonite Studies* was the first among the serious Mennonite journals (I refer here to *Mennonite Quarterly Review* and the *Conrad Grebel Review* as well) to take seriously the Mennonite literary community—and to encourage its reading audience to do the same. This is not necessarily a given. As the Mennonites well know, communities are not uniformly eager to hear what their writers have to say. For literature reveals a community to itself as no other field or discipline is likely to do. Because it takes liberties in pursuing so freely what we conventionally refer to as truth. Because literature is, by its very nature, unruly. Because it presumes to enter the territory of human intimacy. Rudy Wiebe observed in 1990: "I see no point in writing imaginatively unless it is done with both a critical coldness and an intense compassion, the simultaneous brilliance and stupidity of human beings deserves nothing less" (96). Indeed.

The sociologist might tell us how it seems we tend to function as a group; the historian or anthropologist might remark on how Mennonites in general—or even certain individuals—have comported themselves in times past. The theologian might write descriptively or prescriptively about the manner in which we might encounter God. But the novelist and the poet presume to utter our innermost thoughts: our desires and fears, anticipations and disappointments. The writer foregrounds the individual close up and often invites the identification of his or her audience in a way none of the other commentators on the nature of experience can do.

In his influential study of nationalism first published in 1983, Benedict Anderson identifies what he calls the "deep, horizontal comradeship" we call community. He speaks of nations in particular as *imagined* communities and observes: they are imagined "because the members of even the smallest [group] will never know most of their fellow-members, meet them, or even hear of them, yet in the minds of each lives the image of their communion"

(6). A journal like the *Journal of Mennonite Studies* and the programs of the Chair have contributed in significant ways to helping Canadian ethnic Mennonites in particular formulate the "image of their communion," to realize their commonalities, to construct their identity as a group of people with a common heritage and as individuals negotiating similar cultural dynamics.

I could comfortably stop here, if this were 30 years ago. There was little need then to qualify or explain the fact that the Mennonite world addressed by the Chair and the *Journal of Mennonite Studies* is, in fact, a Mennonite world narrowly defined. That world encompasses predominantly Russian Mennonites first of all (as opposed to what we call the Old Mennonites, or the Swiss, for example—to cite the two most prominent groups in Canada). But the Mennonites themselves are a multicultural people. We need only consider, just for a moment, the thousands of Mennonites from all parts of the world who met in Zimbabwe last summer for the 2003 Mennonite World Conference to realize that the Mennonite community reaches well beyond our own extended families. But we don't need to look to other continents to take stock of the Mennonites as a multicultural people, for we encounter this phenomenon every day among and within the Mennonite communities of Canada itself. Indeed, it would be possible to focus on a subject like "Mennonites and the challenge of multiculturalism"—the focus of this symposium—without looking outside our domestic Mennonite communities at all. In fact, we risk mimicking the limited and limiting vision of Ronald Sutherland (who spoke of "Canadian" as comprised of only the English and the French) if we persist in imagining "Mennonite" as comprised of only the Russian and the Swiss. Unless, of course, we think of ourselves only as an ethnic group. Ah, there's a quagmire I have no desire to wade into.

These observations raise all kinds of questions, many of which I, as someone who writes about Mennonite literature, have encountered over the last three decades: Who is a Mennonite? How do you define the Mennonite writer? Can you call yourself a Mennonite if you are not a believer? Is a novel about a Mennonite community, composed by a Mennonite unbeliever, a Mennonite novel? I can't help but think that the sorts of questions that dog members of the literary community must find their parallel in Mennonite studies generally. Who are the Mennonites now? How might we describe our newly configured communities? And that persistent, troubling line between ethnicity and religion: where does it belong? Is it ever fixed? Does it matter?

The latter-twentieth-century construction of multiculturalism, which encouraged the Mennonites and other settlers to reconstruct imaginatively their own communities in Canada, has encouraged other immigrant groups, too, to record imaginatively their transition from one world to another. The Mennonites, one of the earliest groups to immigrate to Canada during the last 150 years and among the most prominent documentarists of the migrant experience, have provided a model for other emerging Canadian minority-culture literary traditions. My own experience teaching multicultural literature suggests that this is so: our stories not only reveal us to ourselves but serve to inform and objectify all immigrant experience in this country. We Mennonites need to read each others' stories AND the stories of others who have travelled a path somehow similar to our own, as we continue to document our imaginative *becoming* as a community within the multicultural framework of this country. By listening to each other, all Canadians will, presumably, come to realize also the structure of the "imagined community" we call Canada.

Finally, when we talk about Mennonite thought and writing, we will do well to realize that the texture of our communal and personal existence as Mennonites and Canadians is nowhere more evocatively (and sometimes, also, provocatively) registered than in the published work of the creative writers our communities have produced. Even one individual's struggle to abandon much of what we are, as David Bergen, for example, has seemed in recent years to do, informs us about ourselves. The writers among us recreate and redefine community ceremonies and family relationships that are suggestive of our identity as individuals and as a group. Some of their stories evoke, with a poignant sense of loss, what the particular Mennonite world we once knew had to offer that was gentle, generous, and kind. Others challenge and interrogate the values, dogmas, and traditions that have for many years formed the base of traditional Mennonite community consciousness.

Our writers reveal the dissonances inevitably perceptible in communities under the stress of constant change. They probe ironies and contradictions that reveal the shadows that have fallen, in the Mennonite world, between desire and actuality. Their work suggests, for the most part, that a community can never afford to stop making thoughtful decisions about its place and role in the context of complex environments that never remain the same. What a gift our writers have given, and continue to give, us—about the complex and compelling nature of "the image of our communion." In his Preface to Volume One of the *Journal of Mennonite Studies*, Harry Loewen wrote: "We believe there is a *need* [emphasis mine] for a journal which will reflect, support, and evaluate the emerging and developing literature, art, and culture among Mennonites, with a focus on Canadian Mennonites" (4).

This vision has guided the program in Mennonite Studies we celebrate today. But we mustn't stop here: the need for the complex engagement of our artists in our communities persists, as the challenges of multiculturalism—within our communities and without—multiply.

WORKS CITED

Anderson, Benedict. *Imagined Communities: Reflections on the Origin and Spread of Nationalism*. Revised ed. Verso, 1991.

Brandt, Di. "'The sadness in this book is that I'm reaching for this story...'" *Sounding Differences: Conversations with Seventeen Canadian Women Writers*, ed. Janice Williamson, U Toronto P, 1993, pp. 31–44.

Loewen, Harry. "The Birth of a New Journal." *Journal of Mennonite Studies*, no. 1, 1983, pp. 4–5.

Reimer, Al. "Founding Editor Harry Loewen '*im Ruhestand*': a Tribute." *Journal of Mennonite Studies*, no. 14, 1996, pp. 7–11.

Wiebe, Rudy. "Writing Words." *Prairie Fire: Special Issue on Canadian Mennonite Writing*, vol. 11, no. 2, Summer 1990, p. 96.

Nine

A Mennonite Novelist's Journey (from) Home: Ephraim Weber's Encounters with S.F. Coffman and Lucy Maud Montgomery*

Introduction: Weber, Montgomery, and "Aunt Rachel's Nieces"

What follows is, in large measure, a respectful investigation into the life of a man who grew up among the Mennonites of Waterloo County, Ontario well over a hundred years ago, but who found the Mennonites' way of life not conducive to the realization of his deepest longing: to be a writer. Like so many writers—perhaps like most of us—Ephraim Weber occupied several worlds and was comfortable in none. "I want nothing so much as to write," he wrote Lucy Maud Montgomery in 1903 (in Eggleston, "A-precis [ca. 1959]" 22). As we shall see, Weber would leave the Mennonites in order to realize his longing to be a writer, and—following the pattern of the epics—he would return, finally, to the place from which he had begun and see it differently. He would absorb and confront his heritage—gently enough—in a novel: the

---

* First published as Hildi Froese Tiessen, "A Mennonite Novelist's Journey (from) Home: Ephraim Weber's Encounters with S.F. Coffman and Lucy Maud Montgomery" *Conrad Grebel Review*, vol. 24, no. 2, 2006, pp. 84–108.

great work of his life. Weber, the great-grandson of Benjamin Eby,[1] lived to be 86 years old, and throughout his life he was, as his wife Annie Melrose remarked after his death, "ever the student." "We are climbing the Alps of life," he wrote when he was 27, eerily anticipating a lifetime replete with vocational disappointment. "We mount and slip and fall and rise and fall and rise and mount and tremble." But, he added, the "awful avalanche of adversity must not dismay us" ("Excelsior!" 91).

I will begin by placing what I have to say into the context of my own scholarly interests, which have been focused over the past several decades on the emergence of a significant body of creative literature written by Mennonites in Canada. I have been interested, in particular, in two things: the often-uneasy relationship between the Mennonite writers and their communities, as one affects the other; and the impact that Mennonite literature has had on the construction of Mennonite identity in our time. I am interested in how Mennonite writers respond to their communities, and their communities to them; and in the fact that writers of Mennonite heritage—whether they embrace or reject the communities that nurtured them—contribute, in any case, to the construction/our conception of "the Mennonite" both within the Mennonite community and without. Nowhere are all these dynamics more evident than with respect to the recent (conflicted) reception of Miriam Toews's novel *A Complicated Kindness*, about a disenchanted teenager appalled at what it means to be Mennonite in her small Mennonite prairie town.

Stories make us real, Robert Kroetsch has remarked (*Creation* 36). This investigation hinges on the discovery in Canada's national archives of a story—a narrative in fiction—about Mennonites who lived in or around Kitchener, Ontario, in the early years of the last century. In June 1937—two years after Ephraim Weber had begun to write his novel about Mennonites—Lucy Maud Montgomery wrote to him one of her wide-ranging, lengthy letters (in this case, some 30 handwritten pages). Montgomery and Weber had been writing to each other for over three decades. She ended her letter with a breathless question: "Have you read *Gone With the Wind*!!!" In the body of her letter were comments on the immortality of the soul (on which Weber had delivered a sermon in his Saskatchewan church) and on other things,

---

[1] Benjamin Eby (1785–1853), a prominent churchman, educator, and community leader in what was to become Waterloo, Ontario, was a pioneer of the Mennonite community in Canada.

including the recent abdication of King Edward VIII, who, Montgomery declared, had expressed "senile folly" when he threw away "the crown of the greatest empire the world has ever seen ... for the sake of a middle aged double divorcee!!" Edward VIII, she told Weber in exasperation, ought to have "his royal bottom soundly spanked" (*After* 237). Among these scattered bits of gossip and opinion was her response to Weber's latest letter to her of some seven months before: "You were, when you wrote me, writing a novelette called 'Aunt Rachel's Will,'" she observed. "Is it finished? As you outlined it, it sounded like an 'awfully good' idea and something quite new—a rare thing nowadays when almost everything has been written about and almost every situation exploited" (*After* 235). The novel to which she refers—later called "Aunt Rachel's Nieces"—lies at the heart of this investigation.

The journey I'm about to map began some 15 years ago, when Paul Tiessen and I stumbled upon a collection of letters in the National Archives[2] in Ottawa—letters between the celebrity Canadian author of *Anne of Green Gables*, Lucy Maud Montgomery, and an Alberta homesteader named Ephraim Weber, who had spent the first 26 years of his life among the Mennonites of Kitchener (then known as Berlin). We became aware in Ottawa of other, related collections of letters in the National Archives—letters between Weber and two of his other correspondents (he had as many as 32 at a time): letters to Leslie Staebler, an old high school friend, who would intermittently keep Weber apprised of cultural developments in his home town (mostly of music and theater events); and letters to and from Wilfrid Eggleston, once a student of Weber's and later a distinguished Canadian man of letters. We discovered to our great delight as scholars of Mennonite literature that these collections of letters from Weber to Staebler and between Weber and Eggleston—as well as from Montgomery to Weber—contained recurrent references to the novel Weber had begun to write in 1935: a "yarn," as he called it, set in the environs of Kitchener, about three sisters whose acting out against their Mennonite congregation's rules regarding dress and deportment threatened to lead to a church split.

In his letters, especially those to Eggleston and Staebler, Weber documented his progress while writing this novel, which had a plot strangely evocative of an historical controversy concerning Mennonite women's compulsory wearing of the bonnet in the early decades of the century—a controversy that in 1924 led to a split in Kitchener's First Mennonite Church (where some of Weber's relatives still attended). Disagreement about what women

---

2 Now called Library and Archives Canada.

in the Mennonite church should wear—especially upon their heads—plays a central role in Weber's novel, as it did in the "Old" Mennonite world in which Weber had once lived. I cannot explore the subject of nonconformity in dress here, but I will invoke the words of Melvin Gingerich who observed, in his study of the history of Mennonite costume, that "between 1865 and 1950 in the district and general conferences of the 'Old' Mennonite Church, the name widely used for the branch of the church established in America in the late seventeenth century [the branch of the church under discussion here, more recently referred to as "Swiss"], no [fewer] than 230 resolutions were passed on nonconformity in dress, more than on any other subject" (6).

The controversial material of Weber's novel is surely interesting, but the very existence of the work is itself worthy of attention, as anyone who has followed the emergence of Mennonite literature in Canada over the past few decades would agree. Prominent in the front lines of the current onslaught of Mennonite literary talent—indeed, on the foreground of English literature in Canada—are Mennonite writers like Sandra Birdsell and Rudy Wiebe and David Bergen, who was awarded the Scotiabank Giller Prize for fiction in 2005, and, of course, Miriam Toews, who won the Governor General's Award for fiction in 2004. It has for some time been generally acknowledged that Mennonite literature in English in Canada began with Rudy Wiebe's *Peace Shall Destroy Many* in 1962, so Paul[3] and I were enthralled when we happened upon the references to Ephraim Weber's work of fiction from a quarter of a century before Wiebe. Here was a Mennonite writer who predated the parade of Mennonite writers who had published scores of volumes of fiction and poetry over the past few decades—and remarkably often to national acclaim.

The only trouble was that the novel about which Weber's letters had so much to say was nowhere to be found. Driven by curiosity and a sense of intrigue, we looked everywhere for it. We pressed the people at the National Archives to search for it, thinking it might have gone missing in their miles of shelves; we wrote letters of inquiry to newspapers across the country, and received among the responses some that were modestly useful, some mildly bizarre. Finally we located and visited those of Weber's friends who were still alive—all to no avail. After years of searching we were surprised and elated when a copy of the novel surfaced. We quickly realized that we had unwittingly been within perhaps 20 feet of the manuscript some years before.

---

3 Paul Tiessen, my co-investigator in matters related to the life and work of Ephraim Weber (and literary matters in general).

The charming novel that Weber modestly and affectionately referred to as a "yarn" about three Mennonite sisters "on the border between Mennonitism and the world" was given several names by him before he settled on "Aunt Rachel's Nieces" (Ephraim Weber-Wilfrid Eggleston Letters,[4] 29 May 1937; *Letters Home* 70). He told his literary friends about his new work soon after he began to write it. To Leslie Staebler he wrote in June 1936 that he had "spent countless weeks on a yarn about three Mennonite maids," and went on to describe how it just kept growing. "The story is stretching out to novel length," he wrote Staebler a few months later, "and is probably on the primrose path to the everlasting bonfire. However, the scribbling thereof makes the days short and keeps me from reading myself stupid" (*Letters Home* 70). To Wilfrid Eggleston he explained that "It's a creation of the L.M. Montgomery type, of course: character continuity and atmosphere, &c ... Of one thing I'm sure," he remarked, inimitably, "it is good practice." After briefly outlining the plot, he ventured: "To my knowledge nobody has done this sort of thing" (EW-WE Letters, 18 October 1936). Weber's novel, a playful portrait of three sisters who struggle to be allowed to express their love for the arts in the context of powerful forces in their community, the members of which would rather they submitted quietly to church discipline (especially as it pertained to dress), begins like this:

> Lucinda, Luanna, and Luella were the only ones of her forty nieces and nephews that Aunt Rachel had succeeded in naming permanently. She loved to name them in pairs and sets. A number of times she had tried to have a Mary and a Martha in at least one of the families of the *Freindschaft*; but the parents and relatives, knowing the Bible rather well, would unfailingly object that nobody could foretell which one would develop into Mary, and which into Martha. A Mary named Martha, and a Martha named Mary,—"Ach, how stupid that would be," cried Aunt Selina.
>
> So the maiden aunt and the eldest member of a family of nine felt sweetly gratified when she had completed the building up of a set of Lu's in her youngest sister's family. The babies were not baptized with these names—Mennonites do not baptize infants; but the names were recorded in fancy letters in the family Bible, as well as in the books of

---

4 Hereafter abbreviated as EW-WE Letters.

the registrar of births. To all this the matronly aunt had attended with prompt devotion.[5] ("Aunt Rachel's" 1)

As much as Weber's novel is central to my interests here, it is not the primary subject of this inquiry (I dealt with it in detail in my Edna Staebler Fellows Lecture at the Joseph Schneider Haus Museum in March 2006).[6] The question I was attempting to answer, when I carried on my research for this essay, was: who was the author of this work of fiction—this man Weber, who grew up among the Mennonites of Waterloo County, later homesteaded with his family in the frontier Mennonite settlements in Alberta (then known as the Northwest, for Alberta didn't become a province until 1905), wrote letters to Lucy Maud Montgomery for nearly 40 years, longed achingly to participate in the broader literary worlds of his day, and eventually came to write this work of fiction which, he confided to Staebler, he feared might offend the "old-school Mennonites" (*Letters Home* 71)? What might knowledge of him contribute to our understanding of Mennonite literature in general—and especially to our consideration of one of its dominant themes: the relationship between the writer and his community? This paper is thus a kind of meta-exercise. That is, it reveals something about the subject of investigation, Ephraim Weber, and something about the trail of research that allowed me to discover who he was.

So obscure a man as Ephraim Weber might have escaped attention in an earlier era. But current scholarly conditions have made room for an investigation of the life and work of this minor Mennonite literary figure, and I have invoked many of these conditions in the course of my work. They include such things as the thoughtful attention given over the past few decades to the very notion of minor literatures—such as the Jewish, West Indian, Chinese, South Asian, or Mennonite traditions within Canadian literature. Current scholarship in the humanities demonstrates a formidable interest in life-writing (diaries,

---

5 For permission to publish the words of Ephraim Weber, I am grateful to Abraham Kidd and Margaret Melrose Kidd.

6 As 2005 Edna Staebler Research Fellow at the Joseph Schneider Haus Museum in Kitchener, Ontario, I presented a lecture entitled "The Story of a Novel: How We Found Ephraim Weber's 'Three Mennonite Maids.'" The lecture, conceived as an introduction to Weber's novel, was later published as "The Story of a Novel: How We Found Ephraim Weber's 'Aunt Rachel's Nieces,'" *Journal of Mennonite Studies*, vol. 26, 2008, 159–178.

journals, letters such as those that inform much of my work); it invokes a new respect for the history of print culture in general.⁷

The scholarly ethos that informs this work invites fresh inquiries into the very nature and function of archives (where it becomes ever clearer that we have both gathered and repressed much of our history); and it provokes intellectual curiosity among critical theorists about the sphere of "everyday life"—the "hidden and oft-suppressed" (Gardiner 2) details and banal daily gestures by which people live—those things that are "'left over', and hence of little consequence in relation to such 'superior' pursuits" as politics, history, science, or theology (11).⁸ All these approaches to how scholars in the humanities are able to read the products of culture have encouraged our taking a closeup view of people and events we might once have overlooked. All these scholarly conditions have contributed to the intellectual ground upon which stands the investigation I am documenting here.

Ephraim Weber was by no means, when we first encountered him in the National Archives, completely unknown. His friend Wilfrid Eggleston had written extensively about him in his autobiography entitled *While I Still Remember* and elsewhere. Montgomery scholars like Muriel Millen or biographers like Mollie Gillen acknowledged Weber's existence too—and often drew heavily in their own work from the archival Montgomery/Weber correspondence—all the while sweeping Weber aside as a rather unsophisticated person who, by his own admission, didn't read a word of English until he was 12 years old. (These same Montgomery scholars neglect to mention that in spite of his modest beginnings on a southwestern Ontario farm, Weber would later just miss completing a PhD in German literature at the University of Chicago after winning two gold medals in graduate studies at Queen's.) Paul Tiessen and I wrote several pieces documenting the epistolary

---

7 I refer here to *History of the Book in Canada, Volume 1: Beginnings to 1840*, ed. Patricia Lockhart Fleming, Gilles Gallichan, and Yvan Lamonde, U Toronto P, 2004, and *History of the Book in Canada, Volume 2: 1840–1918*, ed. Yvan Lamonde, Patricia Lockhart Fleming, and Fiona A. Black, U Toronto P, 2005. See my own "Reading and Publishing in Mennonite Communities," in *Volume 2*, pp. 369–372.

8 See also Henri Lefebvre, *Critique of Everyday Life, Vol. 2: Foundations for a Sociology of the Everyday*. Trans. John Moore. Verso, 2002.

relationship between Weber and Montgomery,[9] but the questions I found most compelling throughout our research remained unanswered: who was Weber in the context of Waterloo County's "Mennonite Country"? In what sense was he a Mennonite? What was the nature of his religious education, that he and Montgomery and later he and others of his correspondents should comment so broadly on religious matters? What compelled him to construct, decades after leaving the Mennonites of both Berlin/Kitchener and Alberta, a novel concerning three young women's struggle to express themselves artistically in a Mennonite congregation in his hometown? And what place might his novel have in the literature of the Mennonites of Canada?

In 1937 Weber predicted that if ever he were to "gain any moonish fame," it would be because he had become a "satellite" orbiting "around the greater heavenly bodies of Eggleston and Montgomery" (EW-WE Letters, 15 November 1937). He was to live another 19 years after he made this remark; and four years after his sudden death by heart failure in 1956, it would seem that his prediction began to come true. It was then—in 1960—that Toronto's Ryerson Press first published Eggleston's *The Green Gables Letters*,[10] an edition of Montgomery's early letters to Weber, letters that crossed the continent from Prince Edward Island to the Alberta plains between 1905 and 1909. In 1905 Montgomery and Weber had both been aspiring writers, each with a modest claim to success; by 1909 she was the international celebrity author of *Anne of Green Gables*, and he was, well, still an aspiring writer (when he wasn't occupied as a wrangler or census-taker in the homestead territories of Alberta). Montgomery remained and remains a star in the international literary heavens, and Weber, as he predicted, would appear to have gained a slight bit of literary recognition because of his association with her.

But this essay is not solely concerned with Weber's relationship with Montgomery either—a relationship that, to be sure, drew our attention to Weber in the first place. For it was Weber we were interested in from the start, originating from Kitchener, this late-nineteenth-century Mennonite with an

---

9 See Hildi Froese Tiessen and Paul Tiessen, "Lucy Maud Montgomery's Ephraim Weber (1870–1956): 'a slight degree of literary recognition.'" *Journal of Mennonite Studies*, vol. 11, 1993, pp. 43–54; and "Epistolary Performance: Writing Mr. Weber," in *The Intimate Life of L.M. Montgomery*, ed. Irene Gammel, U Toronto P, 2004, pp. 222–238. See also our Introductions to *Letters Home* and *After Green Gables*.

10 Hereafter abbreviated as *GGL*.

irrepressible longing to be a writer. So we began a search in earnest, not for Ephraim Weber, warmly favored correspondent of Lucy Maud Montgomery, but for Ephraim Weber, Mennonite writer. And the place to begin appeared to be a US-based Mennonite periodical called the *Young People's Paper*, where Weber was known to have published in the earliest days of his writing career.

Weber and the *Young People's Paper*

The *Young People's Paper* was published by the Mennonite Publishing Company in Elkhart, Indiana between 1894 and 1906, and was one of several initiatives of the prominent nineteenth-century Mennonite bishop and evangelist John Fretz Funk. Funk had, in 1864, founded the internationally distributed newspaper *Herald of Truth* (the first newspaper of the Mennonites of North America). Funk was committed to revitalizing the Mennonite church, and, indeed, had a long career as an extremely influential "reformulator of the Mennonite identity," as Rod Sawatsky has put it. In fact, as Sawatsky has remarked, the changes in the Mennonite sensibility "spawned largely through the efforts of John [Fretz] Funk" are now read as the great "'Mennonite awakening'" (33–34).

A quick look at the history of the *Young People's Paper* reveals that Ephraim Weber was one of a stable of men listed as contributing editors over the paper's twelve-year run. As such, he served alongside prominent American Mennonites, indeed alongside some of the most influential figures in the history of the Mennonite Church in North America over the past century, ambitious men who "did much to mold the thought and activities of the church during an important period of awakening and expansion into organized church-wide activities" ("Daniel Henry Bender" 273). These men gave shape to what we now identify as "the Sunday school, mutual aid, publishing, missions, education, historical interpretation, peace work and relief work" of the Mennonite church (Gross 83). As a regular contributor to and contributing editor of the *Young People's Paper*, Weber was in effect swept up among the most influential configuration of leaders in the Mennonite church of his day.

The *Young People's Paper* began in 1894 as an eight-page publication released biweekly. Reflecting on the paper at the end of its eleventh year, Bishop Funk described it as one "that will not teach the Young Christian to be worldly—and follow all the vanity and follies of the world, but to be humble and pure ..." (Funk, "Close"). For this paper Weber, in the closing years of the century, wrote over 175 pieces, including poems, collections of aphorisms, and prose reflections of varying lengths—some just a paragraph long, others longer. His first contribution appeared in February 1896. He was then 26 years old and about to move from Berlin to the territory around Didsbury in the Northwest. It was there (in what is now southern Alberta) that Weber's family, under the leadership of his maternal grandfather Jacob Y. Shantz, had begun to homestead barely two years before. For this first column Weber took on an admonishing tone. He addressed his readers directly: "You have been working industriously all day and come home tired," he wrote. "After tea you feel somewhat refreshed. Picking up a paper to read, you notice in some prominent place a poem. Now, this time stop and read it" ("Read" 18). Invoking some of the language he would later use in his letters to Montgomery, to whom he would declare that poetry was "the human soul's magic come out to sun itself in the grace of language," he said in this article that poetry "tends to make us better. It lifts us up out of the mire. It makes life beautiful. It nourishes the better nature of a man" (*GGL* 8). People smothered by the cares of life need "aesthetic culture," he remarked, and the "poverty of the Philistine" is pitiable. "Then form the habit of perusing one poem in your paper," he urged his readers, observing that it will give them "intellectual development and soul culture" ("Read" 18).

Weber would write 13 pieces in all for publication in the *Young People's Paper* in 1896, 44 in 1897, 39 in 1898, 38 in 1899, 32 in 1900, and nine in 1901. Beginning in March 1902, he would write the first of at least 11 letters that year to Montgomery; eight months later, in December, he would move to Philadelphia to pursue his literary fortune—as a guest of Miriam Zieber, a woman who advertised in the *Young People's Paper* her expertise in shaping literary careers (and, incidentally, the person who first suggested to Weber that he write to Montgomery, whose poetry he had so admired).

Weber would leave Zieber and Philadelphia some ten months later, deeply disappointed in his inability to accomplish what he had set out to do. In May 1904, after a sojourn with another literary friend in New Hampshire, and then a short visit with old friends in Berlin (now Kitchener), he would return to Didsbury, from where he would re-establish himself on the prairie and write to Montgomery: "I had the grip for a week, and now except for blistered hands, blistered feet, twitching muscles, aching bones, lame back, gnawing hunger, weariness, homesickness for civilization—I feel first rate. I'm just back from a chase after the cattle. I've been plowing, painting rooms, and milking" (*GGL* 20). He would spend another five sometimes nondescript, sometimes wild and woolly years as a homesteader, before embarking on what for him would become a soul-destroying career as a teacher in small prairie towns.

Teaching would remain a curse for Weber. It was how he made his living, but it was also, he believed, an activity that consumed all his energies and destroyed his soul. "[W]e have to educate the bum, the dandy, the athlete, the moron, and the pair in puppy love," he complained to Eggleston, revealing his failure to see much good in the next generation. The only thing more intolerable than his lackluster and unambitious students were the members of the small-town school boards whose children he taught and—more often than not—refused to advance. These parents drove him to declare: "God made the country, man made the city, and the devil made the small town" (EW-WE Letters, 10 August 1925). But I'm getting a wee bit ahead of myself. Let's return to the younger Weber, the *Young People's Paper*, and the years before Montgomery.

The sensibility that would lie at the heart of Weber's later fiction was readily discernible in much of his work for the *Young People's Paper*. Here, in April 1897, he celebrated the imagination and what he called "the inner man": "Oh the inner man wants sustenance!" he wrote. "Let him out, let him out!" "Open your clay door. The imagination is the key." Invoking a lifelong antipathy towards doctrines and creeds, he criticized preachers for failing to recognize the power of imaginative thought: "when they discourse on the crucifixion," he wrote, "on the mysteries of grace ..., on the soul's communion with its Author, on the Judgement day, on the joys of heaven, [they] would make more impression on their hearers if they wrought more sanctified imagination into it and less theology" ("Imagination" 58).

Not a casual contrarian, Weber nevertheless passionately expressed his belief that there was much wrong with the world and so we should celebrate those who dare both to think independently and to demand change. "If men were as dwarfed and deformed physically as they are intellectually, morally, emotionally, aesthetically and spiritually, what hideous things many of them would be," he declared. It is thanks to "the fault-finding Emerson that we have a nobler morality; thanks to the fault-finding Ruskin that we can use our eyes when we walk the verdant paths of nature and visit the art gallery; thanks to the fault-finding Luther for the popular orthodoxy of justification by faith; blessed be the fault-finding Jesus of Nazareth for a new Christianity. All reformers are fault-finders" ("Craving" 67).

Weber's disposition as a regular contributor to the *Young People's Paper* was mostly pious and scripture-bound; his voice was literary, passionate, cajoling. In 1897, the year the paper carried more of his contributions than any other, his subject matter ranged from devotion and hard work to worldly ambition and the love of Mammon. Among other things, he addressed such subjects as temperance and testimonies, service, and forgiveness. In the three years following, he deliberated on prayer, temptation, God's promises, hospitality, personal growth, independent thought, moral courage, friendship, patriotism, bettering the world, recreation, education, the supernatural, the happy home, the Christian's use of time, penitence, humility, duty, honoring the Lord's Day, the art of letter writing, and Christian zeal.

Weber in the Archives

The articles Weber contributed to the *Young People's Paper* during the years he began to find himself as a writer reveal he was complexly aware of, and largely in step with, the religious sensibility of the Mennonites of his day. After examining what he published there, I wondered what else I might learn about him. To Leslie Staebler he had written from Alberta, in 1902, "I have two or three very nice literary correspondents, to whom I write many a lonely hour and thus enjoy myself exquisitely" (*GGL* 14). Is it possible, I wondered, that Weber had carried on a correspondence with one or more of his fellow contributing editors of the *Young People's Paper*? Or might any of these other editors have referred to him in their letters to each other?

Realizing that many of his collaborators were prominent enough that the archives of the Mennonite church in both Canada and the USA would likely have laid claim to their literary estates, I sent a student in search of Weber in the Mennonite Archives of Ontario at Conrad Grebel University College. Where to begin to look? I decided to start with the lists of names that appeared alongside Weber's on the masthead of the *Young People's Paper*: the other men on the editorial team—Steiner, Hostetler, and Coffman,[11] for example.

We did find an item of interest: a brief typed letter from Hostetler, written on the stationery of the Mennonite Evangelizing and Benevolent Board in Elkhart, Indiana (these men loved their lavish letterheads). It was addressed to S.F. Coffman and dated April 4, 1901. It read, in part: "We are glad to hear of the encouraging work in the Northwest. If you see Ephraim Weber give him my very best regards" (Hostetler). Wow! This line in a letter to Coffman, who would later become so prominent a Mennonite churchman

---

11 Menno S. Steiner, C.K. Hostetler, and Samuel F. Coffman.

in Ontario. It wasn't much but it was certainly something. Then it became even more interesting. The letter was addressed to Weber in Okotoks, Alberta. The single and handsome 28-year-old Coffman had been ordained by Bishop Funk in his early twenties, and would shortly become one of the most highly regarded and beloved bishops among the Mennonites in Ontario. And here he was in Alberta, while Weber was there (Coffman had been seconded by the Waterloo bishops to travel to Alberta—the Northwest—in 1901, to help Mennonite settlers organize themselves into congregations).

I poked around a bit more and was intrigued to discover that the Mennonite Archives of Ontario holds a substantial S. F. Coffman collection that includes not only his daily diary of 1901 but also his 1901 letters from Alberta to his Indiana fiancée, Ella Mann. So I proceeded to sift through the files. (Among the fascinating things I found there was a large number of letters to the dashing young Coffman from so many of the young women he encountered in his ministry—"I'll send you my picture if you send me yours ...").[12]

Coffman in the Northwest

Coffman began to pack for his trip west on February 9, 1901. He left Toronto by Canadian Pacific Railway on February 19 and arrived in Calgary on the 23rd. By March 6 he had traveled to Carstairs, and on Saturday, March 9, he wrote in his diary: "Brother Steckle wanted to go over to Andrew Weber's to get oats for feed. He drove over with the wagon, and I went along with him. We staid [sic] there for dinner. They have the best fixed up place I have seen yet. They have been here about seven years. Their two sons, Ephraim & Manasseh, have places near home" (1901 Diary).

I had to fight not to get drawn into the western adventures of the young Coffman as he narrated them in his diary. I was particularly interested in his reflections on how he spent his leisure time, sketching in pen and ink, or writing poetry and hymns. It appeared to me that the two poets Coffman and

---

12 The Samuel F. Coffman collection at the Mennonite Archives of Ontario includes a series of friendly letters written to Coffman from women during his bachelor years: Elsie K. Bender, Alice Bearss, Ida Bergey, M. Elizabeth Brown, Mary Brubacher, Alda Culp, Mary Denlinger, Sarah Funk, Celesta Hartzler, Lucetta High, Barbara Kratz, Berta Lehman, Lizzie Minnich, Debbie Moyer, Louida Nahrgang, Saloma Rittenhouse, Valerie Rittenhouse, Anna Schact, Barbara Sherk, Rebecca & Sarah Sherk, Linda Shantz, Saphrona Sievenpiper, Mollie Snyder, Sarah Wismer, Bertha Zook, Lena Zook.

Weber had the potential to be what Montgomery would call "kindred spirits." In fact Coffman's reflections suggest that Weber made quite an impression on him. "I have met Ephraim Weber," he wrote to Ella on April 16. "He is a young man yet. But he has a very wide awake appearance and seems to be a very fine young man" ("Letter"). (Weber was actually two years Coffman's senior.) The familiarity between the two men implied in these remarks is sustained in later letters to Ella, where Coffman refers to other members of the Weber family as "Ephraim's father" or "Ephraim's brother."

Weber and Coffman apparently spoke often. Among the conversations Coffman carried on with various members of the community, he recorded the substance of very few. His diary entry for Friday, July 12 was an exception: "This afternoon I rode back to Ephraim Weber's, had a visit there, went to Bro Henry Weber's and staid [sic.] there tonight. Ephraim called too in the evening. Had a very pleasant visit talking of God's use of natural laws in the great changes, miraculous visitations of God upon the earth." As if continuing the dialogue in his own mind, Coffman added: "God cannot go beyond His laws" (1901 Diary).

Coffman's diary reveals something of the texture of that time and place. Serving as an itinerant bishop, Coffman moved constantly from home to home, always engaged with the people around him, invariably busy, trying to be helpful. When he wasn't giving the Mennonite homesteaders shaves and haircuts, he was fixing the pipes of their organs or repairing their sewing machines. He attempted to shoot owls and prairie hens (he never seemed to get very good at that), collected buffalo bones (he took several specimens back east with him, including a vertebra out of which he had made an inkwell), and gathered wild flowers—the greatest of his passions—and then identified, pressed, and mounted them for a collection that numbered upwards of 160 species by the time he left the territory on November 11, 1901.

References to encounters with Weber are scattered throughout Coffman's diary and letters of 1901. On April 9 Coffman wrote, "Ephraim Weber is not at home. [H]e is out taking the census for this district." On May 4 the inevitable: "Ephraim Weber's father is a second cousin to us. Brother Andrew Weber's (Ephraim's father) Grandfather and my Grandmother Coffman were brother and sister" ("Letters"). On May 11: "Rode up to the field where the men were working. Then called on Ephraim Weber's for a little while. He has a very pleasant home." On July 13, Coffman "went over to Brother Andrew Weber's" and "Had a talk regarding the building of a meeting-house. He thinks it ought to be built 30 x 50. This may be a bit too large." July 21: "I taught the Bible class. Ephraim Weber was present today." August 19: "rode over to Bro Henry Weber's. Met Ephraim there again and had a pleasant visit." September 10: "Adjusted the hair spring in Bro Weber's alarm clock so that it may be regulated again. Ephraim Weber came with some cattle he had been hunting. He staid [sic] all night. Had a long talk" (1901 Diary).

On Sunday, September 15 Coffman wrote about helping the new congregation at Carstairs to choose its minister and deacon by the lot. On September 24, Ephraim's brother Manasseh was present when Coffman "[w]rote out a certificate of ordination." By late fall, Coffman, the itinerant bishop, was making his last rounds of the Alberta settlement and saying his goodbyes. He missed saying farewell to Ephraim's father Andrew, who was "away threshing at the Honsburgers," but managed to catch Ephraim on November 8: "Called at Ephraim Weber's too," he recorded, and then hinting at their similar sensibilities and common interests, added, "Got my magazines there" (1901 Diary).

Three days later, on November 11, Coffman was gone. He had spent nine months in Alberta while Weber was there—months during which Weber would see his last nine articles appear in the *Young People's Paper*. Within five days of leaving the Northwest, Coffman was reunited with friends—and specifically with Ella Mann—in Indiana, where he dropped in at the Mennonite Publishing Company and, as he recorded in his diary, "saw Bro Funk." The next day he taught Sunday School and preached. "Bro J.F. Funk was present," he recorded (1901 Diary, November 17). Later that week he and Ella were married.

Weber's Restlessness

In the months during which Coffman and Weber overlapped in Alberta, Weber was growing restless as a writer and beginning to register an increasing spiritual hunger that, he would later remark to Leslie Staebler, he was never able to satisfy—"this universal cry from the centre of the heart for an unchangeable, substantial Something, not to be found in all the wide world of material things." In his own published reflections in the *Young People's Paper* he emphasized Christ as the Bread of Life, but sometimes his remarks seem little more than hollow platitudes alongside his passionate yearning after "fare for the *soul!*" ("Bread" 11).

It is unlikely that Weber and Coffman remained in communication after Coffman left Alberta in 1901 (I've found no evidence of it). Decades later, in the summer of 1935, Weber decided on the spur of the moment to attend a

Mennonite general conference in Kitchener, as a means, he reflected later, "of studying Mennonitism anew, in its latter-day aspects" (*Letters Home* 63). At the conference he was approached by someone who invited him to consider writing a cultural history of the Mennonites. It might have been Coffman who extended the invitation, for he was very active at that conference, as his diary reveals, and as Chair of the Historical Committee he was uniquely poised to make such a gesture. It was this invitation that prompted Weber to embark on the cultural reflections that would become his novel "Aunt Rachel's Nieces" instead.

Weber and the Mennonites

My search for Weber's "Mennonitism" was richly rewarded in the Mennonite Archives of Ontario, the S.F. Coffman collection in particular. A visit to the Mennonite Church Archives USA in Goshen, Indiana, where the John F. Funk collection occupies the largest swath of shelves, offered other resources, especially some that cast light on the wider Mennonite world into which Weber—as contributing editor of Funk's publishing enterprise the *Young People's Paper*—had inadvertently inserted himself. Here my search for information on Weber the Mennonite began much as my search in the Mennonite Archives of Ontario had begun. And once more it was C.K. Hostetler (who edited the *Young People's Paper* for most of the time Weber served as contributing editor) who led to the most interesting of my discoveries. Among the Hostetler papers was a neatly written four-page letter that began "Dear friend" and was signed "Sincerely and fraternally, Ephraim Weber." Dated 29 December 1898, from Didsbury, Alberta, it was clearly a response to Hostetler's request for a sort of spiritual autobiography. Much of Weber's candid self-description, which he wrote then with the understanding that it was not for publication, bears quoting:

> I grew up in a beautiful farm home on Lancaster St. near Berlin, Ont. I loved farming ere I was in my teens even. ... I attended school at Bridgeport, a near village, where I had many trials and tears—as all timid boys have at school; I learned slowly the first five years. After that I got over my extreme bashfulness and made faster progress. But after I was twelve I had to work on the farm in the summer, only attending the five winter months. One winter

> I worked in the Berlin Button Works, which employment was uncongenial to me. Most Winters I went to school again and kept on until July. When I passed entrance to High School I had now discovered a new kingdom, whose winding highways lured me on and on …

Weber relates his substantial trials with high school—issues of confidence, issues related to health. He continues:

> Then I went to Model School, passed and taught a public school, and in six months my dilapidated nerves gave out. I quit teaching and left for the Sanitarium, Battle Creek, Mich. where I sojourned four expensive months, with no improvement. A few months after leaving Battle Creek, I immigrated to our balmy Alberta, hoping simple life and easy open air work would in a few years have at least a [salutary] effect on me. So it has proved, only slower than even my little faith had made me expect. I am here thirty-three months.
>
> …
>
> I work about 200 days a year on our several farms. The remaining hundred I retire to my "literary den," which is simply my brother's unoccupied, sod-roofed log shack. But a "snug little kingdom" it is.

Weber proceeds to describe how, as a bachelor, he has served as "cook, dairymaid ['the merchants pronounced (his) butter splendid'], washwoman, mistress and servant." Remarking that his people have a church and a Sunday School, and that they struggle with apathy, he observes:

> As a rule new countries are not interested in intellectual and spiritual striving, and our colony is no exception. I have been teaching for ten years in S.S.—ever since my conversion, which took place among the pine stumps on the lovely Lancaster farm as I was plowing with an ox-team.

"I was twenty-eight in November," he reports. "I should soon be old enough to know what my life-work is to be, should I not?" he asks provocatively, and then goes on:

> You will already have conjectured what I do in my "den". Here the hours pass quickly and sweetly in utter uninterruptedness. I read, reread, write, rewrite and criticize other men's writings, with a view of disciplining my mind into clear thinking. My purpose is to chisel my thick head into an essayist's. It is only several months since I gave up the notion of re-entering the ranks of the pedagogues and came to a definite conclusion to prepare myself for writing. (Letter to C.K. Hostetler)

Five years later, when his engagement with the *Young People's Paper* had come to an end, and just three months after S.F. Coffman had returned to Ontario, Weber would write a first letter to Leslie Staebler, his old friend from Berlin High School. The world he knew on the Alberta plains, he remarked in February 1902, had grown "painfully leathery and metallic" (*Letters Home* 5). Still, he had decided "to continue" in his "den" until November. "My solitude has not oppressed me quite so much lately," he wrote. "This morning, for instance, the sun without and the 'sun within' and the unworldly quiet make an ideal Indian summer in this retreat of mine. I can read and think and exult in here as I cannot do elsewhere" (*Letters Home* 6).

A month later he would write his first letter to Lucy Maud Montgomery, dated March 12, 1902, and confess that he had not been productive as a writer but had "dabbled off and on at composition for ever so long a time" ("A-precis" 1). Buoyed by her engaged response to his first letter, he wrote her again the day her first letter arrived. She had inquired about his literary work. "Ah me," he replied, "'tis 'the pitifulest infinitesimal fraction of a product.'" But he had produced it in God's name. He used "to send short poems and articles to *Young People's Paper*, Elkhart, Ind. for a dollar each," he told her, but one day an Alberta wind caught up his "unprotected periodicals, goldenly laden with gems from [his] pen," and carried them "into the wilderness." He had never "been zealous enough for [his] lost brain children to organize a search party." He conjectured playfully that "Probably some of the poems are holding sweet communion with the wild roses, at whose prickly feet I hope they have by this time settled to rest from their flighty ways" (2–3).

The disappearance of Weber's saved-up issues of the *Young People's Paper*—poignantly described in this poetic flourish—takes on particular significance when one considers it in light of his move, during 1902, away from so much of what had defined his identity. In his letters to Montgomery, his voice takes on a tenor markedly different from the pious, admonishing tone of his writing for Elkhart only months before. He wrote at least 11 letters to her before the end of 1902. In their flurry of letters, he and Montgomery tested their interests and sensibilities with each other, and found they had much in common, including their metaphysical absorption of nature. He had recently given himself up to the night, he said. "I was the night and the chinook and the grass and the horizon and the wild roses and Wordsworth and the frogs," he wrote. "I don't know how to talk about it. I was infinitely refreshed" (*GGL* 16).

By December 1902 Weber had moved to Philadelphia "to widen [his] life," to expand, as he called it, his "narrow existence" ("A-precis" 32). In Montgomery he had found, earlier that year, someone with whom he could test what it might mean to be a writer. And what it might mean to be a Mennonite—and what it might mean NOT to be a Mennonite. It was in his fourth letter to her, written on May 10, 1902, that he had confessed he was "brought up a Mennonite." He asked her, "Have you ever heard of Mennonites?" (5).

In his letter to Montgomery of June 6, Weber conflated religion and poetry, declaring that the more he thought "over God and life and nature and salvation and everything, the deeper and more missionful" did this art of poetry they shared seem to be. He continued, "It is a serious and profound undertaking to reach into the flying chaos of thought and emotion and bring out into black-and-white a hint of the Infinite, for whom mortals are thirsting so. Isn't this, dear friend, what we're trying to do? To me, God is a poet, and there is no poetry in which He is not" ("A-precis" 7–8).

Weber's early letters to Montgomery both effected and documented his movement away from the Mennonite community. He confided to her that he sensed another world opening up for him. He thought many of the "old ways and creeds" were obsolescent, and declared that he was not living the kind of life he would want to, that he was "in a transition stage from the old to the new" ("A-precis" 11). In September he was more specific about what this transition might entail, and—implicitly invoking his devotional writing for the *Young People's Paper* in the years just past—he declared that "[I] shan't do any more Sunday schooly, preachy, wishy-washy, willy-nilly writing" (12). Religious problems were of special interest to him, he told Montgomery in October, because he was "in a transition from the old thought and creed to some new and undefined life" (13). "To save my soul," he told her in January 1903, he couldn't "settle down into any ready made faith" (16). He had taught a Bible class for 14 years and knew the Bible extremely well, but he had begun to rethink what he now called the "wonder-book." He declared that the Bible is fine as "literary pabulum" and "all gold" as "a book of altruism and ethics." It is "greatest of all literature" and "an inspired record of revelation and a means of spiritual salvation," he acknowledged. Yet he wondered "how much of it [was] final and absolute truth" (21).

During the earliest months of his association with Montgomery, Weber questioned the formal assumptions that had created the framework of his Mennonite faith. By December 1903, realizing that the culture into which he was born offered him no entry—indeed blocked his path—relative to the literary world he longed to inhabit, he stepped away from the Mennonites: "What an advantage [you've had] to be *born* into reading!" he exclaimed to Montgomery. "I had to grind and chisel myself into it. Our [people] are not at all for intellect and culture. My parents have never heard of Shakespeare" ("A-precis" 28). On another occasion he wrote: "I didn't read anything until I was an adult. Such was my heredity and environment, and to this day I suffer from it" (*GGL* 9).

Yet it was to his Mennonite world that Weber returned some 30 years later—now with the distance of someone who had been gone from home a long time, and with a gentle sense of irony mixed with unmediated affection for most of those he had left behind. It was then—after so long an absence—that he recognized the potential for fiction of the Mennonite world he had once known and, wondering where this recognition would lead, he began to write the novelette that would not stay short and that became "Aunt Rachel's Nieces."

About this novel—the great work of his life—he would much later remark to Eggleston: "The Mennonite reader may find it interesting but Mennonites are poor readers!! However, 'tis writ.... What ... value it may have I'm not in a position to know" (EW-WE Letters, 4 November 1937). In 1945 he would recall the novel he had sent to several publishers around the time he had completed it, but not since 1938: "Reread some of it lately and was surprised how interesting I found it. But the Dickens of it," he added, "is that it takes an educated Mennonite or ex-Mennonite to feel the interest, and there aren't many such" (28 February 1945).

Ephraim Weber's conflicted relationship with the world of his ancestors is familiar enough among Mennonite authors. As seems to be the case with writers—both among Mennonites and in other literary communities—he carried his ancestors with him long after he thought he had left them behind. In 1946 Weber wrote about his life's ambitions to Eggleston: "I will strive, I will practice, till I've worn out my corporal functions totally; then I'll yearn, yearn, yearn, till the dark is too chilly and the silence too mighty; then I'll distill into an essence or evaporate into a fragrance—but not, never, yield to extinction" (EW-WE Letters, 5 September 1946).

I won't speculate here on the degree to which my investigations into Weber's life—or the planned publication of his novel, "Aunt Rachel's Nieces"—might rescue Weber from extinction.[13] But I will observe, finally, that the investigative search that allowed me to see something of who this man was and how he occupied various landscapes of Canadian culture and the ethos of the Mennonites of his day has comprised—for me—an extraordinarily exciting journey.

WORKS CITED

Bergen, David. *The Time in Between*. McClelland & Stewart, 2005.

Coffman, Samuel F. 1901 Diary. Hist. Mss. 1.1.2.1.4.26, Samuel F. Coffman Family Fonds, Mennonite Archives of Ontario.

———. Letter to Ella Mann, 16 April 1901, Hist. Mss. 1.1.1.1.3.2, Samuel F. Coffman Family Fonds, Mennonite Archives of Ontario.

"Daniel Henry Bender." *The Mennonite Encyclopedia*, vol. 1, Mennonite Publishing House, 1959, p. 273.

Eggleston, Wilfrid. "A-precis [ca. 1959]." Unpublished precis of Ephraim Weber's unpublished letters to L.M. Montgomery, 1902–04. MG 30 D282 (now R4882-5-2-E), Wilfrid Eggleston Papers, Library and Archives Canada, Ottawa.

———. *While I Still Remember: A Personal Record*. Ryerson Press, 1968.

Funk, John F. "Close of Volume XI [of *YPP*]." John F. Funk Collection, Hist. Mss. 1-1-10, John F. Funk 101/13, "H[erald] O[f] T[ruth] articles"—about Periodicals—*Young People's Paper*," Mennonite Church USA Archives, Goshen.

Gardiner, Michael E. *Critiques of Everyday Life*. Routledge, 2000.

Gillen, Mollie. *The Wheel of Things: A Biography of L.M Montgomery, Author of Anne of Green Gables*. Harrap, 1975.

Gingerich, Melvin. *A History of Mennonite Costume*. Mimeographed manuscript, [1964?].

Gross, Leonard. "The Doctrinal Era of the Mennonite Church." *Mennonite Quarterly Review*, vol. 60, January 1986, pp. 83–103.

Hostetler, C.K. Letter to S.F. Coffman, 4 April 1901, Hist. Mss. 1.1.1.2.9, S.F. Coffman Fonds, C.K. Hostetler letters, Samuel F. Coffman Family Fonds, Mennonite

---

13 The novel remains unpublished.

Archives of Ontario.

Kroetsch, Robert, Pierre Gravel, and James Bacque. *Creation*. Including the Authors' Conversations with Margaret Laurence, Milton Wilson, J. Raymond Brazeau. New Press, 1970.

Millen, Muriel. "Who Was Ephraim Weber?" *Queens Quarterly*, 68, 1961, pp. 333–336.

Montgomery, Lucy Maud. *Anne of Green Gables*. L.C. Page, 1908.

———. *The Green Gables Letters: From L.M Montgomery to Ephraim Weber, 1905–1909*, ed. Wilfrid Eggleston, Borealis Press, 2001. [Abbreviated as *GGL*.]

———. *After Green Gables: L.M. Montgomery's Letters to Ephraim Weber, 1916–1941*, ed. Hildi Froese Tiessen and Paul Gerard Tiessen, U Toronto P, 2006.

Sawatsky, Rodney. *History and Ideology: American Mennonite Identity Definition through History*. Pandora Press, 2005.

Toews, Miriam. *A Complicated Kindness*. Knopf, 2004.

Weber, Ephraim. "Aunt Rachel's Nieces." Unpublished novel. MG 30 D282 (now R4882-5-2-E), vol. 42, Wilfrid Eggleston Fonds, Library and Archives Canada, Ottawa.

———. *Ephraim Weber's Letters Home, 1902–1955: Letters from Ephraim Weber to Leslie Staebler of Waterloo County*, ed. Hildi Froese Tiessen and Paul Gerard Tiessen, MLR Editions Canada, 1996. [Abbreviated as *Letters Home*.]

———. "Excelsior!" *Young People's Paper*, 5 June 1897, p. 91.

———. Letter to C.K. Hostetler, 29 December 1898. John F. Funk Collection, Hist. Mss. 1-1-2, John F. Funk Correspondence and Papers, Box 116 (Green), Biographical sketches—Ephraim Weber, Mennonite Church USA Archives, Goshen.

———. Letters to Wilfrid Eggleston. MG 30 D282 (now R4882-5-2- E), vol. 33–34, Wilfrid Eggleston Fonds, Weber-Eggleston Letters, Library and Archives Canada, Ottawa. [Abbreviated as EW-WE Letters.]

———. "Read the Poem." *Young People's Paper*, 1 February 1896, p. 18.

———. "The Imagination in Devotion." *Young People's Paper*, 10 April 1897, p. 58.

———. "The Craving for Growth." *Young People's Paper*, 24 April 1897, p. 67.

———. "The Bread of Life." *Young People's Paper*, 11 February 1901, p. 11.

Wiebe, Rudy. *Peace Shall Destroy Many*. McClelland & Stewart, 1962.

Ten

Mennonite/s Writing: State of the Art?*

The debates are ongoing. One thing, however, has already become clear: a society's dealings with the past can no longer be happily divided into "history proper," identified with the work of professional historians, and "nonhistory" or "improper history," identified with all the rest.

Ann Rigney, "Portable Memory"

IT WAS JEFF Gundy, convener of "Mennonite/s Writing: Across Borders," who suggested to co-panelists Ann Hostetler and me the focus of our plenary session at the October 2006 Bluffton conference on Mennonite/s Writing—the fourth conference since the inaugural (Waterloo/Grebel) convention of 1990, entitled "Mennonite/s Writing in Canada." Jeff issued the theme: "State of the Art?" At the conference some months later he went on, as he was to confess in his inimitably exuberant way, to "make some wild generalizations and utter some perhaps contentious personal opinions" about writing ("Marriage" 59). Ann Hostetler explored "the grace of confession" ("Playing" 54), asserting with hope that Mennonite literature might create a matrix "in which the wild yeasts of dissenters and shunned can be kneaded back into the community to provide new flavors that can nourish us all" ("Playing" 58). Poets both, Jeff and Ann composed, for that panel, evocative personal essays about the writer's impact upon the world.

* First published as Hildi Froese Tiessen, "Mennonite/s Writing: State of the Art?" *Conrad Grebel Review*, vol. 26, no. 1, 2008, pp. 41–49.

My own prevailing scholarly interest in literary communities compelled me—the sole Canadian and the "Russian" Mennonite among the three of us—to reflect, especially in the context of a mostly American audience, on the world of Mennonite literature north of the border, especially among Russian Mennonites. I chose to focus my remarks on Mennonite literature that fairly explicitly engages Mennonite experience and, as is my wont, to foreground the constantly shifting relationship between Mennonite writers and Mennonite communities. I began with some general comments, and closed with a few observations about something of singular interest to me: the emerging role of literature in the construction of Mennonite cultural memory.

So, what shall I say? That I am elated that the interest in Mennonite literature persists, in spite of Al Reimer's observation at the first "Mennonite/s Writing" conference, at Conrad Grebel University College, that by the end of that May weekend in 1990 we would have said all there was to be said on the subject and that the whole phenomenon of Mennonite writing was likely to fade away in any case. We'd do best, he suggested then, to fold up our tents and move on to other things.

Well, Mennonites certainly didn't stop writing after that first convention. Rather, they persisted in finding their voices and telling their stories. Seven years later, in 1997, inspired and emboldened by the conference on Mennonite/s Writing in Canada, the indomitable Ervin Beck convened a second conference, focused on American Mennonite writers in particular, at Goshen College. Five years after that, in 2002, the third conference, and the first explicitly international gathering, was sponsored jointly by Goshen and Grebel, and once more efficiently and artfully organized by Ervin Beck at Goshen. And in 2006 we were together once more, thanks to the vision, efficiency, and untiring good will of Jeff Gundy and the Bluffton team. The Bluffton conference revealed that, insofar as Mennonite/s writing was concerned, we were richer than ever.

I and others have often enough remarked that Mennonite literature as we know it today was inaugurated—on our side of the border at least—with the publication of Rudy Wiebe's first novel *Peace Shall Destroy Many* in 1962. Unlike earlier Mennonite literary efforts in Canada (and there were some—most notably by Arnold Dyck, who wrote gently and humorously, in German or Low German, of the Mennonites he knew), Rudy Wiebe had the temerity to write in English; moreover, he was published by McClelland &

Stewart, at the time and for some years to come Canada's premier publisher of literary work. And much to the chagrin of many members of the Mennonite community, Wiebe's landmark first novel was reviewed in periodicals across the country and read from coast to coast.

If the first conference gathered together Rudy Wiebe and the mostly Winnipeg-based writers who followed in his wake—Canada's first generation of Mennonite writers—the one in Bluffton in October 2006 foregrounded an emerging new generation. Back in the day, as my son would say, I wrote a brief piece in the *Canadian Mennonite* called "The Writers are Coming, the Writers are Coming." Hurrah! Almost 45 years after *Peace Shall Destroy Many*, new writers continue to appear in the ever more readily discernible Canadian Mennonite literary landscape—as well as in the United States. Indeed, Mennonite writers north of the increasingly conflicted Canada/USA border have, particularly over the past 20 years or so, poured out—often to national acclaim—fiction and poetry and life writing and essays that have appeared in all the major literary magazines of the country and with the imprint of the now many Canadian publishers that function as the support network of this remarkable literary phenomenon.

"Mennonite sells," Sandra Birdsell's Random House promoter declared to a public audience in Waterloo not long ago. A few months later, a popular national Sunday morning radio show on Canada's premier broadcaster, the CBC, hosted a panel focusing for half an hour on what the show's host, the respected journalist Michael Enright, referred to as "the Mennonite Miracle." Enright was quoting *Prairie Fire* editor Andris Taskans, who had so named what he called "the largely Manitoban explosion of writers that started with Patrick Friesen and Sandra Birdsell and also includes Di Brandt, Miriam Toews, and Armin Wiebe." This "blossoming of largely secular Mennonite writers," Taskans went on, is "[w]hat people will remember about writing in Manitoba during the final quarter of the 20th century" (qtd. in "In Country").

Saying this, Taskans echoed an observation made by the influential Canadian writer and critic Robert Kroetsch—friend and mentor to a number of Mennonite writers—when he convened the closing panel at the first conference on Mennonite writing in 1990. There Kroetsch observed that when he toured England's Lake Country it seemed every rock had been sat on by "a Wordsworth or a Dorothy, at least." He had been struck by "all of this heavy inscription." He felt that when he toured southern Manitoba there too "everything had been inscribed," adding that "in Canada finally we have a landscape that is a literary text and that might be the greatest accomplishment of the Mennonite writer so far as that vast text that is southern Manitoba is concerned" ("Closing" 224). It's worth remarking, in this context, that Mennonite writers have begun to inscribe other Canadian landscapes as well, most notably the West Coast. Just two weeks before the Bluffton conference, a new anthology of Mennonite writing by West Coast writers, *Half in the Sun*, was published. About the same time *Rhubarb* magazine devoted a special issue to this compelling new group of writers. And an issue of *Rhubarb* featuring the literature and visual art of Mennonites from Ontario appeared in the fall of 2007.

So, Mennonite writing is more than alive and well in Canada. Between the Goshen conference in 2002 and the Bluffton conference in 2006, Rudy Wiebe, Patrick Friesen, David Waltner-Toews, David Elias, Sarah Klassen, Armin Wiebe, Victor Enns, Barbara Nickel, Sandra Birdsell, Di Brandt, Vern Thiessen, Miriam Toews, and David Bergen—and others: a younger generation of writers like Melanie Cameron and Carrie Snyder, for example (both of whom read from their work at Bluffton)—published new work. Several are recipients of—or have been shortlisted for—major regional and national literary awards. Most notable, perhaps, are dramatist Vern Thiessen and novelists Miriam Toews and David Bergen, who were respectively—and in sequential years, beginning in 2003—recipients of Canada's most significant national literary prizes.

Breakthroughs such as these contribute to the announcement of a "Mennonite Miracle." One of the most provocative elements of this striking epithet is that it has been invoked specifically to denote, as Taskans remarked, "secular" Mennonite writers. At the risk of evoking a stormy protest from people I know and people I don't, who insist that there can be no such thing as a secular Mennonite, that the term is an oxymoron, I might remark that each of David Bergen and Sandra Birdsell and Miriam Toews, all agreeable enough to be spokespeople for the "Mennonite miracle," declared themselves on national radio to be reasonably comfortable with that "secular Mennonite" nomenclature. As am I.

For in Canada at least, Mennonite literature has tended to be more an ethnic or cultural phenomenon than a religious one. I would argue, for example, that unlike my Portuguese Catholic or Iranian Muslim students, or my Bosnian Orthodox or Indian Hindu friends, all of whom claim separate (though often intricately connected) cultural and religious identities, I am—in the language of the diversity of Canada's heritage groups—Mennonite Mennonite: Mennonite (religious denomination) Mennonite (cultural heritage designation). My religion is Mennonite. My heritage designation is not "Russian," even though my ancestors occupied a "Russian" landscape for some two hundred years. Nor is it Dutch or German, even though the languages I learned in my Canadian home originated in the Dutch and German regions of Europe. Culturally and religiously I am Mennonite, but the two identical-sounding terms I invoke when I say this do not mean the same thing.

Some years ago, Di Brandt, at a conference in Millerstown, Pennsylvania, declared that she couldn't become a writer until her father died, for, as she put it then, "he owned all the words." Questions related to the ownership of language have troubled Mennonite writers at least since Deacon Block, in *Peace Shall Destroy Many*, berated Joseph Dueck for speaking out in the presence of outsiders. We know that even in our day, "not just anyone, finally, may speak of just anything" (Foucault 216). But many of the writers among the Mennonites are fairly blithely challenging that notion. If Di Brandt's father owned the language of her Mennonite home, so too did patriarchs for centuries claim proprietorial rights to the language of Mennonite communities. Included among them were confessional historians and theologians. It should come as no surprise—though it sometimes leaves me bemused—that a course offered at Conrad Grebel University College called "Contemporary Mennonite Thought" should focus on theology alone—suggesting that among Mennonites only theologians have thoughts worth remarking upon.

Like post-colonial writers writing back to their imperial centres, demanding that they have a right to tell their own stories—to describe life as they have experienced it—Mennonite writers are in effect writing back as well, and declaring that the *official* stories of Mennonite communities and congregations are not the only stories to be told. And in Canada, where Mennonite writers have gained access to national and international publishers as well as to the national media, all sorts of people are listening. In 2006, in a national cultural project called "Canada Reads," Miriam Toews's *A Complicated Kindness* was chosen as the one novel that the whole country should read and talk about. During the "Canada Reads" campaign (a kind of "American Idol" for books), many sets of eyes read and many ears heard (on national public radio) this passage, spoken near the front of Toews's novel by the teenaged narrator Nomi Nickel:

> We're Mennonites. As far as I know, we are the most embarrassing sub-sect of people to belong to if you're a teenager. Five hundred years ago in Europe a man named

> Menno Simons set off to do his own peculiar religious thing and he and his followers were beaten up and killed or forced to conform all over Holland, Poland and Russia until they, at least some of them, landed right here where I sit ... Imagine the least well-adjusted kid in your school starting a breakaway clique of people whose manifesto includes a ban on the media, dancing, smoking, temperate climates, movies, drinking, rock 'n' roll, having sex for fun, swimming, make-up, jewellery, playing pool, going to cities, or staying up past nine o'clock. That was Menno all over. Thanks a lot, Menno. (Toews 5)

Some months ago, I was at a weekend strategic planning session at Grebel. Foremost on the agenda was the question about where the College should find itself, say, three or five years from now. A committed Grebel alumnus, now a young professor at the University of Toronto, spoke up forcefully and often. We must support the research activities of the Grebel faculty, he demanded; these, after all, are the scholars who will tell the Mennonites who they are, where they're from, and where they might steer the Mennonite enterprise for decades to come. That he was referring exclusively to historians and theologians soon became evident. We must support and encourage those academics who are committed to the task of telling our story, he urged, adding, without an ounce of humor, "otherwise Miriam Toews will have the last word."

I'm not sure Miriam Toews would want the last word. In fact, although her comments about Mennonites (as she experienced them in her smallish rural city of Steinbach, Manitoba) have been almost as controversial, it could be argued, as the early work of Rudy Wiebe, she actually remains remarkably positive about these people and the "complicated kindnesses" she has observed among them. In fact, the remarks of the young scholar at that weekend meeting say much more about a Mennonite community's conflicted sensibility, its ambivalence about the fiction writer and the projects of literature, than they do about the vision articulated by any individual writer. Every new Mennonite writer who addresses matters related to the Mennonites reveals the power of literature both to shape and bring into circulation characters and images that are shared across generations, and to "'de-stabilise' memories by provocatively opening up cracks in the consensus" (Erll and Rigney 114). The Mennonite community expressed shock at the appearance of Rudy Wiebe as a writer of fiction in 1962. Today, members of the community are bewildered that there are so many Mennonite writers and that, unlike Joseph Dueck, Wiebe's dissenting mouthpiece in *Peace Shall Destroy Many*, they have come to stay.

A quick survey of the past several years' worth of Mennonite periodicals, both popular and scholarly, will reveal that Russian Mennonites in particular have begun to memorialize—with cairns and other physical monuments—their experience in the former Soviet Union. In the context of a flourishing interest throughout the wider culture in archives, monuments, nostalgia, and memory, Mennonites have become actively engaged in questions concerning who will preserve their past, who will construct the cultural memory of their people.

In an August 2006 special issue of *European Journal of English Studies* entitled "Literature and the Production of Cultural Memory," editors Astrid Erll and Ann Rigney assert that "Over the last decade, 'cultural memory' has emerged as a useful umbrella term to describe the complex ways in which societies remember their past using a variety of media." They go on:

> [A]ttention has been shifting in recent years to the cultural processes by which memories become shared in the first place. It has become increasingly apparent that the memories that are shared within generations and across different generations are the products of public acts of remembrance using a variety of media. Stories, both oral and written, images, museums, monuments: these all work together in creating and sustaining "sites of memory." (111)

Literary texts "play a variety of roles in the formation of cultural memory," Rigney has observed elsewhere, not least as media by means of which "disparate local memories" are channeled and framed (Rigney 374). By communicating and sharing among members of a community images of the past, cultural memory serves to "stabilize and convey" a society's "self-image" (Kansteiner 182). Literature, it could be argued, plays a significant role in the production of cultural memory, and so also in the construction of community, offering the reader of a literary text "the possibility of adhering to a community, as an outsider, without laying down particular criteria that have to be met" (Culler 37). That is, a novel might offer a kind of homeland to those who have been deemed community outsiders, alongside "the insider's view" readily available to adherents to community norms.

So, what do we observe when we speak of the state of Mennonite writing in Canada in the first decade of the twenty-first century? That we have a veritable choir of voices, and that several of the more prominent ones have an audience that stretches well beyond the borders of any Mennonite community. That the Mennonite audience as a whole remains conflicted about its writers, even as elements in the larger world celebrate their achievement. That the writers among us are as often embraced—almost as trophies—by theologians, historians, musicians who recognize the particular impact and resonance of their work, as they are dismissed by others who also recognize that same impact and resonance. Here lies the crux of the matter. When we started to talk in conference settings about the writers among us—the conferences on Mennonite/s writing since 1990—we spoke often of the relationship between the writer and the Mennonite community, which was more often than not resistant to what the writer had to say. The ground has shifted, I think. The cat is out of the bag. The conserving community is losing ground. Miriam Toews and others are not demanding the last word; but it is their words, I am suggesting here, that are in large measure shaping—in this age of monuments and monumentalizing—the new cultural memory of the Mennonites.

WORKS CITED

Culler, Jonathan. "Anderson and the Novel." *Diacritics*, vol. 29, no. 4, Winter 1999, pp. 20–39.

Erll, Astrid, and Ann Rigney. "Literature and the Production of Cultural Memory: Introduction." *European Journal of English Studies*, vol. 10, no. 2, August 2006, pp. 111–115.

Foucault, Michel. "The Discourse on Language." *The Archaeology of Knowledge*. Pantheon, 1982.

Gundy, Jeff. "The Marriage of the *Martyrs Mirror* and the Open Road, or Why I Love Poetry Despite the Suspicion that it Won't Save Anybody." *Conrad Grebel Review*, vol. 26, no. 1, 2008, pp. 59–71.

Hostetler, Ann. "Playing the Sacred Harp: Mennonite Literature as Confession." *Conrad Grebel Review*, vol. 26, no. 1, 2008, pp. 50–58.

"In Country: David Bergen." *Quill & Quire*, June 2005, www.quillandquire.com.

Kansteiner, Wulf. "Finding Meaning in Memory: A Methodological Critique of Collective Memory Studies." *History and Theory,* no. 41, May 2002, pp. 179–197.

Kroetsch, Robert. "Closing Panel." Tiessen and Hinchcliffe, pp. 223–242.

Rhubarb: A Magazine of New Mennonite Art and Writing, no. 11 (West Coast), 2005.

Rhubarb: A Magazine of New Mennonite Art and Writing, no. 15 (Words and Images from Ontario), 2007.

Rigney, Ann. "Portable Monuments: Literature, Cultural Memory, and the Case of Jeanie Deans." *Poetics Today,* vol. 25, no. 2, Summer 2004, pp. 361–396.

Neufeld, Elsie K., ed. *Half in the Sun: Anthology of Mennonite Writing.* Ronsdale, 2006.

Tiessen, Hildi Froese, and Peter Hinchcliffe, eds. *Acts of Concealment: Mennonite/s Writing in Canada.* U of Waterloo P, 1992.

Toews, Miriam. *A Complicated Kindness.* Knopf, 2004.

Wiebe, Rudy. *Peace Shall Destroy Many.* McClelland & Stewart, 1962.

Eleven

An Imagined Coherence:
Mennonite Literature and Mennonite Culture*

I AM CURRENTLY WORKING with a number of writers and literary critics from Canada and the USA to plan an international conference on "Mennonite/s Writing" to take place in 2012. This will be the sixth such event since the inaugural conference on "Mennonite/s Writing" hosted by my home university at Waterloo back in 1990, 20 years ago. It's the creative literature of the Mennonites—perhaps even more than the Mennonites' theological or sociological or historical discourses—that has consistently drawn widespread attention in North America over the past few decades. In fact, it is without a doubt the literature produced by writers nurtured within the diversity of Mennonite communities across Canada and the USA that is most palpably shaping how many Mennonites are seeing themselves in our day (and, of course, how Mennonites are being perceived by others). Mennonite literature is certainly stimulating many, many readers and others to reflect on the sometimes decorous and sometimes audacious images of Mennonite culture circulating among and around us. Somehow, in spite of the fact that Mennonite writers are widely revered for their beautiful, vivid,

---

* Previously unpublished, this essay was presented as an invited lecture on a panel convened in November 2010 in recognition of the inauguration of the program in Mennonite Studies at the University of the Fraser Valley.

life-affirming works evoking the rich textures of human passion and fear and desire and hope, there are people who still harbor limiting stereotypes about these writers' powerful and illuminating works. It would be best to sweep these reductive stereotypes away.

If we address the relationship between Mennonite literature and Mennonite culture we cannot avoid saying what we mean by "Mennonite." The term "Mennonite" is, as you all know, a deeply political term. It's a contentious term because, perhaps quite rightly, the many people who would like to own it do not agree on what it means. In Canada practice makes it clear that "Mennonite" is both a religious and an ethnic term. It means at least these two things, just as many other words we use every day have multiple meanings. I like to think of it this way: my course in Canadian multicultural literature draws students from a range of backgrounds. Among them: a Kurdish Muslim, an African Sikh, a Dutch agnostic, a Bengali Hindu, a Portuguese Catholic, a Mennonite Catholic. As for me? I am a Mennonite Mennonite (that is, a member of each and both ethnic (or cultural) and religious Mennonite communities: an inheritor and an adherent). I find it useful—perhaps necessary—to accept that "Mennonite" is both a religious and an ethnic (or cultural) term and that the border between these two instances of the term is fluid, forever shifting.

A Mennonite writer, it seems to me, is a writer who knows from lived experience what it means to be a Mennonite, and Mennonite writing is writing such a writer produces. Some might want to narrow the scope, to say that Mennonite writing might be confined to writing-about-Mennonites such a writer produces. But regardless of whether or not a "Mennonite" writer's work deals explicitly with Mennonite subject matter, the writing tends to be richly informed by the experience of his or her having been "Mennonite."

Many of the Canadian writers we identify as Mennonites would describe themselves as having no committed relationship with any particular congregationally-based Mennonite community, even though they were likely nurtured within one. Still, in the vast majority of cases, they would acknowledge explicitly and/or implicitly that their sensibility, their thinking, their view of the world and responses to it, are richly shaped by the nature of their experiences as Mennonites—just as James Joyce's work, for example, was indelibly inscribed with his Dublin-based Irish Catholicism, even though he spent his almost entire writing life outside of Ireland. Among these Mennonites, whom some would once have referred to as *abgefallen*, fallen away, are Andreas Schroeder, for example, who declares himself a "defunct" Mennonite—a Mennonite no longer active as a Mennonite; or this year's Giller Prize nominee David Bergen, who no longer considers himself to be in any way religious; or the well-known poet Di Brandt, who holds that the Mennonites among whom she grew up betrayed and abandoned her; or Vern Thiessen, one of Canada's most widely-produced playwrights, who has little contact with any Mennonites outside of his own family, but whose most recent play *Lenin's Embalmers*, a dark comedy produced this year in New York and by Jewish theatre groups in Winnipeg and Toronto, is, he has declared, "deeply rooted in [his] upbringing in a Mennonite home" (qtd. in Prokosh).

It's worth remarking, before I go on, that Mennonite literature as we know it in Canada today has been written almost exclusively by Mennonites of Dutch/North German heritage—the folks we in Ontario call "Russian Mennonites" (these are Wiebes and Dycks and Klassens and Friesens). There are very few writers among Canadian Mennonites of Swiss/South German heritage (the Snyders and Zehrs and Brubachers and Erbs of southwestern Ontario), never mind among the vast range of "new" Mennonites we find in many Canadian urban centres—the Hispanics and Chinese, and Hmong and Koreans, for example. As someone interested in the emergence not only of Mennonite literature, but also of multicultural literatures in Canada, I have observed how Canadian literatures by people other than the British and the French have followed Canadian immigration patterns: a few decades after a strong wave of immigration a new literature might begin to appear. Hence we now have Canadian literatures expressive of a range of Chinese, Ukrainian, South Asian, and Italian ways of being in Canada, among others. Any group needs to find its voice (and, of course, learn the language) before individuals within it will begin to produce a literature reflective of their particular cultural reality. So, just as I assume a Serbian Orthodox literature and an Iranian Muslim literature will find a firm footing within the Canadian literary landscape soon enough, I am eagerly awaiting the new Mennonite literatures that are sure to emerge among the many Mennonites living in Africa and India, for example, but also among Hispanic and Chinese and Hmong and Korean Mennonites here in Canada. These new literatures will surely illumine Mennonite worlds altogether different from the worlds of Rudy Wiebe or Andreas Schroeder or Patrick Friesen or Miriam Toews. But these new literatures have not yet been written. Hence my reflections today will address the Mennonite literature we can claim now, even as we anticipate the diversity of "Mennonite literatures" we can anticipate in future decades.

"Mennonite culture." I take this to mean, on the one hand, what we would once have fairly easily spoken of as Mennonite "community"—the actual, day-to-day communal world of Mennonites who meet face to face in everyday settings and hold in common assumptions, attitudes, beliefs and practices. Just as compelling, though, in the context of our discussion today, is another manifestation of culture or community—this one not actual, but imagined, as historian Benedict Anderson might say. Perhaps that's what we are really talking about when we talk about Mennonite culture: not so much any coherent reality Mennonites actually share, but rather an imagined coherence, a more-or-less shared mental image of "Mennonite culture," if you will.

One could probably safely say that the Mennonite reader who picks up a literary text by a Mennonite writer is not looking for religious instruction. In this vein, I'm often reminded of a statement Canadian literary critic Clara Thomas made during the 1990 conference on Mennonite/s Writing in Waterloo. She remarked that although Rudy Wiebe's "*The Blue Mountains of China* [for example] is a magnificent epic and religious novel ... it does not and cannot," she said, "identify [her] to [herself]" as do the novels of Margaret Laurence, for example, "written from a background so close to [her] own" (130). Both Clara Thomas and Margaret Laurence were Scottish Presbyterians. Well, the fiction of Rudy Wiebe and the fiction and poetry of Sarah Klassen or David Waltner-Toews, for example, written from a background so close to mine, identify me to myself, and for that I am immensely grateful. Like all fine works of literature, they cast light on elements of the human condition as we might find it expressed in any affecting literary work, but in their particularities they say something special to me and, I'm sure, to many of you. I "know" the mother in Sarah Klassen's poems or in Rudy Wiebe's memoir, for example. I have sat beside women just like her; I have eaten her baking; I have heard women just like her speak and sing and weep and pray.

When I attended a production of Mennonite playwright Vern Thiessen's *Lenin's Embalmers* at the Toronto Jewish Theatre a week ago, I was struck by these remarks in the program notes: "As our mandate, we embrace and celebrate the Jewish story—stories about our history, stories about our beliefs, and stories about our struggles and triumphs."[1] For a member of a Mennonite community the next best thing to a Mennonite writer telling a Jewish story (as in Vern Thiessen's play) is a Mennonite writer telling a Mennonite story. And that it happens all the time is cause for celebration. In Canada the Fraser Valley is one of the vigorous centres of Mennonite writing. And a program in Mennonite Studies such as has been established here has the opportunity to encourage this work—so often an enthralling exploration of Mennonite history, beliefs, struggles and triumphs.

---

1 This statement appears also in various of the Harold Green Jewish Theatre Company's statements of self-description.

We could think of much of Mennonites' writing about Mennonites as an act of cultural memory. Historical narratives in both fiction and poetry have a prominent place in Mennonite writing, where literary texts about Mennonites, by Mennonites, function as "public acts of remembrance"—as monuments recalling, sometimes critically, sometimes nostalgically, a past for whom the Mennonites no longer have living witnesses. Such terribly important writing serves to construct Mennonite self-understanding over and over again. It contributes to the ongoing and dynamic construction of what some would call the Mennonite "imaginary"—the aggregation of dominant and commonly-embraced narratives through which the community imagines itself, both preserves and reforms itself, and presents itself to others.

Where Mennonite literary texts reflect not on the past but on the present, they give voice to some of the challenges contemporary Mennonites might encounter when they try to find meaning in their inevitable and repeated negotiations between the Mennonite individual they once knew themselves to be and the accommodated self the wider world compels them to become. These readers share with the characters in the contemporary Mennonite fiction they read various ways of testing any number of possible responses they might make to the modern world as they encounter it—and to the Mennonite community, whether actual or imagined.

Mennonites sometimes look to the Jews for a kind of paradigm for their own much shorter range of experience as a community where religion and ethnicity are intertwined and amended by periods of intense suffering and sacrifice, and where self-understanding is shaped by a diasporic reality—by the fact that they are a scattered people, living in dispersion. But the Jews, the definitive diasporic community, have a homeland; the Mennonites do not. As one of Rudy Wiebe's characters in *The Blue Mountains of China* declares, were the Mennonites to have a homeland, it would be no place on earth. Perhaps the Mennonites' homeland is, as Wiebe seems to suggest, the New Jerusalem. Perhaps we could also say that the Mennonites' homeland resides between the covers of books: the Bible, the *Martyrs Mirror*—and (is it so outrageous to say this?) the Mennonite literary discourse of the twentieth and twenty-first centuries.

I would go so far as to say that Mennonite literature, indeed, offers any current or past member of the Mennonite community a kind of homeland. Those who have remained inside the congregationally-based actual community, as well as those who have found themselves on the margins of it, or even further afield, or in an in-between space—all can find some kind of homeland here: a place they can insert themselves without the threat of someone telling them they do not belong. The book, the narrative, makes available a common discourse—an evocative, recognizable assemblage of words and codes and images—that holds together the "imagined community" all can declare as their own.

Literary texts by Mennonite writers are, of course, embraced by audiences that extend far beyond any Mennonite readership. One need only think of the international success of Miriam Toews's *A Complicated Kindness*, for example (with rights sold to at least 15 countries, and over a quarter of a million copies sold in Canada alone), or the explosive, if conflicted, popular response to Rhoda Janzen's *New York Times* bestseller *Mennonite in a Little Black Dress*. But today we are talking about Mennonite literature and its relationship to Mennonite culture. Texts like *A Complicated Kindness* and *Mennonite in a Little Black Dress* certainly serve, among other things, to stimulate conversation among Mennonites—reflective conversation about love and betrayal and community and family and faith and history and loss and home.

American poet Robert Frost once wrote: "Home is the place where, when you have to go there, / they have to take you in" ("The Death"). I belong to a generation of Mennonites among whom many did not find Frost's observation to be true. Many of my friends were excommunicated or dis-invited from the Mennonite church and hence, because the Mennonites have tended to conflate religious and cultural identities, from their home communities. There are a lot of Mennonite exiles out there. My husband Paul speaks of them as the lost ones, those who have fallen into what he calls the *Mennochasm*. You can count them all the way through Mennonite literature. People like Peter Neufeld in Patrick Friesen's *The Shunning* or Nomi Nickel and her mother Trudie and her sister Tash in Miriam Toews's *A Complicated Kindness*, or Mike in Di Brandt's poem about this lost generation: "where / was God when all these young men / felt their souls crumble to dust" she asks, "& where's my long lost brother / Mike who might have inherited the / earth with me Menno where's Mike" ("at Basil's," *Agnes* 11). Mennonite religious dogma often makes it hard for Mennonites to think of these lost souls as our own. But they are. And I know that often Mennonite literature has been and is for these exiles a place of refuge.

I teach some Jewish literary texts in my course on Canadian multicultural literatures and am frequently struck by what seems to me to be the key difference between Mennonites and Jews, as revealed in their respective Canadian narratives. The characters in Jewish stories often appear to be trying to get away from the overbearing confines of community and family, it seems; and their attempts at escape are often rendered humourously. They really have a hard time escaping because no one, it seems, is prepared to let them go. One would not have to read a lot of Mennonite literature to observe that the Mennonite community, in contrast, has been quite content to shed its people one by one, to shun them (formally or informally), or simply to let them quietly drift away. Many Mennonite writers themselves, especially pioneers like Rudy Wiebe, have been, now and then, at least wished away. (They tend to refuse to leave because the community of their imaginations is big enough to contain both themselves and those who would turn them away.)

Creative writers, whether or not they are more-or-less traditional believers, tend to live on the margins of the community. It's their perch: they see things more clearly from there. It's from there they speak. And there have always been forces within the community eager to silence them. Like any community with a certain common self-understanding, the Mennonites have shared a fairly firm idea about who can speak, and where and when. In Rudy Wiebe's prophetic first novel *Peace Shall Destroy Many*, Joseph Dueck, who dares to speak in an unauthorized setting, is harshly criticized by the Deacon, who represents the enforcement of the way things always were. Dueck does not remain within the community for long. Women in general did not, until recent decades, have a voice in Mennonite congregations, as any reading of the poetry of Di Brandt, for example, reveals. Literary critic Magdalene Redekop has remarked, "I feel a kinship with Mennonite writers of fiction and poetry, not because they assert the same values as I do, but because they ... are willing to ask questions—to dissent. The writers who are on the periphery, challenging the very idea of being Mennonite, may paradoxically be the most true to the spirit of the Reformation dissenters" (46).

One young Mennonite academic told me recently that where Mennonites do not stand against the system, where they are not prepared to question all the "givens" by which we tend to live, to dissent at any level of our contemporary worldly existence, they have no right to identify themselves with their dissenting ancestors. So, might it be that our writers should be acknowledged as prominent among our current reformers?

Mennonite writing has compelled us to recognize that life among Mennonites is richly informed not only by centuries-old dogma and cultural habits so ingrained that we barely recognize that they're there, but also by great diversity, even within the most traditional of communities. We know there are dozens of different Mennonite groups in Canada. But this isn't the sort of diversity I am speaking of. I'm referring to something closer to home—literally. Indeed, every Mennonite family is a wee bit different from every other. To be sure, some Mennonites have expressed dismay that the fiction of Miriam Toews or the poetry of Di Brandt or the creative nonfiction of Rhoda Janzen—or, for that matter, the work of any one of the dozens of Mennonite writers active today—might give readers out there a so-called distorted sense of what or who the Mennonites are. The Mennonites are at once all the things they are said to be in writing such as this. Yet any one Mennonite person or community might be none of the things these authors have put forth so publicly. My own life as a Mennonite woman is richly informed by the poetry of Di Brandt, for example, but her experience as a Mennonite woman is by no means identical with mine. It could be that this is one of the most important things Mennonite writing has brought to the community: a recognition that Mennonites do not all have to be the same to be authentic. And they are not the same—neither within our congregations nor without. Mennonites might have avoided a lot of pain and suffering had they recognized this to be true.

Sometimes I teach literature in the context of a Department of Peace and Conflict Studies. That's an odd place to study poems and stories, you might think. Peace Studies are usually offered through the prisms of Political Science or History—disciplines concerned most of all with issues generally apprehended on a grand scale. Literature, to be sure, trades in ideas just as these disciplines do, but not on a macro-level. In literature we find the particular—the individual, the singular. In literature each one of us finds a place to insert ourselves at a human, an intimate level. It's an oh-so-human enterprise. And spiritual at the same time, as Rudy Wiebe observed decades ago when, in response to an interviewer's question, he remarked with characteristic insight that the role of literature is to reveal what mankind, by the grace of God, is capable of. Indeed. In literature we observe the result of someone's longing to explore and express what it means to be human—sometimes, if we're lucky, what is means to be Mennonite.

There has been an outpouring of fine literature among Mennonites over the past half century. In another forum we could talk about how it was that that came about. Suffice it to say, here, that some doors had to be opened to allow it to happen, and kept open to allow it to persist. A new centre for Mennonite Studies like this one can keep the doors open. It has the opportunity, among any number of other things, to nurture and celebrate the diversity of artistic expression that the Mennonites of the Fraser Valley, by the grace of God, are capable of.

WORKS CITED

Brandt, Di. *Agnes in the sky.* Turnstone Press, 1990.

Frost, Robert. "The Death of the Hired Man." 1914. Academy of American Poets, www.poets.org.

Prokosh, Kevin. "Playwright had help finding humour in horror." *Winnipeg Free Press,* 21 October 2010, www.winnipegfreepress.com.

Redekop, Magdalene. Personal Statement. *Prairie Fire,* vol. 11, no. 2, Summer 1990, p. 46.

Thomas, Clara. "Western Women's Writing of 'The Childhood' and Anne Konrad's *The Blue Jar.*" *Acts of Concealment: Mennonite/s Writing in Canada,* ed. Hildi Froese Tiessen and Peter Hinchcliffe, U Waterloo P, 1992, pp. 129–142.

Twelve

The Case of Dallas Wiebe: Literary Art in Worship[*]

I was born to be a shepherd. I was trained to be a shepherd and I still want to be what I was destined to be. I want to sit on the ground, watch my flocks by night and wait for the glory of the Lord to come upon me ... Now there ain't no pastures. And because there ain't no pastures there ain't no sheep. And because there ain't no sheep there ain't no shepherds. And because there ain't no shepherds there's no one out there waiting for the Messiah to come. And because no one's waiting, He won't come. Someone has to sit and wait. No one's waiting and we're all lost.

Dallas Wiebe, *Skyblue's Essays: fictions*

IS IT POSSIBLE to discuss the literary arts in worship without addressing—or embracing—the literary artist? My reflections here, on "the word" and worship, take into account both my commitment to the presentation and performance of the literary word (what I will here loosely refer to as "poetry") in the context of worship, and my conviction that Mennonite congregations would do well not only to literally listen to the words of creative writers from

---

[*] First published as Hildi Froese Tiessen, "The Case of Dallas Wiebe: Literary Art in Worship." *Journal of Mennonite Writing*, vol. 3, no. 3, 2011.

inside and outside their communities, but also, where possible, to engage the writers themselves.

I have always found inspiration and sustenance, sometimes refuge and comfort, in poetry—even as I recognize that poetry might very well be, also, disturbing and unsettling. I know what it means to realize, as someone has said, that *I don't quite know what I know until the poet gives utterance to it; and then I know I knew it all along.* Poetry does have the capacity to focus the imagination and to stir us to see the ordinary in extraordinary ways. Sometimes it draws us away from the messy and frightening parts of our lives and gives us space to breathe. Sometimes it draws us back to the nitty-gritty of living, and compels us to reflect freshly on the conditions in which we carry on.

Because I believe that a good poem or a passage of creative prose, read with grace and understanding, can enlarge our ability to comprehend the full scope of human existence, I have for several years now organized and performed Sunday morning poetry services once a year in my home church. Among the poets whose work I have featured is the late Dallas Wiebe (1930-2008), perhaps at once the least likely and most compelling of spiritual guides.

The work of the early Dallas Wiebe might not have come immediately to mind to someone looking for literature to read in church. In his grad student years he had, after all, as Bethel College History Professor James Juhnke remarked in a letter to me last year, "written a lot of insulting poetry and prose about Bethel College and other Kansas places and people of his origin." Indeed, seemingly since his earliest years, Dallas had harboured a rather unorthodox perspective on church and community—as well as on the social dynamics of family and class—as he recalled in an interview I conducted with him in his Cincinnati home in 1998, about "growing up Mennonite." Seemingly comfortable with what a reasonably long life had revealed to him, he spoke—as Dallas tended always to speak—with an inimitable tone of oddly empathetic, probing candor:

> I didn't like going to church, I don't mind telling people. I found it terribly boring and tiresome. It was awful to go to church because it was sometimes terribly, terribly hot in the church in Kansas. It was awfully uncomfortable ... I enjoyed reading. I have always been a reader. And I don't know why because the rest of our family is not and I read and read and read and read. And I loved reading the Bible. I loved reading anything and I really liked Sunday School and I liked memorizing Bible passages ... I enjoyed that. I thought that was fun. And I liked singing ... one of the

things I started doing (because the sermons were so long and so boring and so tiresome I thought it was just awful) was I started reading the hymn book while the sermon was going on. So nowadays I will often ask people, do you read hymn books? And they look at me as if I am crazy ... they look at me like you read hymn books, why would you read hymn books? And I say don't you want to know what you're singing? Don't you realize what is there? Some of this stuff that's in this book doesn't make any sense. It really doesn't. The words of some of those hymns don't make sense. They're stupid ... There are a couple in this new hymnal ... that are just screwy. They don't make any sense. They're silly. At any rate some of them are great. There are some really wonderful verses in some of those hymns and I discovered that when I was reading them and I still read them. I read the new hymnal. I read it straight through ... I never was very religious, I just wasn't, I'm just not and I wish I could be like some of those people are ...

Dallas Wiebe, like Skyblue the Badass—who appears in his work as what Dallas himself described as "the irresistible hero both funny and sad ... the eternal striver"—was, as Paul Tiessen has observed, filled with both serious mischief and serious purpose.[1] It could be argued that Dallas was—even in his formative years—more thoughtful and reflective about church than most people who fill the benches on a Sunday morning. And so it's not surprising that he was deeply affected when he was invited to read from his work in a Kansas Mennonite community he had left over 40 years before, in the fall of 1997, just months before he recalled for me the observations about church I've quoted here. It was serendipitous that he should have occasion, then, to perform his own words in a setting he had left in 1954, when he had moved to the University of Michigan (Ann Arbor) and then finally to Cincinnati, where he would spend over three decades as a professor of English and mentor to young writers. He would speak often of how much that Sunday morning service—his performance and the warm reception he received—had meant to him.

He had never planned that Sunday's performance. Perhaps it was providential that he was called upon just then, when he seemed, one might say, spiritually primed. It happened like this: Anna Kreider Juhnke, who taught in the English

---

1 See "Literary Refractions" (121).

Department of Bethel College then, wrote in a recently-recovered family letter[2] that on a Friday in the fall of 1997 she had "stopped at the post office and found a letter from Dallas Wiebe that he would be in Newton [that] weekend for a family reunion!" Her pastor Darrell Fast had decided to use a lot of pilgrimage hymns that Sunday, and, in place of a sermon, "three pilgrimage stories: from the Bible (Elijah going to Mt. Horeb and hearing the still small voice), from *Pilgrim's Progress*, and from Dallas Wiebe's book, *Our Asian Journey*, about the Claas Epp trek to Central Asia to meet the Lord's return." Hearing from Anna about Dallas's presence in his own hometown, Darrell called Dallas at his motel and invited him to end that weekend's Sunday morning service with a reading from his novel.

"That was a great climax to the service," Anna recalled, "and Dallas got a round of applause." James Juhnke reflected later: "I assume that Dallas was moved by his welcome at Bethel College Mennonite Church [BCMC] because it represented a return to Kansas roots from which he had been alienated." In fact, Juhnke continued, the event "might be called 'The Triumphant Return of a Repentant (Maybe) Skyblue.'" Dallas's novel *Our Asian Journey*, after all, Juhnke observed, "was part of a pilgrimage of circling back toward reconciliation—reconciliation with his people and with God. As he said, he wrote that entire book to justify one sentence about God's love." Well, Dallas, in spite of what Juhnke says here, was not prone to contrition. In fact his work, apart from its sometimes startling "edge," revealed from the very beginning his spiritual propensities: his committed nonconformity made him no less a striver.

For that Sunday morning event, James Juhnke recalled, "Dallas wore very informal clothes—faded jeans and flannel shirt—quite distinctive among the BCMC coats and ties. He read his manuscript with passion, and the congregation applauded enthusiastically, which was unusual for this 'Mennonite high church' congregation." Juhnke continued:

> I think BCMC's welcome of Dallas had something to do with a Mennonite need to come to terms with the story of Claas Epp and the Great Trek, and with the way that story and those people have been misunderstood and unfairly discredited in Mennonite communities. In a sense, Dallas was able to memorialize his despised ancestors on his own

---

2 Used with permission. I would like to thank James Juhnke for permission to quote from both Anna Kreider Juhnke's letter and his own communication with me.

terms. (Take that, C. Henry Smith, and all you other pious progressive Mennonite historians.)[3]

Shortly after Dallas Wiebe died in May 2008, Paul Tiessen and I received in the mail a CD with a message from him, declaring that he had wanted to save friends and family the trouble and expense of gathering for his memorial service. So, on the first day of his 79th year, in anticipation of his death, he had recorded his own memorial, including readings of his own poetry and prose: a favorite Skyblue essay on confession (from which I derive my epigraph), a passage from *Our Asian Journey*, and some of his most recent poems, including "God Speaks to the Geriatric Convention," quoted below, and others. It was fitting that his service was made up almost entirely of his readings from his work.

The first time I featured some of Dallas's poetry in church, a theologian friend called me later that day to declare that he had experienced a remarkable sense of "worship" that morning, and to confess that he had been so moved by the service he had had to leave the sanctuary early, for fear of losing his composure in public. (When he stepped into the lobby he found another member of the congregation, pacing, similarly affected.) Dallas's words had had a profound impact on them both. The poems I had read that day were taken from a volume Paul Tiessen and I published in 2008. Dallas had approved the proofs of this small, limited-edition volume (50 numbered copies) entitled *Monument: Poems on Aging and Dying* shortly before he died of heart failure on May 1 that year. His own first copy of the book was still in the mail when he passed away. The following three poems[4] are included in that volume; they offer a voice distinctive enough to unsettle or inspire a particular kind of Sunday morning.

God Speaks to the Geriatric Convention

You should read the Old Testament
to see how old people
messed up my world
and the price
you have all had to pay
for it.
You should consider the idea of covenant,

---

3 Juhnke adds: "Truth is, Mennonites have not gotten Claas Epp and the Great Trek out of their system. That remains an unfinished process."

4 Used with permission, with thanks to Ericka Wiebe and Jeff Hillard.

the agreement to live
according to my laws
and what happens
when you don't.
You should remember
that my justice and your justice
are not the same thing.
You should keep in mind
the words "abomination,"
"wrath" and "scourge."
You should never forget
that I'm omniscient, omnipresent
and omnipotent—and you're not.
You should imagine
that when you walk
through the valley of the shadow of death
that I am the one
who casts the shadow.
You should acknowledge
that even a good shepherd
eats mutton,
and that's why
he leads you to green pastures
and still waters.
You certainly know
that if someone prepares a table
before you, someone
has to pay the bill,
and that the oil
that runs off your head
is expensive.
You've probably guessed
that goodness and mercy
are in short supply
and that your share
may not be available.
If you plan to dwell in my house,
you may need a reservation.
But be of good cheer.

Lift up your eyes
 to the everlasting hills
 and I'll do what I can
 to focus your bleary vision.
Raise your feeble voices
 in my adoration
 and I'll provide a catchy tune.
Warble, wobble and twitch
 into a dance of praise
 for my grace
 and I'll tap and clap along.
Never forget that only I know
 what eternity is like.
I hope you like surprises.
Have a good day.

Let's Pretend

Each morning I arise and pretend
 that I'm alive.
It's a good way to start the day
 even though the heartbeat's a little slower,
 the blood a little thinner
 and the appetite fails completely.
Putting on shoes and clothes is an act of faith
 that I will last out the day.
Swallowing pills is an act of trust
 that my cardiologist knows what he's doing.
Going to the bathroom
 seems a waste of time.
I pretend that breakfast is nourishing.
I pretend the sun is shining.
I pretend that the clocks are working.
Nothing deters my imagination
 as I sweep my porch,
 collect the mail and pay my bills
As if I had all time before me
And it was just another day

out of a multitude of days.
Which it is
  except each one could be my last one.
"Let's pretend," I say to myself,
  "that I have a future.
Let's pretend that there is much to be done
  and that there is time for the doing."
As I pretend,
  I remind myself
  not to buy new socks,
  not to check out long books from the library
  and never to buy green bananas.

A Morning Prayer in Old Age

Lord, let my knees bend
  one more time.
Let my ears hear and my eyes see
  one more day.
Let the words of my mouth
  not be slurred.
Let the meditations of my heart
  not fibrillate,
  and let me breathe enough.
Help me to rise from my bed,
  to bend over and put on my socks,
  to stay upright while putting on
  my underclothes, a shirt and trousers.
Help me to tie my shoelaces.
  Grant me the strength
  to descend the stairs
  and sit down for breakfast.
Grant me the ability
  to close my hands
  on the handle of a cup
  and on the handle of a spoon.
Grant me the skill
  to lift the cup to my lips
  and the spoon to my mouth.

Grant me the courage
to drink my tea and chew my food,
to swallow and not choke.
Sustain my attention
so that I take the right pills
in the right number.
Sustain the miracle of blood circulating
without clotting
and without the arteries closing.
Bestow upon my ears
the ability to resonate
to a Mozart sonata.
Bestow upon my voice
the power to whisper
this prayer aloud.
Bless me with thought
so that at noon
I can remember
what I prayed for at dawn.
If all is well, Lord,
when darkness falls,
Anoint my sleep
with the hope of rising
one more time.

WORKS CITED

Juhnke, James. Emails to the author. 14 December 2010, 2 February 2011, 10 March 2011.

Tiessen, Hildi Froese. "Literary Refractions [an introduction to Dallas Wiebe's 'Can a Mennonite Be an Atheist?']." *Conrad Grebel Review*, vol 16, Fall 1998, pp. 120–121.

Wiebe, Dallas. *Monument: Poems on Aging and Dying*. Sand Hills Books, 2008.

———. *Skyblue's Essays: fictions*. Burning Deck, 1995.

Thirteen

Homelands, Identity Politics, and the Trace: What Remains for the Mennonite Reader?*

THE WINTER OF 2012 was a rich season for avid readers of what many have come to refer to as "Mennonite" literature. A series of public readings and lectures by and about Mennonite writers at Conrad Grebel University College in Waterloo, Ontario, drew audiences of over a hundred on Wednesday evenings week after week from January to March. At the end of March the sixth international conference on Mennonite/s Writing, this time held at Eastern Mennonite University in Virginia, attracted similar numbers of readers and writers over four days—all presumably interested in the phenomenon of Mennonite literature that had begun to take shape as a literary fact in Canada in the decade before the first conference on Mennonite/s Writing was convened in Waterloo, Ontario, in 1990. It was mostly self-identified Mennonites who gathered at these events in 2012. There are Mennonites, it would appear, who like to read texts and gather around authors who, in the midst of a range of subjects, tell stories and evoke language, settings, and circumstances that resonate, often at a profound level, with their own experience.

---

* First published as Hildi Froese Tiessen, "Homelands, Identity Politics, and the Trace: What Remains for the Mennonite Reader?" *Mennonite Quarterly Review*, vol. 87, 2013, pp. 11–22.

It is clear that while Mennonite writing in Canada has evolved over the years, its keenly engaged though sometimes skittish Mennonite readers have grown into a palpable, though by no means monolithic, audience. This paper is in part driven by my respect for and curiosity about that audience, which by its very existence makes implicit demands on the writers whose works they read—demands occasionally resisted by the writers themselves, who sometimes feel constrained by their Mennonite readers' real or assumed assumptions or expectations.

Initially, the audience's postulations about the literary works they read would have been framed, in large measure, both by Mennonites' experience of the apparently coherent Canadian Mennonite world of the mid-twentieth century—augmented by the collective trauma represented by Rudy Wiebe's first novel, *Peace Shall Destroy Many* (1962)—and by the dynamic identity politics that came into play in the world-at-large in later decades, when the apparent integrity of the Canadian Mennonite world clearly began to fragment. The present Mennonite audience of Mennonite literary texts, while invoking with less urgency the assumptions, identifications, and imperatives of past decades, continues to read and ponder the plethora of literary productions by writers of Mennonite heritage. Given this keen interest, the question inevitably emerges: What do these Mennonite readers expect of the Mennonite text? Indeed, what do they want of Mennonite writers? And can the writers—do they, will they—deliver on these expectations? What follows is a foray into the landscape these questions inscribe.

Homelands

When I was invited, a few years ago, to present a paper on Mennonite/s writing in the context of studies in diaspora,[1] I inadvertently drew laughter from my audience by confessing that when I began to think about Mennonites and diaspora, the first thing that came to mind was the Mennonite *literary* diaspora of recent decades: the dispersal of many of the first generation of English-language Canadian Mennonite writers from Winnipeg—the city with one of the largest concentrations of Mennonites in the world, and the centre,

---

[1] That paper, entitled "'Well then, Eric Reimer, where are you going?' Mennonites Writing Diaspora," was prepared for a panel at *Narrating Mennonite Canada: History and/as Literature*, a colloquium hosted by Smaro Kamboureli and Robert Zacharias at the TransCanada Institute, University of Guelph, February 27, 2009. Other members of the panel were Royden Loewen and Rudy Wiebe.

the point of origin (if we are to accept the trope of the myth of origins and assume we can identify a beginning) of English-language Canadian Mennonite writing. They include Rudy Wiebe, who had settled in Winnipeg but who was in effect cast out by Manitoba Mennonites after the publication of his first novel; David Waltner-Toews, who declared himself a refugee; Patrick Friesen, who was drawn to the west coast; Sandra Birdsell, who transplanted herself to Regina; Di Brandt, who was lured to Windsor and then Brandon; and Miriam Toews, who decamped to Toronto, to name a few.

A review of some of the texts that make up the multidisciplinary scholarly literature on diaspora reveals that an abiding assumption underlying much of the work on the subject is that to speak of diaspora is to engage the concept of "homeland." Texts by writers of Mennonite heritage in Canada suggest that these writers would likely not readily agree on the nature and identity of a Mennonite "homeland"—if they could be persuaded to ponder the notion of homeland at all, with its suggestions of fixity, cultural authenticity, and the purity of origins. In *The Blue Mountains of China* (1970) Rudy Wiebe has a character posit for Mennonites the sort of homeland claimed by Jews and invoked in classic discussions of diaspora; for the Mennonites, he says adamantly, there is no such place on earth. Patrick Friesen and others have invoked the New Jerusalem as another kind of homeland: the place members of my parents' generation might have invoked when they looked heavenward in a posture of hope or despair and declared that they wanted to "go home." Sarah Klassen and others reference Anabaptist points of origin that prevailed in the era of the martyrs—what Di Brandt refers to as "the burning times." Others, including Sandra Birdsell, in effect locate the Mennonites' point of departure in the last century, in the villages and estates of what the ancestors referred to simply as "Russia."

No matter what place Canadian Mennonites designate as "home," and no matter how long it's been since their ancestors left their "homeland," it could be argued that Canadian writers of Mennonite heritage have, during the most recent half century of Mennonite/s writing, tended to think of themselves as not so much connected to a particular location of origin as situated within a distinctive cultural construct defined by diverse and compelling narratives of heritage and history. Their work seems to draw upon and to confirm a particular, if tenuous, sustaining culture that could be read as a shared sense of continuity.

Many writers of Mennonite heritage in Canada have written about, or invoked, fragments at least of a shared cultural past. Cultural theorist Stuart Hall has suggested that people bear "the traces of [the] particular cultures, traditions, languages, systems of belief, texts and histories" that have shaped them. Sometimes they take "a symbolic detour through the past" as they move into the future (361). Writers of Mennonite heritage, whether they have grown up as the children of immigrants or as descendants of immigrants who settled in Canada one or more generations before, even when their subject matter is not overtly "Mennonite," presumably draw upon collectively shared representations of the past and a certain continuity of meaning. That is, they would seem to share some imputed commonalities or a certain "life-in-common": what one commentator refers to as that "small currency of a community's existence, its way of life, values, and so on" (Booth 39). And, of course, in their texts—even while they might eschew the limits of one fixed identity—they have reconstructed those pasts and their traditions: made them visible to Mennonites and others, and, to a degree at least, stabilized them.

At the same time, as we have observed in the growing body of Mennonite literary texts over several decades, various writers of Mennonite heritage in various contexts have resisted, in diverse gestures and tones, being identified as "Mennonite writers"—in effect invoking a gesture by Philip Roth: "I am not a Jewish writer; I am a writer who is a Jew" with "I'm not a Mennonite writer; I am a writer ..."[2] Many Canadian Mennonite writers have been compelled to ponder the question of how to slough off a cultural heritage rich with literary potential and with an ever-larger audience keen to encounter "Mennonite" material, and at the same time continue to write, as writers tend to put it, "what they know." Such a writers' dilemma has found its way into Mennonite fictions, where it is carried by characters confronted with these sorts of questions: What does that religious and/or cultural heritage have to do with me? How do I negotiate this ethnic landscape without becoming entrapped by it? What would it mean to be a writer who has stepped outside all Mennonite circles altogether? What does the Mennonite *reader* want of me anyway? Indeed, in recent decades the very notion of "homeland"—if I can return to that trope—is progressively losing its place in communal memory. Experience and identity is grounded, instead, in the complex textures of real lived experience, here and now—most often in some palpable place in the Canadian landscape, often the Canadian prairie, frequently in or near Winnipeg.

So, what am I saying? That what we have come to call Mennonite/s writing in Canada is richly diverse and in a state of flux. Mennonite pasts might remain prominent in Mennonite historical narratives, but the narrators and

---

2 Roth is qtd. in Wisse, 11.

characters in fiction and the speakers in poems are not necessarily concerned with how to negotiate—especially not in any conventional ways—religious and cultural landscapes dominated by the forceful community-endorsed oppressors that readers encountered in the narratives of *Peace Shall Destroy Many*, *The Shunning*, *The Salvation of Yasch Siemens*, and even *A Complicated Kindness*, or in the work of Di Brandt and others. They are less concerned with that landscape than with the here and now, where other cultural forces prevail—forces perhaps just as powerful as those identified in these prominent literary texts, but diverse and profuse and "worldly" and unstable. In the new Canadian Mennonite writing, history and tradition are no longer authoritative. They needn't be thrown out, but they have lost their claim to normativity.

As a literary historian I am interested in this dynamic, not least because the new Mennonite literature and its readers are asking different questions than those that have been foregrounded in Mennonite literature and Mennonite literary studies over the past few decades. Many writers, for example, are less interested in origins than in milieus; less concerned with group history than with individual becoming; less compelled by essential identity than by multifaceted identifications. They are taken less with traditional notions of community than with what feminist materialist Rosi Braidotti calls "multiple ecologies of belonging" (19). Many writers embrace the option of shucking off their inherited role as the children or descendants of immigrants affected by their forebears' values and beliefs. They have not had the experience of living in a language not their own. They choose not to look upon themselves as marginal. They are not taken with notions of displacement, exile, and deterritorialization, but rather assert the liberty to locate themselves in a "worldly" present. And so in their work identity politics and essentialisms are, in large measure at least, replaced by expressions of where and how they, as individuals, are living in the present—among "imminent and contingent expression[s] of ... earthly place-time" (Hroch 52). And most of their Mennonite readers share with them these conditions.

Were any of today's Mennonite writers or readers to presume to invoke something like a "homeland"—a place of beginning and consummation—to define what we've come to call Mennonite literature, they might do well to appropriate instead an understanding articulated by Gilles Deleuze and Félix Guattari in another context altogether, when they speak of a literature emerging "as a result of an ambience or milieu rather than an origin, of a becoming rather than a history, of a geography rather than a historiography, of a grace rather than a nature" (96–97). Mennonite writing—even the historical literary text—persists, that is, as a contingent expression of the here and now.

Identity Politics

Literature, writer Bruce Bawer observed in *The Hudson Review* in 1995, is "passing through an Age of Identity Politics, when ... many writers view themselves (and are viewed by others) as representatives of certain identity groups ... and view literature, moreover, as an outpouring of group consciousness, an articulation of group solidarity, and a means to group empowerment" (19). Mennonite literature in Canada emerged in the era of identity politics. The year after the publication of Rudy Wiebe's first novel in 1962, the federal government set up the Royal Commission on Bilingualism and Biculturalism to ensure wider recognition of the basic cultural dualism of Canada: English and French. The Royal Commission met from 1963 until 1969, and while it prompted the government to frame new terms of reference related to biculturalism (most notably, perhaps, the Official Languages Act), it also precipitated in citizens of non-English and non-French background an acute sense of the government's seeming willingness to ignore, in its official deliberations, the abiding links of the *non*-English/*non*-French to their own heritage. The Royal Commission's myopic obsession with biculturalism (oddly sustained by academics like Ronald Sutherland, who traveled from university to university in the early 1970s proclaiming that Canadian literature must be defined only in terms of the struggle between the English and the French) prompted urgent queries from the implicitly disenfranchised "other" ethnics that could be summed up in the question: "What about *us*?" What resulted from the unrest of these "others" and the spirit of the times (during which all Canadians were discovering a new interest—especially after the spectacular success of Expo 67—in what it might mean to be Canadian) was an emerging understanding that we now accept as the Canadian "given" of multiculturalism.

In September 1971, the same year the Canadian government announced a multicultural policy within a bicultural framework, Mennonites in Winnipeg, as if recognizing themselves in a new way as an ethnic group under the new regime, founded the *Mennonite Mirror*, a magazine published ten times per year, featuring Mennonite cultural activities in general, and literary productions in particular. In 1972 the federal government established a Multicultural Directorate within the Department of the Secretary of State "to assist in the integration of multicultural policies and programs." Multiculturalism—which refers, in the language of the Canadian Charter of Rights and Freedoms (1982), to "the preservation and enhancement of the multicultural heritage of Canadians"—has since then remained a dominant feature of Canada's cultural landscape (Dewing). And throughout the next decade writers among the Mennonites—from novelist Rudy Wiebe to poets Patrick Friesen, Victor Enns, and David Waltner-Toews; translator Al Reimer; and children's author Barbara Smucker—began to mirror their people to themselves in volumes of fiction and poetry rooted in Mennonite experience. A deluge of Mennonite literary works in English followed, with the arrival in the 1980s of poets Audrey Poetker, John Weier, Di Brandt, and Sarah Klassen, and writers of fiction Sandra Birdsell and Armin Wiebe; and in the 1990s and later, Rosemary Nixon, David Elias, Miriam Toews, David Bergen, and Carrie Snyder, as well as Barbara Nickel, Carla Funk, Dora Dueck, Vern Thiessen, and others.

Mennonites were not alone in finding their voice (as some would put it) in those decades. Since the literatures of Canada tend to follow immigration patterns, and Canadian immigration policy had for the most part restricted access to Canada by people outside the preferred, nonthreatening Western European immigrant groups, it took a while for the now prominent Asian and South Asian and West Indian writers, for example, to begin to write out of their ethnocultural experience in a Canadian setting. Mennonite writers, representative of one of the earliest of Canada's minority literature cultures, were not alone in the geographical hotbed of Mennonite writing—Winnipeg and southern Manitoba—as Kate Bitney and Andris Taskans remarked in their "Introduction" to a 2007 collection of new Manitoba writing, where they observed, for example: "the past three decades saw the rise in Manitoba of writers from a Mennonite background, the coming of age of a new generation of Jewish writers and the development of an Aboriginal writing community" (5). Soon enough, writers of Chinese or Sri Lankan or Jamaican descent also stood alongside the Mennonites, who had themselves followed groups like the first generation of Jewish writers in developing Canadian literatures tinged with the distinctive markers of their identity.

While I speak of identity politics, it might be useful to admit that I am driven, in my own pursuits relative to Mennonite literature, by my own desire that creative writers who can offer me resonances of a view of the world screened through experiences of having been a Mennonite—as multifarious and divergent as those experiences might be—will continue to write, to give voice to memories and understandings, experiences or sensibilities—however strong or slight—I am able to imagine we might have in common. As a Mennonite reader, I recognize and resonate with something in their work, not only by virtue of their ability to invoke, perhaps, our common historical memory, but also because of their capacity to evoke the conflicted sensibility of an ambivalent, somewhat cynical, urban, assimilated, perhaps agnostic, postmodern Mennonite.

Ethnic identity is not passed on as a simple inheritance; it is revised and reinvented by successive generations, and by the unique individuals of which these generations are comprised. Mennonite writers traveled a substantial distance from *Peace Shall Destroy Many* to *A Complicated Kindness*; Mennonite readers have traveled that distance too. The new Mennonite writing reflects—often discretely, even unconsciously—a dynamic that suggests what it means to be a Mennonite in the complex, multidimensional worlds we now occupy. Reader and writer (here I borrow some of the language of Dan Miron, in his study of "New Jewish Literary Thinking") could be said to share a "perception of reality through (or also through) the screen of the experience" of *being* a Mennonite in the world—an experience "that can be as divergent and multifarious as that of being in love"(307).

None of this is meant to suggest "Mennonite" should be taken as a totalizing or fixed category, or that writers of Mennonite heritage should in any sense be defined by any one strand of their being, any more than Mennonite readers should be. Our Mennonite ancestors might have imagined that they could transport a culture from one place in the world to another, but, as human geographer Tim Cresswell has observed, "The idea of culture as a coherent whole located and bounded [has been] effectively deconstructed by a new focus on transnationalism and flows of people and commodities which effectively deterritorialized identity" (18). Rudy Wiebe knew that, and told us about it as early as *Peace Shall Destroy Many*. The place any one of us might occupy in the world today, as Benzi Zhang, in his study of Chinese diaspora poetry in America has observed, is "a site of cultural transliteration." Identity, he remarks, lies at the "intersection of various cultural crossings" (137).

The works of writers of Mennonite heritage, although they might bear traces of what we might call family resemblances, do not function as a kind of data set. Mennonites anywhere in North America give expression to diverse sets of "practices, bodies of knowledge, conventions, and lifestyles" developed independent of any community of origin (Featherstone qtd. in Zhang 137). We have no option, by now, but to deconstruct the term "Mennonite" when we use it as a modifier for the literature of contemporary poets and novelists and dramatists of Mennonite heritage. But that doesn't mean we need to abandon the term. Perhaps we need to redeploy it, to release it from difficulties associated with past usage.[3] The past, W. James Booth has observed, "leaves its traces on our character, our values, sentiments, and habits" (25). But, he

---

3 I would like to acknowledge Linda Nicholson and Steven Seidman for their discussion of similar matters in their "Introduction" to *Social Postmodernism: Beyond Identity Politics*.

continues, citing Galen Strawson's oft-quoted, provocative observation, "The past can be present or alive in the present without being present or alive as the past" (36). Elsewhere Strawson has observed: "The past can be alive—arguably more genuinely alive—in the present simply in so far as it has helped to shape the way one is in the present, just as musicians' playing can incorporate and body forth their past practice without being mediated by any explicit memory of it" (432). Finally, as we exit an era of identity politics, we do not need to get rid of history and memory and tradition, but rather simply to challenge their claims to normativity.[4]

Traces

In a paper she gave at the first conference on Mennonite/s Writing in 1990, Canadian literary critic Clara Thomas declared that the work of Margaret Laurence was able to identify her to herself as the works of Rudy Wiebe were not able to do. This comment has remained with me these twenty-some years, and I have made reference to it in my writing now and then, always inserting an inverted corollary: that the work of Rudy Wiebe, for example, identifies me to myself in a manner that the novels of Margaret Laurence do not.

Like the late Margaret Laurence, Clara Thomas is a Scottish-Canadian Presbyterian; in 1990—and perhaps even today—we might think of both these women as members of the "invisible majority" in Canada: members of the group Canadian Mennonites once unselfconsciously referred to simply as "the English." Perhaps Thomas's statement had such an impact on me because of its startling suggestion that even members of a dominant "Anglo-Canadian" majority might find traces of themselves—intimations of their heritage, sensibilities—in works of literature. I had come to regard the literature of "the English" in Canada as so normative that I did not recognize the traces that evoked from Thomas what was for me so surprising a declaration. Before I began to read Rudy Wiebe the literatures of Canada were always, to a certain degree, alienating; they always told someone else's story. In fact, people I might recognize as culturally "like me"—figures who might identify me to myself (to use Thomas's phrase)—never made an appearance, not even as minor characters. It was no wonder, then, that I and other Mennonite readers had taken so much pleasure in the work of writers of Mennonite heritage introduced to regional, national, and international audiences during

---

4 Thank you to Petra Hroch, who has adopted this insight from Deleuze.

the closing decades of the twentieth century. Like most Mennonite readers of my generation, I learned to read Mennonite literature in an age of identity politics, and certain dynamics and challenges endemic to that age influenced how each of us came to see ourselves. "In a sense, we haven't got an identity until somebody tells our story," Robert Kroetsch observed in an interview with Margaret Laurence. Yes. "The fiction makes us real," he added (*Creation* 63). Aha.

This paper began to take shape in the aftermath of a conversation with a young academic, Petra Hroch, working in feminist materialist philosophy. Returning from a scholarly conference in the USA following several months of study in the Netherlands, Hroch lamented, in passing, that for the most part American intellectual feminism had not moved beyond identity politics— beyond a consideration of basic, rather conventional questions related to the representation of women—unlike many predominantly European feminist philosophers who celebrate and build upon feminist thought as productive of a plethora of innovative intellectual paradigms. The notion of moving beyond identity politics in feminist philosophical thinking must have implications I could adapt for Mennonite literary studies, I thought, a field where identity politics often runs us aground as we try to find ways of talking about the writers who ostensibly share our memories and sensibilities—and, at the same time, try to refrain from entrapping the writers and their readers (including ourselves) in limiting, confounding essentialist discourse.

It must be clear, as I proceed, that I recognize that writers who have been identified and/or have self-identified as "Mennonite" are by no means circumscribed only by an audience that self-identifies as Mennonite; Mennonite writers are read across the nation and around the world—by readers who know they are Mennonite, and by others as well. But it is perhaps only the Mennonite *reader* for whom the recognition of a writer as Mennonite has any lasting resonant meaning. My deliberations about Clara Thomas and Margaret Laurence have led me to numerous questions, this among them: if literary productions of writers of Mennonite heritage were to be found by virtually all readers, for the most part, to be "mainstream" in the sense that Margaret Laurence is "mainstream"—that is, if the general reader were to cease to recognize the literature of Mennonites as distinctive—what remains of, or in, these texts for the reader who self-identifies as a Mennonite? Would Mennonite readers who celebrated the emergence of what Andris Taskans has referred to as the "Mennonite miracle" be left, in those circumstances, without texts that in some way "identify them to themselves?" as Thomas observed of the work of Laurence? That is, if the new "Mennonite" literary text were to prove to be, simply, utterly everyone's text—the normative "universal" text—what might remain to allow the Mennonite reader to say that *this text is particular*; in fact it "identifies me to myself"?

It could be that Mennonite writers, in the words of Robert Kroetsch about writers in general, "write books, not in search of [their] identity, but against the notion of identity" (*Lovely* 188), that they dare what Kroetsch calls "that ultimate *contra-diction*: … uncreat[ing] themselves into existence" *(Lovely* 63). When they succeed at this "uncreating" and the Mennonite text is in effect no longer recognizable as a "Mennonite" text, what then? In such a circumstance, is a reader like me, who embraces the text that I find resonant, the text that identifies me to myself as a Mennonite, once more bereft of texts that somehow invoke for me my particular heritage, history, sensibility? Perhaps there is comfort for someone like me implicit in Kroetsch's famous observation that "[t]here is always something left behind. That is the essential paradox. Even abandonment gives us memory" (*Lovely* 2). What compels us, he observes, is "always a question of trace. What remains of what does not remain?" (*The Hornbooks* 8). When the Mennonite text becomes the mainstream text, the Mennonite reader might come to covet or cherish the trace of which Kroetsch speaks—the trace, we might say, possibly "visible only to those who know where to look" (del Toro). It could be that the public in general might cease identifying texts as Mennonite or writers as Mennonite. Even then, though, we might hope that the Mennonite *reader* would persist, to embrace the trace: the absent presence—however slight or penetrative—that remains, to identify the Mennonite reader to herself.

WORKS CITED

Bawer, Bruce. "Violated by Ideas: Reflections on Literature in an Age of Identity Politics." *The Hudson Review*, vol. 48, no. 1, 1995, pp. 19–33.

Bitney, Katherine, and Andris Taskans, eds. *A/Cross Sections: New Manitoba Writing*. Manitoba Writers' Guild, 2007.

Braidotti, Rosi. *Nomadic Theory: The Portable Rosi Braidotti*. Columbia UP, 2011.

Booth, W. James. *Communities of Memory: On Witness, Identity, and Justice*. Cornell UP, 2006.

Cresswell, Tim. "Introduction: Theorizing Place." *Mobilizing Place, Placing Mobility: The*

  Politics of Representation in a Globalized World, ed. Ginette Verstraete and Tim Cresswell, Editions Rodopi B.V., 2002, pp. 11–31.
Deleuze, Gilles, and Félix Guattari. *What is Philosophy?* Trans. Hugh Tomlinson and Graham Burchell, Columbia UP, 1994.
Del Toro, Guillermo. (Director and writer.) *Pan's Labyrinth*. Warner Brothers/Picturehouse, 2006.
Dewing, Michael. "Canadian Multiculturalism." Parliamentary Information and Research Service, Report Number PRB 09-20E, www.parl.gc.ca.
Hall, Stuart. "Culture, Community, Nation." *Cultural Studies*, vol. 7, no. 3, 1993, pp. 349–363.
Hroch, Petra. "Sustainable Concepts: Pedagogy, Politics, and a Planet-Yet-to Come." *For a People-Yet-to-Come: Deleuze, Politics, and Education*, ed. J. Wallin and Matthew Carlin, Palgrave, 2014, pp. 49–76.
Kroetsch, Robert. *The Hornbooks of Rita K.* U Alberta P, 2001.
———. *The Lovely Treachery of Words: Essays Selected and New.* Oxford UP, 1989.
———, Pierre Gravel, and James Bacque. *Creation*. Including the Authors' Conversations with Margaret Laurence, Milton Wilson, J. Raymond Brazeau. New Press, 1970.
Miron, Dan. *From Continuity to Contiguity: Toward a New Jewish Literary Thinking*. Stanford UP, 2010.
Nicholson, Linda, and Steven Seidman. "Introduction." *Social Postmodernism: Beyond Identity Politics*, ed. Linda Nicholson and Steven Seidman, Cambridge UP, 1995, pp. 1–35.
Strawson, Galen. "Against Narrativity." *Ratio*, vol. 17, no. 4, 2004, pp. 428–452.
Zhang, Benzi. "Of Nonlimited Locality/Identity: Chinese Diaspora Poetry in America." *Journal of American Studies*, vol. 40, no. 1, 2006, pp. 133–153.

Fourteen

After Identity: Liberating the Mennonite Literary Text[*]

THIS CHAPTER BEGINS with a number of assumptions: (1) that critics of Mennonite literature are in the company of a vast number of scholars who have determined that the literary-critical approaches of recent decades—in which critics (and writers) found themselves "in deep conversation with their historical contexts and the social worlds or publics they engage" (Edwards 232)—are inadequate as interpretive strategies; (2) that, even though scholars of Mennonite literature do not share all the concerns (about race, nation, etc.) of a range of literary critics focused on other minority culture literatures in North America, they might be richly informed by the stimulating critical conversations about "identity" and "after identity" occurring in fields such as Jewish American literature or Asian American literature, for example; and (3) that any discussion of identity issues relative to Mennonite/s writing remains a vexing matter not least because concerns about identity in general continue to challenge the complexly layered landscape of Mennonite communities across North America and beyond.

---

[*] First published as Hildi Froese Tiessen, "After Identity: Liberating the Mennonite Literary Text." *After Identity: Mennonite Writing in North America*, ed. Robert Zacharias, Pennsylvania State UP, 2015, pp. 210–225.

It is worth observing, at the outset, the diversity of people who identify themselves as Mennonites and the heterogeneous nature of the tag "Mennonite," routinely used to identify people by creed and culture first but most often qualified by distinguishing identifiers such as "Canadian" and "American," or by epithets such as "Swiss" and "Russian," or in terms of migratory groups such as *Kanadier* and *Russländer*, or by denominational divisions such as Mennonite Brethren, Bergthaler, Kleine Gemeinde, and many others. (Margaret Loewen Reimer's *One Quilt Many Pieces: A Guide to Mennonite Groups in Canada* lists a few dozen denominational groups in Canada alone, quite apart from the many distinctive language-based clusters among them: German, French, Hispanic, Chinese, Vietnamese, Korean, Arabic, Punjabi, and others.) Furthermore, when literary critics speak of Mennonite literature, they tend to refer to writing produced only by individuals identified with certain groups within the North American Mennonite community, which itself, even in its immense diversity, represents barely 30 percent of the world's 1,775,000 Mennonites.[1] Moreover, other sorts of modifiers, such as *ethnic* or *secular*, are much more readily acknowledged as appropriate descriptors of Mennonites in Canada than they are of Mennonites in the United States, where Mennonites are generally regarded as a religious group, and where the word *ethnic* has troublesome resonances not generally detected by most Canadian Mennonites, who have long seen themselves—and have been seen in the public eye—as belonging to both religious and ethnic communities.

This essay barely begins to explore one aspect of an emerging subject for the literary critic interested in Mennonite/s writing: Mennonite literature "after" (i.e., "apart from" or "in pursuit of" or "regarding" or "subsequent to") "identity." This subject doggedly confronts anyone working in the field, in particular the editors of the two journals at present devoted exclusively to Mennonite/s writing: *Rhubarb* magazine and *CMW Journal* (online)[2], in which editorial declarations concerning "who is a Mennonite writer" and "of what does Mennonite writing consist" might include statements such as this one from the frontmatter of *Rhubarb*, asserting that the magazine accepts work "by non-Mennonites about Mennonites" as well as by writers "who self-define as Mennonites, whether practicing, declined, or resistant," or this announcement from the editor of *CMW Journal*, which describes the "emerging writers" of

---

[1] These were numbers of baptized members in 2012 (Mennonites practice adult baptism). In 2022, the number was 2.13 million members. See the World Directory of the Mennonite World Conference, www.mwc-cmm.org.

[2] The *CMW Journal* is now titled the *Journal of Mennonite Writing*.

a recent issue simply as "those who have spent formative years with or who have chosen to hang out with Mennonites."[3]

What would it mean to edit a journal or magazine devoted to "Mennonite" writing, or to compile an anthology featuring Mennonite work, or to convene a conference on Mennonite/s Writing if none of the work presented or discussed made any explicit reference to things Mennonite or none of the writers self-declared as Mennonite? What does the multiply inflected term "Mennonite/s writing" signify? How is the term useful? How does it serve writers or readers? What would it mean to define it in relatively exacting ways? In what manner do we need to retain some version of it? What if it disappeared altogether? Do any of these questions have any import for anyone beyond the relatively few who make it their business to ask?

This essay acknowledges the rich diversity that exists within the ever-expanding panorama that is Mennonite/s writing—a range of work much of which in no palpable way addresses distinctive ways of "being Mennonite," work including the eclectic range of poems and fictions published in specialized and mainstream magazines, journals, and anthologies. That valuable work poses a particular range of identity questions within the field of Mennonite/s writing. What concerns me here is one thing in particular: the ways in which any literature that has been, and continues to be, encompassed by the circle of Mennonite/s writing has been or might be affected, inflected, refracted, or infected by what critic Wai Chee Dimock refers to as "literary causality" derived from "a territorial [or territorialized] jurisdiction" (*Through Other Continents* 3) generally identified, in this case, by the descriptive moniker Mennonite—and the sorts of illuminations and new possibilities that might proceed from this investigation.

This essay (which borrows language and insights from outside the Mennonite circle) urges us not to abandon identity issues in Mennonite writing altogether but to probe them vigorously—especially as the work of more and more writers who self-identify as Mennonite appears in print—and to explore avenues of interpretation that would foreground perspectives other than those rooted in identity categories. The chapter applauds the direction proposed by those who have urged the critics of Mennonite/s writing to move in new directions; to open up the conversation; to liberate the texts, the writers, the readers, and the critics themselves from a propensity to foreground referential knowledge and historical situations that have often tended to precede and guide—and limit—the accessibility of texts and reader response.

---

3 Quoted from a 26 April 2013 email circulated by *CMW Journal* editor Ann Hostetler.

During the era of identity politics and multiculturalism, the idea of identity in large measure "structured the field imaginary"[4] of any number of minor or major literatures, including Mennonite/s writing, in which deeply held assumptions about the relationship between literary texts and their contexts prevail. Although Mennonite writing continues to flourish in both Canada and the United States, introducing a vast range of voices and narratives, not only in novels and other major works but also via little magazines in print and online, critical responses to Mennonite literature—especially those written by commentators of Mennonite heritage—have tended to work with the tacit assumption that identity categories will, in large measure, continue to direct the reading and to condition the experience of Mennonite literary texts. Only recently have scholars begun to reframe the critical discourse related to Mennonite/s writing in Canada and the United States, to move beyond the familiar conventions of identity-based criticism and launch new conversations that a 2013 symposium identified as critical conversations about Mennonite/s writing "after identity."

Critics of Mennonite/s writing are by no means alone among literary critics looking for fresh ways to talk about the relationship between literature and identity or seeking ways to discuss literature without referring to matters related to identity. From the encouragement of French literary theorist Pascale Casanova, who, in the context of what she calls "the world republic of letters," advocates the abandonment of "habits of thought that create the illusion of uniqueness and insularity" (5), to the exhortation of Americanists such as Brian T. Edwards, who has observed that "the relationship between text and context needs to be reconsidered: the link is too stable when the text is understood as the translation of historical context and vice versa" (233), the call has gone out for critics across the spectrum of local, national, and world literatures to invent new critical discourses, to dislocate texts from their original contexts, to disturb notions of "national" or ethnic authenticity, to abandon what Michael P. Kramer refers to rather roughly as the "critical narcissism" whereby context precedes and guides reading ("Critical").

Mennonite literature is a small player in a vast landscape of writing that has "come of age" in recent decades and now finds itself in an era in which

---

4 I borrow this phrase from Michael Millner on American studies (541); see also Donald E. Pease. "National Identities, Postmodern Artifacts, and Postnational Narratives." *boundary 2*, vol. 19, no. 1, 1992, pp. 1–13.

that anchoring concept, "identity," is spoken of in terms of exhaustion (e.g., Palumbo-Liu 765; Roof 1; Millner 541) and abandonment (Lee passim); it is referred to as a concept "under erasure" and "no longer serviceable" (Hall 1–2). Resisting the urge to abolish identitarian categories even while recognizing that notions of identity have left critics with a range of vexing questions, Stuart Hall and others suggest that critics might make the effort to reconceptualize identity (2). Inspired by Dimock's assertion that the "'immortality' of literature must be understood ... as the continual emergence of interpretive contexts" ("Theory" 1065), the Mennonite reader and critic could be informed and enlightened by considering what it might mean to ease the Mennonite text away from its context, and by exploring what it might mean to dislocate and relocate it, and so, as Judith Roof has remarked in her commentary on "post-identity," to offer, in the world of Mennonite/s writing, "a glimmer through a tear in what once seemed to be the very fabric of culture" (5).

Because the critic of Mennonite literature would not be alone in exploring various means of escape from what Casanova calls the "intrusion of history" (xiii) and Paul Giles refers to as "the magic circle between text and context" (263), a consideration of the concerns and commentaries of other critics of literatures grounded in identity might be instructive here: the thinking of Benjamin Schreier, for example, who has composed a range of responses to what he identifies as the "fraught relationship between historiography and literary practice" in American Jewish literature ("Editor's Introduction" 1), or the stimulating commentaries offered by Asian American literary critics who have challenged in recent years "the assumed coherency if not the ultimate efficacy of Asian Americanness [for example] as a viable subject category" (Chen 186). These critics and many others are engaged in exploring, in various guises, the question that draws our attention here: how do we speak of a body of writing that has been identified, as Dimock (as I have already observed) puts it, by an adjective "derived from a territorial [or territorialized] jurisdiction" that has turned it into "a mode of literary causality" (*Through Other Continents* 3)—while abjuring references to its identity?

It might be useful to pause briefly here to make it clear that throughout this discussion I use the term "identity" as a concept closely related to notions of context and historicity. Among those who have tried to clarify the concept is French philosopher Paul Ricoeur, who has observed that the concept of identity tends to have "two major uses" (115). The first use refers to identity in the way that I, and most of the critics whom I refer to here, make use of it—to suggest sameness, or (Latin) *idem*, or (German) *Gleichheit*. When we speak of identity in this mode, we refer, according to David J. Leichter, in his commentary on Ricoeur, to the external projection of identity over the course of time; static and reductive characterization; "the habits, ethos, or ideology that defines an individual or a group"; or the norms, traditions, and practices through which a community might be identified (for a more expansive discussion, see Leichter 120–121). Ricoeur's second distinctive use of the term "identity" refers to identity as selfhood, or (Latin) *ipse*, or (German) *Selbstheit*: inner identity, the fluid and indeterminate self that persists despite changes in habit or opinion or desire (see Leichter 120). These two forms of identity, in the simplest terms, answer two questions: "What are you?" and "Who are you?" The apparent propensity of readers of identity-based texts to conflate or confuse these two conceptions of identity has created the kind of circumstance that has compelled many a writer of Mennonite heritage, for example, to balk at being identified as Mennonite because she observes that such identification can confine or conceal her as a writer, as a dynamic individual, and relegate her to a fixed type. I have heard many a Mennonite writer declare, in exasperation, a version of Philip Roth's frequently cited self-description, suggestive of Ricoeur's two forms: "I am not a Jewish writer; I am a writer who is a Jew" (qtd. in Wisse 11). One would not have to search far to discover any number of interviews with or articles by Mennonite writers (the novelists Rudy Wiebe, Miriam Toews, or David Bergen, for example) who address—sometimes sympathetically and sometimes irascibly—what it means for them to be known as Mennonite writers. One could trace, of course, among members of the Mennonite community, a propensity of both writer and reader alike to represent each other as "types."

Some commentators on matters of identity in literature, without reference to Ricoeur, have implicitly equated the two forms of identity that he identifies with two paradigmatic approaches to the literary text. They have urged critics to attend to the variable internal structures of a text (to engage in a form of close reading that, if they were to adopt his model, would be equivalent to a form of inner identity) and thus to avoid the pre-emptive constraints of context and historicity—a text's external structures, equivalent, these commentators might observe, to the static and reductive qualities associated with what Ricoeur identifies as *idem*, sameness, *Gleichheit*. As long as Mennonite writers and readers insist on *identifying* each other—corralling each other's being and sensibility by invoking sameness and stability—each might pre-empt the response of the other and perhaps limit the potential scope of the literary texts that span the spaces between them.

Vexing questions about identity have drawn the attention of American studies critics for a few decades now, including Edwards, who recently observed that placing texts (we'll say Mennonite texts) "in deep conversation with their historical contexts and the social worlds or publics they engage" has resulted in the construction of "a formidable framework." He continues, "Yet that critical structure has outlasted the conditions within which it was created" (232). Indeed. One could make the case that a number of large literary gestures in the landscape of Mennonite writing fairly directly address the very matter that Edwards identifies. Central characters in works as diverse as Wiebe's *Sweeter than All the World* or Toews's *A Complicated Kindness*, for example, among others, investigate the troubled and troubling relationship between historical "givens," or the "formidable framework" of which Edwards speaks, and contemporary conditions that belie their relevance—or even their palpable presence—for citizens of postmodern North America. Such a disjuncture between apparently moribund, or simply disappeared, social and religious understandings and the conditions that confront characters finding themselves compelled to negotiate the postmodern world lies at the heart, also, of Rhoda Janzen's bestselling American memoir, *Mennonite in a Little Black Dress*, in which the principal character literally travels back into a past context so incongruous with her modern worldly life that it appears quaint at best and ridiculous at worst.

So what does one speak of when one purports to address the issue of context/historical identity relative to Mennonite/s writing? A description of the social context in which Canadian Mennonite writing in particular emerged (the historical trajectory of American Mennonite history and American Mennonite/s writing, in many senses, is another matter altogether) could be borrowed from commentators who observe that the Jewish artist in America, for example, arose "at a time of crisis" and "during the transition from religious tribalism to worldliness."[5] Or from other prominent Jewish critics who—observing in 1977 that "the tensions of immigrant life" and "the tug-of-war between tradition and assimilation" (Kramer citing Irvin Howe, "Art" 306) no longer dominated the Jewish American experience—feared that Jewish literature had lost its subject and would disappear. Howe was wrong, but his comment is worth our attention. How do we speak of Mennonite writing in Canada now that virtually all members of the Mennonite community have

---

[5] See Greene and Peacock (91), quoting Aharon Appelfeld, commenting on the social contexts of Jewish American writing.

moved well beyond the sorts of conditions to which such commentaries might refer?

How do we speak of Mennonite writing—and how do writers write Mennonite—now? A provocative proclamation by Schreier in his essay on Philip Roth, if we could apply it to Mennonite writing, might be illuminating here: "It is not that Roth's characters do not want to be Jews; it is that they do not know how to describe themselves as Jews" (107). This observation, adapted for use in the world of Mennonite writing, seems to me to strike to the heart of the matter. It is not that characters in Mennonite fiction, for example (or, for that matter, the writers of Mennonite prose and poetry themselves), do not want to be Mennonite; the challenge that confronts fictional and real characters alike is how to identify, describe, or represent the Mennonite in the twenty-first century in North America. Ah, how to both embrace certain treasured aspects of Mennonite identity and escape its imperatives at the same time?

How do Mennonite writers describe their "people"? The task appears to have been relatively straightforward for Julia Kasdorf when she made the attempt in 1992, in her oft-anthologized poem "Mennonites," which begins, "We keep our quilts in closets and do not dance. / We hoe thistles along fence rows for fear / we may not be perfect as our Heavenly Father" and continues "We love Catherine the Great and the rich tracts / she gave us in the Ukraine," and "We love those Nazi soldiers who, like Moses, / led the last cattle cars rocking out of the Ukraine," and so on. Or for Jeff Gundy a year later, when he composed a tongue-in-cheek companion piece, "How to Write the New Mennonite Poem," which begins

> Choose two from old Bibles, humbly beautiful quilts
> Fraktur, and the *Martyr's Mirror* in Dutch.
> Get the word "Mennonite" in at least
> twice, once in the title, along with zwiebach,
> vareniki, borscht, and the farm,
> which if possible should be lost now. (86)

It is interesting to note that both Kasdorf and Gundy implicitly conflate "Swiss" and "Russian" Mennonite experiences here (as well as American and Canadian experiences); in a former paradigm it was convenient and acceptable to do so, when, in Ricoeur's terms, writers and readers tended to be driven in their thinking by *idem* identity: focusing mostly on fixity and sameness. As writers, readers, and texts move beyond relatively stable notions of identity in discussions of Mennonite/s writing, each moves in the direction of foregrounding what Ricoeur calls *ipse* identity: identity that is fluid and indeterminate. We speak here of loosening the hold of a rigid sort of historicist thinking on a field. As we liberate the field, of course, we also liberate texts and writers, many of whom have felt confined by the *idem* identification that in effect has challenged their claims to a certain kind of autonomy. So a younger generation of Mennonite writers, including the authors of many of the kaleidoscope of poems gathered in Ann Hostetler's anthology *A Cappella: Mennonite Voices in Poetry*—Shari Miller Wagner and Keith Ratzlaff and Barbara Nickel, for example—and others, including Cheryl Denise and Becca J.R. Lachman, both assert a particular perspective on accepted common stories of Mennonite heritage and introduce new narratives. In the process, they become, in effect, strikingly comprehensive in their particularity.

But we dare not suggest that identity-based readings of Mennonite poems and fictions are only limiting. Perhaps no one has taken greater pleasure in the texture and light that they have offered than have I. The identity-based critical understandings that have served as prisms for critics and writers alike leave us in a condition perhaps best described by Stuart Hall in an essay aptly subtitled "Who Needs Identity?": identity is "an idea which cannot be thought in the old way, but without which certain key questions cannot be thought at all" (2). So critics of Mennonite writing are left both with readings that have illuminated texts that have seemed to belong to a certain history and sensibility and with a desire, a need, for a new critical language, to freshen and inform the prisms through which they read—perhaps to disrupt, disturb, trouble readings of existing texts structured on notions of ethnic authenticity—and to remove constraints that might inhibit their responses to new literature being composed by a new generation of writers whose work, for the most part, addresses issues substantially different from the issues that earlier generations of writers found most compelling. I have observed elsewhere, in a similar vein, that a new generation of Mennonite writers and their readers are asking questions different from those foregrounded in Mennonite literature in the past. Many of the writers whom we encounter in *Rhubarb* magazine, for example, or in *CMW Journal*, are "less interested in origins than in milieus; less concerned with group history than with individual becoming; less compelled by essential identity than by multifaceted identifications ... taken less with traditional notions of community than with ... 'multiple ecologies of belonging.'" Neither disturbed nor distracted by notions of displacement or exile or deterritorialization, they embrace the freedom to locate themselves in a "worldly" present ("Homelands" 15).

It is not the lives of writers alone, of course, that are inflected by the texture of the postmodern world. Most of their Mennonite readers (critics included) share with them the conditions and concerns of a new generation, though (of course) among them are many for whom the concerns regarding identity and immigration and ethnicity and various forms of "otherness" that many Mennonite texts gave expression to at the height of the era of identity politics remain of substantial interest. The propensity to invoke a sense of historicity persists nevertheless, for example in the theme for an international conference on Mennonite/s writing in Fresno, California, in 2015. The theme, "Movement, Transformation, and Place," while not precluding readings that might circumvent matters of identity, clearly invokes a consideration of matters central to most deliberations that defined the era of identity politics: migration, borders, location, home, and belonging.

What does it mean to speak of Mennonite writing "after identity"? Any determined examination of the landscapes within which this body of work emerged, and continues to exist, will surely reveal that the question has resonances and implications well beyond texts, writers, and critics. Laurence Roth, commenting in a compelling essay on his father's Jewish bookstore in Los Angeles, observes that a people's literature is not only constituted "by authors and texts" but exists also "within social space" (293). Yes. A similar kind of social space was evident in Waterloo, Ontario, during the winter of 2012, when I convened a series of readings and lectures at Conrad Grebel University College at the University of Waterloo, celebrating "the first fifty years" of Mennonite/s writing, "mostly in Canada."[6] Every Wednesday evening, for nine weeks of a Canadian winter, over a hundred readers of Mennonite literature, most of them Mennonites themselves, gathered seemingly with what Morris Dickstein describes as a "sense of communal pride" (325) to listen to and hear about Mennonite writers. Dickstein uses the term "communal pride" derisively; I do not. I speak here of a generation of readers who have paid particular attention to the historicity of the Mennonite texts of the first decades because those texts tended to illuminate worlds that they comprehended collectively and individually in terms of what Alison Landsberg has named "prosthetic memory": that is, like other members of their generation of Mennonites in Canada, they had been informed and affected by narratives in the context

---

6 Video recordings of the reading/lecture series are available online: www.uwaterloo.ca/grebel/events/lecture-series/celebrating-mennonite-literature/videos.

of which they were nurtured or, as Landsberg would say, by "memories of events through which [they] did not live" but took on as their own (1). These memories, it seemed, were challenged and confirmed, elaborated and enlarged in the literary texts that lent them weight and substance—texts embraced by a generation of readers who in various ways might make the claim to be familiar with the religious and cultural topography of their people's texts: to have "been there."

Many Mennonite texts have invited certain limited interpretive approaches—have carried within them what Julia Kasdorf refers to as "autoethnographic announcements" (21): most notably, perhaps, Wiebe's *Peace Shall Destroy Many*, with its explanatory foreword, or Toews's *A Complicated Kindness*, with its comic documentary commentary offered by Nomi Nickel early in her narrative: "We're Mennonites. As far as I know, we are the most embarrassing sub-sect of people to belong to if you're a teenager. Five hundred years ago in Europe a man named Menno Simons set off to do his own peculiar religious thing" (5). So the literature itself announced the nature and scope of the prism through which it was to be read, or at least it offered access through a particular framework of understanding.

In one of his several stimulating articles on American Jewish literature, Schreier asks, rhetorically, do Jewish readers read a Jewish writer for his or her Jewishness? (see "Against" and "New York"). Do Mennonite readers, I wonder, read a Mennonite author for his or her Mennoniteness? (And which "Mennoniteness" would that be?) To some degree at least, I have taken pleasure in the fact that Wiebe's work (as I have put it in the past, citing Canadian critic Clara Thomas) "identifies me to myself." That is, I recognize his characters and the typical gestures of their lives; they are familiar to me. I have shared their meals and heard their singing. The German phrases that they use are immediately legible to me, on several levels. Their history, the structure of their families, and their conflicted piety resonate with my own. Chapter 6 of *The Blue Mountains of China* tells the story of my parents' escape from Stalin's Russia in 1929 more clearly and evocatively than I have ever read or heard elsewhere.

Having grown up as a Mennonite in a culture in which all the public stories, it seemed, belonged to the (apparently) Anglo-Saxon Canadian majority, I learned to embrace Robert Kroetsch's dictum that "fiction makes us real" (36) and I remember the enormous pleasure that I took when the early work of Mennonites writing in English appeared in Canada: Patrick Friesen, Sandra Birdsell, and Di Brandt, for example. I must add, in this context especially, that I do not mean to suggest that any other reader—

Mennonite or not—would share my experiences or my readings of them or of the texts that evoked them. When I first started teaching Mennonite poetry and fiction in southwestern Ontario in the 1980s, my students would often include Mennonite readers, some of whom, by virtue of their being either or both American and "Swiss," for example, declared themselves to be at a substantial remove from the mostly prairie-based, often markedly unsophisticated, characters presented by Canadian Mennonite writers. Some of them expressed shock at the portraits of writers and characters whom they were unable to recognize as Mennonite; the matter of those literary texts (which depicted cultural landscapes so familiar to me) bore no resemblance to their Mennonite experiences.

It is interesting that in the winter 2012 reading/lecture series, even the new, under-forty writers and critics—Darcie Friesen Hossack and Carrie Snyder and Robert Zacharias—failed to draw a younger crowd. The findings of Franco Moretti's rather unconventional literary history came to mind: that literatures tend to remain in place "for twenty-five years or so" and that almost "all genres active at any given time seem to arise and disappear together according to some hidden rhythm" (20). Why? Because the audience changes; the readers vanish. Commenting on the literature of the United States in the middle of the past century, Robert E. Spiller declared that each generation "should produce at least one literary history" because "each generation must define the past in its own terms" (vii). Long before that, Ralph Waldo Emerson had observed, "The books of an older period will not fit this" (88). Mennonite literature seems to be in no danger of vanishing, but the conditions that sustained its origins and the early critical readings of it no longer compel many who have an interest in the field. Much of the new Mennonite writing is a different thing altogether: vibrant and fresh and worldly.

Although Mennonite literature has tended to be monitored and commented on mostly (though by no means exclusively) by critics who are Mennonite, it is worth observing that in Canada, at least, this literature (the principal writers of which are national figures functioning in the top ranks of Canadian literature) did not emerge as a sectarian literature. Almost all of Canadian Mennonite literature has been published by public presses (Turnstone Press is notable here, along with McClelland & Stewart, HarperCollins, and many well-established small publishers and little magazines). The first conference on Mennonite/s Writing took place on a public university campus; it was initiated and sponsored by *The New Quarterly*, the literary magazine based at the University of Waterloo. The conference was attended by a number of prominent Canadian literary scholars, some of whom played significant roles; the conference proceedings were published by the University of Waterloo Press, as was the first collection of Mennonite short fiction: *Liars and Rascals: Mennonite Short Stories*. If those who work in the field are to illuminate one of the paths to Mennonite literature "after identity," then they would do well to continue to invite literary critics outside the Mennonite circle to join (or remain in) the conversation.

When I began to anticipate what it might mean to speak of Mennonite writing "after identity," I was compelled to consider, first of all, the fact that the term "Mennonite writing" contains and conceals a tangle of relations. I wondered whether scholars might do well to dislocate particular "classic" Mennonite texts from the contexts in which they have been written and received (in which they have, in large measure, served as what Jeff Karem calls "objects of desire for ... reading publics" [213]) and relocate them to allow new readings to emerge. Inspired by Dimock's warning against "analytic domain[s] foreclosed by definition" (*Through* 3), I wondered about the impact, for a small but powerful literary movement that we have come to identify as Mennonite, of investigating what might happen if critics were to focus their attention on alternative, non-Mennonite tropes and traces in seminal (and assumed to be seminally Mennonite) works such as Rudy Wiebe's *Peace Shall Destroy Many* (haunted by the shadow of Big Bear and, as Paul Tiessen remarks, shaped in some measure by its first central Canadian, Anglo-Canadian readers[7]). Consider also other notable works like some of the lyric poetry of Patrick Friesen (in which he adopts as muse the great Russian and Soviet modernist poet Anna Akhmatova), Di Brandt's early poems (richly infused with feminist critical theory) or her late verse (a feast for the eco-critic), the Tante Tina poems of David Waltner-Toews (the roots of which are in the work of Ugandan poet Okot p'Bitek), or the fiction of Dallas Wiebe (influenced and informed by the satire of British modernists). I mused about exploring how critical responses to Mennonite works that engage traces and territories "after identity" might liberate texts

---

7 See Tiessen, Paul. "Double Identity: Covering the *Peace Shall Destroy Many* Project," *After Identity: Mennonite Writing in North America*, ed. Robert Zacharias, Penn State UP, 2015, pp. 70–85.

and creators and inspire readers to revisit these texts without the lingering distraction of what Karem calls "the romance of authenticity." Can this literature, I wondered, survive such abandonment?

Any number of critical trajectories that eschew the issue of identity might result in very interesting readings of the Mennonite texts referred to here—and others. Dimock, in her "theory of resonance," offers further encouragement in this vein, asserting that a text is "continually interpretable": "[S]tretched by a growing web of cross-references, often to the point of unrecognizability, a text cannot and will not remain forever the same object" ("Theory" 1061, 1062). If we are to "liberate" the Mennonite text, we could do worse than to take direction from Dimock. Like some of the other critics cited here, she offers valuable perspectives that encourage us to explore and exploit the fact that Mennonite literary texts extend well beyond their originating circumstances.

Such a "liberation" might require some qualification. Some critics of "minoritized" literatures that embody issues of race and/or politics that extend well beyond anything that Mennonites have had to encounter, for example, have suggested that, to emerge safely on the other side of conversations about identity, we might need to consider doing away with the minority subject as a category (e.g., see Chuh; Lee). Mennonite writers in North America have not been compelled to deal with matters of race (even though there are many Mennonites of colour in North America, no prominent Mennonite literary voices have emerged, so far, among them), and Canadian Mennonites especially have not tended to trouble themselves about how the Mennonite fits into the broader culture; in fact, with a few notable exceptions (e.g., the issue of conscription in the Second World War, addressed in *Peace Shall Destroy Many*), Mennonite characters in fiction tend to be much more interested in their places within their own communities than in their situations in society at large. This is not to say that there are no national or racial resonances in their work; Sandra Birdsell was sharply criticized in the *Globe and Mail* by fellow Canadian (i.e., Ukrainian Canadian) novelist Janice Kulyk Keefer for her dismissive treatment of Ukrainians in *The Russländer*, for example.[8] And Rudy Wiebe's treatment of Canada's Native peoples has not been universally applauded. Perhaps centuries of willed isolation from "the world" and things "worldly" have left at least Canadian Mennonites relatively comfortable expressing a separatist sensibility; nevertheless, issues of nation, race, and

---

8 See Janice Julyk Keefer, "Paradise Lost in Russia, Found in Manitoba." Review of *The Russländer* by Sandra Birdsell. *The Globe and Mail*, 29 September 2001, p. D17.

After Identity

ethnicity as they are treated in Mennonite literary texts might bear some further investigation.

It is by no means imperative that critics of Mennonite writing abandon all notions of identity; in fact, as Tina Chen, citing Paula Moya, observes in another landscape altogether, "it is imperative that ethnic studies scholars develop theoretical models for demonstrating how identity is still an indispensable category of inquiry, a site of investigation" (192–193). Moya is speaking here of the need for critics to attend to matters especially of political agency. Chen cites her in the context of a discussion in which she observes that "post-structuralist conceptions of identity (and their accompanying emphases on the impossibility of coherency, the suspicion of realism, and the naïve idealism and essentialism of identity politics) have been embraced in the academy at precisely a moment when minorities are claiming for themselves the right to speak as subjects and agents" (192). Even for Mennonite writers—almost exclusively, until now, North Americans of white European ancestry (though this too is changing, as it should, given the change in Mennonite demographics)—Chen's observations and their implications resonate; after all, the discourses developed and sustained by the identity politics of decades past have offered opportunities for a vast range of minority voices to be heard, not only in the culture at large, I might add, but also within any given minority community itself. The most appreciative and engaged readers of minority literatures in North America, it could be argued, are members of the minority cultures that have produced the liminal texts that in large measure serve to identify their members to themselves.

The challenge, then, is not to forget about identity altogether but to refuse it the front seat that it has occupied for so long in Mennonite literary discourse, to invite new—possibly disruptive—readings; perhaps to abandon the desire to read texts as Mennonite/Mennonites. If critics of Mennonite writing at least temporarily set aside their presumed understandings of what Mennonites are, they might clear away the noise that prevents them from hearing the individual voices in the texts who declare who they are—as individuals, not as members of a collective. Like any literary text, after all, the Mennonite literary text surely has, in Dimock's words, "a force of incipience commensurate with the incipience of humanity" ("Theory" 1064).

WORKS CITED

Braidotti, Rosi. *Nomadic Theory: The Portable Rosi Braidotti*. Columbia UP, 2011.

Casanova, Pascale. *The World Republic of Letters*. Trans. Malcolm DeBevoise. Harvard UP, 2004.

Chen, Tina. *Double Agency: Acts of Impersonation in Asian American Literature and Culture*. Stanford UP, 2005.

Chuh, Kandice. *Imagine Otherwise: On Asian Americanist Critique*. Duke UP, 2003.

Dickstein, Morris. "A Response [to Michael P. Kramer, 'Race, Literary History, and the "Jewish" Question'] from Morris Dickstein." *Prooftexts*, vol. 21, no. 3, 2001, pp. 324–327.

Dimock, Wai Chee. "A Theory of Resonance." *PMLA*, vol. 112, no. 5, 1997, pp. 1060–1071.

———. *Through Other Continents: American Literature Across Deep Time*. Princeton UP, 2006.

Edwards, Brian T. "The World, the Text, and the Americanist." *American Literary History*, vol. 25, no. 1, 2013, pp. 231–246.

Emerson, Ralph Waldo. "The American Scholar." 1837. *Selected Essays*, ed. Larzer Ziff, Penguin, 1982, pp. 83–105.

Giles, Paul. *Virtual Americas: Transnational Fictions and the Transatlantic Imaginary*. Duke UP, 2002.

Greene, Dana M., and James R. Peacock. "Judaism, Jewishness, and the Universal Symbols of Identity: Re-Sacralizing the Star of David and the Color Yellow." *Studies in American Jewish Literature*, vol. 30, 2011, pp. 80–98.

Gundy, Jeff. "How to Write the New Mennonite Poem." *A Cappella: Mennonite Voices in Poetry*, ed. Ann Hostetler, U Iowa P, 2003, pp. 86–87.

Hall, Stuart. "Introduction: Who Needs 'Identity'?" *Questions of Cultural Identity*, ed. Stuart Hall and Paul du Gay, Sage, 1996, pp. 1–17.

Hostetler, Ann, ed. *A Cappella: Mennonite Voices in Poetry*. U Iowa P, 2003.

Jelen, Sheila E., Michael P. Kramer, and L. Scott Lerner, eds. *Modern Jewish Literature: Intersections and Boundaries*. U Pennsylvania P, 2010.

Karem, Jeff. *The Romance of Authenticity: The Cultural Politics of Regional and Ethnic Literatures*. U Virginia P, 2004.

Kasdorf, Julia Spicher. "Mennonites." *A Cappella: Mennonite Voices in Poetry*, ed. Ann Hostetler, U Iowa P, 2003, p. 129.

———. "The Autoethnographic Announcement and the Story." *After Identity: Mennonite Writing in North America*, ed. Robert Zacharias, Pennsylvania State UP, 2015, pp. 21–36.

Kramer, Michael P. "The Art of Assimilation: Ironies, Ambiguities, Aesthetics." Jelen et al., pp. 303–326.

———. "Critical Narcissism and the Coming-of-Age of Jewish American Literary Studies." *Jewish Quarterly Review*, vol. 56, no. 1, 2010, pp. 19–39.
Kroetsch, Robert. *The Lovely Treachery of Words: Essays Selected and New*. Oxford UP, 1989.
Landsberg, Alison. *Prosthetic Memory: The Transformation of American Remembrance in the Age of Mass Culture*. Columbia UP, 2004.
Lee, Christopher. "Asian American Literature and the Resistances of Theory." *Modern Fiction Studies*, vol. 56, no. 1, 2010, pp. 19–39.
Leichter, David J. "Collective Identity and Collective Memory in the Philosophy of Paul Ricoeur." *Études Ricœuriennes/Ricœur Studies*, vol. 3, no. 1, 2012, pp. 114–131.
Millner, Michael. "Post Post-Identity." *American Quarterly*, vol. 57, no. 2, 2005, pp. 541–554.
Moretti, Franco. *Graphs, Maps, Trees: Abstract Models for a Literary History*. Verso Books, 2007.
Palumbo-Liu, David. "Assumed Identities." *New Literary History*, vol. 31, no. 4, 2000, pp. 765–780.
Reimer, Margaret Loewen. *One Quilt Many Pieces: A Guide to Mennonite Groups in Canada*. 4th ed. Herald Press, 2008.
Ricoeur, Paul. *Oneself as Another*. Trans. Kathleen Blamey. U Chicago P, 1992.
Roof, Judith. "Thinking Post-Identity." *Journal of the Midwest Modern Language Association*, vol. 36, no. 1, 2003, pp. 1–5.
Roth, Laurence. "Unpacking My Father's Bookstore." Jelen et al., pp. 280–302.
Schreier, Benjamin. "Against the Dialectic of Nation: Abraham Cahan and Desire's Spectral Jew." *Modern Fiction Studies*, vol. 57, no. 2, 2011, pp. 276–299.
———. "Editor's Introduction." *Studies in American Jewish Literature*, vol. 32, no. 1, 2013, pp. 1–3.
———. "The Failure of Identity: Toward a New Literary History of Philip Roth's Unrecognizable Jew." *Jewish Social Studies: History, Culture, Society*, vol. 17, no. 2, 2011, pp. 101–135.
———. "New York Intellectual/Neocon/Jewish: Or, How I Learned to Stop Worrying and Ignore Ruth Wisse." *Studies in American Jewish Literature*, vol. 31, no. 1, 2012, pp. 97–108.
Spiller, Robert E., ed. *Literary History of the United States*. Vol. I. Macmillan, 1948.
Tiessen, Hildi Froese. "Homelands, Identity Politics, and the Trace: What Remains for the Mennonite Reader?" *Mennonite Quarterly Review*, vol. 87, no. 1, 2013, pp. 11–22.
———, ed. *Liars and Rascals: Mennonite Short Stories*. U Waterloo P, 1989.
Tiessen, Paul. "Double Identity: Covering the *Peace Shall Destroy Many* Project." *After Identity: Mennonite Writing in North America*, ed. Robert Zacharias, Pennsylvania State UP, 2015, pp. 70–85.

Toews, Miriam. *A Complicated Kindness*. Knopf Canada, 2004.
Wiebe, Rudy. *Peace Shall Destroy Many*. McClelland & Stewart, 1962.
Wisse, Ruth R. *The Modern Jewish Canon: A Journey Through Language and Culture*. U Chicago P, 2000.

Fifteen

Beyond "What We by Habit or Custom Already Know," or, What Do We Mean When We Talk About Mennonite/s Writing?*

Identity ... is at once impossible and unavoidable.

Robert Kroetsch, *Excerpts from the Real World*

THIS EXPLORATION OF what we mean when we speak of Mennonite/s writing has its roots in what were, for me, two substantial literary experiences. The first spanned several decades, beginning in the 1970s, when I began to pay attention to the early published fictional writing of Rudy Wiebe. While I was a graduate student in the Department of English at the University of Alberta, a department Wiebe had joined as a young professor of creative writing in 1967,[1] I made a study for a course on the fiction of the Canadian West of Wiebe's first and third novels: *Peace Shall Destroy Many* (1962) and *The Blue Mountains of China* (1970).[2]

---

* First published as Hildi Froese Tiessen, "Beyond 'What We by Habit or Custom Already Know,' or 'What Do We Mean When We Talk About Mennonite/s Writing'?" *Mennonite Quarterly Review*, vol. 90, 2016, pp. 11–28.

1 In 1967 Wiebe moved from Goshen, Indiana to Alberta, where he taught in the Department of English at the University of Alberta.

2 This student project became the first Canadian scholarly article devoted to Wiebe's work. See "A Mighty Inner River" in this collection.

I was, at the time, interested in the fact that these were "Mennonite" texts, but did not think of them as belonging to any sort of Mennonite literary tradition.

In Canada Wiebe had been preceded, to be sure, by other writers of Mennonite heritage, several of whom had published modest chapbooks in German. Most prominent among them was Arnold Dyck, whose major work, in German, included a nostalgic *Bildungsroman* published in installments during the 1940s about Mennonites on the plains of Ukraine,[3] and, in Low German, a collection of humorous stories about two flat-footed Mennonites from southern Manitoba named Koop and Bua.[4] Others, who wrote in English, included Mabel Dunham, an Ontario woman "of Mennonite descent through her mother," who, as early as 1924, began to write historical novels about some of the Swiss American Mennonite pioneers like Benjamin Eby and Sam Bricker, who had contributed to the development of the first Mennonite settlements in Canada, in southern Ontario, in the early 1800s (Bender and Steiner).[5] Another such writer was Paul Hiebert, a Mennonite chemistry professor who won the Stephen Leacock Memorial Medal for Humour in 1948 for *Sarah Binks*, a faux biography of "the Sweet Songstress of Saskatchewan."[6] Sarah Binks had no apparent connection with Mennonites. Moreover, Koop and Bua, Eby and Bricker, and Sarah Binks would have shared few readers in the early 1970s, and were unlikely to be thought of by anyone except, possibly, Rudy Wiebe, in the same breath. In the 1970s, Wiebe was the only author among the Mennonites in Canada writing for a national audience and whose fiction explicitly addressed Mennonite experience. At that time there was nothing that could be identified as a Mennonite "literature." It was when Patrick Friesen, Sandra Birdsell, Di Brandt, Victor Enns, and Audrey Poetker, along with Al Reimer, David Waltner-Toews, Armin Wiebe, and others, began to write and publish, in the 1980s and 1990s—work that was embraced by readers first in Manitoba and then more broadly across Canada, and work that addressed the condition of being Mennonite in that era—that a Canadian public began to see something of a literary phenomenon among Mennonites.

---

3 See Dyck. The novel *Lost in the Steppe* was originally published in five modest volumes (1944–1948) as *Verloren in der Steppe*.

4 Among these was the popular *Koop enn Bua opp Reise* (1943).

5 B. Mabel Dunham's *The Trail of the Conestoga* was first published by Macmillan in Toronto in 1924, with a foreword by W.L. Mackenzie King, then Prime Minister of Canada.

6 The novel was originally published in 1947, by Oxford UP Canada.

This literary movement gained a palpable momentum through the support of hospitable regional publishers (especially Winnipeg's Turnstone Press) and an exuberant, stimulating, wide-ranging drive by the Canadian government to renew its national culture at various levels, from the grassroots to government policy.[7] At that time, Canada was friendly both to the arts and to all shades of the non-Anglo-Saxon "other." Among the Canadian literati, issues of race had not begun to preclude interest in issues related to white ethnicity. In fact, from the late 1980s through the 1990s Mennonite writers of Canada were considered both "other" enough to warrant serious attention in those early years of multiculturalism, and prolific and gifted enough to sustain it. By the mid-1980s I was teaching a course in Mennonite literature at Conrad Grebel College at the University of Waterloo and, following the publication of *Liars and Rascals: Mennonite Short Stories* (1989) and in the context of the Mennonite World Conference assembly taking place in Winnipeg in 1990, I was invited by two prominent Canadian literary magazines—first by *The New Quarterly* (Waterloo) and then by *Prairie Fire* (Winnipeg)—to edit special issues devoted to Mennonite/s writing. At the same time, I was also invited to help plan and convene the first conference on Mennonite/s Writing,[8] an event born in the imagination of Miriam Maust,[9] organized and sponsored by *The New Quarterly*, funded by a combination of institutional and private donors, and hosted in 1990 on the campus of the University of Waterloo.[10]

I mention these developments because they define, in large measure, the substructure of this essay, which is concerned with critical writing about

---

7 The Canadian Multiculturalism Act was passed into law in 1988, preceded by the adoption of a national multiculturalism policy in 1971.

8 The first conference on Mennonite/s Writing took place at the University of Waterloo in 1990. The second and third, hosted at Goshen College in Indiana, took place in 1997 and 2002. The fourth happened at Bluffton University in Ohio in 2006. The fifth took place at the University of Winnipeg in Manitoba in 2009. This was followed by the sixth, at Eastern Mennonite University in Virginia in 2012, and the seventh, at Fresno Pacific University in California in 2015. By the late fall of 2015 there were plans underway for two more conferences, in 2017 and 2020. The 2017 conference took place at the University of Winnipeg, and the most recent conference, delayed twice due to COVID-19, was held in 2022 at Goshen College, in Indiana.

9 The idea of a conference on Mennonite writing originated with Miriam Maust, an American Swiss Mennonite literary scholar and poet who had settled in Waterloo, where she served as one of the poetry editors of *The New Quarterly*.

10 Except for the closing banquet and readings on the last night, which took place at the University of Waterloo's St. Jerome's College and at the country home of Vern and Elfrieda Heinrichs, respectively, the conference—which consisted of plenary sessions only and included as presenters and participants a number of prominent Canadianists, such as Robert Kroetsch, Clara Thomas, Stan Dragland, and John Lennox—took place mostly at Conrad Grebel College.

Mennonite literature. Although scholars like Harry Loewen had begun to write about Mennonite "literary arts" (composed in both German and English),[11] questions about how to speak of this emerging field of "Mennonite literature" began around the time of the special issues and the first conference. It was then that I began to employ the slash in the now commonly-accepted brand "Mennonite/s Writing" to assert, among other things, my ambivalence about using the term "Mennonite" as a bare adjective, a simple signifier. To speak of this new writing phenomenon simply as "Mennonite literature" would have the effect, I feared, of both declaring and delimiting the "essence" of this burgeoning body of literature. Perhaps, I ventured, writing by Mennonites could be referred to simply as "Mennonite writing"; but I knew the label was inevitably more complicated, more knotty than that. Then, as now, the term "Mennonite" signaled numerous divergent, inconsistent, and unstable commitments to identity, and was coded differently within a wide range of chronological, geographic, cultural, and religious settings.

One of the most significant things to happen during those early years of Mennonite/s writing was the development of a critical literature—mostly, at that time, in the form of reviews. Many reviewers did not share my ambivalence about the term "Mennonite" and used the term fairly freely (sometimes indiscriminately) as a definitive modifier to tag or label any and all of the incipient generation of Mennonite writers, their communities, and their texts.[12] As more and more writers of Mennonite heritage and their texts achieved increasing regional, national, and international recognition, many of the writers, while recognizing the value of the new literary label "Mennonite," resisted the label, revealing their own skittishness about being limited or entrapped by it. At the same time, however, some embraced it, revealing their desire to benefit from the growing momentum in the field.[13]

I shared the interest many readers of these early "Mennonite" texts had in ethnography, but with the qualification that the term "Mennonite" as a modifier surely had a different tenor in every literary voice and was,

---

11 See Harry Loewen, "Mennonite Literature in Canada Beginnings, Reception and Study," *Journal of Mennonite Studies*, vol. 1, 1983, pp. 119–132.

12 For a useful list of critical responses to creative work by Mennonite writers, see Ervin Beck's fine bibliographies at www.goshen.edu/academics/english/ervmb/canada/ and www.goshen.edu/academics/english/ervinb/usa/.

13 Any number of informal or formal interviews published at the time revealed these writers' attitudes.

moreover, read differently by every member of a writer's audience.[14] Indeed, I am struck now by the fact that no member of my children's generation is capable of reading any of those early works—whether written by Rudy Wiebe or Di Brandt, or others—in the same way any Mennonite of my generation would have read them; this younger generation simply occupies a different world: the collaboration among reader and text now cannot approximate the collaborations that attended these writers' works when they first appeared in print. Ways of reading, as Diana Fuss has famously observed, are both culturally variable and historically specific.[15]

In order to demonstrate that there was no one way to speak in one voice of all these writers and their communities, and to assert that there was no single entryway into their texts, I embarked on a series of interviews with writers who grew up in Mennonite homes and within Mennonite communities.[16] I asked each of them what it meant for them to be nurtured, as they all were, within a community of Mennonites. Deliberately constrained by my own definition

---

14 It's worth remarking here, in anticipation of some of the questions this essay is likely to raise, that the term "Mennonite" was—and, for some, remains—a contentious term, especially when applied to creative writers like Patrick Friesen, for example, and others who have at some time openly announced a certain distance from the Mennonite communities in which they grew up and the Mennonite churches they once attended. I can recall Patrick Friesen telling me that one of the first times he came to Waterloo to read from his work at Conrad Grebel College in the early 1980s, he was challenged by a senior Mennonite professor of the college to explain how it was he had the temerity to call himself a Mennonite. Friesen was not alone in encountering those sorts of taunts then, taunts that reflected a not uncommon uneasiness and a proprietorial attitude felt and expressed by some about Mennonite identity. Regardless of whether or not you were raised in a Mennonite family, community, and church, these detractors would assert that if you were not an active, baptized member of a Mennonite congregation, you had no right to identify yourself as a Mennonite. Furthermore, anyone who presumed to embrace a cultural or "ethnic" Mennonite identity (as a badge of birth and heritage)—whether that person was a church member or not—faced being derided for being insensitive to "new" Mennonite converts who seemed to have the right to claim one of any number of ethnic heritages, but who, the detractors argued, might feel alienated by assertions of Mennonite "ethnicity." These issues have been, and here and there remain, thorny. Certainly they form part of the substructure beneath the matters with which this article deals.

15 Fuss writes, "Readers, like texts, are constructed, they inhabit reading practices rather than create them *ex nihilo* ... if we read from multiple subject positions, the very act of reading becomes a force for dislocating our belief in stable subjects and essential meanings" (35).

16 Edited and abridged versions of several of these interviews have been published, including "'A Place You Can't Go Home To': A Conversation with Miriam Toews," *Prairie Fire*, vol. 21, no. 3, Autumn 2000, pp. 54–61; "'Where I Come From': An Interview with David Bergen," *Prairie Fire*, vol. 17, no. 4, Winter 1997, pp. 23–33; "'Every Play Should Pose a Good Question': An Interview with Vern Thiessen," *Journal of Mennonite Writing*, vol. 2, no. 7, 2010. Fully derived from an interview is "The Case of Dallas Wiebe: Literary Art in Worship," *Journal of Mennonite Writing*, vol. 3, no. 3, 2011.

of the Mennonite writer as someone who knows by personal experience what it means to be, or to have lived as, a Mennonite, and of Mennonite writing as writing by a Mennonite writer—and compelled by a desire to demonstrate the variety of Mennonite experience, the diversity of texts these writers produced, and the contingency of Mennonite identity—I wanted to head off any tendency within communities of critics, reviewers, and general readers to assume an unexamined commonality among the writers and texts that had come to be identified as "Mennonite." I wanted to preclude or impede the sort of assumptions about unity and cohesion that might constrain or distort the individual text's reception or impact.

So one could say that the first literary experience that lies at the root of this discussion was my growing awareness, in those early years, of a literary movement that was becoming substantially more than a simple clutch of texts. But what was it, then? And how would we proceed to speak or write of it?

This investigation has also been stimulated, in the second instance, by my encounters with several recent, published critical/theoretical observations about a number of the ethnic and ethnoracial, or minority-culture (these are all contentious terms) literatures that have found their place in the literary landscapes of North America. And these literatures are many, of course. Among the more prominent are Afro American, along with Chicano, Native American, Asian American, and Jewish American literatures and their Canadian counterparts, and others. Each of these by now well-established literary traditions includes both creative and critical works, as well as the actual and implied conversations among all those works—exchanges among critics or writers or between critics and writers, most of which are well beyond the scope of this essay. I invoke these conversations here insofar as they offer perspectives on the questions that lie at the heart of my investigation.

Critic Sau-ling Cynthia Wong has observed of Asian American literature that it "may be thought of as an emergent and evolving textual coalition, whose interests are promoted by a professional coalition of Asian American critics" (9). Although the questions I raise here concern what we now call Mennonite/s writing, my observations are concerned less with the primary creative texts that make up "Mennonite literature" than with the critical discourse that continues to develop around them—with critics' participation in what Wong refers to as a "textual coalition." In particular, my reflections are rooted in my belief that the relatively small, though vibrant, field of criticism addressing

Mennonite/s writing[17]—and the question that lies at the core of this inquiry: What do we mean when we talk about Mennonite/s writing?—can be richly informed by some of the critical debates that have engaged critics of other minority-culture literatures that developed alongside Mennonite/s writing within the broad literary panoramas of North America.

The Mennonites, of course, are first of all a religious group; but it is worth reminding ourselves that in Canada Mennonites have had a firm place in the landscape of multiculturalism since the 1970s and 1980s, when multiculturalism was embedded in official policy of the Canadian government as both a sociological/demographic fact and a political ideology. In Canada, Mennonites are widely regarded simply as one of the country's wide spectrum of "ethnic," or minority-culture, groups. It would seem that the place of Mennonites in the USA, where the concept of "ethnic" is otherwise inflected than it is in Canada, is different. This is one of the factors driving my inquiry: What do we mean when we speak of "Mennonite" literature across North America? This essay only begins to frame this question, a question richly informed, as I have already suggested, by scholars pondering similar things in the context of other minority-culture literatures in North America.

In a 2012 article entitled "Affectionate, Anxious, and Perplexed," critic Dean Franco observes that "Jewish American literature study … needs a rethinking of major concepts to account for new or newly understood realities" (14). As several of Franco's colleagues have remarked, scholars of Jewish American literature have been a little late, relative to scholars committed to the study of other "ethnic" (or ethnoracial) literatures, in addressing the perplexing issues endemic to their literary-critical investigations and commentary. In 2014 Benjamin Schreier observed that "of all the 'ethnic' American literary

---

17 It should be noted that the critical work I am referring to throughout this essay is work that, for the most part, takes place within the context of conferences and symposia, essay collections, special issues of journals, and books (such as the 2015 volume on Mennonite literature, *After Identity*). Because of the way these works are defined (as studies of Mennonite writing, for example), they address authors and texts that the critics deem to be representative of a Mennonite writing community or of a Mennonite literary tradition. There are, of course, many books and articles of criticism that offer studies of creative work published by Mennonite writers that are written by critics who take interest neither in Mennonites nor in any Mennonite features in the literary work or works they have chosen to examine. This welcome, often insightful work lies, more or less, outside the scope of my commentary here, though it implicitly addresses some of the issues I raise.

fields, the Jewish American literary field has probably seen the least sustained theorization and self-criticism over the last generation or so" (764). Schreier's observation, offered in the context of substantial theoretical debate in the context of Asian American or African American literatures, might well hold true for Jewish American literature. But the field of Mennonite literature has seen even less theorization of the kind to which Schreier refers—theorizing that would, as he observes in the context of Jewish American writing, both "contest the legibility of the category" (the category of "Jewish" in his context and "Mennonite" in ours) and strive "to decenter and pluralize the field of scholarly labor (in talk of histories, literatures, cultures …)" in literary study (764, 760).

Mennonite literature, to be sure, is a relatively small player in the vast landscape of ethnic literatures that have found themselves in a discursive situation where the concept "identity" that anchored these new literatures and lay at the roots of countless anthologies of minority-culture writing has figured prominently. This troublesome term, identity, lies at the heart of the critical debates.[18] The term is problematic because, as Robert Kroetsch has remarked, it is both unavoidable and impossible (15). For more than a decade now it has been described in terms of exhaustion[19] and abandonment.[20] The late Stuart Hall referred to identity as a concept "under erasure" and "no longer serviceable"; yet it is an idea, he observed, that, paradoxically, "cannot be thought in the old way, but without which certain key questions cannot be thought at all" (1–2).

Perhaps the concept "post-identity," along with other related "posts," begins to offer a way of dealing with the conundrum to which Kroetsch and Hall allude. Or "post-ethnic," which, commentators like David Hollinger remark, reflects a "determination to keep track of the past, to register its legacy without denying the reality of change." It implies, Hollinger goes on to say, "a strong holdover from the past, but a refinement of that legacy in relation to new opportunities and constraints" (176-177). "Post-ethnic" invokes both

---

18 For further discussion of identity issues in Mennonite/s Writing, see Robert Zacharias, ed., *After Identity: Mennonite Writing in North America*. My chapter, entitled "After Identity: Liberating the Mennonite Literary Text," is included in this volume.

19 See, for example, David Palumbo-Liu. "Assumed Identities," *New Literary History*, vol. 31, no. 4, 2000, pp. 765–780; Judith Roof, "Thinking Post-Identity," *Journal of the Midwest Modern Language Association*, vol. 36, no. 1, 2003, pp. 1–5; and Michael Millner. "Post Post-Identity," *American Quarterly*, vol. 57, no. 2, 2005, pp. 541–554.

20 See, for example, Christopher Lee. "Asian American Literature and the Resistances of Theory." *Modern Fiction Studies*, vol. 561, 2010, pp. 19–39.

heritage and adaptation. The "post" in the word, as in "post-colonial," designates "not a chronological but a conceptual frame"; it denotes not a phase but a new perspective, a new way of seeing (Saldivar 575). It "encourages cultural and political dynamics responsive to individual perceptions and ambitions," Hollinger observes, adding that it implies "the experience of being able to really choose" (176).[21]

During recent decades when various "posts" announced their presence and secured their impact upon literary studies, critics devoted to commentary on particular ethnic literatures began to ask new kinds of questions about minority culture texts, even as the literary texts to which they gave their attention proliferated—many of them written in what Kenneth Warren calls a "new register," or composed in such a way as not to address "what we by habit or custom already 'know'" about a particular group (403). Like Warren, Schreier suggests that critics need to find ways of distancing themselves as readers from "the expected recognition" of a population (Jewish, in his case) that is "already conceptually coherent, legible, and historiographically legitimate despite geographical and temporal diversity" (760).

Matters of identity often do not surface prominently in more recent literary texts produced by writers nurtured in minority-culture communities, though legible traces of a particular identity might persist here and there.[22] In recent years, the literary critical work of assembling anthologies and analyzing—often as ethnographic—individual texts that had figured prominently during the emergence of minority-culture literatures, when matters of identity were a strong concern, has in large measure given way to metacritical investigations focused on the assumptions underlying various critical responses to those early texts. These investigations might include addressing questions about what can be said to be distinctive about an African American or a Jewish American or a Canadian Mennonite literary text, for example. Or they might endorse theoretical explorations of what it means to read an ethnic text as an ethnic text—or not. How, in Schreier's words, might literary critics manage

---

21 Hollinger goes on, citing *The New Authentics: Artists of the Post-Jewish Generation*, edited by Staci Boris, Spertus Press, 2008: "A similar dynamic is invoked under the flag of 'post-Jewishness'" as defined, for example, by the organizers of a highly successful exhibition of post-Jewish art at the Spertus Jewish Museum in Chicago in 2008. "The post-Jewish generation," in the words of the Spertus catalog, "focuses on self-definition and on balancing lived experience and heritage in intellectual and daily practice," fostering "an internal, highly personal consciousness as to how one connects with Jewishness today."

22 For a discussion of "the trace" relative to Mennonite/s writing, see "Homelands, Identity Politics, and the Trace: What Remains for the Mennonite Reader?" included in this volume.

to "destabilize the habits and patterns" that still prevail in the language and paradigms of identity politics (763)?

In the spring of 2013, a symposium of several scholars of Mennonite literature convened at Penn State University "to re-frame the critical discourse surrounding Mennonite writing in North America." Gathered around the theme of "after identity," the group began to explore what the organizers, Julia Kasdorf and Robert Zacharias, cautiously referred to as "a certain critical ambivalence" about the role of "cultural identity" in Mennonite literature.[23]

In the midst of these tentative probings into the challenging critical landscape of post-identity and post-ethnicity, critics of Mennonite writing have yet to address what some observers regard as the pressing concerns being debated actively and productively among commentators of other ethnic literatures in North America. Jennifer Glaser, for example, observed in 2013 that scholars of Jewish American studies had recently been "struggling to find a new, more expansive identity and vernacular," a "portal into wider discourses" (327). Specifically, she referred to inquiries that might include consideration of questions such as these: what do we *mean* by terms such as "Jewish American" or "African American" or "Canadian Mennonite" when these modifiers precede the word "literature"? Or what does it mean to read "Canadian (or American) Mennonite literature" as "Mennonite literature"?

To corral and tag any of these minority-culture literatures is to invoke the understanding that they are distinctive. Yet, if they address the question at all, critics struggle to identify the nature and meaning of this distinctiveness— not least critics and reviewers of Mennonite literature, who have tended to signal, rather unselfconsciously, in their use of the word "Mennonite" a certain commonality of narrative, a fairly undifferentiated unity, and to invoke certain cultural or religious markers that are in fact not held in common by Mennonites in the many Mennonite communities in Canada or the USA or, indeed, on other continents where 70 percent of the world's 2,100,000 Mennonites now live. In fact, the Mennonite creative writing that is being published today evokes and documents "multiple, conflicted, and emergent formations" and delivers numerous and varied, inconsistent, and possibly contrary or contradictory expressions of identity.[24] Critics of Mennonite/s writing have tended not to catalog these. We are just beginning to speak of them. How shall we proceed?

---

23 From a memo entitled "After Identity: Mennonite/s Writing in North America" sent by Kasdorf to the author and others on 12 July 2012 and from a follow-up 5 September 2012 memo.

24 My language here is borrowed from Susan Koshy, 318.

If Mennonite literature is, to borrow the language of Wai Chee Dimock writing about American literature, "a simplified name for a much more complex tangle of relations ... a crisscrossing set of pathways, open-ended and ever multiplying," perhaps our present deliberations could be informed by consideration of the multiple expressions of identity embodied not in an apparent literary tradition, but in a particular Mennonite writer's work (3). That is, the multiplicity of subject positions that find expression across a writer's oeuvre might, in fact, provide a paradigm for the wide diversity of texts we now speak of as in some sense "Mennonite." An instructive illustration of such diversity might be found in the verse and prose works of Di Brandt, for example, and the various subjectivities to which they give expression. Among these we might recognize the novice writer full of trepidation, accused of being a rebel, traitor, thief; the eco-poet; the revisionist historian of Anabaptist/Mennonite history; the "Canadianist" literary critic; the feminist theorist; the self-identified survivor of domestic violence; the shunned dissident; the brilliant urban intellectual; the daughter; the mother; the lover; the world traveler; the prairie dweller; the reluctant occupant of seemingly alien "hyper-industrialized" and "environmentally-stressed" landscapes; the Mennonite; the *Kanadier*; the secular Mennonite; the non-Mennonite. To which of these speakers or characters or critics or narrators do we refer when we embrace Brandt or her work, or both, as "Mennonite"? Is this question worthy of consideration? Does it matter that Brandt herself has expressed concern about the nature and legacy and future of Mennonite creative expression, asking:

> what does it mean to be Mennonite? is it a racial/tribal/ancestral thing? is it a land/social practice? is it a political/religious movement? does belonging to a Mennonite church make you Mennonite? does not belonging to a church make you not Mennonite any more? does abandoning the old land/social practices as most Mennonites, not only the writers but everyone else as well, have done in the last half century in NA mean that the Mennonites are no longer Mennonite? (email to the author)

And what do anyone's responses to any of these questions imply for Mennonite/s writing, which we continue to identify and define implicitly and explicitly in various print and other contexts without expressing the urge to explore what it is that we tacitly agree demonstrates some identifiable commonality among producers of Mennonite literary texts or among the texts themselves? What is it, after all, that we implicitly affirm whenever we participate in a conference on Mennonite/s writing, or read a poem or prose narrative, or host or attend readings by "Mennonite writers," or read or contribute to a special issue such as this one? What is it we agree upon—what commonality do we give expression to—when we assert that among the texts we interact with on some of the intersections of our lives is this thing called Mennonite/s Writing?

Within the field of Mennonite literature studies, many of us critics have tended to rely on paradigms of ethnicity produced in the inaugural moment of the field, and so have "run the risk," in the words of Susan Koshy, "of unwittingly annexing the newer literary productions within older paradigms" (317). We have tended to assume, perhaps too often, certain unfolding, "common" narratives—illustrated persuasively, for example, in Robert Zacharias's 2013 study of literary treatments of the Mennonite exodus out of the Soviet Union during the 1920s—rather than to investigate what Koshy identifies as the "premises and assumptions underlying our constructions of commonality" (317). We have tended to presume a kind of coherent Mennonite distinctiveness, for example, instead of acknowledging the highly refractable dynamic of Mennonite identity, or striving to parse the variable encounters between the Mennonite and his or her environments here and now.

During the era of identity politics many of the questions that presented themselves to critics of "ethnic" literatures, including Jewish or Mennonite, appeared straightforward enough, and "ethnic" literary texts tended to be read, as often as not, as exercises in autoethnography, where it was assumed that identity precedes text. But critical eras and fashions shift and, while creative writers continue to publish new and stimulating and provocative texts, we literary critics often lag behind as we struggle to make a particular kind of sense of the diversity of texts produced by the writers we read and study. "Criticism," Franco writes provocatively, "has to catch up to literature" (17).

Critics in some fields of literary discourse, as I have already noted, have made greater strides on this score. Take, for example, commentators on Asian-American literature. A decade ago, Canadian scholars Eleanor Ty and Donald Goellnicht declared in their introduction to a collection of essays entitled *Asian North American Identities* that the term "Asian American" (which tends to subsume Asian Canadians) no longer had "the same resonance" as it had in the early 1990s. Scholars of Asian American literature, they remarked, "recognizing the diversity of identities covered by the umbrella term [Asian American] are less likely today to make ... emphatic statements about 'common experiences.'" Citing Shirley Lim, they observed that Asian American literature is "collapsing under the weight of its own contradictions" (Ty and Goellnicht 1). A number of recent studies in Asian American studies have revealed the deep probing that has sharpened critics' perception of this field and driven them to consider abandoning "the assumed coherency if not the ultimate efficacy of Asian Americanness as a viable subject category" (Chen 186).

Similarly, Kenneth Warren in his provocative 2011 volume *What Was African American Literature?* argued that the conditions that gave rise to African American literature and framed its initial critical reception might very well no longer persist. He observed that "the boundary" creating the "distinctiveness" of that literature had "eroded" (8). Warren asks whether the notion of a distinct and collective African American literature is still viable. Should the prevailing paradigm be challenged?

There is little doubt that the relatively cohesive and distinctive diasporic Mennonite culture that took shape in particular geographic contexts during particular periods in history, and that nurtured each of the writers of the first generation of Mennonite/s writing in English in Canada, has more or less disappeared—or has been transformed by geography and circumstance into something other than what it was. This is not surprising, given that Mennonites—at least Mennonites who write and publish poetry and prose fiction that reach regional and national and international audiences—tend to be subject to the myriad of influences that affect the lives of virtually everyone living in the modern and postmodern Western world.

In the spring of 2015, novelist Carrie Snyder, who belongs to a new, younger generation of Mennonite writers, was featured on a Kitchener CBC radio program just after the release of her novel *Girl Runner*. In response to a line of interview questions that assumed that all Mennonites always and deliberately set themselves apart from the world, Snyder offered a contrarian riff on the often-expressed Mennonite idiom that states that Mennonites are "in the world, but not of the world." She asserted instead that her generation of Mennonites was raised "in the world and of the world." As Snyder averred that morning, the cultural conditions that gave rise to the wave of Mennonite writing we have observed especially since the 1980s play only a minor part in the traditions of many Mennonite writers publishing today—if they persist at all.

Furthermore, a new audience, of a different generation and in a different place geographically, historically, religiously, culturally, even linguistically, reads these texts differently. As Peter Kirkpatrick and Robert Dixon remark in their introduction to a 2012 volume of essays on literary communities in Australia, literary texts in any tradition attract "distinct communities of reading"—whether defined geographically or chronologically or culturally; and in each of these communities each text might, of course, have "fundamentally different meanings" (xii). Perhaps, then, critics would do well to abandon the notion that what we call Mennonite literature can be considered collectively. We might, indeed, appropriate for reflection Warren's provocation that critics ask of a particular assemblage of texts both why anyone would regard them as distinctive and why, collectively, they should be thought of as constituting "a literature." Like individual writers, the writing community we identify as Mennonite is continuously reconstituted, in the words of Katherine Ewing, "in response to internal and external stimuli"; and like individual writers, the community is often projected as whole—even "in the face of radical contradictions"—because as critics we tend to keep "only one frame of reference in mind at any particular moment" (258, 251).[25] This tendency is one of the challenges that confronts us now.

There is no question that creative work by writers who claim a Mennonite heritage or who identify themselves as adherents to the Mennonite faith continues to proliferate. Among the most widely-applauded works of Canadian fiction for 2014, for example, are novels by four Mennonite writers, all of whom have developed a national audience well beyond what they might admit as any sort of "Mennonite base": Miriam Toews, whose No. 1 Canadian bestseller *All My Puny Sorrows*[26] explores the nature of love and the apparent inevitability of death in a complex modern Mennonite family; David Bergen, whose *Leaving Tomorrow* features a protagonist at once repelled, confounded, and comforted by his Mennonite background; Rudy Wiebe, whose *Come Back* foregrounds a protagonist who first came to light as the young Mennonite child Hal Wiens in Wiebe's first novel (1962) *Peace Shall Destroy Many*; and Carrie Snyder, younger than the others, and from a distinctively different Mennonite tradition,[27] whose *Girl Runner* is, according to the author, "entirely un-Mennonite in content" (email to the author). Snyder's novel, after creating a stir at the Frankfurt Book Fair, was released in Canada last fall, and was slated for publication in at least 11 distinct territories, in eight languages, in 2015. In what sense will it—or any other of these novels—be read as a "Mennonite" text? And if any or all of them are, what might that *mean*?

---

25 See Ewing for a discussion of how, as she puts it, "in all cultures people can be observed to project multiple, inconsistent self-representations that are context-dependent and may shift rapidly" (251).

26 The American and British reviews have been spectacular as well.

27 Carrie Snyder was brought up in a family of "Swiss" Mennonites.

And if they are not read as "Mennonite," what is the tenor and range of our response, our embrace?

Citing Michael Kramer and Hana Wirth-Nesher in his study of material culture and Jewish thought in America, Ken Koltun-Fromm observed in 2010 that "there is talk 'about many Jewish American literatures'" (181). We have spoken of at least two Mennonite literatures since the first two Mennonite/s writing conferences were devoted to writing in Canada and in the USA, respectively. Commentators on Mennonite/s writing tacitly acknowledge, also, "bonnet fiction"—or Amish romance novels—as a literature, even while they all but ignore possibly more earnest fiction titles released from Herald Press, the publishing imprint of MennoMedia, a ministry of Mennonite Church Canada and Mennonite Church USA.[28] The 2015 Fresno conference on Mennonite/s Writing hosted a powerful session focused on LGBT writers and texts; in the closing session of the conference some participants voiced the question: "Where are the people of color?" Even though we have seen a few works of fiction published by Mennonites in Germany or Paraguay, for example, we await work that will surely emerge from among the Mennonites in India and Africa and Indonesia and Central and South America and other parts of the world. In what terms will we receive that work? How will we speak of it? Will we be able to resist appropriating it? How will those Mennonite writers beyond our border receive us? Will those writers and their communities resist us? How might we frame the disposition of those writers relative to the Mennonite/s Writing tradition that has established a strong foothold in North America?

The more the literature of Mennonites proliferates, the more diverse are the voices. Yet, while literary critical debates compound among critics and theoreticians writing about other minority literatures—that is, debates about what people *mean* when they speak of any particular literary tradition—there is very little conversation among Mennonite critics that takes into account a "vexed" question: *What is Mennonite about Mennonite literature?*[29] What I am remarking upon here is that both formal and informal responses to Mennonite/s writing have placed unexamined confidence in the notion that Mennonite literature must be considered collectively. In fact, by gathering at the seventh international conference on Mennonite/s Writing in Fresno, California, in the spring of 2015, critics and writers and readers alike once

---

28 See www.mennomedia.org.

29 I borrow this question, this language, from Leslie Morris, on the future of Jewish studies (770).

again tacitly implied that a certain unified essence of "Mennonite" literature persists over time and space. How shall we define it? Does it matter?

To be sure, the first generation of Mennonite literary texts in Canada revealed a struggle against an ethno-religious culture that was more or less coherent within certain temporal and geographical boundaries. Later generations tend not to struggle explicitly against that earlier culture, though they might, like Carrie Snyder, endorse some of the principles of Anabaptism. More or less fully assimilated into dominant cultures, these writers, many of whom refer to themselves as "secular Mennonites," might not even know what form such an earlier culture might have taken.

I am not suggesting that we retire the category "Mennonite" when we speak of certain literary texts. In fact, quite the opposite. Paraphrasing Koshy, "Mennonite/s writing" offers us "a rubric that we cannot not use" (342). But we might be informed by critics outside our circle who have responded in various complex ways to similar literary traditions. That is, we might give some attention to contextualizing the term "Mennonite literature" and particularizing its uses, so that we *critics* of Mennonite/s writing, like the writers themselves, might write in a new register, both acknowledging more fully the capacious and protean quality of the lived experience of Mennonites in the assorted landscapes of Canada, the USA, and beyond—and tracing in critical discourse the fascinating trajectory of Mennonite/s writing as a field in transition.

WORKS CITED

Bender, Elizabeth H., and Sam Steiner. "The Trail of the Conestoga." *Global Anabaptist Mennonite Encyclopedia Online*, April 2011.

Bergen, David. *Leaving Tomorrow*. HarperCollins, 2014.

Brandt, Di. Email to the author. 23 February 2015.

Chen, Tina Yih-Ting. *Double Agency: Acts of Impersonation in Asian American Literature and Culture*. Stanford UP, 2005.

Dimock, Wai Chee. *Through Other Continents: American Literature Across Deep Time*. Princeton UP, 2006.

Dyck, Arnold. *Lost in the Steppe*. Trans. Henry D. Dyck. Steinbach: Derksen Printers, 1974.

———. *The Collected Works of Arnold Dyck*, ed. Victor G. Doerksen et al. 4 vols., Manitoba Mennonite Historical Society, 1985–1986.

Ewing, Katherine P. "The Illusion of Wholeness: Culture, Self, and the Experience of Inconsistency." *Ethos*, vol. 18, no. 3, 1990, 251–278.

Franco, Dean. "Affectionate, Anxious, and Perplexed: Studies in American Jewish Literature." *Studies in American Jewish Literature*, vol. 311, 2012, pp. 11–18.

Fuss, Diana. *Essentially Speaking: Feminism, Nature & Difference*. Routledge, 1989.

Glaser, Jennifer. Review of *Race, Rights, and Recognition: Jewish American Literature Since 1969* by Dean J. Franco. *American Jewish History*, vol. 97, no. 3, 2013, pp. 327–329.

Hall, Stuart. "Introduction: Who Needs 'Identity'?" *Questions of Cultural Identity*, ed. Stuart Hall and Paul du Gay, Sage, 1996, pp. 1–17.

Hiebert, Paul. *Sarah Binks*. 1947. McClelland & Stewart, 2010.

Hollinger, David A. "The Concept of Post-Racial: How Its Easy Dismissal Obscures Important Questions." *Dædalus*, vol. 1401, 2011, pp. 174–182.

Kirkpatrick, Peter and Robert Dixon, eds. *Republics of Letters: Literary Communities in Australia*. Sydney UP, 2012.

Koltun-Fromm, Ken. *Material Culture and Jewish Thought in America*. Indiana UP, 2010.

Koshy, Susan. "The Fiction of Asian American Literature." *Yale Journal of Criticism*, vol. 9, no. 2, 1996, pp. 315–346.

Kroetsch, Robert. *Excerpts from the Real World: A Prose Poem in Ten Parts*. Oolichan, 1986.

Morris, Leslie. "Placing and Displacing Jewish Studies: Notes on the Future of a Field." *PMLA*, vol. 125, no. 3, 2010, pp. 764–773.

Saldivar, Ramon. "Historical Fantasy, Speculative Realism, and Postrace Aesthetics in Contemporary American Fiction." *American Literary History*, vol. 23, no. 3, 2011, pp. 574–599.

Schreier, Benjamin. "Literary-Historical Zionism: Irving Kristol, Alexander Portnoy, and the State of the Jews." *Contemporary Literature*, vol. 55, no. 4, 2014, pp. 760–791.

Snyder, Carrie. *Girl Runner*. House of Anansi P, 2014.

———. Email to the author. 23 May 2014.

Tiessen, Hildi Froese, ed. *Liars and Rascals: Mennonite Short Stories*, U Waterloo P, 1989.

———. "A Mighty Inner River: 'Peace' in the Early Fiction of Rudy Wiebe." *Journal of Canadian Fiction*, vol. 2, no. 4, Fall 1973, pp. 71–76.

Toews, Miriam. *All My Puny Sorrows*. Knopf Canada, 2014.

Ty, Eleanor, and Donald C. Goellnicht. *Asian North American Identities: Beyond the Hyphen*. Indiana UP, 2004.

Warren, Kenneth W. "A Reply to My Critics." *PMLA*, vol. 128, no. 2, 2013, pp. 403–408.

———. *What Was African American Literature?* Harvard UP, 2011.

Wiebe, Rudy. *Come Back*. Knopf, 2014.

Wong, Sau-ling Cynthia. *Reading Asian American Literature: From the Necessity to Extravagance.* Princeton UP, 1993.

Zacharias, Robert. *Rewriting the Break Event: Mennonites and Migration in Canadian Literature.* U Manitoba P, 2013.

———, ed. *After Identity: Mennonite Writing in North America.* Pennsylvania State UP, 2015.

Sixteen

Thirty Years of Mennonite Literature: How a Modest Course Became Something Else (A Fragment of Literary Memoir)*

Y̲OU NEVER KNOW, someone told me once upon a time, with urgency, what sorts of things might spin off from almost anything you do, anyone you know. Well, my experience with Mennonite writing and Mennonite writers might be a case in point. Mind you, I'm not sure my earliest encounters with Rudy Wiebe in 1962, when he was a Young People's sponsor in a Winnipeg Mennonite Brethren Church and I was, briefly, one of his teenage charges, led to anything in particular. Nevertheless, I recognize in retrospect that our meeting then might have been a kind of starting point to my journey into the land of MennoLit.

My work in Mennonite literature began a few years later, in 1970–1971, when Canadian literature courses had barely begun to be offered in undergraduate and graduate programs in Canadian universities. I had the singular opportunity to take a graduate course in Western Canadian Literature in the Department of English at the University of Alberta (U of A) in Edmonton. Rudy Wiebe, after the conflicted reception of his first novel

---

* First published as Hildi Froese Tiessen, "Thirty Years of Mennonite Literature: How a Modest Course Became Something Else." *Journal of Mennonite Writing*, vol. 8, no.1, 2016.

and a sojourn at Goshen College in Indiana (1963–1967), had returned to the U of A, where his position as a faculty member in the English Department did not preclude his work's being included among the assigned reading for that course. So I took the opportunity to write one of my papers on Wiebe's first two "Mennonite" novels: *Peace Shall Destroy Many* (1962) and *The Blue Mountains of China* (1970). That student paper was subsequently published in the *Journal of Canadian Fiction* (1971), and later republished in a collection of essays entitled *The Canadian Novel: Here and Now* (1983); it was the first article on Wiebe's early fiction to appear in a Canadian academic journal,[1] and seems to have linked me to Wiebe's work ever since.

Besides our being participants in the same English department then, Rudy and I attended the same church, Lendrum Mennonite Brethren, in Edmonton—a church that then had an active drama society that staged a full-length play every year. Rudy and I co-directed (not without mainly friendly disagreements) Kobe Abe's *Friends* one year in the early 1970s, and in a subsequent year I directed an adaptation (composed by members of the drama society) of "The Vietnam Call of Samuel U. Reimer," a chapter from Wiebe's *The Blue Mountains of China*. And the junctures between our personal and professional lives, and our shared interests, grew.

Like so many scholars of Canadian literature during that era of vibrant cultural nationalism (under the first Prime Minister Trudeau), I was not a Canadianist. One barely had the opportunity to become one then, since the field was so young and academic mentors who were trained in the literatures of Canada were few. My area of scholarly pursuit was British modernism, which I studied with the Canadian novelist and scholar Sheila Watson. I was focused, in particular, on the nature, the dynamics, and the politics of literary community as it was expressed in the UK after the Great War. It was much later, after I had settled into a vocation focused on the creative work of Canadian and American Mennonites, that I came to realize that I had not shifted as far from my original field of study as I had thought: I might not be studying the figures of British modernism, but I surely remained interested in the nature and dynamics, and even the politics, of literary community—the

---

1 Elmer Suderman's "Universal Values in Rudy Wiebe's *Peace Shall Destroy Many*" appeared in the Kansas-based *Mennonite Life* in 1965.

Mennonite literary community, as it took shape over the last decades of the twentieth century and into the present.

Rudy Wiebe followed me, figuratively speaking, even after I left Alberta and began to move east—first, for a year, to my hometown of Winnipeg (home of Mennonite writing in Canada) and then to Kitchener-Waterloo. That is, the fact that I had published an essay on Rudy Wiebe began to shape my identity as a young scholar, especially when, in 1974, in Waterloo, I found friends and academic conversation partners among the faculty at Conrad Grebel College at the University of Waterloo. I was invited to become a Fellow of the College, and to deliver guest lectures on Mennonite literature in the College's course on Mennonite History, taught by the then College Dean, Rod Sawatsky.

It was at Rod's invitation that in 1983 I developed a course on Mennonite literature and art. I was teaching down the street from Grebel then, at Wilfrid Laurier University, and would not become a full-time member of the Grebel faculty until 1987. For reasons too involved to go into here, the course I taught on Mennonite literature (and art) at Grebel was initially offered not through the Department of English at the University of Waterloo, but rather under the rubric of something called "Interdisciplinary Arts." (My interest in the visual arts part of the course was rooted in my graduate work on modernist art movements, my teaching of film studies at WLU, and my collaborations with my husband Paul Tiessen on developing a small boutique Press—Sand Hills Books—that published the work of photographers and painters, many of them Mennonite.) It was several years later that the course I had developed was renamed and reframed as a literature-only course: "English 218: Mennonite Literature."

During those early years of our settling in Waterloo, I became reacquainted with Harry Loewen, whom I remembered fondly as my high school history teacher at Mennonite Brethren Collegiate Institute (MBCI) in Winnipeg. When Paul and I moved to Waterloo in the 1970s, Harry was a member of the German Department at WLU, and he and I encountered each other often. An eclectic academic with scholarly interests in history and theology as well as literature, he would go on to become the Founding Chair in Mennonite Studies at the University of Winnipeg (1978), where he established the *Journal of Mennonite Studies*. It was in the first volume of that journal (1983) that he published an essay entitled "Mennonite Literature in Canada: Beginnings, Reception and Study." And he taught courses in Mennonite studies in Winnipeg then, courses that included the reading of literary texts by and about Mennonites.

One of Loewen's closest collaborators in those ventures at the University of Winnipeg was Al Reimer, with whom I had taken a senior course in literary criticism as an undergraduate. Ever the most irrepressible of raconteurs, Professor Reimer would regale my student colleagues and me for at least a quarter of the time allotted to any class with stories about his upbringing in Steinbach. He considered himself a refugee from small town Manitoba (where, my aunt told me long ago, as a difficult-to-manage teenager, he was sent by his father to spend a few weeks of being straightened out by my grandfather on my grandfather's farm. My mother's youngest sister added then that it was there that she fell in love with him—though nothing came of her summer crush). Al Reimer would gradually rediscover his Mennonite roots and write substantial works of fiction about both Mennonites in Russia (*My Harp has Turned to Mourning*) and the Mennonites who peopled his own southern-Manitoba Mennonite childhood home (*When War Came to Kleindarp*).

Harry Loewen and Al Reimer belonged to one of the two relatively distinct Mennonite literary communities in Winnipeg in the late 1970s, two groups of people who belonged to two generations. The first of these was comprised of faculty members like Loewen (Mennonite Studies) and Reimer (English) from the University of Winnipeg, alongside Victor Doerksen (German), Elisabeth Peters (German), Roy Vogt (Political Science) from the University of Manitoba, and George K. Epp (who taught at several colleges and universities in Winnipeg and was, for a time, president of CMBC, now Canadian Mennonite University). These scholars, who focused more on German Mennonite literary texts than English, found expression primarily in the *Mennonite Mirror* (the precursor to *Rhubarb* magazine), the *Journal of Mennonite Studies*, certain literary publications of the Manitoba Mennonite Historical Society such as *The Collected Works of Arnold Dyck* (1985–86), and the small, independent Hyperion Press, which published translations of fiction (German to English) by Al Reimer and collections of essays in Mennonite studies such as *Visions and Realities: Essays, Poems, and Fiction Dealing with Mennonite Issues*, edited by Loewen and Reimer.

The second Mennonite community in Winnipeg during those early years when Mennonite literature began to be taught in the university classroom consisted of the younger generation of emerging writers: Patrick Friesen, Victor Enns, Di Brandt, Armin Wiebe, Sarah Klassen, Sandra Birdsell, and others, for whom German (even though most of them understood it—both High

German and Low) was not a language in which they chose to communicate (though instances of code-switching are scattered throughout their work). The members of this younger generation, while they drew the attention of the *Mennonite Mirror* and the *Journal of Mennonite Studies*, were published mostly by strictly secular enterprises such as Turnstone Press and various little magazines across Canada, including, most prominently, Winnipeg's own *Prairie Fire*. None of these literary venues had explicit ties to any Mennonite community.

Loewen and his colleagues were less interested in these "promising young writers" (as this new generation was referred to by members of the older generation in those early years) than in the earlier, German-language writers who had emerged among Canadian Mennonites, most notably Arnold Dyck. Interestingly, Rudy Wiebe's first novel foregrounds the language shift among (Russian) Mennonites in Canada, from German to English—a shift that seemed, to some, to threaten Mennonite self-identity during the second half of the last century. It was Wiebe, who wrote in English of course, along with the new generation of writers Turnstone Press was publishing, who were accessible to a new generation of readers in Canada and who became the subjects of my own investigations when I began to teach Mennonite Literature in 1983.

There were some texts available to be taught in 1983, to be sure: besides the early work by Rudy Wiebe, there were books by Sandra Birdsell, Patrick Friesen, and David Waltner-Toews, for example. In fact 1983 itself was a good year, with new work by Rudy Wiebe (*My Lovely Enemy*) and David Waltner-Toews (*Good Housekeeping*), and Barbara Smucker (*Amish Adventure*). But Armin Wiebe's first fiction, *The Salvation of Yasch Siemens* (1984), Al Reimer's *My Harp Has Turned to Mourning* (1985), Audrey Poetker's *i sing for my dead in german* (1986), Di Brandt's *questions i asked my mother* (1987), and Sarah Klassen's *Journey to Yalta* (1988) had not yet appeared.

There was at least one American whose work was available—if barely: Warren Kliewer, whom I contacted when I began to teach Mennonite writing, and who then generously sent me "the last remaining copies" of his collection of zany stories *The Violators* (1964)—a stash of (by then) slightly musty green-jacketed volumes I sold at cost to my students until they were pretty much all gone. Dallas Wiebe's controversial novel *Skyblue the Badass* (1969) which, in the words of Jeffrey Hillard, "rose provocatively and crashed silently,"

was out of print by 1972. I'm not sure about his collection of stories *The Transparent Eyeball* (1982), but it doesn't really matter because I would not become aware of Dallas's work until 1989, when I contacted him because his name was Wiebe and, like me, he had written a dissertation on the British modernist Wyndham Lewis. I had seen a citation to his dissertation on Lewis in a bibliography and wrote to him, asking whether he was Mennonite, and—because I was soliciting material for the special issues I was editing at the time—whether he was a creative writer (years later I could have Googled him). He responded by sending me the manuscript of *Our Asian Journey*, which he had circulated among several publishers by then, none of whom would publish it. I included an excerpted chapter in *The New Quarterly* special issue (1990), and Dallas, founder of the *Cincinnati Poetry Review* in 1975 and the University of Cincinnati's creative writing program in 1976, came up from Cincinnati that spring for the first Mennonite/s Writing conference in Waterloo. Oh, he was beyond delighted to have found in Waterloo so large a Mennonite literary family. Between conference sessions he expanded for himself the Mennonite family trope, posing for photographs between Rudy Wiebe and Armin Wiebe at every opportunity. It was years later that I once more took off the shelf the novel manuscript Dallas had sent me in 1989, and Paul Tiessen worked with Dallas to bring it to light (1997).[2]

Well. Back to that course in Mennonite literature. Recognizing in the late 1980s that there were individual short stories by Mennonite writers scattered in collections and magazines here and there, I was compelled to assemble a selection of them into a volume I could use as a text. With the support of a grant from the Secretary of State for Multiculturalism in that heady early era of multiculturalism in Canada, and with the aid and support of Gloria Smith, publisher at the University of Waterloo Press, I edited *Liars and Rascals: Mennonite Short Stories*. The first printing (1989) sold out soon enough; there was another printing the following year.

As had been the case with my Rudy Wiebe essay, *Liars and Rascals* made me visible (once more) as a scholar of Mennonite literature. When plans for the 1990 Mennonite World Conference in Winnipeg began to take palpable shape, I was invited to edit a special issue on Mennonite writing for *Prairie Fire* (in Winnipeg, where every year more Mennonite writers were finding

---

2 Dallas Wiebe's *Our Asian Journey* was published by MLR Editions in 1997.

an audience) and for *The New Quarterly* (an ambitious little magazine at the University of Waterloo with an established history of holding annual conferences featuring new Canadian writing). Compelled by Miriam Maust (an American Swiss Mennonite who had settled in Waterloo and was one of the poetry editors of *The New Quarterly*), the editorial team of *The New Quarterly* invited me to work along with them as programmer and host of their annual conference, which would become the first international conference on Mennonite/s Writing.

That conference, which attracted a number of prominent Canadianists along with Mennonite writers and critics in the spring of 1990, and the special issue that was distributed at that event, were both remarkably successful ventures, drawing positive attention not only to *The New Quarterly*, but also to the new minority literature they were celebrating. I remember one of the Canadianists who had been there declaring with great passion every time we would meet at conferences for years afterwards what a remarkable conference that had been. And it was, not least because of the freshness of the idea, and the warmth of *The New Quarterly* hosts, and the fact that every session was a plenary session (we were all in it together), but also because so many Mennonite writers from so many different provinces and states became acquainted with each other there. And developed lasting literary friendships.

Always looking for new things to teach, I was delighted to find that the literature continued to grow. While the writers who were first published in the 1980s published new volumes of work, new voices emerged: David Bergen, then Miriam Toews and others. And, thanks to the generous Author Readings program of the Canada Council for the Arts, most of these writers were able to visit Waterloo, where they offered public readings to a growing southwestern-Ontario Mennonite reading audience (an audience peppered always with interested non-Mennonite literary types) and made themselves available to students in my course on Mennonite/s writing.

In fact the general reading audience for this literature compounded, partly because in Canada, for example, writers like Rudy Wiebe and Sandra Birdsell and David Bergen and Miriam Toews and playwright Vern Thiessen and others were winning major regional and national awards. Partly because many of their texts delivered narratives about Mennonite experience that were not accessible in any other context, and that came to represent a kind of "homeland" to many Mennonite readers who recognized that in some way these oddly familiar stories and poems made them and their Mennonite experience, as Robert Kroetsch would have observed, somehow "real."

The critical response to Mennonite literature, which had begun to coalesce around the early special issues of little magazines and the first conference in 1990, grew as well, and flourished in numerous special issues devoted mostly to literary criticism (in *Mennonite Quarterly Review*, *Conrad Grebel Review*, and *Journal of Mennonite Studies*, for example). Six more international conferences devoted to Mennonite/s Writing followed (and there are at least two more in the works). The new Mennonite literature was foregrounded in *Rhubarb* magazine, a series of "Literary Refractions" in the *Conrad Grebel Review*, Goshen College's Center for Mennonite Writing with its prodigious online journal, special sessions at literary conferences in Canada and Germany, and countless other individual literary activities across North America. Not to mention reviews of new publications, interviews with authors, and scholarly publications (including theses and dissertations in Canada, United States, Australia, Germany, Finland, Sweden, etc.)—all of which provided secondary material for students, scholars, and general readers with interest in the field.

But back, once more, to teaching. Over the years, guests of Conrad Grebel and of the course in Mennonite literature included Canadians Patrick Friesen, Di Brandt, Rudy Wiebe, Victor Enns, Sandra Birdsell, Armin Wiebe, David Waltner-Toews, David Bergen, Andreas Schroeder, along with Americans Jeff Gundy, Jean Janzen, Julia Kasdorf, and others. Many of these performed for Waterloo audiences over and over, as they launched new work. And Paul Tiessen and I had the great pleasure of hosting them in our home, where literary conversations that gathered momentum throughout the evening continued over breakfast the next day and were maybe picked up again during the next visit.

Because Conrad Grebel College was, like Winnipeg, situated in a demographic that included a large population of Mennonites, my classes in Mennonite Literature tended to attract, along with students with some kind of Mennonite heritage and students who knew nothing about Mennonites, members of the community who were keen readers of every new Mennonite novel or collection of poems. Among these mostly "mature" students were "Swiss"

Mennonites who, more often than not, registered wonder and surprise when they encountered the seemingly utterly foreign cultural landscapes occupied by, for example, Armin Wiebe's Yasch Siemens. And always the persistent question: how come all the writers are Russian Mennonites; where are the writers who are Swiss?

By the late 1980s Conrad Grebel College (by 2001 Conrad Grebel University College) had become a centre for Mennonite/s writing, a venue in which Mennonite writers and readers regularly encountered each other. These encounters were frequent, entertaining, informative, provocative, stimulating, inspiring. Moreover, with a committed audience for Mennonite literary events, Conrad Grebel invited writers like Rudy Wiebe, Sandra Birdsell, Julia Kasdorf, and Jeff Gundy to deliver major public lectures on their work. Most of these were subsequently published in *Conrad Grebel Review*.

What began as a relatively small course in Mennonite literature grew over the years to include a committed southwestern-Ontario reading community that early in 2012 gathered weekly for lectures and readings by Mennonite writers and critics in an iteration of my course in Mennonite Literature which, in winter 2012, was offered as an open series that spanned the twelve-week winter term. The series was called "Mennonite/s Writing: Celebrating the First 50 Years." The regular audience of about a hundred and more joined the students in the course to hear Patrick Friesen, Rudy Wiebe, David Bergen, David Waltner-Toews, Darcie Friesen Hassock, Carrie Snyder, and Julia Kasdorf speak about the trajectory of their work as writers nurtured among Mennonites.[3] The conversations among members of the audience continued during those winter evenings long after the guest writer, my students, and I retired to a seminar room where, for the remaining hours of the evening, the rest of the "course" took place. Those were special evenings, in the public space among a keen and buzzing crowd first of all and, afterwards, among my students (who, every week, had immediate access to the writers whose books they were reading).

---

3 See video recordings of the series at www.uwaterloo.ca/grebel/events/lecture-series/menno-lit-videos-2012.

I retired from teaching the following summer, 2012. A year and a half later, in February 2014, I wrote an email note to Rob Zacharias, whom I had come to know during his grad school years, while I sat on the committee supervising his writing of the dissertation that would become his book: *Rewriting the Break Event: Mennonites and Migration in Canadian Literature* (2013). "Patrick Friesen just wrote to me," I said to Rob. "He is hoping to come to Toronto (and Waterloo) to promote a new book in April 2015 ... It occurred to me that Carrie Snyder and Miriam Toews and David Bergen are all bringing out new books later this year. With Patrick, that makes four. It would be lovely if you would get the folks at Grebel to help you sponsor a 2014–2015 reading series." At the same time, I alerted the administrators of the College of this serendipitous opportunity to host another series. Everyone agreed that it would be a good idea to try to carry on the tradition of providing a home to Mennonite/s writing, even though the faculty position I had held, and my role as purveyor of the course on Mennonite literature and as organizer of decades-worth of Mennonite literary events, had come to an end.

When I retired, the literature slot I had occupied full-time for 25 years became a faculty position in Peace and Conflict Studies. The fate of the course "Mennonite Literature" became tenuous. Conrad Grebel University College, which never had a formalized role as a permanent site of literature teaching within the University of Waterloo's established academic structures, now teaches primarily Music, Peace and Conflict Studies, and Theological Studies—with a small program in Mennonite Studies. So the tradition of providing a credible "liberal arts" program, which had already been threatened with the loss of courses in philosophy, for example, and sociology, has been dramatically set back. As has the possibility of the College's providing a venue for the study of Mennonite literature. That work, which had begun to emerge in 1983, continued only informally into 2014-2015, with Rob Zacharias (who was on campus that year as a post-doc working on Mennonite literature in the university's English Department) organizing and hosting readings by the writers launching new work and also by Rudy Wiebe, Di Brandt, and Jeff Gundy.

I have been interested, throughout my literary career, in writing communities, writers in community, writers and communities. Who could have known that a grad-school essay and my subsequent opportunity to teach a course in Mennonite/s writing should have opened the door for me to spend some

30 years and more encountering, observing, engaging, hosting, listening to Mennonite writers, their texts, and their reading community. Ah. It would be a treat if the College that played host to these writers and their readers would find a way for the Grebel tradition in Mennonite literature to continue.

WORKS CITED

Hillard, Jeffery. "Cover Story: Rebel with a Cause … and a Past." *CityBeat* [Cincinnati], 23 September 1999, www.citybeat.com.

Suderman, Elmer. "Universal Values in Rudy Wiebe's *Peace Shall Destroy Many*." *Mennonite Life*, vol. 20, October 1965, pp. 172–176.

Seventeen

"I didn't have words for it": Reflections on Some of the Early Life-Writing of Di Brandt and Julia Kasdorf*

Authorial Addresses

In her essay entitled "The Autoethnographic Announcement and the Story" (published in 2015), Julia Kasdorf reflects on having been prompted, just prior to the publication of her first volume of poetry, *Sleeping Preacher*, in 1992, to compose a preface or afterword that would offer her readers a gloss on the "Amish and Mennonite culture" that figured prominently in her early poems. That suggestion, she recalls, "confounded" her then: "In addition to writing poems, had it also become my job," she asks, "to write prose that would explain my background in rational sociological or anthropological or theological language?" ("Autoethnographic" 21).[1] Citing Mary Louise Pratt's

---

* First published as "'I didn't have words for it': Reflections on Some of the Early Life-Writing of Di Brandt and Julia Kasdorf." *Journal of Mennonite Studies*, vol. 36, 2018, pp. 25–41.

1 This paper was inspired by an essay Julia Kasdorf prepared for a symposium on Mennonite/s Writing at Penn State University in 2013 and subsequently published in *After Identity: Mennonite Writing in North America* in 2015. It revisits and extends my own 1996 essay on Mennonite literature and binary thinking, first presented at the second conference on Mennonite/s Writing,

use of the term "autoethnographic text," Kasdorf goes on to examine several instances of the sort of explanation she had been urged to provide alongside her poems—informative interludes she identified as "autoethnographic announcements." These would function in Mennonite writing, she observes, not only as ethnographic explanations of who the Amish and/or Mennonites are, but also as "declaration[s] of identity" that "temporarily [sort] insiders from outsiders, facts from fictional misrepresentations, and [tell] the truth" (25). In the course of her discussion she identifies Rudy Wiebe's earnest (but, as it turns out, not entirely accurate)[2] "Foreword" to *Peace Shall Destroy Many*, which offers a summary history of the "Russian" Mennonites, as an example of such an explication, along with Rhoda Janzen's satirical "Appendix" to her bestselling *Mennonite in a Little Black Dress* (Janzen's "A Mennonite History Primer" runs 17 pages), and Miriam Toews's two-paragraph fulmination about Mennonites in the opening pages of her immensely popular "Mennonite" novel, *A Complicated Kindness*. Factual or not, informative, playful, earnest, or satiric, the sorts of expositions Kasdorf identifies—elucidations that are variously attached to or embedded within literary texts—were ostensibly composed to provide a context for the primary work to which the "announcement" is attached, though they function in other ways as well, as we shall see.

Kasdorf's essay prompted me to consider other, similar sorts of authorial addresses in Mennonite texts. To be sure, the autoethnographic announcement, as Kasdorf points out, allows an author the opportunity to offer information that would seem (at least to someone, often the publisher) to be necessary for the reader seeking to comprehend the context in which a primary text operates. But there are other sorts of intratextual or extratextual authorial interventions poised to inform the reader—not about the cultural or historical or theological context in which a given work is situated, but rather about the author herself. These addresses, which tend to be distinctly more personal and often evoke a sense of writer-reader intimacy, appear, almost of necessity, outside the main text, but usually alongside it. Or they might be published as

---

in Goshen, Indiana in 1997 and subsequently published as "Beyond the Binary: Re-Inscribing Writing and the Post-Colonial Condition,"; and my 1992 essay entitled "Mennonite Writing and the Post-Colonial Condition," published as the introduction to *Acts of Concealment: Mennonite/s Writing in Canada*, the curated proceedings of the first conference on Mennonite/s Writing, in Waterloo, Ontario in 1990. This essay reflects my interest in literary history and suggests that the dominant paradigms affecting the development of Mennonite literature in some of the most productive early years of that minor literature's present iteration (I refer here to the late 1980s and early 1990s) were significantly influenced by, among other things, available discourses.

2 See Kasdorf, "Autoethnographic" (27).

independent works—essays, interviews. Most often they occur in the form of what Gérard Genette called paratexts[3]: discursive gestures, generally made by the author, that surround or prolong a text—the sort of thing one might find in a foreword, an introduction, a preface, an afterword, or an appendix.

These latter sorts of authorial commentaries do not occur in the work of all Mennonite writers, of course, but they did figure conspicuously in early work by the prominent Mennonite poets Di Brandt and Julia Kasdorf, both of whom, as it happens, were well known among readers of Mennonite literature and beyond in the very years when certain significant events affecting literary-critical thinking (the emergence of the discourse of post-colonialism, for example) were beginning to have an impact on the literary community. The language introduced by post-colonialism not only served to inform and transform the broad literary landscape, but also changed the way writers belonging to minority cultures in particular saw themselves, assessed their condition in the context of the various cultural landscapes they occupied, and performed their role as author.

Looking for Words

In 1989 Di Brandt prophetically anticipated a prominent theme of this essay when she reflected on her earliest writing (her first volume of poems had been published two years before). "I didn't know then what a huge cultural distance there existed between Reinland and Winnipeg," she declared then, invoking the traditional southern-Manitoba Mennonite village in which she grew up and the urban centre to which, she would argue, she migrated as surely as anyone who travels between vastly different cultures is a migrant. She continued: "or rather, I knew it, deeply, intimately, in my bones, but I didn't have words for it." She went on: "The rest of the world, for us, was *other*"; she didn't have the words to span the vast cultural divide that confronted her then (*Dancing Naked* 32).

This paper, which focuses on Brandt's and Kasdorf's early writing, draws attention to the fact that their relatively frequent personal and (in the development of Mennonite literature as a field) influential addresses—which often took the form of prose essays about their early creative work—were composed during a significant international literary moment. To be sure,

---

3 See Gerard Genette and Marie Maclean. "Introduction to the Paratext." *New Literary History*, vol. 22, no. 2, 1991, pp. 261–272.

both poets had to some degree, from the outset of their careers as writers, registered the shaping influence of the critical discourses of feminism and postmodernism, well-established and influential critical perspectives they, as young writers thoroughly engaged with literary concerns—indeed, as critically-engaged academics—encountered as a matter of course. They were not alone among literary figures in coming to the realization that the languages of feminism, which Brandt applauded for "its articulate strategies of resistance and subversion and survival," and postmodernism, which she commended for having "crazy affinities for contradictions and split identities and discontinuous narratives" (*Dancing Naked* 35) were not adequate to address some of the most salient questions arising out of their particular condition. While neither of them was a migrant in the conventional sense of the term (that is, neither was confronted by the experience of having to cross international borders), each struggled, like any number of contemporary minority-culture writers around the world in the late 1980s and early 1990s, to find language adequate to express the condition of trying to move between what were, for them, distinctly different and incompatible cultures. That is, each of them was driven to find language that would capture and convey— and ideally, also, somehow integrate—the divergent experiences of living in her traditional Mennonite or Amish community while also living in "the world" or—as Brandt would say—"the worldly world" ("how i got saved" 27).

The language that would give adequate expression to their experience—a discourse addressing issues related to borderlands and migration and hybridity and the "third space"—arrived with post-colonial theory, which was beginning to make an impact in literary circles just as these poets were beginning to publish their early work.[4] Seeing their home communities—and, in turn,

---

4 It's worth noting that the seminal study of post-colonialism in literature, entitled *The Empire Writes Back: Theory and Practice in Post-Colonial Literatures*, by Bill Ashcroft, Gareth Griffiths and Helen Tiffin, was published in 1989; Homi Bhabha's *The Location of Culture*, equally influential in the field, did not appear until 1994. My own earliest exploration of the instructive value of post-colonial critical thinking in reading Mennonite literary texts was in my introduction to the proceedings of the first conference on Mennonite/s Writing—*Acts of Concealment* (1992). Here I referenced Bill Ashcroft, et al.'s *The Empire Writes Back* (1989). I preface that introduction, entitled "Mennonite Writing and the Post-Colonial Condition," (in this volume) with a quotation from Sandra Birdsell that effectively glosses the discussion of Brandt and Kasdorf in this essay: "Someone asked me about being on the edge or the periphery, and I really don't feel that way. I see myself as being at the centre, but I don't know where that centre is. Maybe it's writing." My subsequent essay entitled "Beyond the Binary: Re-Inscribing Cultural Identity in the Literature of Mennonites" (1996) (also in this volume) was informed by Bhabha's *The Location of Culture* (1994). Subsequent forays into the field of Mennonite literature and post-colonialism include two essays on Rudy Wiebe by Ervin Beck: "Postcolonial Complexity in the Writings of Rudy Wiebe" and "Rudy Wiebe and WB Yeats: Sailing to Danzig and Byzantium," as well as Amy D.

the world beyond them—as distinctive and monolithic, and apparently not yet recognizing that these worlds need not be incommensurable, nor that the potential of inhabiting the space in between these discrete spheres of experience and activity might be productive and liberating, Brandt and Kasdorf turned to personal writing—the kind of writing that would seem to allow them to bridge the troublesome gap between their sectarian communities and their secular environment. "Do we not turn to memoir and other kinds of personal writing to find language to understand the events of our own lives?" Kasdorf wondered later, when she reflected on the highly personal discursive gestures embedded in her early work (*the body* xiii). As for Brandt, striving in 1989, as she put it then, to "write [her]self out of" her culture, she confessed that she found no other way than to compose what she referred to as "another autobiographical story" ("dancing naked" 23). Indeed, it was their own personal writing that, in effect, conveyed each of them across the gap each perceived to exist between the worlds that—in compelling and distinctive ways—had a hold on them.

Registering Ambivalence

Kasdorf's early propensity to register the trope of leaving one cultural landscape to occupy another (and suffering a certain ambivalence about such a move along the way) was not restricted to the prose declarations she composed as commentaries on the experience of writing and publishing her earliest volume of poems. The trope of leaving, and the ambivalence about leaving, resonated throughout *Sleeping Preacher* itself, from the very first poem, where the urban environment in which the poet/speaker was living and the nostalgically rendered agrarian community in which she had been nurtured are featured in juxtaposition. "I don't like New York," the speaker remarks, making use of a compelling symbol of urban worldliness. She goes on, invoking a striking image that expresses her ambivalence about her move to the city while suggesting her deep and abiding attachment to land—presumably the rural terrain she identifies with the home she once

---

Kroeker's MA thesis entitled "'Separation from the World': Postcolonial Aspects of Mennonite/s Writing in Western Canada," and Cheryl Lousley's "Home on the Prairie?: A Feminist and Postcolonial Reading of Sharon Butala, Di Brandt, and Joy Kogawa." All these were published in 2001. Vikki Visvis's "Postcolonial Trauma in David Bergen's *The Time in Between*" appeared in 2013. Sofia Samatar's "The Scope of This Project" and Daniel Shank Cruz's "On Postcolonial Mennonite Writing: Theorizing a Queer Latinx Mennonite Life" appeared in 2017.

knew: "but sometimes these streets / hold me as hard as we're held by rich earth" (3). This prominent trope, that draws attention to how conflicted the speaker is, how difficult it is for her to withdraw herself from the community that brought her up to live in a particular way, in a particular place, is clarified and expanded in the volume's second poem, where the speaker reflects on her relationship with her recently deceased grandmother, Vesta Peachey: "When old church ladies call me her name," she writes, "I must tell them I'm no one they know, / no one who stayed in that Valley of silos / and holsteins." Nevertheless, she confesses, "I have carried her out of that Valley, / Between Front Mountain and Back / I've taken her still clutching / her bulbs and berry canes" (4).

An ambivalence one might find in any number of literary texts by Mennonite authors is evident as a constant dynamic accompanying this leaving of the old world; but evident, too, is the celebration of the one who has had the courage to leave, the rebel with the temerity to refuse the constraints enforced by and represented in the home community. Instructive in this regard is the parenthetical and paratextual note at the end of Kasdorf's volume of poems, which offers a gloss on the figure who is featured in the title of the collection: the "sleeping preacher"—a figure whose "spirit preaching" made him "unaccountable to the processes of community censure," given that he might very well be delivering "the direct voice of God" (61). Aha. The sleeping preacher had found a way to claim a place in the community even while released from its constraints. This poet would surely covet such a role. Consider how she extends the celebration of escape in another poem, entitled "Riding Bike with No Hands," in which she speaks of learning to ride a bicycle, and revels in the "quickening" she felt "long ago when Daddy let go." She recalls how she "coasted off in the lawn" then, "exquisitely balanced," and "absolved from all attachment" (57).

The recurring theme of a difficult withdrawal from the culture of one's birth is seminal in the early prose commentaries of Brandt, too, who finds an equally dramatic way of expressing her troubled condition of trying to negotiate between two worlds of experience, declaring with inimitable drama that when she began to write she had been living with her heart and soul "somewhere halfway between sixteenth-century northern Europe and the Old Testament, and [her mind and body], at least some part of them, in twentieth-century Canada" (*Dancing Naked* 33).

Self-fashioning

Life-writing—as life-writing—among Mennonite authors has received until now only scant critical attention.[5] Here I am focusing on one aspect of this field, not on memoirs or autobiographies, those readily recognizable *bona fide* genres, but rather on some pithy and, to some degree, intense, personal appeals to the reading audience Brandt and Kasdorf made early in their careers—their exercises in what is now generally identified in literary circles as the practice of "self-fashioning" (a term influentially used by Stephen Greenblatt in 1980). "Self-fashioning"—using publishing opportunities to create a public persona and perform a self (even if conceived as a fiction)—afforded each of these young poets and essayists whose relatively exotic subject matter was not quite as comfortably received initially as it would be in the years ahead (in the heyday of so-called ethnic literatures and multiculturalism) the opportunity to confirm her authority and authenticity as a writer; to direct, through urgent-seeming personal appeals, the reading of her work. This is not to say that these poets soon abandoned their personal appeals to the reader; as late as 2001, Kasdorf wrote: "I want to disturb you too, my reader, even as I would like to seduce you sweetly through the pages of this book" (*the body* xvi). Self-fashioning was particularly useful to these writers in the early years when the practice allowed them to shape and limit the public narrative that would determine how both they and a particular minor literature might be received.

In their particular context, the practice of self-fashioning allowed these brilliant poets to create a legitimate space for themselves and their out-of-the-ordinary work, and to claim what Kasdorf would later call "the important, somewhat glamorous roles of transgressor and exile" ("Sunday Morning" 7). In a similar vein, Brandt, in retrospect, reflects on "writing [herself] into scandal and success" (*Dancing Naked* 10). Each one of them was—and recognized herself to be—a trailblazer, after all, and found currency in embracing her role as the bold, even audacious individual who would dare to challenge boundaries generally accepted by other participating members of her community. "This act of rebellion and subversion shatter[ed] my identity as I knew it at that time," Brandt declared later, adding that she had "to recognize in [her]self

---

[5] A notable major study in the area is Jesse Hutchison's 2015 PhD dissertation for the University of Waterloo, entitled "Private People in Public Places: Contemporary Canadian Mennonite Life Writing." Hutchison focuses on autobiographical writing by Di Brandt, Connie Braun, Katie Funk Wiebe, Miriam Toews, and Rudy Wiebe.

the 'rebel traitor thief,' willing to sell out, blow up, throw away the family stories and the official narratives of the culture, for art." Would she be killed, she wondered, "for this act of utter betrayal?" (*Dancing Naked* 10). Yet, as their colleague and contemporary Patrick Friesen would observe of his own role as a transgressive poet, these young women were prepared to proceed with one foot in, one foot out of their community, as Brandt observes in her tribute to Friesen composed in January 1992. Here she commends Friesen, whom she identifies as a significant mentor, for demonstrating "how to locate yourself on the edge of a community, dangerously, precariously, the cutting edge, without falling in or out" (*Dancing Naked* 58–59). That is, Brandt and Kasdorf were, as another Mennonite poet of the time, Sheri Hostetler, remarked, willing to trouble the cultural and religious environment that had nurtured them—but, they were, at the same time, not prepared to leave, to go away.[6] So they were confronted not simply with the challenge of escape, but with the task of bridging apparently incommensurate worlds. They needed to figure out a way of writing across the gap, of embroidering a bridge of words that would allow them to function within both of the divergent landscapes they then occupied almost alternately. The practice of self-fashioning—of placing themselves as real, live figures negotiating a treacherous cultural landscape—offered them at least a provisional discourse. Through personal writing they were able to begin to map the unfamiliar terrain in which they found themselves.

At a colloquium on Western Canada in the German city of Trier in 1989, Di Brandt observed that "what Germans find shocking about the new Mennonite writing is its confessional quality its nakedness" ("dancing naked" 23). Indeed, she and Kasdorf appeared to be willing to reveal a lot about themselves while they attempted to straddle two worlds, using personal narrative and a coaxing voice to forge a link between them. While addressing—often intimately—the full range of her readers, each of Brandt and Kasdorf was able to establish a position for herself both inside and outside that place we so often and so casually refer to as the Mennonite community. And each poet's persuasive and affecting description of what it meant for her to relate to the place from which she said she feared being displaced would resonate throughout the early development of Mennonite writing. In

---

6 See Hostetler's various pieces throughout *Mennonot: For Mennos on the Margins*, a modestly-produced literary magazine created/edited by Sheri Hostetler and Steve Mullet. This informative and humourous, thoughtful, and instructive little magazine, devoted to giving voice to Mennonites who don't conform to conventional Mennonite stereotypes, appeared in 13 issues, published from 1993 to 2003.

fact, this compelling narrative of alienation and displacement—identified by fellow poet Jeff Gundy in 2005 as the "Ur-myth" of Mennonite writing: "the agonistic story of how the most visible and prominent cried out against communal repression and endured the costs" (25) and identified later, by Kasdorf herself, as "the transgressive myth of origins" ("Sunday Morning" 8)—would draw the attention of a range of readers and critics alike. And, given its mesmerizing and paradigmatic dynamic and character, Brandt and Kasdorf's rendition of this "myth of origins" would ensnare their readers' imaginations and be retold by Mennonite writers—and critics—over and over again.

Place

At the first conference on Mennonite/s writing in Waterloo in 1990, Robert Kroetsch memorably commented on southern Manitoba's having been richly inscribed by Mennonite writing. "[I]n Canada," he exclaimed, "finally we have a landscape that is a literary text and that might be the greatest accomplishment of the Mennonite writer" ("Closing" 224). "Paradoxically," Julia Kasdorf wrote in 1991, "*a precarious sense of location* is exactly what has fueled much of my writing so far" (emphasis added, *the body* 46). Indeed, an investigation of geographic place in Mennonite writing has enormous potential. From the sumptuous, dizzying evocation of prairie in the prose and poetry of Di Brandt to celebrations of the land writ large in the giant fictions and reflective essays of Rudy Wiebe; from the evocative conjuring of more intimate midwest American spaces in the poems of Jeff Gundy to the diverse, oftentimes nostalgic summons of the turn-of-the-twentieth-century Russian steppes in the works of Sandra Birdsell or Dallas Wiebe, Mennonite writers have suggested that place—where you are, the landscape you inhabit—matters.

"It is impossible for me to write the land," Brandt swoons. But she does write it: "This land that I love, this wide, wide prairie, this horizon, this sky, this great blue overhead, big enough to contain every dream, every longing." She goes on, deliciously: "It was heaven, the prairie was" (*So this* 1). Evocations of these myriad, often magnificent topographical places might seduce the reader, but they fall short of telling the whole story about Mennonite writers and place. If the individual's position relative to a particular natural landscape is worth exploring in Mennonite writing, so too, of course, is the individual's position relative to the panorama of human beings who make up her community. We know that the individual can readily be placed within—and displaced from—either: from her geographic location and from another sort of place, her cultural and spiritual and genealogical home.

The "place" of community a number of writers spoke of in the early years of the present surge in Mennonite writing—especially the 1980s and 90s—was a narrow, oppressive enclave resistant to forces of change. Few would deny that that common ground so many Mennonite writers identified in their work has shifted or, in many instances, disappeared altogether in these past decades, thanks to what Julia Kasdorf efficiently calls "cultural change and strategic assimilation" ("Autoethnographic" 34). But the transformation Kasdorf registers is not just a matter of cultural change and assimilation; it's about how Mennonites have come to think about being Mennonites in the world and how they have come to think of the world itself, and their place in it. The binary paradigms and the very language some Mennonite writers depended upon to describe the conditions of that common ground, even so recently as a few decades ago, are, we all know, no longer available as persuasive tools.

But in the late 1980s and early 1990s both Brandt's and Kasdorf's descriptions of their vulnerable condition as writers caught between worlds were powerful, resonant performances. When Brandt wrote of "finding myself in exile" and "living my inheritance on this black earth among strangers" (*questions* n.p.) and Kasdorf of her own "fear of abandonment and dislocation" (*the body* 43), each appealed, on the one hand, to the "worldly" reader, who found her exotic; and, on the other, to the empathetic reader among the Mennonites—the one who took solace in asserting that she was not one of the throng who would threaten the Mennonite writer who dared to speak in public. The persuasive statements Brandt and Kasdorf appended to their early work were skillfully constructed and efficiently performed tropes invoked during a particular era when boundaries were, to borrow the words of Hilary Fraser, "at once so momentous and so permeable" (197)—and therefore, one might add, so troublesome and disorienting. The particular exercises in self-fashioning that served Brandt and Kasdorf then would have had scant persuasive impact as little as a decade later. Not only had the wide world changed, and the literary world with it; so too had the language available to address persuasively how any writer might negotiate the various places she occupies.

Struggle for Cultural Legitimacy

"I'm British, I'm English," Rudy Wiebe asserted in a mock interview called "The Blindman River Contradictions," published in 1984. In this piece he would later designate a "story," a cleverly contrived "fake" interview that masquerades as an apparently brazen piece of self-fashioning, Wiebe directs a sharp focus on the practice of self-fashioning and makes light of it (while not failing to reveal, playfully, a few things about himself). "I never had anything to do with Mennonites," he declares; "that's a fiction I made up because of course in western Canada there's much more point to being ethnic than to being English." He continues, observing that he "had the races of the world to choose from and ... made a really bad choice; I should have chosen Jewish," he says, "which would have given me tremendous literary contacts in ways I can never have as a Mennonite" (347).

Wiebe was, of course, not alone in chronicling the place of self-fashioning in that pre-Facebook world, just as he was not alone in registering a minority-culture writer's struggle for cultural legitimacy and in conceding that it was the non-Mennonite world that would make his literary reputation. To be sure, while Mennonite writers like Brandt and Kasdorf railed against the Mennonite community that would seem at once to reject and to smother them, while they planted in the public consciousness the image of the Mennonite writer as oppressed outsider, as ambivalent escapee from a narrow and oppressive—and exotic—minority environment, they too were among those who found a way to stake a claim in the worldly world of the "English" that, after all, appeared for most twentieth-century North American writers, for a long while, to offer the only legitimate base for a substantial literary career. These writers faced having to negotiate not only the cultural terrains in which they lived their apparently bifurcated lives, but also the dominant culture's literary landscape that threatened to elude them and ignore their work if they did not choose astutely how to represent themselves and their personalized narratives. And while each fashioned her literary persona for all, she shaped how all her readers grew to comprehend the dynamics that defined the Mennonite writer's relationship to her audiences, and forged a compelling paradigm that would markedly affect the trajectory of Mennonite/s writing.

Beyond Fixed Points of Departure and Arrival

The appeals Brandt and Kasdorf made in their early work were personal and expressed with urgency: "i hate having to choose between my inherited identity & my life: traditional Mennonite versus contemporary Canadian woman writer, yet how can i be both & not fly apart?" (Personal 183), Brandt complains, while Kasdorf declares without equivocation: "I've had it both ways—to be in the community and in the world—which of course means to have it neither way" (*the body* 46).

Julia Kasdorf and, a few years earlier, Di Brandt, predated the wide-ranging and enormously influential language adopted by literary theorists and others around the world at the time that Homi Bhabha published his seminal work *The Location of Culture* in 1994, and introduced the notion of the interstitial space between worlds and declared that space integrative and productive. Bhabha's fresh way of writing about people moving between regions and between cultures was barely reaching public consciousness when Brandt and Kasdorf began to find their way as writers. Had these young Mennonite poets absorbed the language of post-colonial theory at the beginning of their careers, would they have described their worlds—and their ability to negotiate them—differently? Not that they might have described the details of their experience otherwise, but that they might, for example, not have accepted the implication that the multiple cultures they occupied were in some real sense monolithic and exclusive. And what about that dominant paradigm Jeff Gundy identified as the "Ur-myth"? Had these poets found a way, early on, to name and occupy a "third space," might they have had a very different impact on how we have come to imagine the development and dynamic of Mennonite writing, or even life generally among late twentieth-century Mennonites?

In 2011 Benjamin Schreier, a critic of American Jewish literature to whose work I have made reference elsewhere,[7] observed of Philip Roth's characters that it's not that they "do not want to be Jews; it is that they do not know how to describe themselves as Jews" (101). One might say that a similar, parallel condition confronted also, for a while, powerful and influential minority-culture writers like Kasdorf and Brandt, who found themselves burdened with the challenge of describing themselves as Mennonites (while attempting to elude what they perceived as the negative impact of embracing such a definition).

---

7 See, for example, my "After Identity: Liberating the Mennonite Literary Text," *After Identity: Mennonite Writing in North America*, ed. Robert Zacharias, Pennsylvania State UP, 2015, pp. 210–225. Included in this volume.

And one might add that Mennonite writers' often conflicted encounter with such a challenge has had a significant and lasting impact on the development of the Mennonite literary scene. It's not, for example, that these young poets wanted to escape absolutely the traditional places they had known, but rather, as they themselves remarked, that they didn't have the words to explain what their modern condition between places might mean—that it didn't necessarily imply, as the young Brandt feared, that she might fly apart, or, in the words of the young Kasdorf, that she might be condemned to occupying no place at all.

To be sure, the issue of the availability of language—of words adequate to express what one is driven to say—would not have been a novel concept for someone like Kasdorf, who, in her first collection, muses on the subject in a gentle poem about the speaker's father, who was clearly challenged, she observes, by the inadequacy of words for expressing a full range of human experience: "When he came home / from college, dreaming at last in English," she wrote of her father, "he reached for words that didn't exist / in Pennsylvania Dutch, to talk with his aunts, / and for the first time wondered what you could think / if all you spoke was a language with words enough / for cooking and farm work and gossip" (*Sleeping Preacher* 12).

As for Brandt, her own understanding of the complexities of discrete languages and discourses was embedded in her understanding of the world from the beginning, as she observes when she speaks of the three languages that punctuated her existence while she was growing up: Low German (*Plautdietsch*), High German, and English. "We had very strict rules about not mixing these languages up, nor ever speaking them in the wrong place" she wrote. "And so we did this complex weekly juggling act between three profoundly different conceptual and linguistic paradigms, without ever batting an eye. It wasn't really translating that we did, going from one language to the other, so much as stepping from one paradigm clearly into the other, and then back again" (*Dancing Naked* 33–34).

The critical discourses available for expressing the condition of these writers, each of whom were in a genuine sense migrants even without crossing international borders, defined and delimited the paradigms each understood to be definitive of her own experience as surely as did the distinctive languages Brandt spoke of here. As long as the dominant discourse defining migrancy offered a binaristic paradigm limited to fairly rigid notions of here and there, the language of writers trying to come to terms with the condition of the migrant was limited. Paul Carter observed usefully in 1992 that the binary oppositions of here and there, them and us (most commonly thought of in relation to the migrant, but equally applicable to the person who moves between any two cultures) might be supplanted if we were prepared to regard movement between places, locations, cultures "not as an awkward interval between fixed points of departure and arrival, but as a mode of being in the world" (101). Simply "being in the world" had been a challenge for both Brandt and Kasdorf, each of whom had accepted her condition as embodying the imperative that she move awkwardly between fixed points.

In 1991 Julia Kasdorf wondered about what it was that set her, as a Mennonite, "apart from the mainstream." When, one day, she might "break through this invisible sphere that both comforts and confines," would she, she wondered, "be released into ... what? The world, whatever that means?" (*the body* 46–47). At about the same time, in 1992, she began an investigation into the life of Joseph W. Yoder, who, she wrote, emerged for her "as a heroic author who refused to yield to the religious community of his birth and who was able to write his own life, defining himself and his truths in terms that were broader than his relationship to that community and its God." Yoder's story, she observed, "maps a progression from identification with traditional family and sect to identification with the democratic, pluralistic nation, propelled by education and creativity" (*Fixing* 239). In other words, Kasdorf observes that Yoder landed in, and functioned within, the "world." She notes that her study of Yoder had begun as an investigation of "how anyone from an ethnic or traditional background can become an artist without breaking ties with his place and people of origin"; but it became something else. She became "more interested in understanding how this particular Amish-born individual became an American, engaged in public life and discourse, even as he maintained conversations with individuals from his community of birth" (*Fixing* 13). Years later she registered her recognition that the boundary she had assumed existed between her Mennonite culture and "the broader culture" ("Autoethnographic" 28) had disappeared. She had borrowed the term "contact zone" from Pratt, who spoke of it, Kasdorf observed, as "the social space in which 'cultures meet, clash, and grapple with each other.'" The "contact zone," she wrote then, was "no longer out there somewhere" (23, 34).

So, finally, when we examine the personal writing, the acts of self-fashioning, in the writing of these poets, we encounter much more than we might have anticipated. That is, by constructing bridges that would allow them to span the apparently disparate worlds they occupied early in their careers, both Brandt and Kasdorf—through personal writing—very effectively addressed the restrictive binary logic of their time. Through personal writing often offered merely in snatches, often in paratexts and personal essays, these poets came to define how they themselves—and the condition of the Mennonite writer, and the dynamic of the Mennonite literary community, and the character of much of the work we call "Mennonite/s Writing"—grew to be seen in the last decade of the twentieth century. Shortly after Brandt and Kasdorf began to publish their early work, the discourse of post-colonialism, that embraced the notion of the binary-defying "third space" and that pervaded and shaped how minority literatures and their authors came to be seen, offered them an alternative paradigm—a fresh discourse—that allowed each one of them to express herself in a manner that was not circumscribed by binaristic and monolithic models. This alternative paradigm encompassed and integrated divergent and emerging ways of being in the wide world.

Kasdorf, in an essay dated 2000, reflecting on her regular trips between New York City and her home place in central Pennsylvania, invoked this new paradigm when she declared that what invigorated her "was not an arrival at either end but the suspension of the demands that either destination placed on me. I liked being able to think in the free space between places," she wrote, "and the ways that my own travel could make a connection between them." She proceeded to embrace "the experience of embodying a connection between disparate locations," declaring that from childhood she had "learned to love the anticipation of arrival and also to follow a road between the traditional community and the non-Mennonite world. Now that distance is not as great as it once seemed" (*the body* 8). Di Brandt, later in her career, would similarly invoke the fresh paradigms theorists had developed to permit and support a new way of thinking about being a member of a minority culture within a broader context. "I have been writing myself back into life ... grieving my lost identity, pasting together the shattered bits of myself piece by piece in new configurations as I learn to relocate myself in the contemporary world," she wrote in 1996 (*Dancing Naked* 10), suggesting the emergence of a new perspective. The liberating language she adopted was most evocatively expressed in the exclamation recorded in the title of her second collection of essays, in 2007: "So *this* is the world," she exclaimed with palpable exuberance, "and here I am in it."[8]

---

8 Emphasis mine. The expression "this is the world & here i am in it" appears first in Brandt's published work in the opening poem of her second volume of poems, *Agnes in the sky*. Brandt makes frequent use of this resonant phrase, including in the concluding essay of *So this is the world & here I am in it*, where she writes, "I've been ... trying as hard as I can to understand what that idealistic, crazy, stubborn, ecstatic, beautiful, terrible heritage was about, and what it means to me, and to everything, now. *So this is the world, and here I am in it, one of the many lost & found, if you can believe it across all this space*" (210–211).

WORKS CITED

Beck, Ervin. "Postcolonial Complexity in the Writings of Rudy Wiebe." *Modern Fiction Studies*, vol. 47, no. 4, 2001, pp. 855–886.

———. "Rudy Wiebe and W.B. Yeats: Sailing to Danzig and Byzantium." *Ariel: A Review of International English Literature*, vol. 32, no. 4, 2001, pp. 7–19.

Bhabha, Homi K. *The Location of Culture*. Routledge, 1994.

Brandt, Di. *Agnes in the sky*. Turnstone Press, 1990.

———. *Dancing Naked: Narrative Strategies for Writing Across Centuries*. The Mercury Press, 1996.

———. "dancing naked: narrative strategies for writing across centuries." *The Ethnic Strain: Place & Vernacular Musings: Papers and an Interview*, ed. Wolfgang Klooss and Herbert Zirker, Universität Trier, 1989, pp. 23–32.

———. "how i got saved." *Why I Am a Mennonite: Essays on Mennonite Identity*, ed. Harry Loewen, Herald Press, 1988, pp. 26–33.

———. *questions i asked my mother*. Turnstone Press, 1987.

———. *So this is the world & here I am in it*. NeWest Press, 2007.

———. Personal Statement. *Prairie Fire: Special Issue on Canadian Mennonite Writing*, vol. 11, no. 2, 1990, p. 183.

Carter, Paul. *Living in a New Country: History, Travelling and Language*. Faber, 1992.

Cruz, Daniel Shank. "On Postcolonial Mennonite Writing: Theorizing a Queer Latinx Mennonite Life." *Journal of Mennonite Writing*, vol. 9, no. 4, 15 December 2017.

Fraser, Hilary, Stephanie Green, and Judith Johnston. *Gender and the Victorian Periodical*. Cambridge UP, 2003.

Friesen, Patrick. "Poet Patrick Friesen: One foot in, one foot out." Interview by Sheri Hostetler, *Mennonot: For Mennos on the Margins*, vol. 1, Fall 1993, pp. 5–7.

Greenblatt, Stephen. *Renaissance Self-Fashioning: From More to Shakespeare*. U Chicago P, 1980.

Gundy, Jeff. *Walker in the Fog: On Mennonite Writing*. Cascadia, 2005.

Janzen, Rhoda. *Mennonite in a Little Black Dress: A Memoir of Going Home*. Henry Holt, 2009.

Kasdorf, Julia. "The Autoethnographic Announcement and the Story." Zacharias, pp. 21–36.

———. *the body and the book: Writing from a Mennonite Life: Essays and Poems*. Pennsylvania State UP, 2009.

———. *Fixing Tradition: Joseph W. Yoder, Amish American*. Pandora P US, 2002.

———. *Sleeping Preacher*. U Pittsburgh P, 1992.

———. "Sunday Morning Confession." *Mennonite Quarterly Review*, vol. 87, no. 1, 2013, pp. 7–10.

Kroeker, Amy D. "Separation from the World: Postcolonial Aspects of Mennonite/s Writing in Western Canada." MA thesis, University of Manitoba, 2001.

Kroetsch, Robert. "Closing Panel." *Acts of Concealment: Mennonite/s Writing in Canada*, ed. Hildi Froese Tiessen and Peter Hinchcliffe, U Waterloo P, 1992, pp. 223–242.

Lousley, Cheryl. "Home on the Prairie?: A Feminist and Postcolonial Reading of Sharon Butala, Di Brandt, and Joy Kogawa." *Interdisciplinary Studies in Literature and Environment*, vol 8, no. 2, 2001, pp. 71–95.

Samatar, Sofia. "The Scope of This Project." *Journal of Mennonite Writing*, vol. 9, no. 2, 15 May 2017.

Schreier, Benjamin. "The Failure of Identity: Toward a New Literary History of Philip Roth's Unrecognizable Jew." *Jewish Social Studies: History, Culture, Society*, vol. 17, no. 2, Winter 2011, pp. 101–135.

Tiessen, Hildi Froese. "Beyond the Binary: Re-Inscribing Cultural Identity in the Literature of Mennonites." *Mennonite Quarterly Review*, vol. 72, 1998, pp. 491–501.

———. "After Identity: Liberating the Mennonite Literary Text." Zacharias, pp. 210–225.

Toews, Miriam. *A Complicated Kindness*. Knopf, 2004.

Visvis, Vikki. "Postcolonial Trauma in David Bergen's *The Time in Between*." *Ariel: A Review of International English Literature*, vol. 44, no. 2, 2013, pp. 169–194.

Wiebe, Rudy. "The Blindman River Contradictions: An Interview with Rudy Wiebe." *Rudy Wiebe: Collected Stories, 1955–2010*, U Alberta P, 2010, pp. 346–356.

———. *Peace Shall Destroy Many*. McClelland & Stewart, 1962.

Zacharias, Robert, ed. *After Identity: Mennonite Writing in North America*. Pennsylvania State UP, 2015.

Afterword

"Some Hidden Rhythm": On Being Right There, Right Then

It is clear that there is another generation out there and boy can they write!

Victor G. Doerksen, in *Mennonite Mirror*

I. Some Hidden Rhythm

It's been quite an adventure to revisit a selection of the essays I wrote about Mennonite/s writing over the past 50 years. I am grateful to Robert Zacharias, editor, and Sue Sorensen, publisher, for inviting me to rediscover (with both pleasure and consternation) that body of work; for giving me the impetus to explore and understand some of the uneasiness I had sensed, from time to time, about my writing and the conditions that affected it; and for providing an occasion for me to ponder some of the questions that, for lack of time or courage, I had not paused to address when I was confronted by them. The more I revisited what I had written, the more I came to see afresh what I had grasped imperfectly all along. I had not re-read most of these essays since proof-reading them just before their original publication.

Among the things I was able to see and appreciate with greater clarity was this: I had simply been, somehow, all those years, in the right place at the right time. I had been given an astonishing range of opportunities to observe at close hand and to comment upon a singular literary phenomenon that was dynamic and vibrant, produced by creative individuals ready to give voice to their own blends of talent, acute observation, insight, and magnanimity—individuals poised to write brilliantly about Mennonite worlds they had known.

The essays gathered for this volume (along with other pieces I wrote during that same period of time, not collected here) respond to, and to some degree document, the ever-emergent confluence of national and multicultural histories, literary and literary-critical movements, personal and cultural sensibilities, and publishing opportunities that nurtured and sustained the literary phenomenon we have come to identify with Mennonite/s Writing, a term that, since I settled on it as the title for the 1990 conference, has become something of a brand or trademark denoting a field of literary activity centred around texts written by authors who are Mennonites.[1]

The essays in this volume consist of extended observations about a particular phase of Mennonite/s writing and explore how a group of literary works can come to occupy and shape a unique cultural landscape framed by historical, social, religious, and/or geographical conditions. These essays address some of the ways a literature that had—and, to be sure, has—a palpable impact on the culture and self-understanding of Mennonites in North America emerged and, by the turn of the twenty-first century, had begun to morph into something no longer readily legible in terms of the particular values and beliefs, the points of reference and habits of thought, the assumptions and stereotypes that had earlier defined it. The aggregation of Mennonite literary texts that began to give expression to an era some 20 years before the turn of the last century has since grown ever larger and substantially more diverse. I dealt principally with the emergence and initial flourishing of that literature—in a period primed to foster it.

Working my way through my own essays—and inevitably revisiting the creative and critical activity of others who accompanied my literary journey—I was also struck by several other things. One is that the particular body of creative work around which I focussed my thinking and writing

---

1 In my address to the September 2022 Goshen conference, the ninth in a series of international conferences focused on "Mennonite/s Writing," I explained what I have meant by that term, where the slash in the first word, "Mennonite/s" allowed it to function as both an adjective and a noun while the second word, "Writing" served as a noun and a verb. I use the terms "Mennonite writer" and "Mennonite writing" and "Mennonite literature" as shortcuts referring to writing produced by authors who, as I've suggested elsewhere, know what it means to be Mennonite. (I tend not to refer to writing *about* Mennonites as "Mennonite writing" or "Mennonite literature.") See my "Fourteen Reflections," p. 142.

was remarkably definable and limited, even as the landscape of Mennonite literature was simultaneously expanding and morphing. And two, that even though I gave voice to them in various ways and venues, I hadn't satisfactorily come to terms with some interconnected central questions embedded within my own work which included, in the simplest of terms, these: how do I bring my reading and experience, my tools and insights, to bear on the new work being produced by the Mennonite writers who were increasingly diverse and cosmopolitan? How do I—given the nature and trajectory of my own critical thinking—best address the work of the amazing new writers whose experiences as Mennonites are distinctly non-ethnological and whose audiences (often eager enough for new literary texts ostensibly tinged with traces of Mennonite experience) are themselves, more than ever before, various and international?

My essays reveal that I was struggling with these related questions and effectively avoiding them at the same time. In fact, I was responding to the range and diversity of creative work that was making up an ever-enlarging field in a manner I had criticized in readers of Mennonite texts all along: exercising the urge to address the phenomenon of Mennonite writing as if it were a whole, as if one could, in effect, transfer one's understanding of one text by one Mennonite writer to one's comprehension of a text by another (well, maybe I'm being a little hard on myself here). I had always been ready to say that wouldn't work. I was, to be sure, and to an appreciable degree, on the verge of being stymied by the variety of new texts by writers identified as Mennonite and the pace at which those new texts were appearing, by the enthralling chutzpah of the new writers themselves, and by the rapidly-shifting general literary-critical landscape, with its own often ideologically-driven imperatives.

Among the more compelling insights my re-reading offered me was the fact that far from being a haphazard collection of reflections on Mennonite/s Writing, the essays gathered here have a rather peculiarly defined beginning and end. While I worked to make sense of patterns I discerned in my own writing, I came to see that the literary era to which I had been responding (a literary period I detected as a distinctive historical phase only after it was well under way) seemed now, in retrospect, also to have had a discernible span. That is, both the assemblage of my own essays and the cluster of texts these essays engage seem now, in retrospect, to have comprised a perceptible (and in many senses, parallel) surge, wave, or phase.

In my "After Identity" essay, published in 2013 and included in this volume, I quote Robert E. Spiller's declaration that each generation "should produce at least one literary history" because "each generation must define the past in its own terms" (vii). Long before that, as I observed in that same essay, Ralph Waldo Emerson had declared: "The books of an older period will not fit this" (88). I had the temerity to observe, then, ten years ago, something I didn't fully comprehend until years later: that although "Mennonite literature seems to be in no danger of vanishing ... the conditions that sustained its origins and the early critical readings of it no longer compel many who have an interest in the field. Much of the new Mennonite writing is a different thing altogether: vibrant and fresh and worldly" ("After" 220). The last sentence here, of course, needs no qualification. But it seems to me that the vibrant new literature we enjoy now invites us, as readers interested in the field, to look back to ask what exactly we are, in effect, leaving behind. My revisiting my own work propelled me towards that question perhaps more than any other.

I will invoke, on this matter, the work of Franco Moretti, whose innovative thinking about literary history I first encountered while preparing my paper for the symposium on post-identity issues in Mennonite/s writing hosted by Julia Kasdorf and Robert Zacharias at Penn State University in 2013.[2] Moretti was interested in a certain kind of quantitative literary history (in dates and numbers, trends and patterns) that led him to this observation in 2003: literature "remains in place for a generation or so" (83). The literary world, he argued, demonstrates "brief bursts of invention" determined by what he referred to as a "hidden pendulum of literary history" (80). Literary genres, he wrote, "seem to arise and disappear together according to some hidden rhythm" (82). Every 25 or 30 years the pendulum reaches the end of its arc and recedes while something else takes its place.

So, if we were to think of Mennonite writing in terms of waves or eras, what might we observe? I've worked for years with the notion that—as many acknowledge—there was a surge of writing by creative writers of Mennonite heritage during the 1980s and onward, until the early years of the twenty-first century, when writing by Mennonites persisted in a new register and a more dispersed and variable pattern. I would argue that Rudy Wiebe bridged an interval in the general history of twentieth-century Mennonite writers between, say, the generations of Arnold Dyck who published work, in German, mostly during the 1940s–60s[3] and Patrick Friesen, a prominent Mennonite author who emerged forcefully in the 1980s. Similarly, one could say that Miriam Toews and David Bergen are perched at the intersection between

---

2 The scholarship from this event appeared in Robert Zacharias's edited collection, *After Identity*.

3 See *The Collected Works of Arnold Dyck*, 4 vols., ed. Victor G. Doerksen, George K. Epp, Harry Loewen, Elisabeth Peters, Al Reimer, Manitoba Mennonite Historical Society, 1985–1986.

the generation that began with Patrick Friesen and his contemporaries and the next wave: the new writers whose work we are reading now. Of course, there are no fast borders between these eras of literary activity, nor do the eras necessarily resemble each other. Moreover, any number of writers—including, to be sure, Rudy Wiebe—would seem to be part of more than one generation. But a reader of Mennonite literary work from the past 60 years or so can see that contexts and themes, form and focus, voice and audience, for example, shift palpably enough as time goes by. The texts we are reading now by writers who identify as Mennonites (even work by writers who might span more than one generation) have a different character, gist, and texture than the principal texts we were reading a few decades ago.

This concept of the generation is compelling for various reasons including, for me, the fact that I was privileged to be in the right place at the right time while the surge of Mennonite literary activity that began to take shape in the 1980s was gathering momentum. And my work was my attempt to engage that wave, which was swirling all around me. I was very attentive to it; developed a way of thinking about it; explored how critics who were focused on other, parallel literary developments in Canada and beyond were grappling with questions resonant in literatures expressing similar dynamics; and struggled to find a meaningful way to respond with sensitivity and insight to what has followed—which is, as I've remarked, in so many ways a discernible departure from what prevailed before.

It's important to note that with these remarks, of course, I am neither announcing nor predicting an end to Mennonite literature. But I am suggesting that this literature as we've tended to define it—like any literature we might comfortably call "Victorian" or "modernist" or "post-colonial," or any genre we might identify as the "novel of manners" or "theatre of the absurd"—might readily appear, in retrospect, as having been a discrete happening, a wave that emerged, grew ever more prevalent, and then in some sense receded. Not to disappear altogether but, while braiding into itself strands from the past and drawing from what it once was, becoming something discernibly different. Across North America (and beyond) we are now reading many "Mennonite" texts that belong to a younger generation, texts that again are distinctly fresh. And we take pleasure in embracing these texts as Mennonite writing. I wonder how that term informs the way we read them, if at all? If, 30 years from now a collection of work called "On Mennonite/s Writing" were published, what sort of textual material might it contain?

The Jewish literary historian Benjamin Schreier observed in 2021 that there was an "irruption" of Jewish American writers in the 1950s; he pointed to writers like Bernard Malamud, Philip Roth, Norman Mailer, and others bursting into the American literary scene. This "breakthrough" that Schreier identifies as "the primal scene of the Jewish American literary field" was, he observes, chiefly legible "through an ethnological lens" (734). This is simply one of several instances in Schreier's analysis of Jewish American literature where it might be instructive to substitute for the term "Jewish" the word "Mennonite." Quite apart from any prevailing myths of origin concerning Mennonite/s writing, Canadian Mennonite literature "irrupted" at a particular time, as surely as did the American Jewish literature of which Schreier speaks—but a few decades later. And the "breakthrough" that Andris Taskans, long-time editor of the literary magazine *Prairie Fire*, called the "Mennonite miracle" was, to be sure and for a time at least, "the primal scene" of Mennonite/s Writing. Taskans identified this Mennonite literary landscape as a "largely Manitoban explosion of writers that started with Patrick Friesen and Sandra Birdsell and also includes Di Brandt, Miriam Toews, and Armin Wiebe" along with David Bergen.[4] The panorama of Mennonite literature Taskans put a name to expanded exponentially (both figuratively and geographically) after its initial advance. It certainly looks (and reads) different(ly) now.

So, what might we remark upon when we revisit those early years when Mennonite writing irrupted, initially in Canada? Beginning in the 1970s the government of Canada had set out to fund literary activity through the Writing and Publications Program (WPP) of Canada's federal multiculturalism directorate. By that time Canada was rapidly beginning to see itself as not only bicultural (English and French) but also multicultural in its make-up. Canada, which was, of course, not alone in finding itself in a multicultural moment, was undergoing rapid change, and soon its cultural texture would be transformed further and the meaning and uses of "ethnic" altered so as to call into question claims of cultural distinctiveness some citizens of European ancestry might earlier have taken for granted.

As the literature of the surge in Mennonite writing reveals, most of the Mennonites who had begun to write in English in Canada were raised in contexts that were decidedly ethnic. Among other cultural markers that might set them apart, these writers were, for the most part, bi- or tri-lingual. If not the children of German-speaking immigrants, they were at least migrants from neighbourhoods, towns, or villages where German and/or Low German

---

4 "This blossoming of largely secular Mennonite writers is what people will remember about writing in Manitoba during the final quarter of the 20th century," Taskans was quoted as saying. See *Quill & Quire*, 8 July 2005.

had been one of the languages of their childhood. They were in a transitional mode between cultures. In a sense they—and many of their characters—were nomads: individuals in transit. And their writing gave voice to this condition. They were positioned, as poet Patrick Friesen put it (in German) on the closing page of his 1984 collection, *Unearthly Horses*, "in between," with "one foot in fire" or, as he says elsewhere, with "one foot in, one foot out."[5]

In my Introduction to the special issue of *The New Quarterly* focused on new Mennonite/s Writing, published in 1990, I wrote: "Mennonite literature as it exists in Canada today is unique because the very particular experiences about which these people write will not ever recur" (12). To be sure, the prominent writers of that era wrote for everyone, and about more than Mennonite experience. But when they wrote about the Mennonite worlds they knew, they often gave voice to a shared sensibility, a heritage they held in common. For one thing, as if invoking a dominant trope from Rudy Wiebe's epically prophetic first novel, they were very aware of cultural distinctives and seemed to regard the world of the "English" (that is, anything or anyone *not* Mennonite) as reasonably inhospitable, if not threatening. And they were often, at the same time, compelled, even though most often not bound, by the fairly rigidly-defined and tightly-monitored religio-cultural world of the sectarian communities in which they were nurtured. Their propensity to give way to code-switching—the appeal to German in the English texts of Rudy Wiebe, Patrick Friesen, Armin Wiebe, Sarah Klassen, David Waltner-Toews, Audrey Poetker, and others—reveals something of the remnants of the ethnic cultural experience that identified (at the least) their residual connection to their people.

I have always been interested in the expanded literary text. That's another way of saying that I have a persistent interest in literary community as a phenomenon, and in broader literary contexts. Among the plethora of factors that inevitably come into play for a literary movement such as the one I have obsessed about for half a century, I would never want to dismiss the individual text; but I am most persistently intrigued by how authors and texts and contexts interact with each other. The literary work is, to be sure, a thing unto itself and deserves a certain kind of attention as such. I was trained in New Criticism, which assumes that the work of art is a coherent unit that offers within itself everything one needs to comprehend it. That sort

---

5 See Patrick Friesen, *Unearthly Horses*, p. 75: "*ich stehe / zwischen nein / ein fusz im feuer / ja.*" See also "Poet Patrick Friesen: One foot in, one foot out," an interview with Friesen by Sheri Hostetler in *Mennonot*, 1993, pp. 5–7.

of reading, I have found, is satisfactory in a limited way. But I have always wanted to know more about the larger world out of which a work and its author emerged. To be sure, I read in order to savour the virtuosity of the literary moment, but I think I am not alone in taking particular pleasure in recognizing a gesture or an emotion that is somehow uncannily familiar. I appreciate how creative people make art out of an everyday that resonates with my own experience. After all, although the ethnological ground sustaining the early literary expressions of Mennonite writers has receded, the fact that they experienced a distinctive culture and the ways in which that culture has been explored in literary texts prevails.

Although they worked independently, the Mennonite writers active during those twenty-some last years of the twentieth century were generally aware of, and supportive of, each other. They were conscious of sharing a common heritage—whether that heritage might be traced back to recent domestic life, the experience of "prosthetic" memories[6] of colonization or migration, or more distant Anabaptist beginnings. In fact, many of the stories and poems they wrote happened to be reflective of a plethora of larger narratives encompassing their wider communities' social, historical, theological, geographic, and literary histories. Although their work tended to invoke a range of subjects and themes that might be found in any community, written by members of any cultural enclave, much of their work took on a "Mennonite" flavour that members of Mennonite communities at the time might identify with a particular generation living during a particular era. Indeed, much of the work of that era addresses, sometimes implicitly and sometimes explicitly, the question of what it might mean to be Mennonite in Canada in the last decades of the twentieth century—though the subject matter of most of their work does not, by any means, adhere merely to the distinctive features of that particular heritage group.

When I began to study the literatures of Mennonites, I was initially interested in fine creative work produced by talented writers whose formative experiences—in home, church, and community—might most resonate with, and illumine, my own experiences and those of my Mennonite peers. I hesitate to make observations like this for fear of being accused of unfettered nostalgia. I am wary, too, of the prospect of being chastised for appearing to be on the wrong side of an ideological divide focused on the contested concept of "ethnicity," for instance, or for striking what might appear to be

---

6 See Alison Landsberg, *Prosthetic Memory: The Transformation of American Remembrance in the Age of Mass Culture*. Columbia UP, 2004.

an exclusionary posture relative to other Mennonites who do not share my specific history as the child of refugees from Mennonite colonies of the former Soviet Union in 1929.[7] In spite of the dominant ideologies circulating now, I remain interested in how my familial and wider forebears struggled to make the world—insofar as they were able to understand it—more hospitable, more inspiring, more humane. I believe that few are more propitiously poised to convey the singularities of a particular tradition—the specific texture suggestive of a distinctive culture—than the writers nurtured within that tradition.

Of course, like the Mennonite writers whose work I have tended to embrace, I can lay claim to influences and experiences, encounters and relationships, obsessions and commitments that lie well outside what we might take to be "Mennonite." In fact, I'd be hard-pressed to describe how my own reading of texts or my writing embodies or reveals anything one could describe as intrinsically or inherently "Mennonite." But I do find in many of the prominent works of this era at least tacit invocations of people, objects, and understandings among whom/which I grew up. I'm thinking of Rudy Wiebe's *Peace Shall Destroy Many* and *The Blue Mountains of China*, Patrick Friesen's *The Shunning*, David Waltner-Toews's Tante Tina poems, Armin Wiebe's *The Salvation of Yasch Siemens*, Sandra Birdsell's *Night Travellers*, Audrey Poetker's *i sing for my dead in german*, Di Brandt's *questions i asked my mother*, as well as work in poetry and prose by Sarah Klassen, John Weier, and so many others. Of course the work of writers whose Mennonite tradition is different from my own is often also familiar enough and uniquely evocative. I am thinking of the memories invoked by Jeff Gundy's writing about the ceremony of foot-washing he experienced as a young adult growing up on the prairies of Illinois,[8] for example, or the poignant impact of Raylene Hinz-Penner's vivid recollection of items of material culture like "[c]arved wooden plaques or plaster mottoes: *As for me and my house, we will serve the Lord*" adorning the walls of her childhood Mennonite home near the Oklahoma/Kansas border.[9]

Because of their common experiences, Mennonite writers and readers of the era of which I speak share a greater than usual understanding of certain subtexts, as would the members of any reasonably cohesive group of people

---

7 Both my grandfathers were lay ministers in their respective villages and were therefore identified by the state as kulaks; both fled with their families in the late fall of 1929, when they were threatened with exile.

8 See Jeff Gundy, "Walking Beans." *Flatlands*. Cleveland State U, 1995, pp. 54–55.

9 See Raylene Hinz-Penner, "Georgia O'Keeffe Comes West." *Conrad Grebel Review*, vol. 16, Winter 1998, pp. 73–85.

living in similar circumstances at the same time. In my essay on "Critical Thought and Mennonite Literature" (included in this volume), I remark on the distinctive "tastes, smells, sounds of extended family gatherings, the inimitable rhythm of Low German and the tug of certain High German expressions of piety," that most Mennonites of the generation that is my focus here hold in common (240–241). Also familiar would be the powerful emotional force of four-part congregational singing, the paradoxical sense of belonging to a minority group and at the same time living self-consciously, or not, on the margins—or near the centre—of the dominant culture. Members of this cohort of Mennonites might share, also, ambivalence about matters related to faith and salvation, hazy memories of certain Bible passages rehearsed in Sunday School and church, nagging questions about the operation of class and patriarchy and ecclesiastical power within the community in which they grew up, and the compelling, sometimes disturbing, revelations of Mennonite/Anabaptist history from the martyrs onward.

The works of the period of which I speak reveal something of Mennonite communities' disproportionate urge towards boundary maintenance while they foreground something of the smothering effect of the often rigidly-defined moral codes that have tended to govern Mennonites' lives. In these works inquiries into personal meaning and community memory take on a particular hue. Foregrounded are questions about nonconformity and worldliness, and intimations of a Puritanical discomfort with overt expressions of sexuality. Motifs that might be found in the narratives of any number of minority groups tend to take on a particular Mennonite character here: I am thinking of recurrent allusions to familiar hymns, for example, or to the recognizable culture of specific religious institutions, from the congregation to the summer camp. The obsession with personal salvation and the end times is not exclusive to Mennonites, of course; nor are the dynamics of a religiously justified patriarchy, nor the challenging sense of belonging to a peculiar, sectarian people. But the framework in which these subjects are addressed in work by authors corralled as members or scions of the "Mennonite miracle," for example, is distinctive, embedded as it is in almost half a millennium of Mennonite theology as well as in Mennonite history, from the horrors of martyrdom in early modern Europe to the bewildering trauma of Mennonite experience in post-revolutionary Ukraine and other territories of the former Soviet Union. Many of the stories of the era of which I write here are set amongst various peculiar practices of Mennonite community life: characteristic rituals of Sunday afternoon visiting, for example, or the invocation of distinctive ethnic markers, including traditional foods and the use of Low German or Pennsylvania Dutch idioms to convey an idiosyncratic form of self-deprecating humour.

As I observed in my 2003 address on "Critical Thought and Mennonite Literature," many of the creative writers who published work in the closing decades of the last century recreate and redefine community ceremonies and family relationships that were then readily identified as typical of Mennonite institutional, community, and family life. Many of them present that once familiar world objectified—made strange. To a large degree they evoke, and provide commentary on, fragments of Mennonite experience that, in the context of a seemingly more coherent world of belief and community practice, were once assumed to make sense. Some of the narratives and poems they wrote then evoke, with a poignant sense of loss, what the particular Mennonite world the writers might have known had to offer that was kind, thoughtful, and sympathetic. Others present a more critical appraisal of the Mennonite communities they knew, by challenging and interrogating the values, dogmas, ceremonies, and traditions that for many years formed the base of the Mennonites' community consciousness, a consciousness that publicly defined itself in terms of Christian discipleship and elevated religious experience, chastity and fidelity, mutual aid, truth-telling, hard work, and traditional ways (and that was acknowledged—often reluctantly, but time and again—as falling short of these ideals).

The fiction and verse of this era reveal dissonances and discontinuities inevitably perceptible in communities under the stress of constant change. Constructed at a distance from conventional contexts, some of them appear to mock—sometimes hilariously and outrageously, often with a gentle touch—aspects of a world-view that many Mennonites would still find familiar. Finally, they "probe ironies and contradictions that reveal the shadows that have fallen, in the Mennonite world," between word and context, memory and practice, desire and reality ("Critical" 245). And so much has changed. So much has faded away (even while much, surely, has remained the same).

I am not suggesting that Mennonite writers who now populate a new era of Mennonite writing no longer pay attention to their cultural history (and it's important to note that there are, of course, many varieties of Mennonite cultural history) nor to the dynamics of Mennonite family or community life. But the texture of their lives is, for the most part, vastly different from what it was before. Where these writers address the conditions of Mennonite experience at all, they frequently tend to be more deliberate about marking the distance between themselves and the community that was. Mennonite narratives, images, tropes, themes are not utterly abandoned in some of the

Mennonite writing of recent years, but often what we might call the old territory that seems to have been left behind is explored, when it is addressed at all, from alternative perspectives, invoking less familiar paradigms. Consider works of fiction like Elina Penner's *Nachtbeeren* (2022), Erwin Wiens's *To Antoine* (2022), Sarah Klassen's *The Russian Daughter* (2022), or David Bergen's *Away From the Dead* (2023), for example. Or Jonathan Dyck's graphic novel *Shelterbelts* (2022). Or Sofia Samatar's memoir *The White Mosque* (2022). Or collections of poetry like Sarah Ens's *Flyway* (2022) and Connie Braun's *Unspoken* (2016). So much literary treasure. So much to explore, so much to unpack. So much momentum.

In my 2015 essay "After Identity: Liberating the Mennonite Literary Text" (also included in this volume) I cited a statement Benjamin Schreier made in an essay on Philip Roth, that "It is not that Roth's characters do not want to be Jews; it is that they do not know how to describe themselves as Jews." I was struck by this observation then, and adapted it: "It is not that characters in Mennonite fiction, for example (or, for that matter, the writers of Mennonite prose and poetry themselves) do not want to be Mennonite; the challenge that confronts fictional and real characters alike is how to identify, describe, or represent the Mennonite in the twenty-first century in North America" ("After" 216). In many cases, of course, they might take little or no notice of anything Mennonite at all. But many do, and they do it from uncommon perspectives, and with fresh eyes.

In 2021 Schreier observed that when one considers Jewish writing in America one might observe that the scholarly focus has "shifted from the object of literary representation to its subject, from Jews as a community written about to Jews as a community writing" (736). This remark is applicable to recent developments in Mennonite writing. Readers of Mennonite literature, too, have in large measure moved away from a principally ethnological focus to attend, instead, to the simple fact that Mennonites are writing—about any number of things and for a world-wide audience. This way of looking at what is taking place in the field offers a range of opportunities and challenges for writers of Mennonite heritage and the characters who populate their fiction, for their readers and critics as well, all of whom might change—or might very well have changed—their focus from a Mennonite community portrayed to a Mennonite community producing.

II. Being Right There, Right Then

I set out in this afterword to offer a perspective on what I'm now thinking about Mennonite writing after having had the opportunity to focus on the field for so long. I ended up composing a kind of personal "state of the art," all the while overwhelmed by the plethora of poetry and fiction and life writing that continues to populate the teeming landscape of Mennonite literature. But I wanted to provide, as well, something more limited and immediate: a context for the selection of essays gathered in this volume—to illustrate my assertion that during that irruption of Mennonite writing concentrated in the last two decades of the last century I had found myself, so often, right there, right then. In fact, I was given a vast range of opportunities to explore Mennonite/s writing during the decades represented in this collection, and beyond.

I was born at just the right time to find teachers, mentors, and friends among some of the most prominent Mennonite figures writing in the early years. I grew up in Winnipeg, then the fourth largest city in Canada, in a neighbourhood that had Mennonites on almost every block. I was nurtured in a family that communicated in German, Low German, and English every day and attended a German-language Mennonite church. I was taught in a Mennonite high school by, among others, Harry Loewen, later Chair of Mennonite Studies at the University of Winnipeg; and then by a clutch of Mennonite professors in the English Department at United College (later the University of Winnipeg). There was novelist Al Reimer, who taught literary criticism when, during our fourth-year seminar, he took a break from regaling the class with stories of his boyhood in Steinbach (the mostly Mennonite town made unforgettable years later by Miriam Toews). There was Peter Pauls, who taught me Shakespeare, and who was the translator of the classic German Mennonite novel *Eine Mutter* (1932) by Peter G. Epp.[10] Also there at the time were Mennonites Lloyd Siemens (with whom I studied the poetry of Thomas Hardy) and Kay Unruh (who taught me new ways to think about theatre). The impudent Jack Thiessen, prominent lexicographer and primary contributor to the development of Low German literature, was at United College then, too, but I did not study with him.

When I got to grad school at the University of Alberta in 1969, Rudy Wiebe, who had arrived in Edmonton from Goshen College in 1967, was there. His Mennonite epic *The Blue Mountains of China* appeared during my

---

10 Translated as *Agatchen* (Hyperion Press, 1986).

first year at U of A (and he would win his first Governor General's Award for *The Temptations of Big Bear* the year I left). In 1969 I married Paul Tiessen, whom I had met at a wedding in Winnipeg the year before and with whom I had begun an animated discussion about art and literature that has so far lasted 55 years. The impact of this conversation partner on my life and work has remained constant, stimulating, incalculable. In 1973 Paul took a teaching position at the University of Manitoba and we moved from Edmonton to Winnipeg. While I was preparing to write my comprehensive exams that year, in anticipation of my dissertation on the dynamics of literary community among British modernists, my first article appeared in print: the study of Rudy Wiebe's first and third novels—both works of fiction that offered sensitive interpretations of Mennonite communities. This was just before Patrick Friesen and Victor Enns and David Waltner-Toews started publishing poetry chapbooks with Winnipeg's notable (and, for Mennonite writers, enormously impactful) Turnstone Press.

I had written that first article—number one in this collection—for a course in Canadian literature while I was at the U of A in 1971-72. That article, published in the *Journal of Canadian Fiction* in 1973, and re-issued in 1978 in a critical anthology on the Canadian novel,[11] identified me with Mennonite literature just as people were becoming aware of the emergence of Mennonite writers in Canadian literature. It must have been while I was composing that paper on Wiebe's novels that, on the 5th of October 1971, I made a note to myself (a note I was to rediscover years later); the capitalizations reveal that I thought I was on to a terrific insight: "IDEA: Why not edit Menn. short stories?" There weren't many short stories by Mennonite writers to be collected in 1971, but by the 1980s more and more short stories by Mennonites were appearing in print, often published in ephemeral and/or hard to find literary magazines.

It was the 1980s that formed the crest of the wave that Andris Taskans christened the "Mennonite miracle." In 1980 Patrick Friesen published *The Shunning*; Sandra Birdsell's *Night Travellers* appeared in 1982, and David Waltner-Toews's *Good Housekeeping* in 1983. Armin Wiebe's *The Salvation of Yasch Siemens* was published in 1984. It was clear that Rudy Wiebe would not be the last Mennonite writer.[12] In fact, interest in the literature of writers of Mennonite heritage was great enough by then, even in southwestern Ontario,

---

11 John Moss, ed. *The Canadian Novel: Here and Now*, Vol.1. U Toronto P, 1978, pp. 169–181.

12 See Maurice Mierau, "Why Rudy Wiebe Is Not the Last Mennonite Writer." *Conrad Grebel Review*, vol. 22, no. 2, Spring 2004, pp. 69–82.

that I was invited to develop a course in Mennonite literature at Wilfrid Laurier University, where I had been teaching part-time since January 1975, and at Conrad Grebel College, where I started teaching part-time in 1983. By then I was intent on acting on that 1971 exclamatory note, not least because I wanted access to an anthology of Mennonite stories I could use as a text.

So I began to make inquiries and send out invitations. I started with writers whose work I knew and admired: Rudy Wiebe and David Waltner-Toews. I had heard Sandra Birdsell being interviewed by Peter Gzowski on national radio when her first collection of stories, *Night Travellers*, appeared in 1982, and made contact with her. Sara Stambaugh I had come to know in grad school where she was a young faculty member in Victorian literature. I hadn't at first known she was a Mennonite. Nor that she wrote fiction. But there she was. Victor Carl Friesen was a few years ahead of me in the same English graduate program. Katie Funk Wiebe was well known as a writer (though not as a writer of fiction) in Mennonite circles of the day. Andreas Schroeder (already well known for his extraordinary work with the Writers' Union of Canada) had been writing full-time for over a decade. Someone introduced me to then New York-based Warren Kliewer, who would eventually send me all remaining copies of *The Violators*, his pioneering collection of wacky short stories, to distribute to my students. And he would compliment me grandly in letters, declaring that his generation of Mennonite writers in the USA (including Dallas Wiebe and Elmer Suderman) had often expressed to each other the wish that they had known someone with my penchant for pulling people and texts together.

In 1984 I published a little article in the *Mennonite Reporter* called "The Writers are Coming, the Writers are Coming," and applied to the Secretary of State for Multiculturalism for funding for what would become *Liars and Rascals: Mennonite Short Stories* (1989). By then both our boys, born in the 1970s, were in school; my PhD dissertation was behind me; and I had expanded my teaching to Conrad Grebel College, then a vibrant centre of scholarly activity focussed on Anabaptists/Mennonites. Personal computers and the internet had not yet splintered the comradery this small institution so effectively nurtured in its daily morning coffee breaks where top-flight academics in Anabaptist and Mennonite history and theology regularly held forth and argued passionately with their colleagues: specialists in ethics, Biblical studies, sociology, music, and peace studies. Here I enjoyed a swift and comprehensive introduction to the cerebral landscape of Anabaptist Mennonite thinkers.

In 1985 I was invited by Cal Redekop, then Director of the Institute of Anabaptist and Mennonite Studies at Conrad Grebel, and his co-director, archivist/historian Sam Steiner, to give a plenary address at a 1986 conference sponsored by four Canadian Mennonite academic institutions and entitled "Toward a Mennonite Self-Understanding." Gerry Noonan, a Canadianist from Wilfrid Laurier University, and John Ruth, whose landmark early critical study *Mennonite Identity and Literary Art* had been published in the USA in 1978, prepared formal responses to what I had to say in what appears, here, as the second of my essays.

In the May 1985 prospectus for that paper, which I then called "Artists' Responses to Mennonite Ethnicity: an Extended Metaphor for Exploring the Role of Art and Literature in Mennonite Self-Understanding," I wrote that although Mennonite readers had gradually become reasonably comfortable with fiction, specifically "with stories peopled by characters who are identifiably not Mennonites, stories set outside the boundaries of their community," many "still shun the fictions that arise from within the community—the stories that in their very telling probe their individual and corporate identities as Mennonites (and so, in turn, record and forge the myths that define them)." But, I observed optimistically, Canada was experiencing "a Mennonite literary and artistic awakening" and attitudes towards the arts were shifting ("Literature" n.p.).

Ervin Beck and Jeff Gundy attended that 1986 conference at Conrad Grebel. Each of them would go on to become a significant figure in the field of Mennonite literature. Ervin would host the second Mennonite/s Writing conference at Goshen College eleven years later, in 1997; and he and I would co-chair the third conference, also at Goshen, in 2002. In 2006 Jeff Gundy hosted (and I co-chaired) the fourth conference, at Bluffton College. Those partnerships between us and our colleges were the direct result of the vision of Robert Kreider, a prominent academic and supporter of the arts who, along with his family, established, at Bethel College, the Marpeck Fund, designed to encourage academics at the various Mennonite colleges in North America to collaborate and remain in conversation with each other.[13]

I was blessed to have steady support from my own institution, Conrad Grebel College, and especially from my friend and administrative mentor there, Rod Sawatsky who, like me, had moved to Waterloo from Winnipeg in 1974. Rod, who knew of my 1973 article on Rudy Wiebe, invited me in the early 1980s to lecture in his Mennonite history class—on Wiebe and the band of Mennonite writers emerging out of Manitoba at the time. In

---

13 See https://marpeck-fund.bethelks.edu/.

the meantime, my husband Paul persuaded me that it would be a good idea for us to start a publishing company that might focus on the visual arts: photography and painting by mostly regional artists, many of whom happened to be of Mennonite heritage. So we founded Sand Hills Books, which published several titles over the next few years, including *People Apart* (1977), David L. Hunsberger's photographs of Old Order Mennonites in Waterloo County; *Rebecca's Nancy: a story of a little Mennonite girl* (1978), an award-winning children's book; *Mennonite Country* (1978), Peter Etril Snyder's pen- and-ink drawings of Old Order Mennonites, with a text by an Amish memoirist, Andrew Herrfort; and *Forever Summer, Forever Sunday* (1981), Peter Gerhard Rempel's early-twentieth-century studio photographs of Mennonites in the Mennonite settlements of Ukraine.[14] This last volume would have a distinct impact on both Sandra Birdsell's and Rudy Wiebe's 2001 novels: *The Russländer* and *Sweeter Than All the World*,[15] as well as on the literary imaginations of other Mennonite writers like Sarah Klassen and David Waltner-Toews. Interestingly, the trope of "Forever Summer, Forever Sunday" as well as the photographic images in that Sand Hills Books volume remain intertwined with Mennonite writing, as in the cover image of Erwin Wiens's 2022 twentieth-century Mennonite historical fiction, *To Antoine*.[16]

The network of support I was able to rely upon was sturdy and profoundly enabling. For *Liars and Rascals*, the Secretary of State for Multiculturalism was ready with funding for both publishing costs and the cost of permissions. The lamentably short-lived University of Waterloo Press, headed by the indefatigable Gloria Smith, offered constant support. My close friend and literary colleague Margaret Loewen Reimer, associate editor of the *Canadian Mennonite*, was always ready to be a partner in conversation and to promote both local and national literary events focused on Mennonite writers and their work. Conrad Grebel College offered moral and material endorsement, and the Canada Council consistently granted stipends and travel support for

---

14 David L Hunsberger, et al., *People Apart: Portrait of a Mennonite World in Waterloo County, Ontario*. Sand Hills Books, 1977; Joan Reimer Goman, *Rebecca's Nancy: a story of a little Mennonite girl*. Sand Hills Books, 1978; Peter Etril Snyder, *Mennonite Country: Waterloo County Drawings*. Sand Hills Books, 1978; and *Forever Summer, Forever Sunday: Peter Gerhard Rempel's Photographs of Mennonites in Russia, 1890–1917*, ed. John D. Rempel and Paul Tiessen. Sand Hills Books, 1981.

15 See my essay on the connection among these works in this volume. At the conference on "The Russländer Mennonites: War, Dislocation, and New Beginnings" in Winnipeg, on 14 July 2023, Sandra Birdsell conveyed clearly once more the formative influence of this book on her writing of *The Russländer*.

16 See Erwin Wiens, *To Antoine*. Gelassenheit Publications, 2022.

readings, enabling me (with Paul's unabating collaboration) to host writers at the College (and in our home) several times a year for many years.

If my little essay on Rudy Wiebe in 1973 alerted some folks to my interest in Mennonite writing, it was the appearance of *Liars and Rascals* in 1989 that announced my presence as someone more than usually engaged with the subject—both in Waterloo (where Kim Jernigan and her colleagues at *The New Quarterly* invited me to program a conference, assemble a Special Issue on new Mennonite writing, and edit a volume of conference proceedings[17]) and Winnipeg (where a committee that included Di Brandt, Maurice Mierau, Andris Taskans, and others—conscious of the fact that the Mennonite World Conference would be meeting in Winnipeg in the summer of 1990—invited me to curate another special issue and to host its launch during the grand world-wide Mennonite event).[18] The eighties became the nineties and, even though the term "Mennonite miracle" would not be coined until 2005, when Andris Taskans set this literary phenomenon firmly into "the final quarter of the 20th century" (qtd. in "In Country"), it was widely evident that something quite extraordinary in the world of Mennonite literature was taking place.

By 1991 the *Mennonite Mirror*—instrumental in stimulating interest in the arts among Mennonites in Winnipeg—ceased publication after 200 issues over 20 years, and the literary scholars whose work had supported that periodical while championing also the generation of German/Low German Mennonite writers Arnold Dyck and Fritz Senn (and, to a lesser degree, the emerging generation of younger writers)—Al Reimer, Victor G. Doerksen and Harry Loewen—retired from their academic positions and the latter two moved away from Winnipeg. Moreover, several of the writers who could be said to have anchored the Mennonite writing community that had been grounded in Winnipeg, the prairie city that remains the centre of the Mennonite world in Canada, moved away as well: Patrick Friesen to Vancouver, Di Brandt to Windsor, Sandra Birdsell to Regina. Later, Miriam Toews to Toronto.

These apparent losses to the Mennonite literary community in Winnipeg in particular were offset by other developments. Rosemary Deckert Nixon, for example, then living in Calgary, where she was mentored by Aritha van Herk, a prominent former student of Rudy Wiebe, emerged as the first writer

---

17 See *The New Quarterly*, vol. 10, no.1–2, 1990. Special Issue. *Mennonite/s Writing in Canada*, and *Acts of Concealment: Mennonite/s Writing in Canada*. U Waterloo P, 1992.

18 I am referring here to *Prairie Fire*, vol. 11, 1990. Special Issue. *New Mennonite Writing*.

of her generation among the Swiss Mennonites in Canada.[19] Like virtually all the other Mennonite writers, Nixon had grown up in the west, in her case in a part of Saskatchewan settled by Swiss Mennonites from Ontario during the first decade of the twentieth century. Nixon's first collection of stories, *Mostly Country*, was published by Edmonton's NeWest Press in 1991. In 1992, David Elias's first collection of stories, *Crossing the Line*, set in the southern borderlands of Manitoba, was published by Orca, a small press in Victoria, British Columbia. The following year David Bergen's first work of fiction, a collection of stories entitled *Sitting Opposite My Brother*, was published by Turnstone Press, followed in 1996 by his first novel, *A Year of Lesser*, published by HarperCollins. That same year the first novel of another significant new Mennonite writer, Miriam Toews's *The Summer of My Amazing Luck*, was published by Turnstone Press. Both these new works of fiction received very positive responses from readers and critics alike. Bergen, who observed in an interview in 1997 that he dreamed in *New Yorker* print, was fortunate enough to have his novel be given a notable mention in the *New York Times Book Review*.

In 1998, Victor Enns, poet and arts administrator, began to publish a new journal, *Rhubarb: The Magazine of New Mennonite Art and Writing*, under the auspices of Winnipeg's Mennonite Literary Society. I was invited, along with writers Rudy Wiebe and Julia Kasdorf, and impresario Garry Enns, to sit on the Advisory Board, and would subsequently edit or co-edit two of its 42 issues.[20] Unlike the special issues I would edit for the *Conrad Grebel Review* and the *Journal of Mennonite Studies*, which were conference proceedings, the special issues of *Rhubarb*, like the special issues of *The New Quarterly*, and *Prairie Fire*, were compilations I curated, often starting with a plethora of submissions. I composed introductions, of course, for all of them.

Those special issues and the many other venues where I invited or curated or hosted and introduced Mennonite writers and/or their work were a constant and dynamic backdrop to all the more formal writing gathered

---

19 Nixon had already published a number of stories by the time her first collection appeared. Among these were two stories in *Liars and Rascals: Mennonite Short Stories*, ed. Hildi Froese Tiessen, U Waterloo P, 1989. Although Nixon was the only writer of Swiss Mennonite heritage in Canada at this time, she was preceded by Mabel Dunham, best known for her 1924 novel *The Trail of the Conestoga*, and Ephraim Weber, whose novel "Aunt Rachel's Nieces," completed in the 1940s, remains unpublished, its manuscript preserved in Library and Archives Canada. See my "A Mennonite Novelist's Journey (from) Home: Ephraim Weber's Encounters with S.F. Coffman and Lucy Maud Montgomery" in this volume.

20 *Rhubarb*, vol. 15, 2007. "Words and Images from Ontario," co-edited with Margaret Loewen Reimer; and *Rhubarb*, vol. 41, 2017, published as *11 Encounters with Mennonite Fiction*.

in this volume. I remember sitting in conversation with a writer of both poetry and fiction around the time I was assembling material for the 1990 special issues of *The New Quarterly* and *Prairie Fire*. He made no attempt to disguise the fact that it seemed unreasonable that I alone should be the arbiter of what might be included in both volumes. When I revisit my large assemblage of files from those projects now, I realize that I was too busy doing the work (as they say) to fret about my curatorial decisions then. I was pretty much alone in Waterloo as far as knowledge of who was writing literature we might think of as Mennonite, and where those authors might be found. My Winnipeg colleagues, who were for various reasons more connected with what was happening in the world of Mennonite/s writing, made suggestions for whom I might contact, to be sure; but they left the final decisions to me. This was before email, before texting. We were not in regular contact with each other, and we all had things to do. Notices were published, invitations sent out, and I took pleasure in reading every new submission from writers known to me and not. And I beat the bushes as I had done in preparation for *Liars and Rascals*.

Among the writers I had not heard of then was Dallas Wiebe, who (I discovered later) was known in American Mennonite literary circles as a writer and founding editor (1975) of the *Cincinnati Poetry Review*, where he would publish the work of then-emerging American Mennonite writers like Jeff Gundy, Julia Spicher Kasdorf, and Jean Janzen. Although I did not know this then, Dallas was in touch with other American Mennonite writers of his generation: Warren Kliewer and Elmer Suderman. I found Dallas while I was doing research in British modernism: his dissertation had focussed on the London literary crowd that had been my focus as well. When I found a reference to his work in an academic bibliography, I couldn't let go of the fact that his name was Wiebe and that he was clearly interested in literature. Was it possible, I asked him in a letter out of the blue, that he was a Mennonite—and could it be that he was a creative writer too? He was both, and sent me, in response to my query, the manuscript of his novel *Our Asian Journey*, which he had grown tired of submitting to publishers, none of whom seemed interested in this giant, esoteric tome. Perhaps, he wrote, I would find something in that manuscript I could use? I did. I selected a chapter for inclusion in *The New Quarterly*. The full text of *Our Asian Journey* was finally published in 1997, when Paul Tiessen decided to revisit the manuscript Dallas had sent me and published it under the imprint MLR Editions Canada. In 2022 Sofia Samatar's scintillating memoir entitled *The White Mosque* brought Wiebe's work back to light. The exceptionally talented Samatar is one of the extraordinary new writers of today offering a new perspective on Mennonite/s writing, giving voice to new paradigms.

In anticipation of the 1990 *Prairie Fire* special issue, my colleagues in Winnipeg forwarded names to me, including poets Leonard Neufeldt and Audrey Poetker, and fiction writers Lois Braun, Douglas Reimer, and David Bergen, whose several short fictions had all won national recognition. I was able to contact David by letter in Vietnam, where he was on assignment with Mennonite Central Committee. I included in each of those special issues of 1990 two parts of an interview I had conducted with Patrick Friesen. Patrick, such a magnificent performer of his own evocative lyrical texts, had, in 1981, initiated readings in Waterloo to promote *The Shunning*, his 1980 long poem published by Turnstone. He had asked Paul, who was a member of the English Department at Wilfrid Laurier University at the time, whether Paul and I would host him while he gave readings in the region. For several days the Friesen family moved in—Patrick and his wife and two children, the youngest of whom was five. It was the first of many visits from Patrick, and it was during one of these visits that he and I sat in my breakfast nook while I conducted that memorable interview. To this day Patrick insists that on several occasions during the interview, while I left the room to attend to something related to house or family, he re-wound the tape to erase sections where he feared he might have revealed too much. I was never able to find evidence of this tampering!

I mention the interviews with Patrick Friesen because they represented the beginning of a major project I would undertake in the years to come: interviews with 27 writers of Mennonite heritage who were prepared to talk about what it meant for each of them as an author and as a member of a particular family to be nurtured in a Mennonite community. Those interviews, which began in the summer of 1993 and for which I received funding from the Social Sciences and Humanities Research Council, took place in various venues including my own home in Kitchener-Waterloo, the Winnipeg homes of Miriam Toews (whose mother picked up her children from school while we talked) and Sarah Klassen (who fed me tea and Platz), the Manitoba Arts Council office of Victor Enns in Winnipeg's Exchange District, Rudy Wiebe's living room in a funky, historic section of Edmonton, a quiet upper room in Dallas Wiebe's Cincinnati home, and the house Andreas Schroeder built on a high bank on Canada's Sunshine Coast. I arranged to meet Al Reimer and Audrey Poetker at the University of Winnipeg, as well as the irrepressible Jack Thiessen who, predictably I suppose, filibustered the two hours we spent together.

The interviews revealed to me two things most prominently: firstly, that there was a period of time when "growing up Mennonite" in Canada and the USA meant something in particular, and writers who grew up within a Mennonite context would have been able to articulate what that meant; in fact, so much of their work gave expression to that experience. And secondly, the fact that the writers whose work we had been reading since the early 1980s were unique not only as individuals but also as Mennonites. Indeed, as I had anticipated, their reflections revealed how distinctive were each of their personal histories. Sandra Birdsell or Sarah Klassen or Miriam Toews or Julia Kasdorf, for example, might very well be able to identify with elements of each other's experience in a Mennonite community, but a reader of the work of one would do well to avoid carrying over that work's postulations about Mennonites into an interpretation of the work of another. I have remarked often enough, for example, that although I can readily understand and appreciate what it might have meant for Di Brandt to grow up as a woman of a particular generation among Mennonites, her experience does not come close to mirroring my own.

I had wished to publish all those interviews in a collection that would reveal the rich and diverse texture of Mennonite family and community life during the last half of the twentieth century, a collection that would weave in a broad range of figures active during the period when Mennonite writing was becoming a brand. Dallas Wiebe, for example, who had a place in the American literary scene as early as the 1960s, and Andreas Schroeder, who had been writing full-time since the early 1970s, and Vern Thiessen, younger than these others, whose work as a playwright was gaining recognition across Canada around the turn of the century. I regret that other projects took priority over preparing the interviews for publication, and most of them remain only in the form of unedited transcripts.[21]

---

21 Among the authors I interviewed were David Bergen, Sandra Birdsell, Di Brandt, Lynette D'Anna, Victor Enns, Elizabeth Falk, Patrick Friesen, Jeff Gundy, Raylene Hinz-Penner, Jean Janzen, Julia Spicher Kasdorf, Sarah Klassen, Barbara Nickel, Rosemary Deckert Nixon, Audrey Poetker-Thiessen, Magdalene Redekop, Al Reimer, Andreas Schroeder, Sarah Stambaugh, Jack Thiessen, Vern Thiessen, Miriam Toews, David Waltner-Toews, John Weier, Armin Wiebe, Dallas Wiebe, Rudy Wiebe. Most of the interviews have been transcribed, but only a few, including abridged versions of the interviews with Patrick Friesen, David Bergen, Miriam Toews, and Vern Thiessen, have been published; the article in this volume entitled "The Case of Dallas Wiebe: Literary Art in Worship" is largely based on my interview with the author in his Cincinnati home. The published interviews (including the interviews with Patrick Friesen, conducted earlier than the others) are: "'Zen, Grace, and Flying': An Interview with Patrick Friesen, part I," *The New Quarterly*, vol. 10, no. 1–2, 1990, pp. 119–125; "'hooked, but not landed': A Conversation with Patrick Friesen," *Prairie Fire*, vol. 11, no. 2, 1990, pp. 152–159; "'Where I Come From': An

I introduced myself to Vern Thiessen at a public reading of his Governor General's Award-winning play *Einstein's Gift* (2003), in Edmonton, during a period when, beginning in the early 1990s, and continuing at intervals for at least a decade, Paul and I spent reading weeks—or parts of sabbaticals—at the U of A. Paul worked on various projects in the archives there, and I divided my time between writing projects and reading current critical work in what was then variously called multicultural literature or ethnic literature or the new literatures in English. The languages of any number of discourses had begun to shift by then—in anticipation, perhaps, of the sweeping imperatives we encounter every day now, while the words and idioms with which we were once reasonably comfortable grow increasingly unstable, their usage challenging and sometimes treacherous. One was compelled—then as now—to stay alert.

So much was changing in those days. Academic journals were just beginning to consider whether or when they would publish online. Most did not, so I would settle into the Rutherford Library's Periodical Reading Room and work my way through shelves and shelves of journals in the arts. These were physical objects, volumes I would amass in huge piles on one of the great wooden library tables before sitting down to see what literary, and other, scholars were saying about the turbulent conditions that prevailed in those changing times. What we came to refer to as the culture wars had begun, and the large field of literary scholarship itself was in transition, constantly changing as academics often found themselves, alternately, barely able to recognize the discipline in which they had been trained and embarrassed by the categories with which they had once comfortably addressed their work. Who would dare say "Commonwealth Literature," for example, when "the new literatures in English" allowed one to evade the politics inherent in that earlier term, now deemed offensive? I struggled—not always successfully—to be alert and sensitive to the pitfalls that come with working in an unstable discursive environment in a volatile ideological landscape.

By the mid-nineties everyone, it seemed, was turning their attention to Mennonite writing, and my colleague Arnold Snyder, Anabaptist historian and then editor of the *Conrad Grebel Review*, invited me to solicit and curate instances of poetry, short fiction, and life writing by Mennonite authors for a regular section of the journal we agreed to call "Literary Refractions." The

---

Interview with David Bergen," *Prairie Fire*, vol. 17, no. 4, 1997, pp. 23–33; "'A Place You Can't Go Home To': A Conversation with Miriam Toews," *Prairie Fire*, vol. 21, no. 3, 2000, pp. 54–61; and "'Every Play Should Pose a Good Question': An Interview with Playwright Vern Thiessen," with an introduction, *Journal of Mennonite Writing*, vol. 2, no.7, 2010, online.

first iteration of this new project appeared in Fall 1996, where I observed that "Stories of Mennonite experience have in large measure been provided by historians and theologians who have functioned as the self-appointed guardians of the Mennonite master-narrative," and suggested that the stories composed by Mennonite creative writers, "by their very particularity, ... question the sustainability" of those prevailing larger narratives ("Literary" 1996, 217–218).

The *Conrad Grebel Review* "Literary Refractions" appeared in virtually every volume of the journal from 1997 until 2003. I prefaced every entry I curated with a brief introduction. In winter/spring 1997, for example, I invoked "the literature of the 'new' Mennonite ethnicities" ("Literary" 1997, 135), expressing anticipation of writing that might be self-consciously Mennonite but written in a different register altogether, writing we've seen recently, for example, in the compelling, outrageous fiction of the Russian-born, Mennonite, (*Spät-*)Aussiedler, German novelist Elina Penner, whose widely-acclaimed, bittersweet debut novel *Nachtbeeren* (2022)[22] offers fresh iterations of the lingering question: "What do home and community really mean?" (Venner 68). In a preamble to a "Literary Refraction" in 1998 I anticipated the emergence of the new era of which I have spoken here, an era announced in the work of writers like Stephen Beachy, Kirsten Eve Beachy, Jessica Penner, Elina Penner, Casey Plett, Carrie Snyder, Jonathan Dyck, Sofia Samatar, Rachel Yoder, and many others. I expressed there an eagerness to recognize and explore "the diverse and multiple sites of cultural identity" to which contemporary Mennonites—no matter the variety of forces shaping their world—might lay claim ("Literary" 1998, 71).

In 1997, the year after the *Conrad Grebel Review* launched the "Literary Refractions" feature, Goshen College hosted the second conference on Mennonite/s Writing. The conference, convened by Ervin Beck, focussed on Mennonite/s Writing in the USA. I was invited to give a plenary address and spoke about what was on my mind at the time. I was exploring a sense I had then that, among Mennonite writers, some appeared to be claiming a preferred "outsider" status, positioning themselves implicitly as the only people who had a critical perspective on what was happening within the larger Mennonite community. In fact, I was set to argue, the writers were in large measure illuminating a condition not unique to them but shared by many of their readers as well. Influenced by the thinking of critics like Homi Bhabha, I had taken an interest in the concepts of margins and liminality:

---

22 The novel, so far available only in German, has been described by Berlin-based novelist Christian Dittloff as "always funny and dangerous at the same time."

the in-between space, the third space, the place of possibility for writers and readers alike. Why were the works of certain writers of poetry and creative prose so richly and urgently embraced by so many readers? It wasn't only their often-brilliant expressions of particular inclinations and gestures, but also the compelling suggestion that any person at the margins can claim a voice. The experience of being or feeling in some sense like an "outsider," I observed, is not exclusive to the artist, though perhaps only the artist can adequately give expression to that state. That essay, "Beyond the Binary: Re-Inscribing Cultural Identity in the Literature of Mennonites," was published in the edited collection *Migrant Muses*,[23] and is included in this volume as well.

Most of the essays gathered in this volume were published after the "Beyond the Binary" paper of 1998 and address developments in what we have come to refer to routinely as "Mennonite/s Writing." Among related projects was my work with Paul Tiessen on the writing career of Ephraim Weber, a Canadian Mennonite writer whose American ancestors settled in southwestern Ontario around 1800. Weber (1870–1956) is best known as one of two principal correspondents of Lucy Maud Montgomery, author of the Canadian classic *Anne of Green Gables* (1908). After doing a considerable amount of research in Library and Archives Canada and the Mennonite Church USA Archives, Paul and I published Montgomery's letters to Weber[24] and collaborated on a number of essays illuminating Weber's relationship with Montgomery and his shadowy role as an ambitious Mennonite writer with little literary success. He was, it might be said in the context of all I've written here, unfortunate in being in the wrong place at the wrong time when he wrote his novel "Aunt Rachel's Nieces"—"a gentle satire of the world of Kitchener area Swiss Mennonites during the 1920s, when questions of decorum and dress raged in the churches."[25] By the time he was willing to share with a friend a full draft of that novel in 1945 (after it had been rejected by a number of publishers) it was clear that Weber had been writing simply as if for an Edwardian world, for an audience that no longer existed. "A Mennonite Novelist's Journey (from) Home," one of my essays on Weber's life and work, is included here; a companion essay, "The Story of a Novel:

---

23 See John D. Roth and Ervin Beck, eds. *Migrant Muses: Mennonite/s Writing in the U.S.* Mennonite Historical Society, 1998, pp. 11–21.

24 See Hildi Froese Tiessen and Paul Tiessen, eds. *After Green Gables: L.M. Montgomery's Letters to Ephraim Weber, 1916–1941*. U Toronto P, 2006.

25 See Hildi Froese Tiessen and Paul Tiessen. "Weber, Ephraim (1870–1956)." *Global Anabaptist Mennonite Encyclopedia Online*, 2006, www.gameo.org.

How We Found Ephraim Weber's 'Aunt Rachel's Nieces'," can be found in the *Journal of Mennonite Studies*.[26]

The Mennonite/s Writing conferences were gathering momentum when Goshen College hosted the third of these conferences (under the leadership of Ervin Beck) in 2002. Because it was the fortieth anniversary of Rudy Wiebe's *Peace Shall Destroy Many*, I invited and curated a chapbook in celebration of that anniversary, to be presented to Wiebe at the event.[27] The 48 individuals who contributed personal tributes to Wiebe in that volume included Robert Kroetsch, Joy Kogawa, Aritha van Herk, Margaret Atwood, as well as fellow Mennonite writers Patrick Friesen, Di Brandt, Sarah Klassen, Al Reimer, Maurice Mierau, and others.

In the meantime, the joint work Paul Tiessen and I were engaged in as publishers of art books persisted from the late 1970s until 2010, when I delivered three illustrated public lectures on the Connecticut-based visual artist Woldemar Neufeld,[28] including "Woldemar, Kate, Dietrich and Victor," a one-hour, 260-slide presentation featuring Neufeld in the context of his small circle of Mennonite artist peers. Neufeld, who would spend his career painting New York City and rural Connecticut as well as Ontario's Waterloo County, was stepson to Jacob H. Janzen, a bishop and prominent man-of-letters among Mennonites in the mid-twentieth century who was unreservedly supportive of his stepson's artistic pursuits. Janzen had published an article in 1935 called "The Literature of the Russo-Canadian Mennonites," which was re-published in 1946, in the first issue of the groundbreaking Kansas-based magazine *Mennonite Life*. Janzen's article ends with this exaltation: "Would God that I could see a new generation of poets and artists arise among us. But even if I do not see my hopes realized in my lifetime, new poets will come.

---

26 See Hildi Froese Tiessen. "The Story of a Novel: How We Found Ephraim Weber's 'Aunt Rachel's Nieces,'" *Journal of Mennonite Studies*, vol. 26, 2008, pp. 159–178.

27 See Hildi Froese Tiessen, comp. *Rudy Wiebe: a tribute*. Sand Hills Books, 2002.

28 See Hildi Froese Tiessen and Paul Tiessen. "Neufeld, Woldemar Heinrich (1909–2002)." *Global Anabaptist Mennonite Encyclopedia Online*. 2006. www.gameo.org/encyclopedia/contents/N4846.html. Volumes featuring Neufeld's artwork include Paul Tiessen and Hildi Froese Tiessen, eds., *Waterloo Portfolio: Woldemar Neufeld's Paintings and Block-prints*. Sand Hills Books, 1982, as well as Laurence Neufeld, Monika McKillen, Paul Gerard Tiessen, and Hildi Froese Tiessen, eds., *Woldemar Neufeld's Canada: A Mennonite Artist in the Canadian Landscape 1925–1995*, Wilfrid Laurier UP, 2010. See also Hildi Froese Tiessen and Paul Tiessen, "Woldemar Neufeld 1909–2002: From Waldheim, Russia to New Milford, Connecticut," in Laurence Neufeld and Monika McKillen, eds. *New Milford Portfolio: Woldemar Neufeld's Paintings and Blockprints of New Milford, Connecticut*. New Milford Tricentennial Commission in collaboration with the Woldemar Neufeld Estate, 2006, pp. 12–26.

Here is to the future belle-lettres of our own a hearty, VIVAT! CRESCAT! FLOREAT!" (28).[29] It was this article that I quoted in my 1989 introduction to *Liars and Rascals*, and, in effect, cited in the title of that book. The mention of Janzen here makes me feel as though I've come full circle!

And indeed I have.

In 2022, I composed a piece entitled "Fourteen Reflections After Some 32 Years" for presentation at the conference on Mennonite/s Writing, once more hosted by Goshen College, that fall.[30] That conference was to have taken place earlier but had been postponed due to Covid two years in a row. My work during those two years of "sheltering in place" took me into archives in my own home: organizing, digitizing, and transcribing over four thousand fabulously detailed and energetic and revealing family letters from the last century and more and perhaps a dozen journals of various lengths (almost all in German) that had been stored, by family now gone, in two steamer trunks in the basement. But before I immersed myself in that massive project I raided my personal archive where, after recovering letters I had received from David Waltner-Toews some 50 years ago, I settled in to write a long essay on the life and career of this poet, novelist, veterinarian, epidemiologist, and popular science writer.[31] I had published two of David's stories in *Liars and Rascals* in 1989, and he was among the first of the Mennonite poets Turnstone Press published in the late 1970s. Here too I felt as if I was coming back to some sort of beginning.

And I was.

One might be hard-pressed to overplay the enthusiasm and excitement felt by virtually all the participants at that most recent, September 2022, conference on Mennonite/s Writing, the ninth of these conferences since 1990. To be sure, there were some critics and writers who had been at the first conference—most notably Patrick Friesen, whose reading of his own work was as mesmerizing as it had been decades before. But the 2022 conference was, for the most part, a gathering of a new crowd of remarkable fresh voices, their work in the context of Mennonite writing—and their individual relationships with a wide range of Mennonite communities—markedly different from that of the earlier generation who had so dramatically announced their presence in

---

29 Transl. "may it live, grow, flourish."

30 See my "Fourteen Reflections After 32 Years." *Mennonite Quarterly Review*, vol. 97, April 2023, pp. 135–148.

31 See my "Portrait of an Epidemiologist as a Young Man: Reflections on the Poetic, Peripatetic Life/Lives of David Waltner-Toews." *Hamilton Arts & Letters*, vol. 13, no. 2, online.

the closing decades of the last century. It was as if the most dominant *object* of literary representation from the earlier era—Mennonites thoughtfully negotiating their existence within Canada and the USA—had given way to its *subject*, which was now, more clearly than ever before, simply writers writing (and readers reading). In the fall of 2022, 32 years after the first conference on Mennonite/s Writing and some 40 years since the irruption of that first great wave of Mennonite writing, Mennonites who write and read, compose and consume, once more found pleasure in being together. But a palpable shift had taken place, so that what they had gathered to celebrate was, decidedly, much less "Mennonites as a community written about" than "Mennonites as a community writing."[32]

WORKS CITED

Bergen, David. "'Where I Come From': An Interview with David Bergen." *Prairie Fire*, vol. 17, no. 4, Winter 1997, pp. 23–33.

Doerksen, Victor. "Apres Nous?" *Mennonite Mirror*, vol. 20, no. 10, June–July 1991, p. 17.

Friesen, Patrick. *Unearthly Horses*. Turnstone Press, 1984.

"In Country: David Bergen." *Quill & Quire*, June 2005, www.quillandquire.com.

Janzen, Jacob H. "The Literature of the Russo-Canadian Mennonites." *Mennonite Life*, vol. 1, January 1946, pp. 22–25, 28.

Moretti, Franco. "Graphs, Maps, Trees." *New Left Review*, vol. 24, Nov–Dec 2003, pp. 67–93.

Samatar, Sofia. *The White Mosque*. Catapult, 2022.

Schreier, Benjamin. "Jewish American Literature Against the World." *American Literary History*, vol. 33, no. 4, Winter 2021, pp. 733–755.

Tiessen, Hildi Froese. "After Identity: Liberating the Mennonite Literary Text." *After Identity: Mennonite Writing in North America*, edited by Robert Zacharias, Pennsylvania State UP, 2015, pp. 210–25.

———. "Critical Thought and Mennonite Literature: Mennonite Studies Engages the Mennonite Literary Voice." *Journal of Mennonite Studies*, vol. 22, 2004, pp. 237–246.

———. ed., *Liars and Rascals: Mennonite Short Stories*. U of Waterloo P, 1989.

---

32 I am here, once more, adapting phrases from Benjamin Schreier.

———. "Literary Refractions [an introduction to Sarah Klassen's 'The Mile East']." *Conrad Grebel Review*, vol. 14, no. 3, Fall 1996, pp. 217–218.

———. "Literary Refractions [an introduction to Rosemary Deckert Nixon's 'Mennonite Your Way' and 'Letters from Zaire' and David Waltner-Toews's 'Letters from Indonesia.']." *Conrad Grebel Review*, vol. 15, no. 1–2, Winter–Spring 1997, p. 135.

———. "Literary Refractions [an introduction to Raylene Hinz-Penner's 'Georgia O'Keeffe Comes West']." *Conrad Grebel Review*, vol. 16, no.1, Winter 1998, pp. 71–72.

———. "Literature and Fine Arts in the Development of Mennonite Self Understanding." Typescript. 2 pp. [10 May 1985].

———. "Mennonite/s Writing in Canada: An Introduction." *The New Quarterly*, vol. 10, 1990, pp. 9–14.

———. "A Mighty Inner River: 'Peace' in the Early Fiction of Rudy Wiebe." *Journal of Canadian Fiction*, vol. 2, no. 4, Fall 1973, pp. 71–76.

Venner, Catherine. Review of *Nachtbeeren [Nightberries]* by Elina Penner. *World Literature Today*, vol. 97, no. 4, 2023, p. 68.

Zacharias, Robert, ed. *After Identity: Mennonite Writing in North America*. Penn State UP, 2015.

Author's Note

One could say that this book has been over fifty years in the making. I am delighted to be able to express gratitude to the many who contributed to its contents. I will begin in the near present and thank the anonymous commentators who encouraged Rob Zacharias, editor, and Sue Sorensen, publisher, to gather and publish selections from my work. Thank you, Rob and Sue, for your courage, inspiration, precision, and forbearance. And thank you also to others whose fine work contributed to this project: Katie Doke Sawatzky, Jonathan Dyck, and others on the team at CMU Press. I would like to acknowledge, also, the various funding agencies that directly enabled the work collected here, including the Social Sciences and Humanities Research Council of Canada, the Canada Council for the Arts, the Marpeck Fund, the Academic Development Fund of Conrad Grebel University College, the Ontario Work/Study Plan, the Edna Staebler Research Fellowship at the Joseph Schneider Haus Museum, TRACE (Teaching Resources and Continuing Education, University of Waterloo), and the Secretary of State for Multiculturalism, Canada.

Thank you to the writers and critics, colleagues and friends who, in a variety of ways, over decades, warmly supported my excursions into the world of Mennonite/s writing. Among those who encouraged and energized me are Kirsten Beachy, Ervin Beck, David Bergen, Sandra Birdsell, Di Brandt, Connie Braun, Daniel Shank Cruz, Harold Dueck, Howard Dyck, Judith Dueck, Maggie Dyck, Gloria Eby, Leonard Enns, Victor Enns, Marlene Epp, Fran Martens Friesen, Patrick Friesen, Jeanette Froese, Laureen Harder-Gissing, Hans-Jürgen Goertz, Arlene Groh, Jeff Gundy, Heidi Harms, Vern Heinrichs, Peter Hinchcliffe, Darcie Friesen Hossack, Ann Hostetler, Kim Jernigan, Julia Spicher Kasdorf, Grace Kehler, Sarah Klassen, Warren Kliewer, Robert Kroetsch, Martin Kuester, Harry Loewen, Mary Ann Loewen, Royden Loewen, Kristen Mathies, Miriam Maust, Ana Milanovic, John Moss, Jesse Nathan, Elsie K. Neufeld, Leonard Neufeldt, Hope Nisly, Sylvia Peters, Alf Redekopp, Magdalene Redekop, Al Reimer, Jim Reimer, Margaret Loewen Reimer, John Rempel, Jim Pankratz, Flora Roy, John Roth, Lorna Sawatsky, Rod Sawatsky, Irene Schmidt, Andreas Schroeder, Mary Shier, Gloria Smith, Arnold Snyder, Carrie Snyder, Sam Steiner, Andris Taskans, Jack Thiessen,

Vern Thiessen, John E. Toews, James Urry, Gary Waller, David Waltner-Toews, Jo-Anne Unruh, Piet Visser, Carol Ann Weaver, Dallas Wiebe, and Rudy Wiebe.

My heartfelt thanks go to my soulmate, partner in all things, literary collaborator, and indefatigable champion and supporter, Paul Tiessen. I would like to dedicate this volume of work on Mennonite/s Writing to Paul and to our family of children and grandchildren for whom we are infinitely grateful. I can imagine no greater source of inspiration, no greater reward.

Acknowledgements

"A Mighty Inner River: 'Peace' in the Early Fiction of Rudy Wiebe." Original publication in *Journal of Canadian Fiction*, vol. 2, no. 4, Fall 1973, pp. 71–76. Reprinted by permission of the author.

"The Role of Art and Literature in Mennonite Self-Understanding." Original publication in *Mennonite Identity: Historical and Contemporary Perspectives*, edited by Calvin Wall Redekop and Samuel J. Steiner, UP of America, 1988, pp. 235–252. Reprinted by permission of the author.

"Mother Tongue as Shibboleth in the Literature of Canadian Mennonites." Original publication in *Studies in Canadian Literature*, vol. 13, no. 2, 1988, pp. 175–183. Reprinted with permission.

"Mennonite Writing and the Post-Colonial Condition." Original publication in *Acts of Concealment: Mennonite/s Writing in Canada*, edited by Hildi Froese Tiessen and Peter Hinchcliffe, U Waterloo P, 1992, pp. 11–21. Reprinted by permission of the author.

"Beyond the Binary: Re-inscribing Cultural Identity in the Literature of Mennonites." Original publication in *Mennonite Quarterly Review*, vol. 72, no. 4, 1998, pp. 491–502. Reprinted with permission.

"Mennonite Literature and Postmodernism: Writing the 'In-Between' Space." Original publication in *Anabaptists and Postmodernism*, edited by Susan Biesecker-Mast and Gerald Biesecker-Mast, Pandora Press, 2000, pp. 160–174. Reprinted with permission from Cascadia Publishing House.

"Between Memory and Longing: Rudy Wiebe's *Sweeter Than All the World*." Original publication in *Mennonite Quarterly Review*, vol. 77, no. 4, 2003, pp. 619–636. Reprinted with permission.

"Critical Thought and Mennonite Literature: Mennonite Studies Engages the Mennonite Literary Voice." Original publication in *Journal of Mennonite Studies*, vol. 22, 2004, pp. 237–246. Reprinted with permission.

"A Mennonite Novelist's Journey (from) Home: Ephraim Weber's Encounters with S.F. Coffman and Lucy Maud Montgomery." This article was originally published in *The Conrad Grebel Review*, vol. 24, no. 2, Spring 2006, pp. 84–108, and appears here with the publisher's permission.

"Mennonite/s Writing: State of the Art?" This article was originally published in *The Conrad Grebel Review*, vol. 26, no. 1, Winter 2008, pp. 41–49, and appears here with the publisher's permission.

"An Imagined Coherence: Mennonite Literature and Mennonite Culture" was presented as part of a panel at University of the Fraser Valley in November 2010. Used with permission of the author.

"The Case of Dallas Wiebe: Literary Art in Worship." Original publication in *Journal of Mennonite Writing*, vol. 3, no. 3, 2011, www.mennonitewriting.org. Reprinted with permission.

"Homelands, Identity Politics, and the Trace: What Remains for the Mennonite Reader?" Original publication in *Mennonite Quarterly Review*, vol. 87, no. 1, 2013, pp. 11–22. Reprinted with permission.

"After Identity: Liberating the Mennonite Literary Text." Original publication in *After Identity: Mennonite Writing in North America*, edited by Robert Zacharias, U Manitoba Press, 2015, pp. 210–225. Reprinted with permission.

"Beyond 'What We by Habit or Custom Already Know,' or, 'What Do We Mean When We Talk About Mennonite/s Writing?'" Original publication in *Mennonite Quarterly Review*, vol. 90, no. 1, 2016, pp. 11–28. Reprinted with permission.

"Thirty Years of Mennonite Literature: How a Modest Course Became Something Else." Original publication in *Journal of Mennonite Writing*, vol. 8, no. 1, 2016, www.mennonitewriting.org. Reprinted with permission.

"'I didn't have words for it': Reflections on Some of the Early Life-Writing of Di Brandt and Julia Kasdorf." Original publication in *Journal of Mennonite Studies*, vol. 36, 2018, pp. 25–41. Reprinted with permission.

Index

Achebe, Chinua, 93
A Cappella: Mennonite Voices in Poetry (ed. Hostetler), 219
Abe, Kobe, 238
Acts of Concealment (ed. Tiessen and Hinchcliffe), 8, 10, 15, 78
After Identity (ed. Zacharias), 225, 260, 270
Agnes in the sky (Brandt), 100, 174
Akhmatova, Anna, 213
All My Puny Sorrows (Toews), 232
Amish, 11, 54, 233, 249, 250, 252, 262
Amish Adventure (Smucker), 241
Anderson, Benedict, 133, 172
Anne of Green Gables (Montgomery). 19, 139, 144, 291
Anzaldúa, Gloria, 86–88
Arnason, David, 76
Ashcroft, Bill, 10, 72, 73, 76, 77, 252
Asian North American Identities (ed. Ty and Goellnicht), 230
Atwood, Margaret, 41, 67, 74, 292
Away From the Dead (Bergen), 278
Bakhtin, Mikhail, 86
Bal, Mieke, 111–113
Bammer, Angelika, 82
Bawer, Bruce, 194
Beachy, Kirsten Eve, 290
Beachy, Stephen, 290
Beck, Ervin, 8, 16, 160, 222, 252, 282, 290, 292
Bender, Elizabeth Horsch, 5, 220
Bender, Harold S., 62, 66
Bergen, David, 12, 131, 132, 135, 140, 162, 170, 195, 206, 232, 243–246, 270, 272, 278, 285, 287, 297
Bergthaler Mennonites, 202
Berlin High School (Kitchener), 154
Bethel College, 180, 182, 282
Bhabha, Homi, 10, 87, 88, 90, 252, 260, 290
Big Bear (TV series), 100, 101

Birdsell, Sandra, 7, 12, 38–41, 50, 61, 67, 71, 77, 111–121, 128, 1230, 132, 140, 161, 162, 191, 195, 211, 214, 220, 240–245, 252, 257, 272, 275, 280–284, 288
Bitney, Kate, 195
Blue Jar, The (Konrad), 132
Blue Mountains of China, The (Rudy Wiebe), 16, 23–35, 39, 40, 67, 76, 77, 130, 172, 173, 191, 211, 219, 238, 275, 279
Bluffton University, 17, 159–162, 282
Booth, W. James, 192, 196
Boym, Svetlana, 112
Braidotti, Rosi, 193
Brand, Dionne, 10, 73, 74
Brandt, Di, 7, 8, 16, 18, 41, 61, 67, 79, 81, 82, 95–106 *passim*, 114, 128, 130, 161–163, 171, 175, 176, 191, 193, 195, 211, 220, 223, 229, 240, 244, 246, **249–265**, 272, 284, 288, 292
Braun, Connie, 278, 297
Braun, Lois, 67, 287
Bricker, Sam, 220
Brodsky, Joseph, 121
Cameron, Melanie, 162
Camrose Review, 39, 50
Canada Council for the Arts, 41, 243, 283
Canada Reads, 163
Canadian Broadcasting Corporation (CBC), 100, 161, 231
Canadian Charter of Rights and Freedoms, 194
Canadian Literature (journal), 5
Canadian Mennonite (journal), 161, 283
Canadian Mennonite University (incl. Canadian Mennonite Bible College), 2, 10, 240
Canadian Novel: Here and Now, The (ed. Moss), 238
Canadian Pacific Railway, 149
Capital (Kroeker), 57
Carter, Paul, 89, 261
Casanova, Pascale, 204, 205

Case of Lena S., The (Bergen), 132
Catherine II, 24, 63
Center for Mennonite Writing, 244
Center for Mennonite Writing Journal, 202, 209
Chair in Mennonite Studies, University of Winnipeg, 17, 127–128, 239
Chambers, Iain, 82, 87, 95, 96, 105
Chase, Malcolm, 112
Chen, Tina, 10, 205, 215, 231
Children's Friend, The, 45
Cincinnati Poetry Review, 242, 286
Coffman, S.F., **137–158**
Cohen, Matt, 10, 74
Collected Works of Arnold Dyck, The, 240
Come Back (Rudy Wiebe), 232
Community of Memory, A (Gundy), 89
Complicated Kindness, A (Toews), 138, 163, 164, 174, 193, 196, 207, 211, 250
Confino, Alon, 118
Conrad Grebel Review, 9, 10, 15, 133, 244, 245, 285, 289, 290
Conrad Grebel University College, 6, 8, 11, 14, 116, 127, 148, 160, 163, 189, 210, 221, 239, 244–247, 281–283
Cresswell, Tim, 196
Crossing the Line (Elias), 132, 285
Cruz, Daniel Shank, 6, 253, 297
Culler, Jonathan, 18, 165
Dames, Nicholas, 113, 165
Dancing Naked (Brandt), 98, 249–265 *passim*
Days of Terror (Smucker), 40, 41
Deleuze, Gilles, 193, 197
Denise, Cheryl, 209
Dickstein, Morris, 210
Dimock, Wai Chee, 10, 203, 205, 214, 229
Diviners, The (Laurence), 77
Dixon, Robert, 231
Doerksen, Victor, 240, 267, 284
Dueck, David, 116
Dueck, Dora, 195
Dueck, Lynette, 132
Dunham, Mabel, 46, 220
Dustship Glory (Schroeder), 57
Dyck, Aganetha, 41, 54, 55
Dyck, Arnold, 37–59, 65–70 *passim*, 78–80, 131, 133, 160, 220, 240–241, 270, 284
Dyck, Ed, 130

Dyck, Jonathan, 278, 290
Eastern Mennonite University, 17, 189
Eby, Benjamin, 138, 220
Edwards, Brian T., 201, 204, 207
Eggleston, Wilfrid, 137–147 *passim*, 156
Eine Mutter (Epp), 279
Einstein's Gift (Thiessen), 289
Eleventh Commandment, The (Schroeder), 132
Elias, David, 131, 162, 195
Emerson, Ralph Waldo, 147, 212, 270
Enns, Garry, 285
Enns, Victor, 41, 67, 130, 162, 195, 220 240, 244, 280, 285, 287, 297
Ens, Sarah, 278
Epp, Claas (*see* Great Trek)
Epp, George K., 240
Epp, Peter G., 279
Epp, Reuben, 63
Erll, Astrid, 164–166
European Journal of English Studies, 165
Ewing, Katherine, 232
Excerpts from the Real World (Kroetsch), 219
Expo 67 (Montreal), 194
Falk, Gathie, 41, 54, 55
Fast, Darrell, 182
Festival Quarterly, 5, 115
First Mennonite Church (Kitchener), 139
Flores, Juan, 88
Flyway (Ens), 278
Forever Summer, Forever Sunday, 190–126 *passim*, 283
Franco, Dean, 225, 230
Frankfurt Book Fair, 232
Fraser, Hilary, 258
Fresno Pacific University, 17, 210, 233
Friends (Abe), 238
Friesen, David, 128
Friesen, Gerhard (*see* Fritz Senn)
Friesen, Patrick, 7, 8, 39, 41, 43, 50, 61, 66, 67, 114, 130, 131, 161, 162, 171, 191, 211, 213, 220, 223. 240, 241, 244–246, 256, 270–273, 280, 284, 287, 292–294
Friesen, Victor Carl, 281
Frost, Robert, 174
Frye, Northrop, 129
Funk, Carla, 195
Funk, John Fretz, 145, 149, 151, 152
Fuss, Diana, 223

302

Index

Genette, Gérard, 251
Giles, Paul, 205
Gillen, Mollie, 143
Gingerich, Melvin, 140
Girl Runner (Snyder), 231–232
Glaser, Jennifer, 228
Globe and Mail, 214
Goellnicht, Donald, 230–231
Gone With the Wind (Mitchell), 138
Good Housekeeping (Waltner-Toews), 55, 241, 280
Good, Merle, 53
Good, Phyllis, 53
Goshen College, 160, 162, 238, 244, 279, 282, 290 292, 293
Governor General's Awards, 40–41, 67, 140, 280, 289
Great Trek, 182–183
Green Gables Letters, The, 144
Griffiths, Gareth, 252
Guattari, Félix, 193
Gundy, Jeff, 7, 8, 16, 87–90, 159, 160, 208, 244–246, 257, 260, 282, 286, 297
Gzowski, Peter, 162
Half in the Sun (ed. Neufeld), 162
Hall, Stuart, 10, 83–84, 87–88, 94, 105, 191, 205, 209, 226
Harder, Hans, 42
Harder, Jo-Anne, 116
HarperCollins, 212, 285
Hebdige, Dick, 93
Herald of Truth, 145
Herald Press, 233
Herrfort, Andrew, 283
Hiebert, Paul, 220
Hillard, Jeffrey, 183, 241
Hinz-Penner, Raylene, 275
Hirsch, Marianne, 111
Hollinger, David, 226, 227
Hossack, Darcie Friesen, 212, 297
Hostetler, Ann, 6, 8, 16, 159, 203, 209
Hostetler, C.K., 148, 152, 154
Hostetler, Sheri, 85, 256
Howe, Irvin, 207
Howells, Coral Ann, 99
Hroch, Petra, 193, 197–198
Hudson Review, 194
Hunsberger, David L., 283

Hutcheon, Linda, 10, 74, 82, 95–96, 99, 101–102, 105
Hutchison, Jesse, 255
Huyssen, Andreas, 94, 112
Hyperion Press, 240
I Hear the Reaper's Song (Armin Wiebe), 41
i sing for my dead in german (Poetker), 68, 132, 241, 275
Impossible Uprooting, The (Waltner-Toews), 116, 117
Institute of Anabaptist and Mennonite Studies (Conrad Grebel), 2 8 2
Interdisciplinary Colloquium on Western Canada, 256
Janzen, Jacob H., 292–294, 41, 48, 49, 64, 65
Janzen, Jean, 244, 286
Janzen, Rhoda, 174, 176, 207, 250
Joseph Schneider Haus Museum, 142
Journal of Canadian Fiction, 23, 238, 280
Journal of Mennonite Studies, 10, 128, 129, 131, 133– 136, 239–244 *passim*, 285, 292
Journey to Yalta (Klassen), 109, 119, 132, 241
Joyce, James, 170
Juhnke, Anna Kreider, 181, 182
Juhnke, James, 180–187 *passim*
Kanadier Mennonites, 111, 202, 229
Karem, Jeff, 213–214
Kasdorf, Julia Spicher, 7, 8, 16, 18, 81–91 *passim*, 208, 211, 228, 244, 245, **249–265**, 270, 285, 286, 288
Keefer, Janice Kulyk, 73, 214
Keith, W.J., 76–77
Kidd, Abraham, 142
Kidd, Margaret Melrose, 142
King, William Lyon Mackenzie, 220
Kirkpatrick, Peter, 231
Klassen, Sarah, 109, 114, 119, 130, 132, 162, 172, 191, 195, 240, 241, 273, 275, 278, 283, 287, 288, 292
Kleine Gemeinde, 202
Kliewer, Warren, 55, 56, 85, 241, 281, 286
Kogawa, Joy, 292
Koltun-Fromm, Ken, 233
Konrad, Anne, 132
Koop, Wanda, 41
Koshy, Susan, 228, 230, 234
Krahn, Cornelius, 5
Kramer, Michael P., 204, 207, 233
Kreider, Robert, 282
Kroeker, Allan, 41, 57
Kroeker, Amy D., 253

Kroetsch, Robert, 10, 71–80 *passim*, 87, 95, 98, 100, 138, 161, 198, 199, 211, 219, 226, 244, 257, 292
Lachman, Becca J.R., 209
Landsberg, Alison, 210, 211
Laurence, Margaret, 130, 172, 197, 198
League of Canadian Poets, 41, 67
Leaving Tomorrow (Bergen), 232
Lee, Christopher, 226
Leichter, David J., 205, 206
Lendrum Mennonite Brethren Church, 13, 238
Lenin's Embalmers (Thiessen), 171, 172
Levine, Naomi, 129
Lewis, Wyndham, 13, 242
Liars and Rascals (ed. Tiessen), 8, 10, 15, 42, 84, 213, 221, 242, 281 283–286, 293
Library and Archives Canada (incl. National Archives), 138–143 *passim*, 285, 291
Lim, Shirley, 230
Lipsitz, George, 114, 119
Location of Culture, The (Bhabha), 90, 252, 260
Loewen, Gerhard, 76
Loewen, Harry, 76, 128–136 *passim*, 222, 239, 240–241, 279, 284
Loewen, Royden, 7, 127
Lost in the Steppe (Dyck), 42, 44, 45, 56, 66
Lousley, Cheryl, 253
Lovely Treachery of Words, The (Kroetsch), 71, 87, 98, 199, 211
Lowenthal, David, 121
Luther, Martin, 62, 147
Lyotard, Jean-François, 95
Mailer, Norman, 272
Malamud, Bernard, 272
Manitoba Arts Council, 287
Manitoba Mennonite Historical Society, 240
Manitoba Writers' Guild, 41, 67
Mann, Ella, 149, 151
Marpeck Fund, 282
Martyrs Mirror, 14, 173, 208
Maust, Miriam, 221, 243
McClelland & Stewart, 65, 130, 160, 212
Melrose, Annie, 138
MennoMedia, 233
Mennonite Archives of Ontario, 148–158 *passim*
Mennonite Brethren, 13, 202, 232, 238
Mennonite Brethren Collegiate Institute, 12, 128–129, 239

Mennonite Brethren Herald, 45, 115
Mennonite Central Committee, 287
Mennonite Church USA Archives, 152, 291
Mennonite Church Canada, 233
Mennonite Church USA, 233
Mennonite Country (Snyder), 283
Mennonite Encyclopedia, 9, 47, 66
Mennonite Evangelizing and Benevolent Board, 148
Mennonite Identity and Literary Art (Ruth), 6, 83, 282
Mennonite Identity: Historical and Contemporary Perspectives (ed. Redekop and Steiner), 17
Mennonite in a Little Black Dress (Janzen), 174, 207, 250
Mennonite Life (journal), 5, 48, 238, 292
Mennonite Literary Society, 6, 42, 285
Mennonite Mirror, 5, 115, 194, 240, 241, 267, 284
Mennonite Publishing Company, 145, 151
Mennonite Quarterly Review, 5, 10, 133, 244
Mennonite Reporter, 84, 115, 281
Mennonite World Conference, 134, 202, 221, 242, 284
Mennonite Writers' Fellowship, 5
Mennonite/s Writing conferences, 2, 8. 10, 11, 17, 71, 79, 130, 159–167 *passim*, 169, 172, 189, 197, 203, 212, 219–236 *passim*, 242–245, 249, 250, 252, 268, 282–294 *passim*
Mennonites and the Artistic Imagination (Reimer), 10
Mennonites and the Challenge of Multiculturalism conference, 127
Mennonitische Volkswarte, 49, 52
Mennonot, 85, 256, 273
Midcontinental, 5
Mierau, Maurice, 130, 280, 284, 292
Migrant Muses (ed. Roth and Beck), 291
Millen, Muriel, 143
Millner, Michael, 204, 226
Miron, Dan, 196
Montgomery, Lucy Maud, 19, **137–158**, 291
Monument: Poems on Aging and Dying (Dallas Wiebe), **183–187**
Moretti, Franco, 10, 212, 270
Morris, Leslie, 233
Mostly Country (Nixon), 132, 285
Moya, Paula, 215
Mullet, Steve, 256
Musil, Robert, 112

My Harp Has Turned to Mourning (Reimer), 132, 240, 241
My Lovely Enemy (Rudy Wiebe), 45, 100, 241
Nachtbeeren (Penner), 278, 290
Neufeld, Woldemar, 15, 41, 292
Neufeldt, Leonard, 287
Neuman, Shirley, 96, 101
New Quarterly, 8, 15, 213, 221, 242–243, 273, 284–286
New York Times, 174
New Yorker, 285
NeWest Press, 285
Ngũgĩ wa Thiong'o, 72
Nicholson, Linda, 196
Nickel, Barbara, 131, 162, 195, 209
Night Travellers (Birdsell), 38, 132, 275, 280–281
Nixon, Rosemary, 284–285, 103–105
No Strangers in Exile (Harder), 42
Noonan, Gerry, 282
Official Languages Act, 194
Old Order Mennonites, 283
Older Than Ravens (Doug Reimer), 132
Ondaatje, Michael, 10, 75, 82
One Quilt Many Pieces (Margaret Loewen Reimer), 202
Orca Publishers, 285
Our Asian Journey (Dallas Wiebe), 182, 183, 242, 286
Palumbo-Liu, David, 226
p'Bitek, Okot, 213
Patterson, Nancy Lou, 76
Pauls, Peter, 130, 279
Peace Shall Destroy Many (Rudy Wiebe), 9, 16, 23–35, 40, 65, 66, 85, 97, 100, 114, 130, 140, 160–65, 175, 190, 193, 196, 211, 213–14, 219, 232, 238, 250, 275, 292
Pease, Donald, 204
Penner, Elina, 278, 290
Penner, Jessica, 290
People Apart, A (Hunsberger), 283
Peters, Elisabeth, 240
Pilgrim's Progress (Bunyan), 46, 182
Playing Dead (Rudy Wiebe), 101
Plett, Casey, 290
Poetker, Audrey, 67-8, 132, 195, 220, 241, 273, 275, 287
Prairie Fire (journal), 8, 9, 15, 161, 221, 241–42, 272, 285–87
Pratt, Mary Louise, 249, 262
Presbyterian Church, 130, 172, 197
Queen's University, 143

questions i asked my mother (Brandt), 102, 132, 241, 258, 275
"Quiet in the Land?" conference, 85
Quill & Quire, 272
Random House, 161
Ratzlaff, Keith, 209
Rebecca's Nancy (Goman), 283
Redekop, Cal, 282
Redekop, Magdalene, 6–8, 175, 297
Regehr, Ted, 7
Reimer, Al, 6, 78, 84, 129–32, 160, 195, 220, 240–41, 279, 284, 287, 292, 297
Reimer, Doug, 132
Reimer, Margaret Loewen, 10, 202, 283, 297
Rempel, John D., 115
Rempel, Peter Gerhard, 115, 121–23, 283
Rempel, Tina, 118
Rewriting the Break Event (Zacharias), 246, 307
Rhubarb (journal), 15, 162, 202, 209, 240, 244, 285, 307
Richards, I.A., 129
Richler, Mordecai, 73
Ricoeur, Paul, 205
Rigney, Ann, 159, 165
Roman Catholic Church, 48
Roof, Judith, 205, 226
Roth, Laurence, 210
Roth, Philip, 192, 206, 208, 260, 272, 278
Royal Commission on Bilingualism and Biculturalism, 194
Rudy Wiebe: A Tribute (ed. Tiessen), 292
Russian Daughter, The (Klassen), 278
Russländer Mennonites, 12, 111, 115, 116, 118, 283
Russländer, The (Birdsell), 113, 116, 128, 214, 283
Ruth, John 6, 83–4, 282
Salvation of Yasch Siemens, The (Armin Wiebe), 41, 54, 67, 132, 193, 241, 275, 280
Samatar, Sofia, 253, 278, 286, 290
Sand Hills Books, 116, 239, 283, 307
Sarah Binks (Hiebert), 220
Saskatchewan Writers' Guild, 41, 67
Sawatsky, Rod, 145, 239, 282, 297
Schreier, Benjamin, 10, 205, 225, 260, 271, 278, 294
Schroeder, Andreas, 41, 50, 57, 67, 130, 132, 170–71, 244, 281, 287, 288
Scotiabank Giller Prize, 140

Secretary of State Multicultural Directorate, 115, 194, 221, 242, 281, 283, 297
Seidman, Steven, 196
Senn, Fritz (Gerhard Johann Friesen), 49, 131, 133
Shantz, Jacob Y., 146
Shantz, Susan, 41
Shaw, Christopher, 112
Shelterbelts (Dyck), 278
Shunning, The (Friesen), 67, 132, 174, 193, 275, 280, 287
Siemens, Lloyd, 279
Sing Me No More (Lynette Dueck), 132
Sitting Opposite My Brother (Bergen), 132, 285
Skyblue the Badass (Dallas Wiebe), 181, 241
Skyblue's Essays: Fictions (Dallas Wiebe), 179
Sleeping Preacher (Kasdorf), 81–82, 89, 249, 253, 261
Slemon, Stephen, 77
Smith, Gloria, 242, 283, 297
Smucker, Barbara, 401, 131, 195, 241
Snyder, Arnold, 289, 297
Snyder, Carrie, 162, 195, 212, 231–234, 245–246, 290, 297
Snyder, Peter Etril, 283
Social Sciences and Humanities Research Council of Canada (SSHRC), 8, 287, 297
Spiller, Robert E., 212, 269
Staebler, Leslie, 139, 141, 148, 151, 154
Stambaugh, Sar,a 41, 281
Steiner, Sam, 282, 297
Stephen Leacock Medal for Humour, 220
Steppe: A Novel (Weier), 132
Stone Angel, The (Laurence), 77
Strawson, Galen, 197
Stubbs, Andrew, 77
Suderman, Elmer, 5, 238, 281, 286
Summer of My Amazing Luck, The (Toews), 285
Surplus at the Border (Reimer), 10
Sutherland, Ronald, 131, 134, 194
Sweeter Than All the World (Rudy Wiebe), 18, 109–128, 207, 283
Swiss Mennonites, 9, 76, 103–104, 111, 285, 291
Taskans, Andris, 7, 161, 195, 198, 272, 280, 284, 297
Tefs, Wayne, 77
Temptations of Big Bear, The (Rudy Wiebe), 100, 280
Thiessen, Jack, 130, 132, 279, 287, 297
Thiessen, Vern, 162, 171–172, 195, 243, 288–289, 298

Thomas, Clara, 77, 130, 172, 197–198, 211
Tiessen, Paul, 8, 18, 115, 139, 143, 181, 183, 213, 239, 242, 244, 280, 286, 291–292, 298
Tiffin, Helen, 77
To Antoine (Wiens), 278, 283
Toews, Miriam, 12, 131–132, 138, 140, 161–166, 171, 174, 176, 191, 195, 206, 232, 243, 246, 250, 270, 272, 279, 284–88
Toronto Jewish Theatre, 172
Toronto Star, 50
"Toward a Mennonite Self-Understanding" conference, 282
Trail of the Conestoga, The (Dunham), 46
Transparent Eyeball, The (Dallas Wiebe), 242
Turnstone Press, 212, 221, 241, 280, 285, 293
Ty, Eleanor, 230
Unearthly Horses (Friesen), 66, 273
University of Alberta, 13, 130, 219, 237, 279
University of Chicago, 143
University of Cincinnati, 242
University of Manitoba, 240, 280
University of Michigan, 181
University of the Fraser Valley, 17
University of Toronto, 164
University of Waterloo, 116, 130, 210, 213, 221, 239, 243, 246, 297
University of Waterloo Press, 242, 283
University of Winnipeg (incl. United College), 13, 17, 128–130, 239–40, 279, 287
Unruh, Kay, 279
Unspoken (Braun), 278
van Herk, Aritha, 284, 292
Vancouver Art Gallery, 41
Vidler, Anthony, 112
Visvis, Vikki, 253
Violators, The (Kliewer), 55, 241, 281
Visions and Realities (ed. Loewen and Reimer), 43, 49, 240
Vogt, Roy, 240
Voice of Peace, 45
von den Vondel, Joost, 48
Voth, Norma Jost, 116
Wagner, Shari Miller, 209
Waltner-Toews, David, 41, 49, 55, 61, 66–68, 105, 109, 114, 116, 119, 130–131, 162, 172, 191, 195, 213, 220, 241, 244–245, 273, 275, 280–281, 283, 293, 298
Warren, Kenneth, 227, 231

Watson, Sheila, 238
Weber, Ephraim, 15, 18, **137–145**, 148, 150–152, 156, 291–292
Weeks, Jeffrey, 87
Weier, John, 130, 132, 195, 275
Weir, Lorraine, 77
What Was African American Literature? (Warren), 231
When War Came to Kleindarp (Reimer), 240
While I Still Remember (Eggleston), 143
White Mosque, The (Samatar), 278, 286
Wiebe, Armin, 41, 54–56, 61, 67–68, 114, 130, 132, 161, 162, 195, 220, 240–245, 272–275, 280
Wiebe, Dallas, 18, 85, **179–187**, 213, 241, 257, 281, 286–288, 298
Wiebe, Erika, 183
Wiebe, Katie Funk, 281
Wiebe, Rudy, 6, 8, 9, 13–18, **23–35**, 3–40, 45, 50, 61, 63, 65–67, 74, 76–77, 79, 85, 95–97, 100–102, **109–125**, 128, 130–133, 140, 160–165, 171–176, 190–191, 194–197, 206–207, 211–214, 219–220, 223, 232, 237–246, 250, 257, 259, 270–271, 273, 275, 279–287, 292, 298
Wiens, Erwin, 278, 283
Wilfrid Laurier University, 14, 129, 239, 281-82, 287
Wilson, Robert, 94
Wirth-Nesher, Hana, 233
Wong, Sau-ling Cynthia, 224
Writers' Union of Canada, 40-1, 67, 281
Year of Lesser, A (Bergen), 285
Yoder, Joseph W., 262
Yoder, Rachel, 290
Yost, Erma Martin, 41, 49, 53
Young People's Paper, 145–55
Yúdice, George, 88
Zacharias, Robert, 5, 212, 226, 228, 230, 267, 270, 307
Zhang, Benzi, 196
Zieber, Miriam F., 146

About the Author

Hildi Froese Tiessen is one of the foremost scholars of Mennonite literature today. Raised in Manitoba, Hildi Froese Tiessen earned her BA at University of Winnipeg and MA and PhD at University of Alberta. She taught English and Peace & Conflict Studies (1987–2012) at Conrad Grebel University College, University of Waterloo, where she also served as academic dean. Before her retirement she was literary editor of *Conrad Grebel Review* and on the editorial board of *Rhubarb* magazine. She has served on the Centre for Mennonite Writing advisory board and on the editorial board of GAMEO, the Mennonite Encyclopedia. She is the editor of *Liars and Rascals* (1989), an anthology of short fiction by Mennonite authors, and also *11 Encounters with Mennonite Fiction* (2017). With Paul Tiessen, she is the editor of *After Green Gables: L.M. Montgomery's Letters to Ephraim Weber* (2006). As founding principals of Sand Hills Books, she and Paul Tiessen have edited and published several volumes featuring the painting and photography of artists of Mennonite heritage. She lives in Kitchener, Ontario.

About the Editor

Robert Zacharias is Associate Professor in the Department of English at York University in Toronto and has held postdoctoral positions at University of Toronto and University of Waterloo. His publications include *Rewriting the Break Event: Mennonites and Migration in Canadian Literature* (University of Manitoba Press, 2013) and *Reading Mennonite Writing: A Study in Minor Transnationalism* (Pennsylvania State University Press, 2022), and, as editor, *After Identity: Mennonite Writing in North America* (Pennsylvania State University Press, 2015). He is co-editor, with Smaro Kamboureli, of *Shifting the Ground of Canadian Literary Studies* (Wilfrid Laurier University Press, 2012). He is Associate Editor of the *Journal of Mennonite Studies* and sits on the Advisory Board of *Journal of Mennonite Writing*.